Praise for the Previous Editions

From Amazon Customers

- Simple and lucid explanation of important issues. A good buy!!!
- Very good book, easy to understand.
- Nice book on environment with case studies which attract your attention.
- This book is the best when it comes to not just studying but also gaining a deep knowledge on the ongoing Environmental Crisis.... The reason for this is the way this book has been written. The Author, R. Rajagopalan, being a keen Environmentalist himself, has tried to present the current situation of crisis in a very simple language to the readers. It just can't get any better than this. When I first started reading this book, I just did it for the sake of the subject from which questions will be asked in Entrance Examination. But now, I just can't stop myself from reading it and that is only because of the way the author has managed to connect with readers on all the issues and terms. Truly a masterpiece and should be read by everyone no matter if they are giving some exam or not.
- Still halfway to finish the book, but I can vouch for this book as an excellent read if you need to understand environmental issue better in a simple and convincing way. Basic to advanced terminologies have been simplified to communicate readers in an easier way. Good for academic purposes and for avid environmentalists too.
- The book is excellent for undergraduate courses of Environmental Studies. Moreover, it's very helpful for different competitive examinations such as PSC, UPSC etc.
- The book is reader-friendly and easy to understand. The case study given at beginning of each chapter makes it still more interesting.
- Great book for anyone who is interested in knowing about environment. Can be used for lots of purposes, not just for exams.
- A great book to study fundamentals of Environment Studies. An advantage of this book is that in every chapter there will be two interesting case studies. It will be in our memory for quite a long time and comes to your rescue even if you forget the principles especially during MCQ exams.
- Perfect book to study... In a very precise and lucid manner it covers everything required... plus develops interest in the subject too.
- Great book to attain clarity on basics of environment, ecology, biodiversity, and climate change. ...Absolutely love this book. Even NCERT books do not come close to its content-quality.
- Finally got the right book for environmental crises... the content of the book is accurate and written in lucid language...
- Undoubtedly the best book I ever read on this subject.
- Better than any book on these topics.
- Methodically written... A must-read book... Very useful... My cordial respect to Mr Rajagopalan, the author, for producing such an awesome book.
- An extraordinary book. The best book on the subject for the general public.

- Very well written work covering many areas in contemporary environmental sciences.
- Great book with lot of case studies.
- Excellent book for beginners!!
- A great work by Rajagopalan. While reading it I feel as if I am reading a romantic novel. It has been presented in a brilliant style.
- Cannot find a better book than this in the market, everything is so simplified and comprehensive, Rajagopalan ROCKS.

From Academics

'I wish to heartily congratulate you on your efforts leading to publishing the book and assure you of the enthusiastic support from faculty and students of BITS, Pilani, Goa, for the cause of Environment.'

–Prof. M.K. Deshmukh, BITS Pilani, Goa Campus

'It is certainly one of the best books I have seen, presented in such an interesting and proactive manner.'

–Shobha Menon, Founder Trustee of Nizhal, a trust for tree conservation

'I have read your book "*Crisis to Cure*" and have found it amazingly interesting and use it almost like a Bible for my Environment classes. The live examples given by you make it more like a storybook.'

–Dr Rashmi Sanghi, LNMIIT Jaipur

'Thank you for writing *From Crisis To Cure*, Mr Gopalan—it's my Bible! I gift it to everyone I feel is sensitive about the subject and there are so many now.'

–Piyali Gupta, Teacher

Environmental Studies

FROM CRISIS TO CURE

FOURTH EDITION

According to the latest UGC syllabus 2023

R. Rajagopalan

Former Professor

Indian Institute of Technology Madras

OXFORD

UNIVERSITY PRESS

OXFORD
UNIVERSITY PRESS

Oxford University Press is a department of the University of Oxford. It furthers the University's objective of excellence in research, scholarship, and education by publishing worldwide. Oxford is a registered trade mark of Oxford University Press in the UK and in certain other countries.

Published in India by
Oxford University Press
22 Workspace, 2nd Floor, 1/22 Asaf Ali Road, New Delhi 110002

First Edition published in 2005
Fourth Edition published in 2023

Second impression 2024

ISBN-13: 978-93-5497-894-4
ISBN-10: 93-5497-894-0

Typeset in Baskerville
by B2K-BYTES 2 KNOWLEDGE, Tamil Nadu
Printed in India by Gopsons Papers Pvt. Ltd, Noida - 201301
Cover image: © Johann Mader/Shutterstock

For product information and current price, please visit www.india.oup.com

This book is dedicated to
the youth climate activists of the world
who might yet save humanity and the planet.

Preface to the Fourth Edition

A Message to the Student and the Teacher

The highest education is that which does not merely give us information but makes our life in harmony with existence.

Rabindranath Tagore (1861–1941)
Writer, Artist, Philosopher, and Nobel Laureate

This book may well be the most important book you will read in your life! It has three messages for you:

- We are in the midst of an almost unstoppable environmental crisis.
- We are not doing enough and on time to save the planet and humanity.
- It is the ethical duty of each one of us to take whatever action we can to conserve the environment.

In December 2003, the Supreme Court of India gave a historic ruling in a case filed in public interest by lawyer M.C.Mehta: Environmental Education should be made compulsory at all levels from Class 1 to the undergraduate degree.

I had then just retired a Professor, IIT Madras, and I saw this ruling as a great opportunity to create environmental awareness among the students of this country. Through my work as the Director, International Ocean Institute (India), I had become alarmed at the rapid deterioration of the environment.

I wrote the first edition of this book in 2004 and followed it up with a series of books at school level. Following the court ruling, school boards and universities introduced environmental education in their curricula. I played a small part in this process by conducting teacher workshops all over India.

Meanwhile, the Indian government passed many environmental laws. NGOs such as the Centre for Science and Environment, New Delhi, were publishing magazines and conducting studies on environment. UN agencies were releasing reports and urging governments to take immediate action.

I had high hopes that, once the governments and the general population understand the seriousness of the situation, efforts will be taken to conserve the environment. In due course, we would bring the global environment back to normalcy.

I was terribly wrong!

In March 2023, the UN Intergovernmental Panel on Climate Change, a body of scientists from all over the world, released a report which included warnings that the world was approaching "irreversible" levels of global warming, with catastrophic impacts rapidly becoming inevitable; and that it was "now or never" to take drastic action to avoid disaster.

This is the fourth edition of my textbook for a course on Environment. This is more than a textbook, however. It is about your life and what is in store for you and the future generations. It is about the present and future of the earth. The text and the stories are meant to evoke surprise and shock, despair and hope, resolve and action. You will surely return to it even after the course. It may change forever your perspectives on life and nature!

This edition fully follows the 2023 'UGC Guidelines and Curriculum Framework for Environment Education at the Undergraduate Level'. It also includes additional topics from the syllabi of some universities. The book is meant for undergraduates of any discipline and assumes no background in mathematics or science beyond the level of the tenth standard.

This book will also be useful for those taking the UPSC civil services examinations. It covers the ecology/environment topics in the syllabi for the preliminary and main examinations.

What are the Special Features of This Book?

This book has variety and something of interest to everyone. Even as you cover the syllabus, learn the concepts, and answer the questions, you will:

- learn about the major environmental problems, such as runaway growth, imperilled ecosystems, disappearing forests, endangered species, dwindling natural resources, escalating pollution, growing population, dangerous toxins, and more;
- find out what is being done about these problems;
- read many true environment-related stories about crises, solutions, successes, failures, interconnections, and inspirational individuals;
- reflect on meaningful quotations, discuss deeper issues, watch films and documentaries, and read related novels; and
- discover how YOU can make a positive difference to the state of the environment by doing projects, joining groups, and taking action at a personal level.

The main text is in a question–answer format (sometimes called the Socratic method). This format promotes effective learning by making you an active learner. I have tried to anticipate the questions likely to arise in your mind. The question format also lends itself to the SQ4R method of effective study explained separately.

The keywords and phrases are listed in the beginning of each chapter. Every chapter ends with a summary, exercises, and deeper questions for reflection. The section 'Enjoy and Educate Yourself' lists feature films and fiction on the theme of the chapter. You will also find an extensive glossary of terms at the end.

Answers to objective questions have been given at the end of the book.

Model papers for universities and for the UPSC civil services examinations have been added.

What is New in This Edition?

Since I wrote the Third Edition in 2015, the global environment has become even more critical and climate change has become a serious issue all over the world. I believe that climate change will be the most serious environmental issue for India and the world in the coming years. Hence, I have made it the integrating theme of this edition. Every chapter begins with a short description of the connection between climate change and the topic in question.

What else is new in this edition?

- Several new topics have been added to cover the UGC syllabus and the syllabi of some universities.
- Several new stories have been included. For additional stories you can access the OUP Online Resource Centre (See below).
- All the stories and the text have been updated to reflect current reports and studies.
- The last unit of the book describes environmental activities you can carry out as an individual and/or in a group; and projects that you can take up.

Online Resource Centre

You will find additional resources on the OUP Online Resource Centre (ORC). Please visit https://india.oup.com/orcs/9789354978944 and follow the instructions. The ORC includes the following resources:

For faculty

- PowerPoint slides

For students

- References including books, websites, and documentaries.
- Additional stories, text, model question papers, references, websites, and films
- Environmental calendar, timeline, organizations, careers, and so on
- Environmental news and updates, major meetings and agreements, new reports, and studies, etc.
- Multiple choice questions

Access also ProfRR.blogspot.com to read my blogs on current environmental issues.

Give me your feedback—point out errors, give suggestions for improvement, ask for additional material, or share stories of your activities. My email address is rrgopalan2005@gmail.com.

Acknowledgements

I wish to thank the reviewers who provided feedback on the previous editions and students who sent me email messages with positive comments and questions. Special thanks are due to Dr. Amrit Sen of Visva-Bharati, Santiniketan, for giving me permission to reproduce his translation of the Tagore poem at the end of the book.

I should also thank all the participants in my programmes (in particular, the alumni of the Auroville workshops) for encouraging me to keep going!

R. Rajagopalan

SQ4R Method and Flash Cards

(Techniques for Effective Study)

What is your preferred way of reading a chapter in a textbook?

If you are a typical student, you would probably read the chapter from the beginning to the end. If you are a 'serious' student, you would underline the important points for easy revision later. Both are passive methods that do not promote learning and remembering.

What is the SQ4R method of study?

The SQ4R method enables you to read a textbook or guide as an active learner so that you understand and remember the material better. Research has shown that this method improves student performance in the examination.

SQ4R is an acronym for a 6-step reading and study method. It was first developed in the 1940s by Francis Robinson (1906–1983), who was a Professor of Psychology at Ohio State University in the US. During World War II, thousands of US army personnel had to be trained very quickly in skills relevant to the war. Based on his research as well as earlier studies on study skills, Professor Robinson came up with the SQ3R method to help the army personnel learn new skills in a short period of time. Later, Robinson's book *Effective Study*, which described the method, became popular with all students in universities and schools. Even today, many US universities recommend this method to the new students. Robinson's SQ3R has re-emerged today as SQ4R (explained below).

What is the key idea behind SQ4R?

SQ4R differentiates between *reading* and *studying*. You can just *read* a novel or a magazine, while you must *study* a textbook or a test-prep guide. In *studying* a book, your aim is to achieve mastery over the topic and to be able to answer correctly all the relevant questions in the examination.

SQ4R recognizes the fact that, while *studying* a book, the most important things you must do often occur *before* and *after* reading, not actually during the reading act itself. SQ4R makes you an active reader of the book, enabling you to learn well and remember the material. SQ4R becomes even more effective when you use flash cards.

What is a flash card?

A flash card is a small card, about 130 mm x 80 mm in size, available in shops selling invitation cards. You write a question, keyword, or phrase on one side of the card. On the other side, you write the answer to the question or an explanation for the keyword or phrase. In this way, you create a deck of cards for each topic and chapter that you study. We will see presently how such cards can be used in conjunction with the SQ4R method.

How can you apply the six steps of SQ4R and use flash cards, while studying a chapter of any book?

SQ4R consists of six related activities: Survey, Question, Read, Record, Recite, and Review. (In the original SQ3R, Robinson had included the recording or writing part in the Read step.)

1. Survey: Before reading a chapter, make a quick survey of what the chapter contains. It is like looking at a map to plan your route before you begin a journey. Read the following (whatever is available):

- Chapter title
- Any introduction given
- Titles of sections, subsections, boxes, and tables
- Main questions addressed
- Keywords and Phrases
- Anything given in bold letters
- Pictures and diagrams
- Conclusions
- Chapter summary
- Questions given under Exercises.

2. Question: As you survey the chapter, focus on the questions that the chapter attempts to answer. This approach keeps your mind alert and concentrated.

- Convert the titles of sections, subsections, boxes, and tables into questions.
- Add questions that you expect the chapter to answer.
- Write down each question on a separate flash card.

As you follow the Survey and Question Steps, try to recall what you already know about the topics. Check whether you can answer any of the questions even without reading the chapter.

3. Read: Read one section of the chapter, looking for answers to the questions you have written down. Separate the key ideas from the supporting details and examples.

Having a question in mind results in:

- an attempt to answer a question with what you know and what you are now learning;
- higher level of concentration and attention while reading to find an answer to the question; and
- increased comprehension due to the brain's activity in its attempt to find an answer to the question.

The approach thus makes you an active reader.

4. Record: As you read a section of the chapter, pick up the flash card with the relevant question and write down the answer as bullet points on the other side of the card. In the case of a keyword or phrase, write the explanation as bullet points. Do not just copy the text, try to write the answer your own words.

If you wish, you can also copy simple and important illustrations from the book or add a diagram of your own. The cards now contain your notes on the chapter. Do not forget to write down the chapter number at one corner of each card.

In addition to writing on the cards, you can also underline or highlight a point on the book but be very selective in this process. You could also write a summary of what you have learned on a special-coloured card.

5. Recite: This is the process of immediate recall of what you have learned. After reading each section:

- Pick up each card and answer orally the question from memory; check your answer by turning over the card.
- If you cannot fully recall the answer, read the relevant section of the chapter again and correct the answer on the card.

- Make up mnemonics if you find it difficult to remember a list of points.

When you can answer all the questions, move to the next section. Follow the steps Read, Record, and Recite for that section. Continue until you complete the chapter.

After completing the chapter, reflect on what you have learned. Ask yourself questions such as:

- What are these ideas and facts based on?
- How can I use them?
- How can I connect these ideas with what I already know – in this subject or a related one?

Such reflection weaves the ideas and facts into your long-term memory.

6. Review: This is the most important step for retaining in memory what you have learned. The best method is to use Spaced Practice, in which you spread out your Review over time. This is the opposite of cramming just before an examination. This is also the opposite of rereading immediately after reading a text. When you space out and review what you learned, you are likely to have forgotten some parts. You are then forced to study those parts again. This very act of forgetting and restudying makes the memory stronger. The Review process is the same as Step 5: Recite.

How much time should you allow between new learning and first Review or between two successive Reviews? Research shows that the optimal amount of spacing for long-term retention is given by the 1:10 rule. That is, if you want to remember the information for 20 days, review the learning every two days.

What is the benefit of using flash cards during the Reviews?

As you review the material in the succeeding days, you will notice that you easily remember the material on some cards. You can then drop those cards from the deck. As you continue the spaced repetition, you will retain more and more of the material in your memory. The deck of flash cards would get thinner, and you will have a much smaller deck to review just before the examination. Retain the dropped cards in proper order – you may want to review them again later.

What is the importance of writing down the answers on cards? In these days of email and text messages, we have lost the art of writing. Every coaching institute and guidebook will tell you how important writing practice is for success in the examination. Flash cards force you to get back into the writing mode.

Writing down the answers improves retention, brings up points you had not understood well, and leads you to more questions on the topic. Further, writing practice improves your speed, which is vital in the examination.

Is the SQ4R method with flash cards the best method of study for all students and all subjects?

Students differ widely in their motivation levels, general work habits, previous education, language competence, and so on. In the same way, books too differ in the way of presentation, difficulty levels of concepts, simplicity of language, format of chapters, and so on. Thus, one method of study may not suit all students and all books. You will have to explore and find the study skill that suits you and the subject best.

What is important is to follow a method of *active* reading, not a *passive* one. Even if you are not comfortable with the actual steps of SQ4R, try to follow the principles of learning it is built upon: Getting the larger context first, examining the book's overall organizational plan, setting specific goals, and then pursuing them, and the use of immediate recall and verbal paraphrase as aids to learning and retention. Try these key elements while studying this book and others. It is very likely that you will learn better, faster, and retain more!

All this may appear to involve too much time and effort. You might say: 'With so many subjects to cover, I do not have the time to follow this method.' Processing a chapter with the SQ4R method will certainly take more time than just reading through it. The quality of learning will, however, be incomparably better and you will also remember the material for much longer. In essence, over the long term, this method will take less time and give you better results. There will be much less need to study the same book again and again.

Syllabus Mapping

In June 2023, the University Grants Commission released the final Guidelines and Curriculum Framework for Environment Education at Undergraduate Level under the New Education Policy (NEP). All the topics listed in this curriculum have been covered in this book as shown below. The sequence of the topics in the book enables a good flow for the facts and arguments.

Syllabus Topic(s)	Covered in Chapter(s)
Unit I. Humans and the Environment	
The man-environment interaction: Humans as hunter-gatherers; Mastery of fire; Origin of agriculture; Emergence of city-states; Great ancient civilizations and the environment; Indic Knowledge and Culture of Sustainability; Middle Ages and Renaissance; Industrial Revolution and its impact on the environment; Population growth and natural resource exploitation; Global environmental change.	1
Environmental Ethics	16
The emergence of environmentalism: Anthropocentric and eco-centric perspectives (Major thinkers); The Club of Rome - Limits to Growth; UN Conference on Human Environment 1972; World Commission on Environment and Development and the concept of sustainable development; Rio Summit and subsequent international efforts.	1, 17
Unit II. Natural Resources and Sustainable Development	
Overview of natural resources: Definition of resource; Classification of natural resources-biotic and abiotic, renewable and non-renewable.	2
Biotic resources: Major type of biotic resources- forests, grasslands, wetlands, wildlife and aquatic (fresh water and marine); Microbes as a resource; Status and challenges.	2
Water resources: Types of water resources- fresh water and marine resources; Availability and use of water resources; Environmental impact of over-exploitation, issues and challenges; Water scarcity and stress; Conflicts over water.	6
Soil and mineral resources: Important minerals; Mineral exploitation; Environmental problems due to extraction of minerals and use; Soil as a resource and its degradation.	7
Energy resources: Sources of energy and their classification, renewable and non-renewable sources of energy; Conventional energy sources - coal, oil, natural gas, nuclear energy; non-conventional energy sources - solar, wind, tidal, hydro, wave, ocean thermal, geothermal, biomass, hydrogen, and fuel cells; Implications of energy use on the environment.	8
Introduction to sustainable development: Sustainable Development Goals (SDGs) - targets and indicators, challenges, and strategies for SDGs.	1, 17

Syllabus Topic(s)	Covered in Chapter(s)
Unit III. Environmental Issues: Local, Regional and Global	
Environmental issues and scales: Concepts of micro-, meso-, synoptic and planetary scales; Temporal and spatial extents of local, regional, and global phenomena.	1
Pollution: Impact of sectoral processes on Environment, Types of Pollution - air, noise, water, soil, thermal, radioactive; municipal solid waste, hazardous waste.	11–13
Transboundary air pollution; Acid rain; Smog	13
Land use and Land cover change: land degradation, deforestation, desertification, urbanization.	7
Biodiversity loss: past and current trends, impact.	9
Global change: Ozone layer depletion.	13
Climate change	14, 15
Disasters – Natural and Man-made (Anthropogenic)	14
Unit IV. Conservation of Biodiversity and Ecosystems	
Biodiversity and its distribution: Biodiversity as a natural resource; Levels and types of biodiversity; Biodiversity in India and the world; Biodiversity hotspots; Species and ecosystem threat categories.	9
Ecosystems and ecosystem services: Major ecosystem types in India and their basic characteristics - forests, wetlands, grasslands, agriculture, coastal and marine; Ecosystem services - classification and their significance.	2
Threats to biodiversity and ecosystems: Land use and land cover change; Commercial exploitation of species; Invasive species; Fire, disasters, and climate change.	9
Major conservation policies: in-situ and ex-situ conservation approaches; Major protected areas; National and International Instruments for biodiversity conservation; the role of traditional knowledge, community-based conservation; Gender and conservation.	10
Unit V. Environmental Pollution and Health	
Understanding pollution: Production processes and generation of wastes; Assimilative capacity of the environment; Definition of pollution; Point sources and non-point sources of pollution.	11–13
Air pollution: Sources of air pollution; Primary and secondary pollutants; Criteria pollutants- carbon monoxide, lead, nitrogen oxides, ground-level ozone, particulate matter, and sulphur dioxide; Other important air pollutants- Volatile Organic compounds (VOCs), Peroxyacetyl Nitrate (PAN), Polycyclic aromatic hydrocarbons (PAHs) and Persistent organic pollutants (POPs); Indoor air pollution; Adverse health impacts of air pollutants; National Ambient Air Quality Standards.	13
Water pollution: Sources of water pollution; River, lake and marine pollution, groundwater pollution; water quality Water quality parameters and standards; adverse health impacts of water pollution on human and aquatic life.	12
Soil pollution and solid waste: Soil pollutants and their sources; Solid and hazardous waste; Impact on human health.	11
Noise pollution: Definition of noise; Unit of measurement of noise pollution; Sources of noise pollution; Noise standards; adverse impacts of noise on human health.	13
Thermal and Radioactive pollution: Sources and impact on human health and ecosystems.	13

Syllabus Topic(s)	Covered in Chapter(s)
Unit VI. Climate Change: Impacts, Adaptation and Mitigation	
Understanding climate change: Natural variations in climate; Structure of atmosphere; Anthropogenic climate change from greenhouse gas emissions – past, present, and future; Projections of global climate change with special reference to temperature, rainfall, climate variability and extreme events; Importance of 1.5°C and 2.0°C limits to global warming; Climate change projections for the Indian sub-continent.	14
Impacts, vulnerability, and adaptation to climate change: Observed impacts of climate change on ocean and land systems; Sea level rise, changes in marine and coastal ecosystems; Impacts on forests and natural ecosystems; Impacts on animal species, agriculture, health, urban infrastructure; The concept of vulnerability and its assessment;	14
Adaptation vs. resilience; Climate-resilient development; Indigenous knowledge for adaptation to climate change. Mitigation of climate change: Synergies between adaptation and mitigation measures; Green House Gas (GHG) reduction vs. sink enhancement; Concept of carbon intensity, energy intensity and carbon neutrality; National and international policy instruments for mitigation, decarbonizing pathways and net zero targets for the future; Energy efficiency measures; Renewable energy sources; Carbon capture and storage, National climate action plan and Intended Nationally Determined Contributions (INDCs); Climate justice.	15
UNIT VII. Environmental Management	
Introduction to environmental laws and regulation: Constitutional provisions - Article 48A, Article 51A (g) and other derived environmental rights; Introduction to environmental legislations on the forest, wildlife, and pollution control.	16
Environmental management system: ISO 14001 Concept of Circular Economy, Life cycle analysis; Cost-benefit analysis	16
Environmental audit and impact assessment; Environmental risk assessment	16
Pollution control and management; Waste Management- Concept of 3R (Reduce, Recycle and Reuse) and sustainability;	11
Ecolabeling and Ecomark scheme	16
Unit VIII. Environmental Treaties and Legislation	
An overview of instruments of international cooperation; bilateral and multilateral agreements; conventions and protocols; adoption, signature, ratification, and entry into force; binding and non-binding measures; Conference of the Parties (COP)	1
Major International Environmental Agreements: Convention on Biological Diversity (CBD); Cartagena Protocol on Biosafety; Nagoya Protocol on Access and Benefit-sharing; Convention on International Trade in Endangered Species of Wild Flora and Fauna (CITES); Ramsar Convention on Wetlands of International Importance; United Nations Convention to Combat Desertification (UNCCD); Vienna Convention for the Protection of the Ozone Layer; Montreal Protocol on Substances that Deplete the Ozone Layer and the Kigali Amendment; Basel Convention on the Control of Transboundary Movements of Hazardous Wastes and their Disposal; Rotterdam Convention on the Prior Informed Consent Procedure for Certain Hazardous Chemicals and Pesticides in International Trade; Stockholm Convention on Persistent Organic Pollutants; Minamata Convention on Mercury; United Nations Framework Convention on Climate Change (UNFCCC); Kyoto Protocol; Paris Agreement; India's status as a party to major conventions	Covered in relevant chapters

Syllabus Topic(s)	Covered in Chapter(s)
Major Indian Environmental Legislations: The Wild Life (Protection) Act, 1972; The Water (Prevention and Control of Pollution) Act, 1974; The Forest (Conservation) Act, 1980; The Air (Prevention and Control of Pollution) Act, 1981; The Environment (Protection) Act, 1986; The Biological Diversity Act, 2002; The Scheduled Tribes and Other Traditional Forest Dwellers (Recognition of Forest Rights) Act, 2006; Noise Pollution (Regulation and Control) Rules, 2000; Industry-specific environmental standards; Waste management rules; Ramsar sites; Biosphere reserves; Protected Areas; Ecologically Sensitive Areas; Coastal Regulation Zone; Status phase-out of production and consumption of Ozone Depleting Substances by India; National Green Tribunal; Some landmark Supreme Court judgements	16 and relevant chapters
Major International organizations and initiatives: United Nations Environment Programme (UNEP), International Union for Conservation of Nature (IUCN), World Commission on Environment and Development (WCED), United Nations Educational, Scientific and Cultural Organization (UNESCO), Intergovernmental Panel on Climate Change (IPCC), and Man and the Biosphere (MAB) Programme.	17 and relevant chapters
Unit IX. Case Studies and Field Work	
Discussion on one national and one international case study related to the environment and sustainable development.	18
Field visits to identify local/regional environmental issues, making observations including data collection and preparing a brief report.	18
Participation in plantation drive and nature camps.	19
Documentation of campus biodiversity.	19
Campus environmental management activities such as solid waste disposal, water management, and sewage treatment.	19

Brief Contents

Contents

Abbreviations and Units of Measurements

(Most frequently used in the book)

Abbreviations

MoEFCC	Union Ministry of Environment, Forests, and Climate Change
IPCC	Intergovernmental Panel on Climate Change
US	United States of America
UN	United Nations
UNESCO	UN Educational, Scientific, and Cultural Organization
UN FAO	UN Food and Agricultural Organization
UNEP	UN Environment Programme
UNFCCC	UN Framework Convention on Climate Change
WHO	World Health Organization
WWF	First known as World Wildlife Fund, later as Worldwide Fund for Nature, now simply as WWF

Units of Measurement

m	Metre
km	Kilometre
sq km	Square Kilometre
ha	Hectare (Thousand Square Metres)
g	gram
kg	kilogram
MW	Megawatt (Million watts)
GW	Gigawatt (Billion watts or Thousand MW)
Tonne	Metric Ton, 1000 kg

Note: ORC refers to the Online Resource Centre of Oxford University Press.

UNIT 1

Humans and the Environment

1 Global Environmental Change, Current Crisis, and Responses

We are in the fight of our lives. And we are losing. Greenhouse gas emissions keep growing. Global temperatures keep rising. And our planet is fast approaching tipping points that will make climate chaos irreversible. We are on a highway to climate hell with our foot still on the accelerator. Humanity has a choice: cooperate or perish.

António Guterres, UN Secretary-General
UN Climate Conference
November 7, 2022

MAIN QUESTIONS ADDRESSED

- What has been the history of man-nature interaction?
- What is the state of the planet?
- What is the scale of the global environmental crisis and what are its causes?
- What is our Ecological Footprint?
- What has been the global response to the environmental crisis?
- What is sustainable development?
- What is the scope of Environmental Studies and why should you study the subject?

KEYWORDS AND PHRASES

Anthropocene, Carrying Capacity, climate change, Doomsday Clock, ecology, Ecological Footprint, environment, Environmental Studies, exponential growth, global warming, Ghoramara, Idea of Progress, Industrial Revolution, sea level rise, Sundarbans, sustainable development, UN Agreements, vulture

(***Note:*** Many of these terms and phrases may be new to you. You may not understand them immediately. Please be assured that all the terms will be discussed in detail in the succeeding chapters. Meanwhile, you can refer to the Glossary at the end of the book for explanations.)

LEAD STORY

THE STORY OF GHORAMARA: CLIMATE CHANGE AND VANISHING ISLANDS

Ghoramara, a tiny island 150 km south of Kolkata in the Sundarbans Delta, will soon vanish under the sea. Between 1972 and 2010, Ghoramara lost at least half of its land to the sea. Two other islands in the region have already disappeared and more are likely to follow.

Every year at least two cyclones hit the Sundarbans islands. The storms have grown increasingly intense, though less frequent. This means more coastal flooding, erosion, and more saline water moving in on the islands.

Man is calling out: *HELP*

Dr Sugata Hazra, an oceanographer with Jadavpur University, gives the following reasons for the erosion and sinking of the islands:

- The sea level is going up and this is caused by climate change.
- Coastal mangroves were cut down to make way for farming. The mangroves used to bind the topsoil, but now the soil is being washed away.
- The farmers also used to dig wells to get fresh water for irrigating their fields. But in time, the underground reservoirs emptied and then collapsed.

The rainfall has also shifted to post-monsoon period affecting food production. This change in the rainfall pattern is also very likely due to climate change.

The change in the climate, ingress of sea water, and the shrinking habitats are also affecting the local species like the Bengal tiger and the Cheetal deer.

Some mangrove species are also being threatened with extinction due to increased salinity as well as pollution from industrial effluents. In 2020, cyclone Amphan destroyed about a quarter of the Sundarbans' mangroves.

There are about 100 islands over an area of 9000 sq km in the Sundarbans. The rising sea could drown many of the islands during the coming decades. About 1.35 million people are currently at high risk from sea level rise, storm surges, and coastal flooding. 2.4 million others face moderate risk.

Already about 10,000 people have become refugees in other islands, while some have moved to Kolkata. Over the next 15 years, 70,000 more could be displaced.

As Ghoramara shrinks in size, its people have been moving further inland or to the larger island of Sagar. However, Sagar itself is under threat now and has already lost around 50 sq km of land — around a sixth of its former area — to coastal erosion. Hundreds of young men and women have had to leave Sagar for Kolkata — the nearest city — or for states like Kerala and Andhra Pradesh in search of employment. What will be the fate of the Sundarbans?

What does the story of Ghoramara indicate?

The islands of the Sundarbans are not unique in their predicament. All over the world, countries consisting of small low-lying islands such as Tuvalu, Kiribati, and the Solomon Islands are facing the effects of the rising sea. The Maldives and Bangladesh could also face severe erosion in the future.

Key Idea
Climate change is the biggest threat that humanity has ever faced but there are other threats such as nuclear warfare and global pandemics.

Sea level rise and severe weather are just two examples of the impact of climate change (Chapters 14 and 15). Almost every aspect of our lives will be affected by this phenomenon.

Climate change is the defining issue of this century. It is the biggest threat humanity has ever faced. The way we respond to this threat will shape the lives of the current and succeeding generations. Hence, the underlying theme of this edition of the book is climate change. It is for you, the reader, to understand the seriousness of the environmental crisis and climate change and join the movement to create a safe and sustainable world.

Scientists and many analysts are clear that we do not have much time. The interconnected issues of climate change, expansion of nuclear arms, global pandemics, growing inequality, and so on demand immediate attention. If we do not act fast, doomsday will be upon us soon (Box 1.1).

BOX 1.1 STATE OF THE PLANET: ***Doomsday Clock - 90 Seconds to Midnight***

The world is just '90 seconds' away from a major catastrophe arising from climate change and nuclear weapons. The Doomsday Clock has been set to 11 hours 58 minutes 30 seconds pm.

The Doomsday Clock was created in 1947 by the Board of the magazine *The Bulletin of the Atomic Scientists. The Bulletin* was founded in 1945 by scientists who created the atomic bomb. Shocked by the devastation caused by the Hiroshima bomb, the scientists wanted to raise awareness about the dangers of nuclear technology.

The Clock is a symbolic indicator that warns the public about how close the world is to a potentially civilization-ending catastrophe. Each year, the magazine's Board analyses threats to humanity's survival to decide where the Doomsday Clock's hands should be set. The closer the Clock is to midnight, the closer we are to global calamity.

In 1947, the Clock was set to 11.53 pm. Since then the Clock was moved forward and backward depending on the state of the nuclear threat. When the US and the erstwhile USSR conducted their first tests of the hydrogen bomb, the hands were moved to 11.58 pm. In 1991, when the world's superpowers signed the Strategic Arms Reduction Treaty, the Clock was set to 11:43 pm.

Now, the Clock has become a universally recognized indicator of the world's vulnerability to catastrophe from climate change, nuclear weapons, and new technologies emerging in other domains.

In January 2023, the Board set the Doomsday Clock to 11:58:30 pm, the closest to global catastrophe it has ever been. Some of the messages of the Board were:

- We move the hands of the Doomsday Clock forward, largely (though not exclusively) because of the mounting dangers of the war in Ukraine.
- Russia's invasion of Ukraine has increased the risk of nuclear weapons use, raised the spectre of biological and chemical weapons use, hamstrung the world's response to climate change, and hampered international efforts to deal with other global concerns.
- The war's effects are not limited to an increase in nuclear danger; they also undermine global efforts to combat climate change. Countries dependent on Russian oil and gas have sought to diversify their supplies and suppliers, leading to expanded investment in natural gas exactly when such investment should have been shrinking.
- Global carbon dioxide emissions from burning fossil fuels, after having rebounded from the COVID economic decline to an all-time high in 2021, continued to rise in 2022 and hit another record high.
- Not only did weather extremes continue to plague diverse parts of the globe, but they were more evidently attributable to climate change.
- Addressing climate change requires faith in institutions of multilateral governance. The geopolitical fissure opened by the invasion of Ukraine has weakened the global will to cooperate while undermining confidence in the durability, or even the feasibility, of broad-based multilateral collaboration.

Is There Really a Global Environmental and Climate Crisis?

Here are some indicators of the current state of the planet, drawn from various reports.

Global warming and climate change

- There are clear signs of global warming and the resultant climate change: Average global temperatures have been rising during the twentieth century and the first decade of the 21st century was the warmest on record. Worldwide, extreme weather including droughts, floods, and storms has become more common. Glaciers all over the world are melting.

- According to the India Meteorological Department (IMD) the year 2022 was the fifth warmest year on record since 1901 and the past decade (2013–2022) was the warmest decade. In 2022, there was an extreme weather event in India on almost every single day of the year. During May–July 2022, the Northeast experienced two waves of devastating floods followed by drought-like conditions.

Water and sanitation

- Two billion people (26% of the world's population) do not have access to safely managed drinking water services, and an estimated 3.6 billion (46%) lack access to safely managed sanitation. By 2025, two-thirds of the world population may suffer water stress.
- Over the last century, India lost 50% of its lakes and wetlands to other uses. 47% of rural households have no tapped water connection.

Biological diversity

- Worldwide, of the known species, 30% of amphibians, 25% of mammals, 12% of birds, 25% of reptiles, and 21% of fish species are threatened with extinction. The current extinction rate is estimated to be 100 to 1000 times the rate at which species naturally disappear.
- More than 10% of India's recorded wild flora and fauna are threatened and many are on the verge of extinction.

Forests

- Over the past three decades, the world lost around 10% of forest cover. Tropical forests are being cleared at the rate of 70,000 to 170,000 sq km annually (equal to 20–50 soccer fields per minute).
- India has lost about 94 million ha of natural forests since 2000. Government reports show an increase in forest cover, but environmentalists question this claim.

Land

- Each year, 6 million ha of agricultural land are lost due to desertification and soil degradation. This loss affects about 250 million people in the world.
- About 40% of India's land has been degraded. We lose 5.3 billion tonnes of topsoil every year. Thousands of hectares of land are diverted every year for industrial and non-agricultural uses.

Pollution

- At least 1 billion people in the world breathe unhealthy air and 3 million die annually due to air pollution. Air pollution levels are still above the World Health Organization (WHO) guidelines in most developing countries.
- According to the World Air Quality Report published by IQAir in March 2023, out of 131 countries studied, India was the world's eighth most polluted one. Also, out of the 50 most polluted cities, 39 were in India. Further, India has the highest rate of deaths caused by chronic respiratory diseases in the world, primarily caused by such pollution.

Ocean and coastal areas

- Overfishing and ocean acidification is placing all of marine life at risk. Large areas of the ocean have become dead zones without any life. Worldwide, 50% of coastal mangroves and corals that perform vital ecological functions have been destroyed.
- Industrial effluents, domestic waste, agricultural runoff, shipping activity, and offshore exploration cause heavy pollution of the Arabian Sea and the Bay of Bengal. Over the past 40 years, India too has lost more than 50% of its mangrove forests.

Energy

- More than 2 billion people in the world go without adequate energy supplies. Even by 2030, nearly 3 billion people, mostly in rural areas in Africa and Asia, will continue to rely on fuelwood for cooking and heating, while about 1 billion people will have no access to electricity.
- India imports more than 80% of its oil needs, primarily to feed the transportation sector.

Population

- The world population reached 8 billion in 2022 and is expected to reach 10 billion by 2100. It took just 12 years for the population to increase from 6 to 7 billion. The largest share of population growth is expected in countries that are currently low-income ones.
- India's population was about 1.3 billion in early 2015. By 2050, with a projected population of 1.65 billion, we will be the most populous country in the world.

Urbanization

- More than half the world's population now lives in urban areas, compared to little more than one-third in 1972. About one-quarter of the urban population lives below the poverty line.
- About 23% of the population in India's million-plus cities live in slums. Just 33% of urban households have access to piped sewage system.

Environmental governance

- International negotiations over several years have not led to any binding agreement on limiting greenhouse gas emissions and tackling climate change.
- While India has many environmental laws and regulations, the implementation has always been lax. In addition, the rules are often seen as impediments to rapid economic growth and the government is always under pressure to relax them.

You can find many more such examples of the crisis in regular and special reports on the state of the world's environment. You will find a list of such reports in the ORC.

The picture is clear: Severe environmental degradation is happening all over the world. What is the reason for this depressing state of affairs? Scientists and environmentalists are clear that human activities have had an enormous negative impact on the environment.

What Was the Initial Impact of Humans on the Environment?

Human impact on the environment was very limited until the end of the Renaissance period (Table 1.1).

How did Ancient Indian Thought relate to Nature and a Sustainable Way of Living?

Indian scriptures such as the Vedas and Upanishads have expressed a profound respect for nature and the idea of taking from nature only what one needs. According to Indian philosophy, the entire universe is to be considered and respected as a form of the Divine.

The Atharva Veda, for example, includes the Prithvi Sukta, hymns to the Goddess Earth. Here is a quote from the Prithvi Sukta:

She who bears plants endowed with many varied powers, may Prithivi for us spread wide and favour us; in whom the sea, and Sindhu, and the waters, in whom our food and corn-lands had their being.

What was the Impact of the Industrial Revolution on the Environment?

The Industrial Revolution began in England and Europe around 1750, when we discovered huge sources of external energy – first it was coal and later oil and natural gas. The steam engine running

TABLE 1.1 Human Impact on the Environment

Period	Human Activities / Impact
2 million years ago	Emergence of *Homo erectus*, hunter-gatherers, ability to control fire
200,000 - 300,000 years ago	Emergence of anatomically modern human species (*Homo sapiens*)
11,000 – 12,000 years ago	Origin of agriculture, domestication of plants and animals, cutting of some forests
2500 BCE (Before Common Era)	Harappan civilization of Indus River valley with high level of public health and citywide sanitation.
1000 – 800 BCE	Emergence of city-states
Late 5th to late 15th Centuries	Middle Ages: Limited impact
14th to 17th Centuries	Renaissance: A turn to science and rationalism; more forests destroyed for heating and building houses.

on coal sparked the rapid growth of industries. Early in the 19th Century came steam locomotives and steamships. This development led to the massive European colonization of countries in Asia, Africa, and Latin America.

The Industrial Revolution also changed man's attitude towards nature by giving an impetus for the Idea of Progress, which has dominated human thinking ever since. The Idea of Progress is based on the following beliefs:

- Humans are a superior species and can indefinitely exploit natural resources.
- Our progress towards a better life will be linear and continuous.
- Science and technology will help us in this quest for ceaseless progress and economic development.

Through colonialism and other ways, the Idea of Progress was conveyed to large parts of the world. Today, most countries swear by this notion of growth and development through science, technology, and industrial expansion.

The first half of the 20th Century saw two World Wars and a lot of destruction. However, once the World War II ended in 1945, there was a rapid industrialization of Europe, Japan, and the US. Further, many countries such as India that became independent also embraced the Idea of Progress.

What factors led to the current Environmental Crisis?

The rapid industrialization led to the current environmental crisis due to two main reasons:

1. We consume natural resources at a rate much higher than that at which nature can regenerate them.
2. As we consume the resources, we are also creating waste and pollution much faster than the rate at which nature can absorb them.

This is an unsustainable way of living and it could only lead to an environmental and social catastrophe.

Surely nature will take care of the environmental problems over time?

The earth has existed for 5 billion years, humanity for 3 to 5 million years, and civilization for 10,000 years. The earth and all its living beings have survived many crises and cataclysmic events. Looking back over centuries, nature seems to have absorbed disturbances and stayed always in balance. Thousands of species have survived over a long period and, consequently, could be expected to continue to exist forever. Will we not survive the current environmental crisis too?

The earth will surely survive this crisis and many species may survive too, but we may be wrong in assuming that humanity will also continue to exist forever. The reason is that there is something different happening now.

In the past, changes in nature were always slow but that is no longer true. Human activities have drastically increased the pace at which things change. What is happening now can be described by a simple mathematical curve or graph—the exponential growth of a quantity with time. This curve is relatively flat in the beginning, but becomes steeper and steeper with time (Read Box 1.2 for an explanation of exponential growth.)

Four such mega phenomena or spikes have been occurring, with profound implications for life on earth. These are the four quantities that are growing exponentially:

- Size of the human population (Fig. 1.2)
- Production and consumption of goods and services (Fig. 1.3)
- Concentration of carbon dioxide gas in the atmosphere (Fig. 1.4)
- Number of biological species becoming extinct every year (Fig. 1.5)

BOX 1.2 CONCEPT: *Exponential Growth*

Suppose you invest ₹1000 in a bank, which gives you an annual interest of 10%. You ask the bank to reinvest the interest earned every year. (We call this compound interest.) At the end of the first year, your account will have grown to ₹1100. At the end of the second year, the balance will be ₹1210 (₹1100 + 110). Thus, every year, an increased amount of interest gets added to the principal. What will be the accumulated amount at the end of 50 years? Guess the amount before reading further!

In 50 years, the amount would have grown to more than ₹117,000! If you did not know the power of compound interest, you would have surely underestimated the value. This kind of increase is called exponential growth.

Compare this growth with the case of simple interest. The initial deposit of ₹1000 will earn a constant amount of interest (₹100) every year. At the end of 50 years, the total amount will be only ₹6000 (original deposit of ₹1000 + interest of ₹5000). You can see for yourself how compound interest makes so much difference. This is the power of exponential growth.

Mathematically, any growth is exponential if the increase is at a constant rate per time period, rather than a constant amount. If you show exponential growth as a graph, the shape of the curve will be like the letter J. Figure 1.1 shows the growth of your investment of ₹1000 at a compound interest rate of 10%. You can also compare the growth with a simple interest of same value.

Many natural phenomena exhibit exponential growth. For example, the population of the world has been increasing exponentially. With every case of exponential growth we associate 'a doubling time'. This is roughly the time it takes for the quantity to double in value. You can get the doubling time by dividing the number 70 by the growth rate of the quantity. This formula is derived from the basic mathematics of exponential growth. World population doubles every 45 years or so.

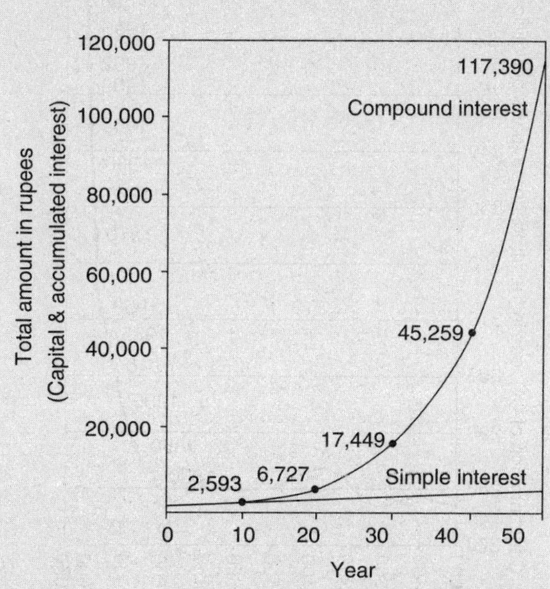

FIGURE 1.1 Curve Showing Exponential Growth

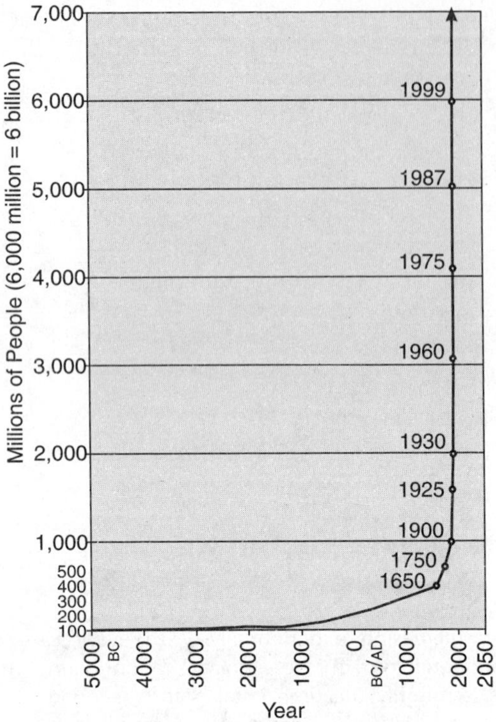

FIGURE 1.2 Growth of Population

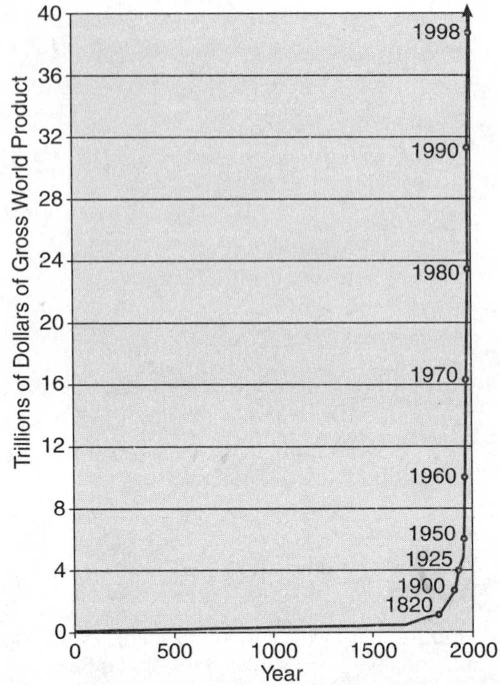

FIGURE 1.3 Growth of Consumption

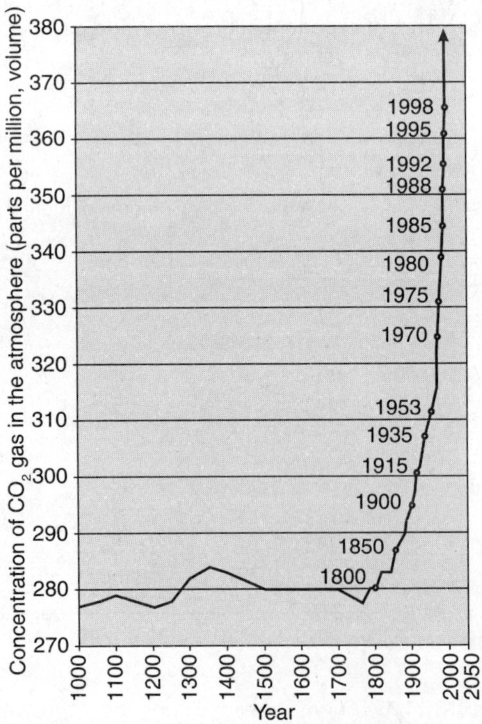

FIGURE 1.4 Growth of Carbon Dioxide Emission

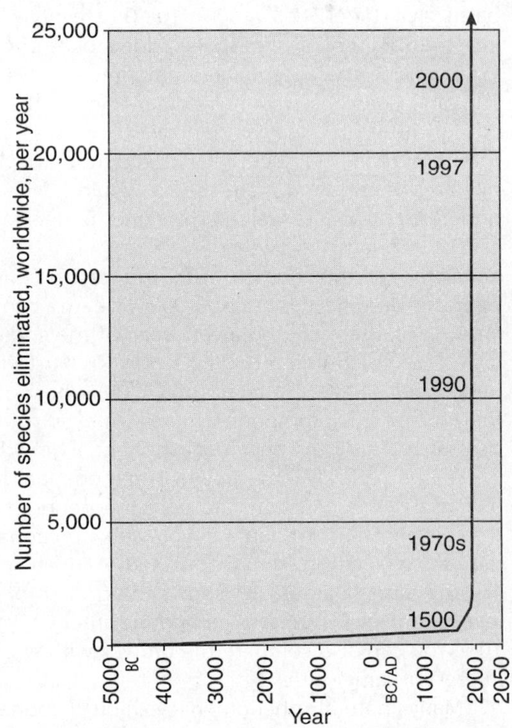

FIGURE 1.5 Growth in Loss of Species

A remarkable fact is that, in each case, the curve was flat over centuries until the spike began in recent times. What makes matters worse is that the four spikes are interconnected, each amplifying the others. Let us take a closer look at these four phenomena.

Are there too many people on earth?

The exponential growth in human population began in 1650 and now, every three days, the size increases as much as it did in a whole century before. We have to provide the existing 8 billion people (and billions more to come) with food, water, shelter, education, medical facilities, and so on. This task looks even more formidable in the light of the impact of the other three spikes.

Are we consuming too much?

The amount of natural resources used up every year began spiking around 1900 and the steady economic growth has led to extraordinary levels of unsustainable consumption. In the mad race to consume more, we are using up the earth's finite resources like topsoil, water, oil, and forests far faster than natural processes can regenerate them.

Are the carbon dioxide emissions too much?

The concentration of carbon dioxide gas in the atmosphere started increasing exponentially since 1800 and the trend continues unabated. The main reason is the burning of fossil fuels like coal and oil. Excessive emissions of carbon dioxide (and other such gases) have reduced the earth's capacity to radiate heat and led to global warming and climate change. We will discuss this issue in Chapters 14 and 15.

Are we losing species fast?

There have been mass extinctions on earth caused by natural changes but they occurred over hundreds of years. For millions of years, the number of extinctions per year seems to have been very low. The ascendance of monoculture and the massive clearing of tropical forests during the last four centuries have decimated plant and animal species. Many biologists believe that we have now entered the fastest mass extinction rate in earth's history. We will cover the enormous negative impact of species loss in Chapters 9 and 10.

We went on exploiting nature so rapidly that we are now living beyond our means. Our 'Ecological Footprint' is getting larger and larger.

What is Ecological Footprint?

Assume that you live in a small house in a city. Let us say that the house is surrounded by a small garden and there is a compound wall that marks your plot of land. Can you isolate yourself in your home and continue to live indefinitely? You cannot, since you need many things from outside: food, water, material of different sorts and so on. Your garden may give you some vegetables, but it cannot provide you all the food items you need. There may be a well on your land, but the water may not be potable and you may have to depend on outside sources for drinking water.

> **Key Idea** Ecological Footprint is the amount of biologically productive land and sea area required to sustain indefinitely an entity such as a person, a city's population, a country, etc. It accounts for the energy, food, water, and materials that the entity consumes and the wastes that it creates.

Suppose we ask the question: How large a land will you need just to sustain yourself completely? That area is your Ecological Footprint.

Let us do a mental experiment. Take the physical area of a city like Chennai and cover it with a huge glass hemisphere. We let in sunlight, but we do not allow any material to enter or leave the enclosure. How long will the city survive? Not many days!

The city cannot produce enough food for all the people. There will be severe water scarcity because the tankers from the surrounding villages will stop entering the city. The enormous amount of solid waste generated every day cannot be sent away or dumped into the sea. The air trapped in the hemisphere will soon become so polluted that people will find it difficult to breathe. The 'Carrying Capacity' (term explained below) of the city area is not sufficient to sustain the lives of the population.

Suppose we are able to expand the size of the glass hemisphere to take in more and more of the surrounding area. Assume also that this area has diverse natural resources like a mini-earth. We can now ask another question: How large should be the area covered, if we want the city to survive indefinitely on the land, water, and energy resources available within the hemisphere? That area is the Ecological Footprint of the city.

Most cities have huge needs and draw their requirements from a very large area surrounding the city. The Ecological Footprint of any large city is many, many times larger than its actual area. Similarly, we can talk about the Ecological Footprint of a country. Or, we can compare the Footprint of a citizen of US with that of an Indian citizen.

We can express Ecological Footprint either in units of area or as the ratio of the area required to the actual area of the entity. For example, if a city requires for its survival an area three times its geographical spread, then its Ecological Footprint is three.

How is our environmental crisis connected to the idea of Ecological Footprint?

The larger the Footprint, the more is the consumption of natural resources and the more is the environmental degradation. Most of the world's cities and many developed countries have Footprints greater than one.

What is the ecological footprint of humanity as a whole?

The answer may surprise you. Humanity's Ecological Footprint is about 1.75. That is, we now require 75% more than the earth's area to sustain our consumption of natural resources! Our Footprint is also increasing steadily.

How is that possible? Common sense tells us that we could not be using resources from an area larger than that of the earth! We have only one earth. If our Footprint is 1.75, how are we surviving at all?

We survive because each year we are using up more than our annual share of the earth's resources. By June, we use up ecological resources that the earth regenerates in the whole year! The rest of the year, we survive by dipping into our quota of the future.

Key Idea Humanity's Ecological Footprint is already 1.75 and we now require 75% more than the earth's area to sustain our consumption of natural resources.

We draw more water from the ground than the amount of natural recharge. We catch fish faster than the rate at which they can re-populate. Our logging of trees is faster than the rate at which new trees grow.

Instead of living within the 'annual interest' that nature gives us, we have begun using up our 'natural capital'. In a sense, we are using resources that rightly belong to our children and grandchildren. We are living beyond our means.

In general, we: are using resources faster than they can regenerate and creating waste faster than it can be absorbed. This is called 'ecological overshoot'. While this can be done for a short while, overshoot ultimately leads to the drastic depletion of resources on which our well-being depends.

Another reason why humanity survives ecological overshoot is that the poorer people on earth consume very little resources. The rest of us consume their share too!

What is Carrying Capacity and How does It Relate to Ecological Footprint?

Carrying Capacity refers to the maximum population of a species that a given land or marine area can support. It is concerned about the present and the future. We can calculate the Carrying Capacity of many non-human species that have easily defined and consistent needs of consumption. For humans, however, calculating the Carrying Capacity is more difficult. That is because human resource consumption, standards of living, and 'wants' (as distinct from 'needs') keep changing over time and space. The productivity of the biosphere and the impact of advances in technology cannot also be easily predicted.

Ecological Footprint, on the other hand, is only concerned with the present and past years. Instead of asking how many people *could* be supported on the planet, the Ecological Footprint asks the question: How many planets were necessary to support all of the people that lived on the planet in a given year, under that year's standard of living, biological production, and technology? This is a question that can be answered through the analysis of available data.

What is Anthropocene?

During the past 10,000 years or so, human civilizations have flourished on Earth by exploiting the bounties of nature. This period is part of the geological epoch is called Holocene. Since the industrial revolution, however, human activities have increased exponentially and generated a global geophysical pressures equivalent to some of the great forces of nature. Such forces inevitably lead to crossing planetary boundaries, placing our future at risk.

Many scientists, led by the late Nobel Laureate Paul Crutzen, have asserted that we have overwhelmed the forces of nature and entered a new geological epoch called the Anthropocene.

What was the Beginning of Environmentalism?

Even by the 1960s, the adverse environmental impact of unbridled economic growth was becoming clear. Books like Rachel Carson's *Silent Spring* (1962), which documented the harmful effects of DDT, set the tone for an environmental movement. In 1972, the Club of Rome, a platform of diverse thought leaders from different countries, published a landmark report, *The Limits to Growth.* This report was the first to model our planet's interconnected systems and to make clear that if growth trends in population, industrialisation, resource use, and pollution continued unchanged, we would reach and then overshoot the carrying capacity of the Earth at some point in the next one hundred years.

The UN Conference on Human Environment in 1972 held in Stockholm was the first international initiative to discuss environmental problems. In 1983, the UN set up the World Commission on Environment and Development (WCED) with Gro Harlem Brundtland of Norway as the Chairperson. The WCED Report, called *Our Common Future,* emphasized the need for an integration of economic and ecological systems. The Commission supported the concept of 'Sustainable Development'.

What is Meant by Sustainable Development?

The WCED Report gave the following definition:

Sustainable development is development that meets the needs of the present without compromising the ability of future generations to meet their own needs.

This definition implies that economic development and environmental conservation could go together. Is this possible or is it just a dream? We will return to this question toward the end of the book (Chapter 17). After we discuss the diverse aspects of the environmental crisis and the possible solutions, we will be in a better position to examine the concepts of sustainability and sustainable development.

What happened after the Stockholm meeting?

After Stockholm, the major effort was the UN Conference on Environment and Development (UNCED), called Earth Summit, held in 1992 in Rio de Janeiro, Brazil. Attended by more than 100 Heads of State and 30,000 participants, UNCED came up with several documents including:

- The Rio Declaration on Environment and Development listing 27 principles of sustainable development
- *Agenda 21,* a detailed action plan for sustainable development in the twenty-first century
- The Convention on Biological Diversity

The implementation of the Rio agreements, however, was very poor. Two more such conferences followed, one in 2002 (Johannesburg, South Africa) and the other in 2012 (Rio de Janeiro again). These conferences came up with more modest but concrete plans of action. But even such plans have mostly remained on paper.

What are the Sustainable Development Goals?

In 2015, the UN General Assembly adopted the 2030 Agenda for Sustainable Development, which listed 17 Sustainable Development Goals (SDGs). Box 1.3 lists the SDGs.

How does the UN Arrive at a Multilateral Agreement on Environment and Other Issues?

The proposal for a new treaty may come from a member state during a speech at the UN General Assembly. If the proposal interests other states, informal and formal discussions will be held on the objectives and provisions of the proposed treaty. Such discussions may go on for months or even years. Finally, a draft treaty is prepared. It may include both binding and non-binding provisions.

BOX 1.3 **UN 2030 AGENDA FOR SUSTAINABLE DEVELOPMENT:** ***17 Sustainable Development Goals to Transform Our World***

1. End poverty in all its forms everywhere.
2. End hunger, achieve food security, and improved nutrition, and promote sustainable agriculture.
3. Ensure healthy lives and promote well-being for all at all ages.
4. Ensure inclusive and equitable quality education and promote lifelong learning opportunities for all.
5. Achieve gender equality and empower all women and girls.
6. Ensure availability and sustainable management of water and sanitation for all.
7. Ensure access to affordable, reliable, sustainable, and modern energy for all.
8. Promote sustained, inclusive, and sustainable economic growth, full and productive employment, and decent work for all.
9. Build resilient infrastructure, promote inclusive and sustainable industrialization, and foster innovation.
10. Reduce inequality within and among countries.
11. Make cities and human settlements inclusive, safe, resilient, and sustainable.
12. Ensure sustainable consumption and production patterns.
13. Take urgent action to combat climate change and its impacts.
14. Conserve and sustainably use the ocean, seas, and marine resources for sustainable development.
15. Protect, restore, and promote sustainable use of terrestrial ecosystems, sustainably manage forests, combat desertification, halt and reverse land degradation, and halt biodiversity loss.
16. Promote peaceful and inclusive societies for sustainable development, provide access to justice for all, and build effective, accountable, and inclusive institutions at all levels.
17. Strengthen the means of implementation and revitalize the global partnership for sustainable development.

The treaty is discussed and adopted at a conference. It could be the regular conference of an existing UN Convention. For example, any new treaty on biodiversity will be discussed and adopted at a conference of the Convention on Biological Diversity. A treaty could also be adopted at a special conference convened for that purpose.

When a treaty is adopted, it is usually called a Convention. The Convention will be opened for signature on a particular day. A state may sign the Convention, but it should also ratify it in due time. The institution of ratification grants states the necessary time-frame to seek the required approval for the treaty on the domestic level and to enact the necessary legislation to give domestic effect to that treaty.

When does a Convention come into force? Typically, the provisions of the treaty determine the date on which the treaty enters into force. It is common to provide for a fixed number of states to express their consent for entry into force. Some treaties provide for additional conditions to be satisfied. For example, a treaty on land conservation may specify that a minimum total area of conservation must be reached before it comes into force. The treaty may also provide for an additional time period to elapse after the required number of countries have expressed their consent or the conditions have been satisfied.

Most conventions conduct an annual Conference of the Parties (COP), which is the supreme governing body of the convention. It is composed of representatives of the member states of the convention and accredited observers. The term 'Parties' is used because of the inclusion of these observers. For example, with many conventions, along with the European states, the Secretariat of European Union is included as an observer. The scope of the COP is to review the implementation of the Convention and any other legal instruments that the COP adopts and take decisions necessary to promote the effective implementation of the Convention.

A new treaty can be a Protocol to an existing Convention. In other words, a Protocol adds provisions to the Convention on some specific aspects. For example, the COP of the UN Framework Convention on Climate Change (UNFCCC) adopted the Kyoto Protocol, which placed limits on emissions by member states.

What Are the Different Scales of Environmental Issues?

Environmental issues can be examined and addressed at micro-, meso-, synoptic, and planetary scales. The concept of scale considers the typical size and lifetime of a phenomenon. The scales refer to the temporal and spatial extents of local, regional, and global phenomena.

Let us consider, for example, the issue of climate change. We can study the changes in climate and weather at different scales of temporal and spatial extents as given below:

- Micro-scale: Changes in your town over a short period of, say, three monsoon months.
- Meso-scale: Changes in India over one year.
- Synoptic scale: Changes in the whole of Asia over five years.
- Planetary scale: Global changes over several decades.

Using different scales will give us different perspectives on the issue.

Could We Define Environmental Studies and Related Terms?

Generally, there are two ways in which we use the term 'environment'. In one, the term refers to what surrounds an entity. Any entity, say a person, any living organism, a citizen, a company, etc., has a certain environment. We thus talk of the home environment, the business environment, the political environment, etc.

In the second way, we use the word to mean just the natural environment: the air, water, soil, living beings, plants, trees, mountains, ocean, etc. The Oxford Advanced Learner's Dictionary defines *environment* as 'the natural world in which people, animals, and plants live'. This book deals with this natural environment.

An entity interacts with its environment, that is, it influences and is influenced by the environment, positively or negatively. For example, the natural environment affects human beings. We in turn have an impact (often a negative one) on the environment.

Ecology is the science that studies the relationships between living things and the environment. It is often considered to be a discipline of biology.

Environmental Science is the systematic and scientific study of the environment and our role in it.

What then is *Environmental Studies*, which is the subject of this book? The two terms, *Environmental Studies* and *Environmental Science*, are often used interchangeably, but we could make a distinction.

Environmental Studies can be defined as the branch of study concerned with environmental issues. It has a broader canvas than environmental science and includes the social aspects of the environment. It does deal with science where necessary, but at a level understandable to the non-scientist.

Why do we say that environmental studies is an interdisciplinary subject?

The subject of environment is inherently interdisciplinary. We study the complex relationships that exist in our natural environment among people, animals, other organisms, water, soil, air, trees, ocean, and so on. The interconnections are numerous and involve many different disciplines. We need inputs from diverse disciplines such as biology, botany, zoology, soil science, technology, oceanography, atmospheric science, economics, sociology, anthropology, and ethics.

A simple rule to remember is that everything in this world is connected. A single act of ours could have unexpected effects. What happened to vultures in India is an example (Box 1.4).

BOX 1.4 CONNECTIONS: *Vultures, Cows, Wild Dogs, and Rabies*

How can there be any connection between vultures, cows, wild dogs, and the incidence of rabies? Here is a remarkable story of environmental connections: a great tragedy, the unravelling of a mystery, and some hope.

In the early 1990s, there were at least 80 million vultures in India and Pakistan. One could see massive flocks of vultures in the sky. Yet, within a decade the vulture population declined by 97–99%. How did it happen?

After examining hundreds of dead birds, scientists discovered that the vultures were dying of kidney failure. Why did the kidney fail? Due to the drug diclofenac! The vultures were eating dead cows and the cows had been given diclofenac, a low-cost painkiller. It turned out that even a small amount of diclofenac was deadly to vultures.

The vulture is the world's most efficient scavenger, but it is also a slow breeder. It lays just one egg every year. Thus the breeding could not match the speed with which the vultures were dying.

Now comes the unexpected connection in the story: When the vulture population declined, wild dogs started eating the dead cows and their population exploded. They also picked up the rabies virus from the cows and transmitted them to other dogs. Rabid dogs started biting villagers and India ended up having the highest rate of human rabies in the world, resulting in about 35,000 deaths a year. (The vultures, with their strong stomach acid and high body temperature, can destroy corpse pathogens such as the rabies virus.)

The story continued: The growing wild dog population was easy prey for leopards, which began entering villages to hunt them. As a result, the leopard population also increased dramatically. There were more man–leopard encounters and many more people were killed.

Another side story: The Parsis leave their dead for vultures to consume and now there were too few vultures to carry out the task!

The story ends with some hope: In 2006, India, Pakistan, and Nepal banned the use of diclofenac for cattle. Meanwhile, Vulture Conservation Centres were also established.

In 2020, the Government of India released an Action Plan for Vulture Conservation (2020–2025). In 2021, India's first captive-bred vultures were set free.

Why should you study environmental studies as a subject?

- Due to the unprecedented environmental degradation, you will soon be living in a very different and difficult world. You must understand the nature and severity of the crisis and your role in it.
- You should move from a linear thinking to systemic thinking that recognizes complex interactions and natural cycles in the world.
- Finally, you must find out what you can do to mitigate the impact of the crisis and how you can join the worldwide movement to save the planet and humanity.

Is There Hope for the Future?

While this book describes the environmental crisis, it also contains many stories of hope, of successful efforts by individuals, voluntary groups, international organizations, and even governments.

Positive actions here and there are not enough, however. We must act individually and collectively to save the planet and the human species through sustainable development.

Ultimately, it is a question of changing one's mindset and taking greater care in the use of natural resources. If that happens to a sufficiently large number of people, we may yet begin to manage the resources in a wise and sustainable way. We will return to this question in the final chapter of the book.

REVIEW: A SUMMARY OF THE KEY POINTS

- Environmental indicators show that the world is facing a global crisis.
- We have entered the new epoch of the Anthropocene.
- Climate change is the defining issue of this century. It is the biggest threat we have ever faced.
- We are the cause of the crisis. We consume natural resources at an ever-increasing rate, without giving nature time to regenerate them.
- We also pollute the world so much that nature cannot absorb all of it.
- Our unsustainable way of living can only lead to a catastrophe.
- The environmental crisis is rooted in our attitude of domination and exploitation of nature, based on the Idea of Progress.
- Many phenomena like population and consumption have been growing exponentially over the past 200 years or so. This has never happened before.
- The concept of Ecological Footprint expresses the amount of land needed to sustain the lifestyle of an entity—a person, a city, a country, etc.
- Humanity's Ecological Footprint is already 1.75. That is, we now require 75% more than the earth's area to sustain our consumption of natural resources.
- There have been several international conferences over the issues of environment and development, but the implementation of the agreements has been poor.
- Any study of the environment has to be an interdisciplinary one.
- If we join forces and change our ways of living, we can still stop the destruction and save humanity.

EXERCISES

Objective-type questions

In each case below, choose the best answer out of the given set of choices:

1. Which of the following statements is true with regard to the global water and sanitation situation?
   (a) Half of the world population does not have access to safely managed drinking water services.
   (b) By 2025, two-thirds of the world population may suffer water stress.
   (c) 75% of India's rural households have no tapped water connection.
   (d) About 7 billion people in the world lack access to safely managed sanitation.
2. Which of the following statements is true?
   (a) Nature can absorb the waste and pollution that we create.
   (b) Even if we continue with our current ways of living, nature will, in due course, take care of the problems that we create.
   (c) Our current consumption levels are unsustainable.
   (d) Natural resources have no limits.
3. Assume that there is a quantity that increases exponentially and we draw the graph of the quantity against time. How would you best describe the curve?
   (a) Its increase is directly proportional to the time. When the time doubles, the quantity also doubles.
   (b) It is a flat curve.
   (c) The curve goes up and down.
   (d) Its value doubles over a fixed time period and the curve becomes steeper all the time.
4. Humanity's Ecological Footprint
   (a) already exceeds the area of the earth.
   (b) cannot exceed the area of the earth.
   (c) now equals twice the area of the earth.
   (d) is less than the area of the earth.
5. Which of the following was **not** a conference on environment?
   (a) Stockholm UN Conference on Human Environment in 1972.
   (b) UN Conference on Environment and Development held in 1992 in Rio de Janeiro.
   (c) World Summit called Rio+10 held in Johannesburg in 2002.
   (d) Conference of the G20 leaders held in New Delhi in 2023.
6. What is the most important environmental issue of this century?
   (a) Scarcity of water
   (b) Climate change
   (c) Population growth
   (d) Shortage of petroleum

Short-answer questions

1. What are the two main causes of the environmental crisis?
2. Explain the concept of Ecological Footprint through an example.
3. List the major international conferences held on environment and development.
4. Define the term 'sustainable development'.

Long-answer questions

1. Explain the root cause of the current environmental crisis through the four spikes.
2. Give a non-mathematical explanation of exponential growth and compare it with linear growth. Give one or more examples.
3. Humanity's Ecological Footprint is 75% more than the earth area. How then are we carrying on our 'business as usual'?
4. Why do we say that any study of the environment becomes an interdisciplinary one?
5. Find out the current status of each of the environmental indicators listed in this chapter. Have any indicators changed for the better?

Think critically: Deeper questions for reflection and discussion

1. There is a view that all our problems and our domination over nature started when we started practising agriculture about 10,000 years ago. Examine this view and give arguments in favour and against.
2. In your opinion, what should be the difference in the way the two subjects, environmental science and environmental studies, are taught to undergraduates?

3. Why are many environmental problems so difficult to solve?
4. What are the implications of living in the Anthropocene?

ENJOY AND EDUCATE YOURSELF

1. Watch the movie *The Day the Earth Stood Still* (2008), starring Keanu Reeves. The film is a powerful reminder that there are consequences to wilful ignorance and inaction about the environmental crisis.
2. Read *Ecotopia: The Notebooks and Reports of William Weston* (1975), a novel by Ernest Callenbach, which describes an ecological utopia. This novel was influential in the environmental movement.

ACCESS THE OUP ONLINE RESOURCE CENTRE FOR MORE

- The story of Kalahandi: From forests to famine
- Connections: Get rid of malaria, but invite the plague
- Connections: Drink coffee in US and make the songbird vanish in South America!
- List of regular and periodical reports on the environment
- References, websites, and films

UNIT 2 Ecosystems and Natural Resources

2 Ecosystems and Natural Resources

The great ecosystems are like complex tapestries— a million complicated threads, interwoven, make up the whole picture.

Gerald Durrell (1925–1995) English naturalist and author

MAIN QUESTIONS ADDRESSED

- What is an ecological system or ecosystem?
- How do materials and energy move through an ecosystem?
- What is the state of our planet's ecosystems?

KEYWORDS AND PHRASES

abiotic conditions, aquatic life zone, biogeochemical cycle, biome, biosphere, biota, carbon cycle, climax ecosystem, community, consumer, decomposer, detrivore, ecological niche, ecological pyramid, ecological succession, ecosystem, ecosystem service, ecotone, Edge Effect, energy flow, food chain, food web, glacier melt, habitat, Himalayas, homeostasis, photosynthesis, population, producer, species, sulphur cycle, trophic level, water cycle

LEAD STORY

THE STORY OF THE HIMALAYAS: CLIMATE CHANGE AND MELTING GLACIERS

'If there is a paradise on earth, it is here, it is here, it is here,' said the Moghul emperor Jehangir while visiting Kashmir in the early seventeenth century. The beauty of the Himalayas is timeless.

The majestic Himalayas are not merely a range of mountains. They are considered to be the cradle of Indian civilization and have exerted great influence over Indian thought, culture, and of course the environment. They are not just the 'abode of snow' (as the name implies), but are venerated as the kingdom of the Gods.

Spread over 2,000 km across South Asia, the Hindu Kush Himalayan region includes all or parts of Afghanistan, Bangladesh, Bhutan, China, India, Nepal, and Pakistan. The mountain range is the source of many rivers that nourish the land, including the great Indus, Ganga, and Brahmaputra.

Husband to wife: *We might as well have gone to the great desert!*

The region contains 55,000 glaciers, 40% of the earth's fresh water, and is a critical source for irrigation, drinking water, and energy to some 1.5 billion people. And now, these glaciers are melting away.

Climate change, which is a result of global warming, is causing the glaciers to melt. It is now clear that global warming is occurring due to human activities, primarily the excessive burning of fossil fuels like oil and coal (Chapter 14).

The meltdown of the glaciers (called glacial retreat) is a complex phenomenon and scientists are still trying to understand the process. They cannot easily measure the rate of meltdown, nor can they predict when all the ice would disappear. They are, however, definite that most glaciers in the Himalayan region are retreating and this process is also accelerating with time.

Excessive meltdown may cause floods initially, but in the long run glacial retreat will reduce the water reaching the rivers. Also, the water from the meltdown is creating large lakes and there is a big risk of these lakes bursting out and causing enormous floods.

Each summer, the melt water feeds the rivers and streams of the region. If the glacial retreat continues, at some stage, normal glacier melt will not be able to contribute to the region's water supply each year.

Climate change is also resulting in less snow in the middle and lower heights of the range. Consequently, many of the Himalayan communities are not getting enough water for irrigation. Overuse of water, increase in population, and depletion of ground water are worsening the water crisis.

The glacial retreat is adding to the irreparable ecological damage already suffered by the Himalayas. Human activities like forest clearing, road construction, and mountaineering have taken a heavy toll. These in turn have led to soil erosion, landslides, and floods. In addition, there are natural calamities like avalanches and earthquakes.

In spite of their scale and grandeur, the Himalayas constitute a fragile ecosystem in delicate balance. That balance may have already been upset, with unpredictable consequences for the entire subcontinent.

CLIMATE CHANGE AND ECOSYSTEMS

Climate change is transforming ecosystems at extraordinary rates and scales, causing widespread species extinction, migration, and behaviour changes.

What do we learn from the story of the Himalayas?

The story shows that even large ecological systems like the Himalayas are being adversely affected by human activities. We can no longer assume that such natural systems would continue to function as before and provide us with the natural resources that we need.

Where do We Start in Our Journey through Environmental Issues?

In this book, we will see how from the Himalayas to Kanyakumari, and in most other parts of the world, human activities are causing severe degradation of the environment. First, however, we should learn about nature itself—the ecological systems, including forests, deserts, ocean, rivers, lakes, etc. That is the task of this chapter and the next few.

What is an Ecosystem?

When you hear the term 'forest ecosystem', what comes to your mind? Immediately you think of trees, animals, birds, butterflies, and so on. The mention of the term 'ocean ecosystem' brings to mind a picture of waves, currents, fish, whales, and so on. An ecosystem (or ecological system) is a region in which living organisms interact with their environment.

Is there a more formal definition of an ecosystem?

Before we can define the term ecosystem in a formal way, we must get to know a few more basic terms. An organism is any living thing—an animal, a plant, or a microbe. A mosquito, a fish, a plant, a rabbit, a tree, an elephant, a human being—all are organisms. A cell is the basic unit of life in organisms. An organism like bacterium consists of a single cell, while most organisms have many cells.

The organisms in this world can be classified into different species. You would know that human beings are a species and so are roses. A species is a set of organisms that resemble one another in appearance and behaviour. The organisms in a species are potentially capable of reproducing naturally among themselves. Generally, organisms from different species do not interbreed and, even if they do, they do not produce fertile offspring.

The members of a species living and interacting within a specific geographical region are together called a population. *Neem* trees in a forest, people in a country, and golden fish in a pond are examples of populations. There is diversity in most natural populations. While there are broad similarities among the members, they do not all look exactly alike nor do they all behave in the same way.

Key Idea
An ecosystem is a community of living organisms (populations of species) interacting with one another and with its non-living physical and chemical environment. The interactions are such as to perpetuate the community and to remain stable under varying conditions.

The term population refers only to those members of a certain species that live within a given area. The term species includes all members of a certain kind, even if they exist in different populations in widely separated areas.

We need one more definition before we can come back to ecosystems. A community is the collection of all the interacting populations of different species existing in a geographical area. It is a complex interacting network of plants, animals, and microorganisms. Each population plays a defined role in the community.

We are now ready for a more formal definition of an ecosystem. (See Key Idea.)

A puddle of water, a stream, a clump of bushes, a thick forest, or a large desert—all are ecosystems. The ecosystems of this planet are interconnected and interdependent.

What is a Biome?

We group similar or related ecosystems on land to form biomes. A biome usually has a distinct climate and life forms adapted to the climate. Deserts, grasslands, tropical rain forests, temperate forests, coniferous forests, and tundra are examples (Chapter 3). A biome is simply more extensive and complex than an ecosystem. It is the next level of ecological organization above a community and an ecosystem.

The non-terrestrial ecosystems are classified into aquatic life zones: Freshwater swamps, marshes, and bogs make up one type of aquatic zone. Lakes and rivers, estuaries, inter-tidal zones, coastal ocean, and the open ocean are the other aquatic zones (Chapter 4).

Note that we often use the term 'ecosystem' instead of 'biome' and 'aquatic life zone'.

What is the Biosphere?

All the living organisms on earth, along with the dead organic matter produced by them, make up the biosphere. That is, the biosphere is that portion of the planet and its environment which can support life.

The biosphere extends to the upper areas of the atmosphere where birds and insects can be found. It also reaches to the deepest root systems of trees, to the dark caves deep in the ground, and to the bottom of the ocean. The biosphere extends to any place where life of any kind might exist.

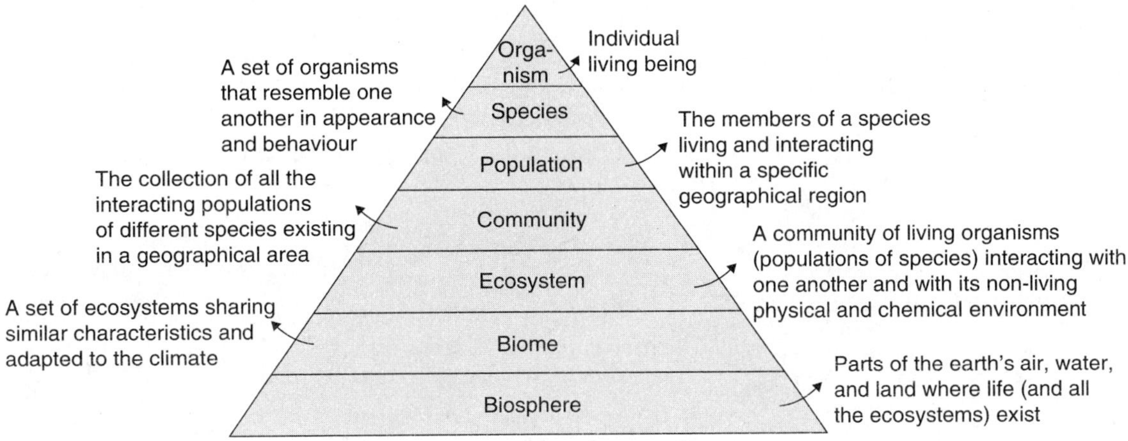

FIGURE 2.1 Levels of Organization in Nature

Thus, the ecology of the earth has different levels of organization, from organism to the biosphere (Fig. 2.1).

What is the Structure of an Ecosystem?

Let us now study ecosystems in greater detail.

The biotic community of species interact with each other and with the abiotic conditions in such a way as to perpetuate the species.

> **Key Idea** An ecosystem consists of a living component, called the biotic community (or biota) and non-living components called abiotic conditions.

The biotic community includes the plants, animals, and the microorganisms. Species in a community are mutually dependent in many ways. For example, in a forest ecosystem, the birds eat the fruits from the trees and build their nests in them. The birds, in turn, spread the plant seeds, helping the propagation of the tree species.

The abiotic conditions of terrestrial ecosystems include water, air, soil, nutrients, minerals, salinity and acidity levels, energy, sunlight, temperature, wind, rainfall, and climate. We could also include the latitude and altitude of the area and the frequency of fires. In short, we define all the conditions under which the organisms live. The abiotic conditions both support and limit the biotic community.

In aquatic ecosystems, the abiotic factors include the depth, turbidity, salinity and temperature of water, chemical nutrients, suspended solids, currents, and the texture of the bottom (rocky or silty).

What is the boundary of an ecosystem?

Where does the sea end and the land begin? Where is the boundary line between a forest and the adjoining grassland? Natural ecosystems rarely have distinct boundaries. In fact, they are never truly self-contained and self-sustaining systems.

An ecosystem gradually merges with the adjoining one through a transitional zone called ecotone. You will find in the ecotone a mixture of species found in both the ecosystems. Often, the ecotone will have additional species not found in either ecosystem. Or, the ecotone may have greater population densities of certain species than in either of the adjoining communities. This phenomenon is called the Edge Effect. Ecotones could be studied as distinct ecosystems.

We can see the Edge Effect in the coastal zone, where the land and the ocean meet. Because of the flow of tides, the coastal zone does not have fixed boundaries on the seaward or landward directions.

> **Key Idea** Ecotones, where two or more ecosystems meet, are very rich in biological diversity. This is called the Edge Effect.

The area is rich in biological diversity and, in particular, it provides habitat for organisms that can survive in water as well as on land. It also contains unique plants like mangroves that thrive in salt water.

An estuary, where a river meets the sea, is even more clearly an ecotone. Here, there is a constant exchange of sea water and fresh water and the biodiversity is very high. An example is the estuary in Chennai, where the river Adyar meets the sea. This area attracts a wide variety of organisms, including many bird species.

What are Food Chains and Food Webs?

All living organisms need energy for doing any biological work such as growing, moving, reproducing, and maintaining themselves. That energy comes from food.

How does any organism get its food? The only way is to eat another organism! An insect is eaten by a frog, the frog becomes food for the snake, and the swooping hawk consumes the snake, and so it goes on. What we have here is a food chain, which is just a sequence of organisms, in which each is the food for the next. An organism is both a predator (eats another organism) and a prey (gets eaten by another organism). All organisms, dead or alive, are potential sources of food for other organisms.

Food chains overlap, since most organisms have more than one item on their menu. Again, an organism could be found on the menus of many other organisms. Thus, we have a complex network of interconnected food chains called a food web (Fig. 2.2).

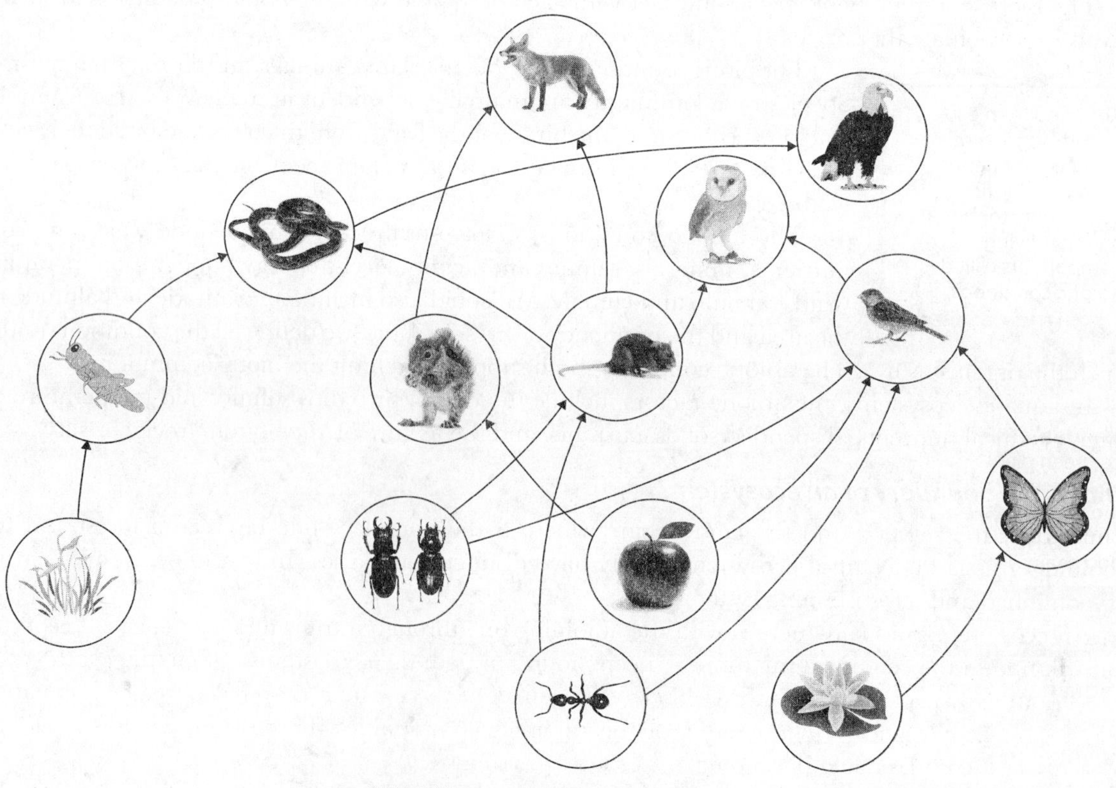

FIGURE 2.2 Example of a Food Web

What is the importance of food chains and food webs?

Suppose species Y in a food chain dies off in an area. Then its predator, species X, will not get its food and hence species X will also dwindle in numbers. Also, species Z, the usual prey of species Y, will multiply in large numbers and may cause other problems. In fact, there will be consequences over the entire food chain. In Chapter 1, Box 1.4, we saw the consequences of the vulture die-off.

Suppose the number of plants in a forest area goes down, the other species in the food web will be forced to adapt or die. For example, deer will have fewer plants to eat. Butterflies and bees will have fewer flowers to pollinate. In turn, predators like lions will have fewer deer to consume. Birds like kingfishers will have fewer insects to eat. Thus, there will be a series of effects on the food web. A similar effect occurs when a non-native species is introduced in an area (Chapter 9).

If every organism must eat another organism for survival, where does the food chain begin?

Obviously, there must be at least one self-feeding organism that produces food and 'eats' it too! Such producers are in fact all around us—the green plants.

Producers take simple inorganic substances from their abiotic environment and make complex organic molecules using solar energy. These are the only organisms in an ecosystem that can trap energy from the sun and make new organic material. All other organisms in this world are, directly or indirectly, dependent on the producers for their food.

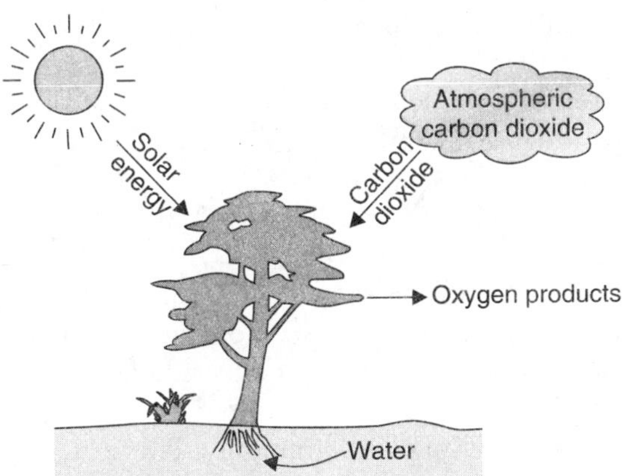

FIGURE 2.3 Process of Photosynthesis

The process used by producers to convert inorganic material into organic matter is called photosynthesis (Fig. 2.3). The green plant takes in carbon dioxide from the atmosphere, water from the soil, and energy from the sun to make a kind of sugar molecule. In the process, it gives out oxygen.

The reaction that takes place can be represented as follows:

carbon dioxide + water + solar energy → sugar + oxygen

The green pigment chlorophyll in the plant traps the solar energy. Hence, we can say that photosynthesis takes place in the leaves.

The world depends on food made by the producers and, fortunately for us, producers come in all types and sizes, from microscopic single-cell algae, through small plants, to giant trees.

> **Key Idea** Producers are green plants that make food through photosynthesis. They form the basis of our food chain.

In addition to producers, there are two other main categories of organisms: *consumers* and *decomposers*. Organisms that feed on producers or other organisms are called consumers. Decomposers get their nourishment from dead organic material (explained later in the chapter).

Does photosynthesis take place in the ocean too?

In aquatic ecosystems, a different process called chemosynthesis takes place. Here specialized bacteria convert simple compounds from their environment into more complex nutrient compounds without sunlight. They use instead, a different source of energy. Deep in the earth's core, heat is generated by the decay of radioactive elements. This heat is released at hot-water vents in the ocean depths. The bacteria use this geothermal energy for chemosynthesis. Later, these bacteria are consumed by many aquatic animals.

What are Trophic Levels?

Each organism in an ecosystem is at a specific feeding stage called the trophic level. All producers are at the first trophic level and are also called autotrophs (self-feeding organisms). All other organisms that must consume other organic matter for their survival are called heterotrophs or consumers (Fig. 2.4).

Consumers are classified as follows:

- Primary consumers or herbivores feed directly on producers and are at the second trophic level. When we eat fruits or vegetables, we act as primary consumers.
- Secondary consumers or carnivores (at the third trophic level) feed on other consumers. When we eat meat, we are secondary consumers.
- Tertiary consumers eat other carnivores and are at the fourth trophic level. Again, we are tertiary consumers when we eat the fish that eats the smaller fish that eats the algae. This chain may go on to one or two more levels.

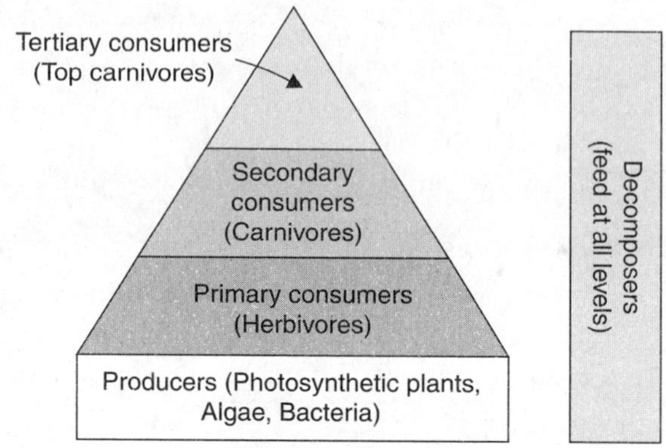

FIGURE 2.4 Trophic Levels

Omnivores eat both plants and animals and hence they feed at more than one level. Human beings, bears, foxes, pigs, rats, and cockroaches are omnivores.

Detrivores are consumers that feed on detritus, which refers mainly to fallen leaves, parts of dead trees, and faecal wastes of animals. Ants, termites, earthworms, millipedes, crayfish, and crabs are examples of detrivores.

What is the role of decomposers?

Decomposers include fungi and bacteria that secrete digestive enzymes, which decompose organic matter into simple sugars. The decomposers then absorb the sugars for their own nourishment. They release the resulting simpler inorganic compounds into the soil and water. The producers take in these compounds as nutrients.

Detrivores and decomposers are essential for the long-term survival of a community. They play the vital role of completing the matter cycle. Without them, enormous wastes of plant litter, dead animal bodies, animal excreta, and garbage will collect on this earth. Also, important nutrients like nitrogen, phosphorus, and potassium would remain indefinitely in dead matter. Then the producers will not get their nutrients and this will make life impossible.

How does food become energy in organisms?

The organisms within an ecosystem are constantly growing, reproducing, dying, and decaying. They need energy for their activities.

When organisms eat food, they take in the chemical energy that is stored in carbohydrates. This energy is released within the cells of the organisms through a process called cell respiration, which is the reverse of photosynthesis. The sugar molecules are broken down in the presence of oxygen and water into carbon dioxide and water and energy is released in the process:

sugar + oxygen + water $\rightarrow$ carbon dioxide + water + energy

Cell respiration makes the stored chemical energy available for biological work. All organisms, including green plants, respire to get energy.

What is an Ecological Pyramid?

The trophic levels form a pyramid. At the base, we have a large number of producers, high energy, and considerable amount of biomass. As we go up the pyramid to higher trophic levels, there are fewer organisms, less energy, and reduction in biomass.

> **Key Idea** It is a fundamental law of nature that energy can neither be created, nor destroyed. It can only be transformed from one form to another. During any such transformation, a part of the energy is lost as less useful heat.

For most ecosystems, the main source of energy is the sun. Producers trap the solar energy and store it as sugar, starch, fats, and proteins. When primary consumers eat the producers, the energy also moves up the trophic level. During the transfer, however, about 90% of the energy is lost to the environment as unusable heat.

As we move up the trophic levels, the amount of usable energy available at each stage declines. Thus, we have a pyramid of energy flow. If the producer has 10,000 units of energy, the primary consumer receives only 1000 units and the secondary consumer gets only 100 units. The tertiary consumer is left with just 10 units. The energy flow is one-directional and the loss at each stage is simply released into the environment (Fig. 2.5).

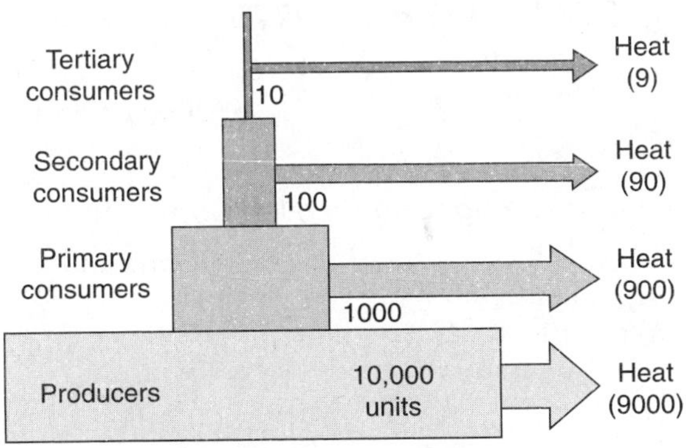

FIGURE 2.5 Pyramid of Energy Flow

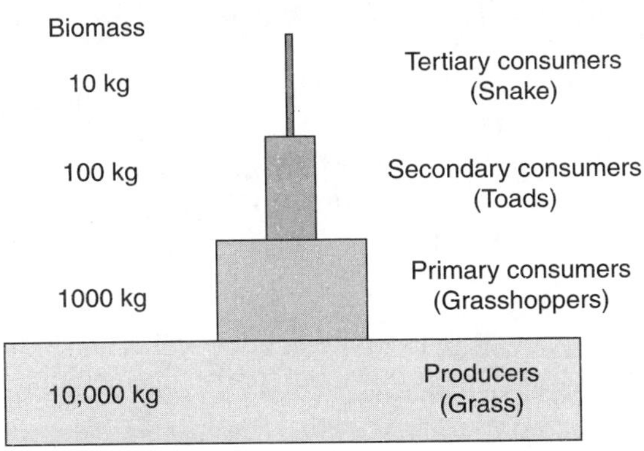

FIGURE 2.6 Pyramid of Biomass

What about matter? Each trophic level contains a certain amount of biomass, which is the dry weight of all the matter contained in the organisms. As we move up the trophic levels, the biomass also decreases drastically. At each level, we lose 90–99% of the biomass. We call it a biomass pyramid.

There are two ways by which the biomass decreases with each level. First, much of the food taken in by a consumer is not converted into body tissues. It is stored as energy to be used by the consumer when needed. Second, much of the biomass, especially at the producer level, is never eaten and goes directly to decomposers (Fig. 2.6).

How does an Ecosystem Get Established?

Consider the rocky surface of a barren hill that is left undisturbed. If there is some rain or moisture, moss starts growing in the minute cracks in the rocks. Slowly, the moss becomes a mat that holds any soil that comes its way. The seeds of small plants start growing on this soil and in turn the plants trap more soil. Shrubs and trees follow and the litter from the trees eliminates the original moss and even the small plants. Over time, more trees grow and ultimately there is a forest. As the big trees grow, many of the small plants under them disappear. This orderly process of transition from one biotic community to another is called primary ecological succession.

What is interesting about ecological succession?

A biotic community grows successfully and its very success makes the area more favourable to another community. When the second community moves in and prospers, the conditions become unfavourable to the first and hence it disappears.

Note also that, for succession to take place, there must be a diversity of species present in the area. It is not a matter of new species developing or even old species adapting to new conditions. The population of an existing species takes advantage of favourable conditions and prospers.

Ecological succession does not go on indefinitely. A stage is reached when all the species are in dynamic equilibrium among themselves and with the environment. This state is called climax ecosystem. During ecological succession, one biotic community gradually makes way to another, the second gives way to a third, and so on, until the climax stage is reached. Major biomes are examples of climax ecosystems.

Climax ecosystems could also change. If the drastic climate changes occur or if alien species are introduced into the ecosystem, a process of adaptation and succession follows. Left undisturbed, an ecosystem always moves towards a state of dynamic balance.

Why do so many hillsides remain barren without ecological succession taking place?

Ecological succession can happen only when an area is left undisturbed. Any interference by human beings disturbs the process. For example, if shepherds take their goats to the hillside every day for grazing, no growth is possible.

What happens if a forest area is cleared by fire or by human beings and then left undisturbed?

In this case, secondary succession takes place. The old soil is still present, but the microclimate in the clearing is different. The appropriate species from the surrounding ecosystem will first reinvade the area. Slowly, each biotic community will give way to another until the clearing becomes indistinguishable from the larger ecosystem.

What is homeostasis?

The self-regulating process by which an ecosystem maintains its stability is also called 'homeostasis'. The term refers to any process by which living things actively maintain fairly stable conditions necessary for their survival.

Homeostasis applies to every living organism in the ecosystem. If homeostasis is successful, the organism continues to live; if unsuccessful, it dies. The stability attained is actually a dynamic equilibrium, in which continuous change occurs yet relatively uniform conditions prevail. Homeostasis dynamically ensures steady-state conditions in climax ecosystems.

What is a Habitat?

Habitat is the area where a species is biologically adapted to live. The habitat of a given species or population is marked by the physical and biological features of its environment such as the vegetation, climatic conditions, presence of water, and moisture, soil type, etc.

How do so many species live together in an ecosystem without fierce competition taking place?

Of course, there are predator–prey relationships, but they do not lead generally to extermination of species. The reason is that each species in an ecosystem finds its habitat and, what is more, its own ecological niche within the habitat.

Key Idea Different species in an ecosystem coexist because each has its ecological niche.

The ecological niche is characterized by the particular food habits, shelter-seeking methods, ways of nesting and reproduction, etc. of the species. It includes all aspects of the organism's existence—all the physical, chemical, and biological factors that it needs in order to live and reproduce. Where the organism lives, what it eats, which organisms eat it, how it competes with others, how it interacts with its abiotic environment—all these aspects together make up its ecological niche. When different species live in the same habitat, competition may be slight or even non-existent because each has its own niche.

What are Cycles in Ecosystems?

We saw that energy flows through an ecosystem in one direction. Matter, on the other hand, moves through ecosystems in numerous cycles. The nutrients that organisms need to grow, live, and reproduce are continuously taken from the abiotic environment, consumed, and then cycled back to the environment.

There are several such biogeochemical cycles (with biological, geological, and chemical interactions), powered directly or indirectly by solar energy. They include the carbon, oxygen, nitrogen, phosphorus, and water cycles. With respect to matter, the earth is essentially a closed system. Matter cannot escape from its boundaries.

How does water circulate on earth?

The hydrologic or water cycle is powered by the sun and gravity. Solar energy evaporates water from the ocean, rivers, lakes, and other water bodies. Plants extract water from the soil through the roots and transport it to the leaves, from where it evaporates. This process is called transpiration.

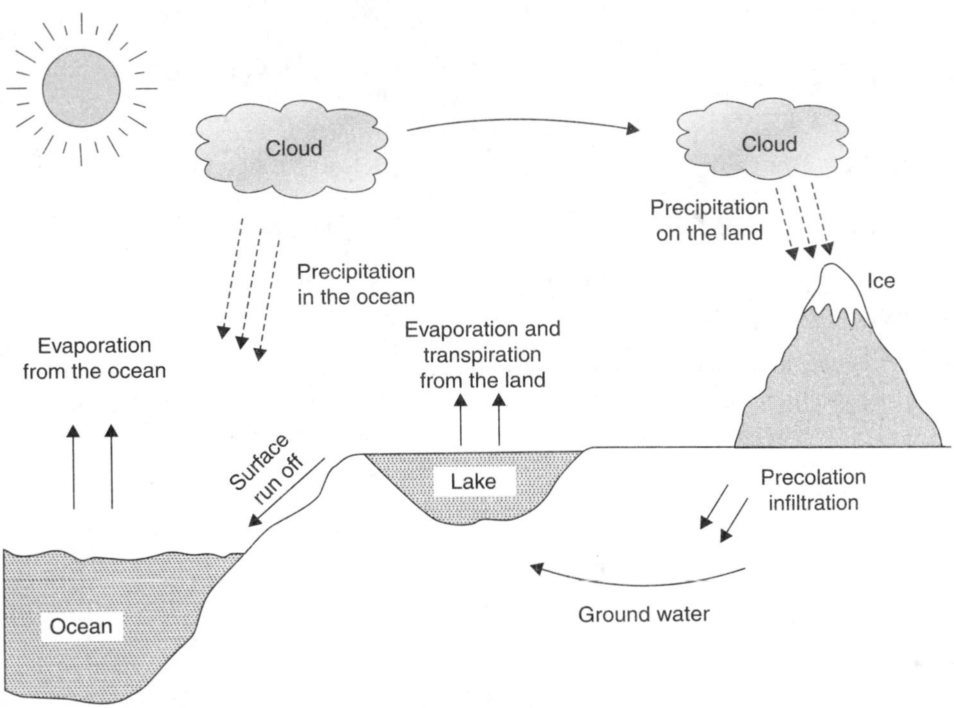

FIGURE 2.7 The Water Cycle

Wind and air move the water vapour through the atmosphere. When the temperature falls, the vapour condenses into tiny droplets that form clouds. The next stage is precipitation as rain or snow, mostly over the ocean and partly over land. The water that falls on land may percolate through the soil and collect in aquifers. Or the water may flow back to the ocean as run-off through the rivers and streams (Fig. 2.7).

We will return to the water cycle in Chapter 5.

What is the carbon cycle?

Carbon dioxide constitutes just 0.035% by volume of the atmosphere and yet it is vital to life. Plants take carbon from carbon dioxide in the air and they use chlorophyll to gather energy from the sun. From these inputs and water, plants make glucose as a basic building block. In this process of photosynthesis, plants release oxygen. Animals breathe in this oxygen, digest their food (that comes from plants), and recombine the carbon and the oxygen to make carbon dioxide, which goes back to the plants. This is called the carbon cycle (Fig. 2.8).

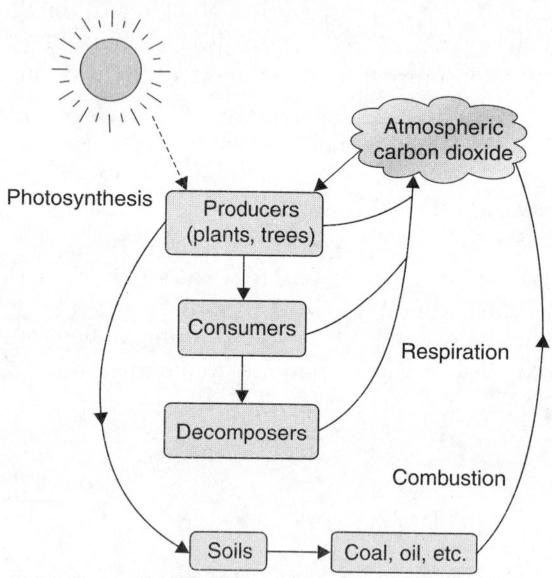

FIGURE 2.8 The Carbon Cycle

When we burn fossil fuels like oil, the carbon in the fuel combines with atmospheric oxygen to form carbon dioxide. Since we burn a lot of oil, there is a huge emission of carbon dioxide. This increase in carbon dioxide concentration upsets the carbon balance in the atmosphere. There are not enough growing plants to absorb all the excess carbon dioxide. Things become worse when we cut down forests and burn more trees.

Normally, carbon dioxide and other gases surround the planet like a blanket and capture the heat. This greenhouse effect is necessary up to a limit. The current excessive level of carbon dioxide, however, leads to a higher temperature, global warming, and climate change.

Like the water and carbon cycles, there are also sulphur, nitrogen and phosphorus cycles in nature (See ORC).

How do We Recognize an Ecosystem?

Ecosystems vary widely in size, complexity, biotic and abiotic components, the sharpness of the boundary, and so on. The key point, however, is that the ecosystem sustains life. Individual organisms or populations cannot sustain life indefinitely. No single species can produce all the food it needs, decompose all its wastes, and reuse the matter to produce more food.

An ecosystem is the minimal grouping of diverse organisms that interact and function together in order to sustain life. That is why we need to focus on ecosystems when we want to conserve a species or to use natural resources in a sustainable manner.

What ultimately sustains life in an ecosystem?

The sun is the primary sustainer of life on earth. It is a huge nuclear fusion reactor running on hydrogen. Energy from the sun flows through materials and living organisms and eventually goes back into space as heat. Only a tiny part of the sun's energy falls on earth, but that is enough to keep the ecosystems going.

What are Ecosystem Services?

We take nature and ecosystems for granted and we take from them whatever we want without worrying about the costs or repayment. Life on earth, including that of human beings, would be impossible without the help of ecosystems.

Ecosystem services are the benefits people obtain from ecosystems. These are the services nature has always provided to all living beings virtually free of cost. There are four kinds of ecosystem services:

- Provisioning services such as food and water (Box 2.1).
- Regulating services such as flood and disease control (Box 2.2).
- Cultural services such as spiritual, recreational, and cultural benefits (Box 2.3).
- Supporting services such as nutrient cycling that maintain the conditions for life on Earth (Box 2.4).

BOX 2.1 *Provisioning Services from Ecosystems*

These are the products obtained from ecosystems, including:

- Food: Plants, animals, etc.
- Fibre: Wood, jute, etc.
- Fuel: Wood, dung, etc.
- Genetic resources used in breeding and biotechnology.
- Biochemicals, natural medicines, and pharmaceuticals.
- Ornamental resources such as skins, shells, and flowers.
- Freshwater

BOX 2.2 *Regulating Services from Ecosystems*

These are the benefits obtained from the regulation of ecosystem processes, including:

- Air quality maintenance: Ecosystems both contribute chemicals to and extract chemicals from the Atmosphere, influencing many aspects of air quality.
- Climate regulation:
  - affecting both temperature and precipitation
  - sequestering or emitting greenhouse gases
- Water regulation
- Erosion control
- Water purification and waste treatment
- Regulation of human diseases
- Biological control of pests and diseases.
- Pollination
- Storm protection by mangroves and coral reefs.

BOX 2.3 *Cultural Services from Ecosystems*

These are the nonmaterial benefits people obtain from ecosystems through spiritual enrichment, cognitive development, reflection, recreation, and aesthetic experiences, including:

- Spiritual and religious values
- Knowledge systems (traditional and formal)
- Educational values
- Inspiration for art, folklore, etc.
- Beauty and aesthetic values
- Cultural heritage values
- Recreation and ecotourism

Cultural services are tightly bound to human values and behaviour, as well as to human institutions and patterns of social, economic, and political organization. Thus perceptions of cultural services are more likely to differ among individuals and communities than, say, perceptions of the importance of food production.

BOX 2.4 ***Supporting Services from Ecosystems***

Supporting services are necessary for the production of all other ecosystem services. They differ from provisioning, regulating, and cultural services in that their impacts on people are either indirect or occur over a very long time. In contrast, changes in the other categories have relatively direct and short-term effects on people. For example, humans do not directly use soil formation services, although changes in this process would indirectly affect people by impacting the provisioning service of food production.

Examples of supporting services:

- Erosion control
- Soil formation
- Primary production
- Production of oxygen through photosynthesis
- Nutrient cycling
- Water cycling
- Crop pollination

Some services, like erosion control, can be categorized as both a supporting and a regulating service, depending on the time scale and immediacy of their impact on people.

What is the monetary value of these ecosystem services that nature provides for free?

A team of ecologists, economists, and geographers tried to answer this question. Led by Robert Costanza, the team first divided the earth's surface into 16 major biomes and aquatic life zones. They then listed 17 goods and services provided by nature in each of these areas and examined over 100 studies that have tried to put a monetary value on such services. Finally, they came up with an estimate of the monetary value of ecosystem services.

Key Idea The ecological, economic, and nonmaterial services provided free by ecosystems and their biodiversity are of enormous value.

Their conclusion was that the ecosystem services were worth more than US$36 trillion per year. This is comparable to the annual gross world product that is estimated to be US$39 trillion. Some experts believe that this is a conservative figure and that the real worth of nature could be much more, even a million times more.

Costanza's estimate involves many assumptions and omissions. Yet, it draws our attention to the enormous value of ecosystem services. Any estimate is better than not attaching any value at all for what we take from nature.

What is the State of the Planet's Ecosystems?

As we will discover in the following chapters, the planet's ecosystems are in deep peril. Human activities, particularly in the 20th Century, have devastated most of the ecosystems on earth and brought us to the edge of total catastrophe.

What is the UN Decade on Ecosystem Restoration (2021–2030)?

On March 1, 2019, the UN General Assembly declared the Decade on Ecosystem Restoration (2021-2030), a rallying call for the protection and revival of ecosystems worldwide for the benefit of people and nature.

It aims to halt the degradation of ecosystems and restore them to achieve global goals. Only with healthy ecosystems can we enhance people's livelihoods, counteract climate change, and stop the collapse of biodiversity. The Decade aims to massively scale up the restoration of degraded and destroyed ecosystems as a proven measure to fight the climate crisis and enhance food security, water supply, and biodiversity.

The UN Decade is building a strong, broad-based global movement to ramp up restoration and put the world on track for a sustainable future. It runs from 2021 through 2030, the timeline scientists have identified as the last chance to prevent catastrophic climate change. 2030 is also the deadline for achieving the Sustainable Development Goals. UN FAO and UNEP are leading the implementation of the Decade.

Ending on a Positive Note: Hopeful Stories

In December 2022, the UN recognized 10 ground-breaking efforts from around the globe for their role in restoring the natural world. The initiatives were declared World Restoration Flagships and are eligible to receive UN-backed promotion, advice or funding. They were selected under the banner of the UN Decade on Ecosystem Restoration. Together, the ten flagships aim to restore more than 68 million ha and create nearly 15 million jobs.

The ten flagships are listed in Table 2.1. Note that India's Ganga Rejuvenation is in the list. Access the ORC for the complete details.

TABLE 2.1 UN World Restoration Flagships

S No	Programme	Country, Countries, or Region
1	Trinational Atlantic Forest Pact	Brazil, Paraguay, and Argentina
2	Abu Dhabi Marine Restoration	UAE
3	Great Green Wall for Restoration and Peace	African Union
4	Ganges River Rejuvenation	India
5	Multi-Country Mountain Initiative	Serbia, Kyrgyzstan, Uganda, and Rwanda
6	Small Island Developing States Restoration Drive	Vanuatu, St Lucia, and Comoros
7	Altyn Dala Conservation Initiative	Central Asia
8	Central American Dry Corridor	Costa Rica, El Salvador, Guatemala, Honduras, Nicaragua, and Panama
9	Building with Nature in Indonesia	Indonesia
10	Shan-Shui Initiative in China	China

REVIEW: A SUMMARY OF THE KEY POINTS

- Ecosystems represent complex interactions among organisms and between them and the environment.
- Energy can neither be created, nor destroyed. It can only be transformed from one form to another; during any such transformation, a part of the energy is lost as less useful heat.
- Organisms have roles like producers, consumers, and decomposers in the food chain; they maintain the flows of matter and energy.
- An ecosystem always moves towards a state of dynamic balance.
- Every species has its ecological niche in an ecosystem.
- Water, carbon, sulphur, phosphorus, and nitrogen are continuously cycled in the biosphere.
- The sun is the primary sustainer of all life on earth.
- Ecosystems provide invaluable services to us.

EXERCISES

Objective-type questions

In each case below, choose the best answer out of the given set of choices:

1. Which of the following statements is true with regard to species?
   (a) The organisms in a species are capable of reproducing naturally among themselves.
   (b) Organisms from different species always interbreed and produce fertile offspring.
   (c) The members of a species living and interacting across the biosphere are together called a population.
   (d) Human beings form a species, but neem trees do not.
2. Which of the following statements is true with regard to ecosystems?
   (a) Ecosystem is different from ecological system.
   (b) There are no interactions between an ecosystem and its environment.
   (c) An ecosystem is a region in which living organisms interact with their environment.
   (d) Ecosystems are the same as populations.
3. Which of the following statements is true with regard to biomes?
   (a) The terrestrial portion of the biosphere is divided into biomes.
   (b) A biome is just a community of populations.
   (c) A biome is just a population of a species.
   (d) Biome stands for biological home.
4. Which of the following is **not** an abiotic condition?
   (a) Water
   (b) Soil
   (c) Temperature
   (d) Bacteria
5. Which of the following statements is true with regard to ecotones?
   (a) We can see the Edge Effect in an ecotone.
   (b) Ecotone stands for ecological tone.
   (c) Ecotone is the sharp line separating two ecosystems.
   (d) Ecotone will not contain the species found in the adjoining ecosystems.
6. What is the basis of all food chains?
   (a) Consumer
   (b) Producer
   (c) Decomposer
   (d) Detrivore
7. Which of the following statements is true with regard to energy?
   (a) There is no loss when mechanical energy is converted into electrical energy.
   (b) Energy can be created or destroyed.
   (c) Whenever energy changes its form, some part is lost.
   (d) As we move up the trophic levels, the amount of usable energy available at each stage remains the same.
8. Which of the following aspects is **not** associated with the ecological niche of a given species?
   (a) Ways in which the given species reproduces itself.
   (b) Other species that consume the given species.
   (c) Food consumed by the predator that consumes the given species.
   (d) Food consumed by the given species.

Short-answer questions

1. Explain the differences between species, population, and community.
2. What is a biome? Give examples.
3. What are the main components of an ecosystem?
4. What are the abiotic factors in terrestrial biomes and aquatic life zones?
5. What is the Edge Effect and what is its importance?
6. Every organism is potential food for other organisms. Then who makes food first to get the chain going?
7. What is the main difference between a producer, a consumer, and a decomposer in an ecosystem? Explain through examples.
8. Explain a food chain and a food web.
9. What happens to the energy flow as we move up the trophic levels?
10. How can we describe the ecological niche of a species?

11. What are biogeochemical cycles? Describe the water and carbon cycles.
12. What is the UN Decade on Ecosystem Restoration?

Long-answer questions

1. Write an essay describing the Himalayas as a mountain ecosystem and explain the ecological problems the region is facing today. Try to add to the information given in this chapter.
2. Describe the processes of primary and secondary ecological succession.

Think critically: Deeper question for reflection and discussion

We, as human beings, are also part of ecosystems. We have, however, overcome the usual barriers and limiting factors faced by other species. We have interfered with the working of most ecosystems and are plundering the resources of ecosystems without any care. What would be the consequences of continuing this trend?

ENJOY AND EDUCATE YOURSELF

1. Watch the children's film *Malli* (1998), directed by Santosh Sivan, which won several awards including the National Award for Best Film on Environment.
2. Relax with the delightful book *The Cartoon Guide to the Environment* by Larry Gonick and Alice Outwater.

ACCESS THE OUP ONLINE RESOURCE CENTRE FOR MORE

- Detailed description of the biosphere and its components
- Explanations of sulphur, nitrogen, and phosphorus cycles
- The story of Sunderlal Bahuguna: A gentle warrior who fought for the Himalayas
- Complete details of the ten UN World Restoration Flagships
- Additional recommended references, websites, and films.

3 Biomes: Forest, Grassland, and Desert Ecosystems

Forests precede civilizations,
deserts follow them.

Attributed to François-René de Chateaubriand (1768–1848)
French author and politician

MAIN QUESTIONS ADDRESSED

- What are biomes?
- What are the features of terrestrial biomes such as forests, grasslands, deserts, and mountains?
- What is the human impact on biomes?

KEYWORDS AND PHRASES

Arctic National Wildlife Refuge, Arctic tundra, Bishnois, coniferous forests, deserts, grasslands, mountains, Silent Valley, temperate forests, Thar Desert, tropical rain forests, Western Ghats

LEAD STORY

THE STORY OF THE WESTERN GHATS: ECOLOGICAL HERITAGE IN PERIL

Older than the Himalayan range, the Western Ghats are a mountain chain that runs almost parallel to the western coast of India. The range extends 1,600 km through six states—Gujarat, Maharashtra, Goa, Karnataka, Tamil Nadu, and Kerala.

The Western Ghats cover an area of 160,000 sq km of which about 70,000 sq km are forested. The Ghats include 16 national parks, 47 wildlife sanctuaries (including tiger reserves), and over 100 sacred groves. 39 sites in the area have been designated as UNESCO Heritage Sites. About 50 million people, including a variety of tribal communities, live in the region.

Animals talking: *Why don't the humans leave us alone?!*

Why are the Western Ghats important for India? These mountains influence the Indian monsoon weather patterns that maintain the warm tropical climate of the region. Acting as a key barrier, the Ghats intercept the rain-laden monsoon winds that come in from the south-west during late summer. The mountain range is the source of 58 major rivers, including the Godavari, Tungabadra, Krishna, and Cauvery. In fact, the Ghats are called the 'water tower of Peninsular India'.

The area is also one of the world's eight 'hottest hotspots' of biological diversity with a species list of over 7000 flowering plants, 500 birds, 140 mammals, 150 reptiles, and 150 amphibians. About 25% of India's biodiversity is found in this region. Many of the species are endemic to this area, that is, not found anywhere else. More than 300 species in the region are on the endangered list.

According to UNESCO, 'The Western Ghats are internationally recognized as a region of immense global importance for the conservation of biological diversity, besides containing areas of high geological, cultural, and aesthetic values.'

During the past 100 years, the forest cover has dwindled dramatically. For example, between 1920 and 1990, in the southern part (Karnataka, Kerala, and Tamil Nadu) about 40% of the original vegetation cover was lost or converted to another form of land use. Large plantations of coffee, coconut, areca, cashew, cocoa, and mango have replaced natural forests.

Logging, urbanization, tourism, encroachment, livestock grazing, building dams and power plants, mining, construction, and other such activities have been increasing in scale and damaging the ecology of the Ghats. Forest fires, often caused by humans, are increasing in the region, leading to degradation of forests and loss of biodiversity, including wildlife. As human settlements grow, there are also increasing man-wildlife conflicts involving elephants, leopards, bears, etc.

Rainfall has been declining in recent decades and climate change is expected to worsen the situation leading to further loss of forests and biological diversity.

Several scientific studies and committee reports have emphasized the need for the protection of the ecology of the Western Ghats. In August 2011, the Western Ghats Ecology Expert Panel, led by Prof. Madhav Gadgil, submitted a report designating the entire Western Ghats as an Ecologically Sensitive Area (ESA) and assigning three levels of ecological sensitivity to its different regions. While environmentalists generally welcomed the report, the six states rejected it saying that it ignored many ground realities.

The government then set up the High Level Working Group on Western Ghats, headed by Dr Kasturirangan. The group's report, presented in April 2013, tried to strike a balance between development and environmental protection. But it was seen as a dilution of the Gadgil Report and, therefore, was unacceptable to environmentalists. But both reports have been criticized by the state governments, political leaders, and mining companies, often without understanding what the reports really recommended.

In July 2022, MoEFCC reissued for the fifth time the draft ESA Notification and the state governments raised their objections. The Centre has now informed the states that a high-level committee will research the landscape, and the draft notification will not be operationalised until this panel submits its report.

There is thus no serious attempt to save the Western Ghats, even as they experience continuous ecological damage.

CLIMATE CHANGE AND FORESTS

Forests currently contribute about one-sixth of global carbon emissions because they are cleared, overused, or degraded. If they are conserved, however, they have the potential to absorb about one-tenth of global carbon emissions projected for the first half of this century.

What does the story of the Western Ghats tell us?

Key Idea Human beings have interfered with and made an impact on 75% of the land area.

In the previous chapter, we learnt how ecosystems function and how they try to reach a state of dynamic balance. However, human beings are now interfering with ecosystems everywhere. The Western Ghats case is an example of the damage that human impact can cause.

How far have human beings explored and disturbed the land on earth?

If we exclude uninhabitable areas of ice, rock, desert, and steep mountains, we have made an impact on 75% of the land area.

Before we learn more about human impact on the environment, however, we should find out more about forests and other natural ecosystems. That is the task of this chapter and the next.

What are the Different Types of Biomes?

Recall from Chapter 2 that we group similar or related ecosystems to form biomes. A biome usually has a distinct climate and life forms adapted to the climate. Tropical rain forests, temperate forests, coniferous forests, tundra, grasslands, deserts, and mountains are examples of biomes. In this chapter, we will learn more about biomes.

Why do different regions have different biomes?

Temperature and precipitation are the two major factors that account for the differences in biomes from region to region. The term precipitation covers all the forms in which water comes down on earth, including rain, snow, hailstorm, etc. Their mean values of temperature and precipitation as well as the way they vary over the year (and even over the day) will determine the kind of biomes we find in an area.

Different climates promote different communities of plants and animals. Again, the types and numbers of organisms may vary from location to location within a biome because of variations in the local climate and soil, and because of the natural and human-caused disturbances that occur in the area. Yet, the regions of a biome have broadly comparable biological communities.

Climate, plants, and animal species of regions vary with latitude and altitude. You can observe these changes as you move from the equator to the poles or from the base to the summit of a tall mountain. Again, in a thick forest, different communities are found at different levels.

What is wonderful is that every species has adapted to the climate and has found its ecological niche in the community. Left undisturbed, the biome reaches a stable state. It continues to be dynamic and undergoes gradual changes over long periods. The trouble comes, however, when humans enter the ecosystem and bring in rapid, often devastating, changes.

Let us now learn more about the different biomes, beginning with forests. Forests still cover about 20% of land on earth. Forests can be classified in different ways and one way is to divide them into tropical rain forests, temperate forests, coniferous forests, and tundra.

What are Tropical Rain Forests?

As the name implies, tropical rain forests are found in the hot and humid regions near the equator. These regions have abundant rainfall (2,000–4,500 mm per year) that occurs almost daily and the temperature varies little over the year. They are found in South and Central America, western and central Africa, South-east Asia, and in some islands of the Indian and Pacific Oceans.

> **Key Idea** Even though tropical rain forests occupy just 2% of the earth, they contain 50–80% of all the terrestrial species.

The enormous plant biodiversity is supplemented by an abundance of amphibians, reptiles, birds, monkeys, and small mammals, as well as predators like tigers and jaguars.

These rain forests are marked by a variety of tall trees and a dense canopy. There are at least three distinct stories or layers of vegetation. The soil is thin, acidic, and nutrient-poor. Little organic matter accumulates since the litter that falls on the floor is very quickly decomposed and the minerals are quickly absorbed by the roots.

Why are tropical forests considered so important?

Apart from preserving immense biodiversity, the tropical forests play a major role in recycling water. In a landmark research study conducted in the early 1980s in the Amazon, scientists found that a forest could return as much as 75% of the moisture it receives back to the atmosphere.

We have always been told that more trees meant more rain. In fact, research shows that the forests could return enough amounts of water to cause the formation of rain clouds. Land that is covered by trees collects and returns to the atmosphere at least 10 times more moisture than deforested land does.

What are Temperate Forests?

Temperate forests have seasonal variations in climate, freezing in winter and warm and humid in summer. The annual rainfall is about 750–2000 mm and the soil is rich.

Temperate forests are found in western and central Europe, eastern Asia, and eastern North America. They have deciduous (leaf-shedding) trees like oaks, maples, ash, and beech, and some coniferous trees like pines. Shrubby undergrowth, ferns, lichens, and mosses are also found.

These forests contain abundant microorganisms, and mammals like squirrels, porcupines, chipmunks, raccoons, hares, deer, foxes, coyotes, and black bears. Birds like warblers, woodpeckers, owls, and hawks, besides snakes, frogs, and salamanders are common.

What are Coniferous Forests?

These forests derive their name from the abundance of coniferous trees like spruce, fir, pine, and hemlock. A coniferous tree produces hard dry fruits called cones. Coniferous forests also contain smaller amounts of deciduous trees like birch and maple. They occur in the northern part of North America, Europe, and Asia.

In these forests, winters are usually long and cold. The precipitation is often light in winter and heavy in summer. The soil is acidic and humus-rich and there is much litter.

The main animals are large herbivores like mule deer, moose, elk, caribou; smaller herbivores like mice, hare, and red squirrels; and predators like lynx, foxes, and bears. They are often important nesting areas for many migratory birds like warblers and thrushes.

What Kind of Forests do We Have in the Arctic?

The forests in the Arctic are called tundra. They occur in the extreme northern latitudes, where the snow melts seasonally. There is no equivalent in the southern hemisphere, since there is no land in the corresponding latitude.

The region has long and harsh winters and very short summers. Precipitation occurs mostly in summer and the annual average is just 10–25 cm.

The species diversity is low but those few species exist in large numbers. Mosses, lichens, grasses, and some dwarf trees are the main plants. The animal species include lemmings, weasels, Arctic foxes, hares, snowy owls, and musk oxen. Many bird species migrate here in summer and feast on the abundance of insects–mosquitoes, black flies, deerflies, etc.

> **Key Idea**
> The Arctic tundra has been adversely affected by oil exploration and military use.

The tundra is a fragile ecosystem. Even a casual hiking on the land causes enormous damage and regeneration is very slow. Large parts of the Arctic tundra have been affected by oil exploration and military use. (Read Box 3.1 on the Arctic National Wildlife Refuge.)

BOX 3.1 ECOSYSTEM: *The Story of the Arctic National Wildlife Refuge—Pristine Nature or Petroleum?*

It is one of the last remaining areas of unspoiled nature and it is now in trouble. The story of the Arctic National Wildlife Refuge (ANWR) in Alaska is a classic case of the environment vs development dilemma.

The ANWR consists of 7.3 million ha of undisturbed tundra, wetlands, and glaciers. It is home to an extremely diverse community of organisms, including polar bears, arctic foxes, peregrine falcons, musk oxen, snow geese, and many other animal species. It is also the calving area for large migrating herds of caribou. More than 150,000 caribou return here after wintering in Canada. All the tundra plant species like mosses, lichens, and dwarf trees are found here. Under a thin layer of soil there is permafrost—tice that does not melt even in summer.

The ecosystem is fragile and finely balanced. Any additional stress can do irreversible damage. Environmentalists have always argued for leaving the area undisturbed. Unfortunately for the region, however, it has deposits of oil!

The US Geological Survey estimates the reserves to be about 7.7 billion barrels. There was always pressure to begin drilling in ANWR, but the US Congress had allowed only exploration, with the condition that its approval was needed for any drilling activity. Over the years, there has been political wrangling on drilling between the Democrats (against) and the Republicans (in favour).

The pro-drilling groups point out that, in neighbouring Prudhoe Bay, oil is already being extracted and the infrastructure for drilling exists. No environmental impact has been reported. What is more, only 1.5% of the total area will be encroached upon. There are sound economic reasons to extract oil from ANWR and reduce dependence on imports.

The environmentalists say that any drilling possesses a permanent threat to the delicate balance of nature. Prudhoe Bay, in fact, has suffered damage—wolves and bears have been decreasing in numbers resulting in an abnormal increase in caribou population. What is more, the oil will not last long but we would have already sacrificed nature. In fact, the production in Prudhoe Bay has peaked and is now declining.

In January 2015, the Obama government released a comprehensive conservation plan for ANWR. The plan recommends that the refuge's coastal plain be federally designated as wilderness based on its extraordinary ecological values and pristine conditions. This landmark decision gives the highest level of protection for ANWR—at least for the present.

In 2020, the Trump administration opened up a part of ANWR for oil and gas development. In 2021, the Biden administration blocked the opening of most of the ANWR to oil and gas interests, but moved forward with a plan that would still allow drilling in about half of its 23-million-acre area. For example, it approved, in March 2023, a massive oil development by ConocoPhillips called the Willow Project. Thus, ANWR continues to be a threatened area.

Chapter 6 describes the state of the forest resources in the world and India.

What are Grasslands?

Grasslands are regions where the average annual precipitation is high enough (250–1500 mm) for grass and perhaps a few trees to grow. The rainfall, however, is erratic and uncertain and hence large groups of trees do not grow. It is hot and dry in summer with incidence of fires.

Grasslands are the vast expanses of plains and rolling hills in the interiors of continents. They are found in central North America, central Russia and Siberia, subequatorial Africa and South America, southern India, and northern Australia.

The soil is rich and deep supporting many grass species, sparse bushes, and occasional woodlands. The animals include large grazing mammals like bison, antelopes, wild horses, kangaroos, giraffes, zebras, and rhinos as well as predators like wolves, coyotes, leopards, cheetahs, hyenas, and lions. Birds, rabbits, and mongoose also flourish in grasslands. There has been a large-scale conversion of grassland into croplands, since they are well suited for agriculture. They are also used as rangelands for animals.

How do We Define a Desert?

Desert is an area where the evaporation often exceeds the precipitation. The typical annual precipitation is between 25 and 50 mm spread unevenly over the year.

Deserts are found mostly in a band 30 degrees north and south of the equator and occupy about 30% of the land surface. This area is increasing with continuous desertification going on in many parts of the world. There is more on desertification in Chapter 7.

The largest deserts are in the interiors of continents, where moist sea air or moisture-bearing winds do not reach. There are also local deserts, which are rain-shadow areas on the downward side of mountain ranges.

How do plants and animals adapt to deserts?

The soil has very little organic matter, but is rich in minerals. The plants have adapted to the dry conditions and conserve water by having few or no leaves. The giant saguaro cactus, for example, has a stem that can expand to store water. Many have thorns or toxins to protect themselves from being grazed.

Some plants have wax-coated leaves that minimize loss of moisture. Others have deep roots that reach the ground water. Alternatively, some have widely spread and shallow roots that collect water after any rain and store it in their spongy tissues.

Desert animals are usually small in size and they remain under cover during the day and come out to feed at night. Many have a thick external shell that minimizes evaporation loss. They can stay dormant during the driest periods. Frogs, reptiles, rodents, jackrabbits, foxes, and owls are some of the desert animals.

During the daytime, the sun heats up the ground and the temperature is high. The night can be quite cold, since the lack of vegetation allows the heat from the ground to radiate away quickly.

Is there any human impact on deserts?

You may think that a dry and hot desert cannot be damaged much by human activity. In fact, the desert ecosystem is quite sensitive and delicate. A heavy vehicle driven on the desert can do enormous damage to the thin topsoil and the sparse vegetation. The disturbed area will take a long time to recover because of the extremely slow rate of growth of vegetation and low species diversity.

Apart from soil destruction, there are other human disturbances to desert ecosystems. The creation of desert cities, depletion of groundwater supplies, land disturbance and pollution from mining, and storage of toxic and nuclear wastes are some of the human activities that cause damage.

> **Key Idea** Even deserts have been affected by human activities.

How can We Describe the Thar Desert?

The Thar or the Great Indian Desert is spread over four states in India—namely, Punjab, Haryana, Rajasthan, and Gujarat—and two states in Pakistan and covers an area of about 446,000 sq km. Though smaller than the Sahara in Africa and the Gobi in Russia, it is the most populated desert in the world with about 13 million people.

The average annual rainfall is between 100 and 500 mm and most of it occurs in a few showers during the monsoon. The only river in the region is Ghaggar, which enters Rajasthan from Punjab and dries up in the desert.

The Thar has no oasis, native cactus, or palm trees. Yet, a variety of flora and fauna thrives in this area. Flowering plants like shrubs and wild grasses, trees like the khejra, babul, and rohida, and fruit trees like ber and pilu are found here.

Sheep, goats, and camels are the common animals used by the people. The Asiatic wild ass, deer species like the black buck and the Indian gazelle, common Indian hare red lynx, jackal, and wild dog are some others. About 23 species of lizards and 25 species of snakes are found here and several of them are endemic to the region. Local communities like the Bishnois have traditionally protected the trees and the animals (Read Box 3.2).

BOX 3.2 INSPIRATION: *The Story of the Bishnois—Giving One's Life for a Tree*

The Bishnois of Rajasthan have been known for their concern for trees, birds, and animals. In 1731, Abhay Singh, the King of Jodhpur, wanted large quantities of wood for burning bricks to build his new palace. He sent his minister, Giridhardas, with woodcutters to cut the trees in the forests near the Bishnoi villages.

Amritadevi, a mother of three, wanted to save the trees. She hugged a tree and begged Giridhardas and the cutters to stop the operation. Her daughters too followed her example. Giridhardas ordered the men to proceed and they cut down the trees and the women.

The news spread and more villagers came to the rescue of the trees. But the felling of the trees continued and by night, 363 people had given their lives in the cause of the forest.

When the King heard the news, he was overcome with remorse. He then banned felling of trees in the Bishnoi forests forever.

The Government of India has instituted the *Amritadevi Wildlife Protection Award*, to be given to village communities that show valour and courage for the protection of forests and wildlife.

The increase of human and livestock population in the desert has led to deterioration in the ecosystem resulting in degradation of soil fertility and vegetation. The desert is on the increase due to overgrazing and deforestation of marginal land.

Are Mountains Distinct Biomes?

Mountains have unique characteristics and can be studied as distinct biomes. Of all the continents, Antarctica is the most mountainous. Elsewhere, thanks to its relative inaccessibility, a mountain often stands out as an island of rich biodiversity in the midst of a devastated landscape.

As you go up a mountain, you will see dramatic changes in climate, soil, and vegetation even over short distances. In a way, moving up a mountain is similar to moving from the equator to the North Pole, since you can experience similar changes in the biomes. Beginning with low deciduous forests, you could move through coniferous forests to alpine tundra and snow.

Mountains perform many ecological services for us. The majority of the world's forests are in the mountains. Apart from being home to endemic species of plants and animals, they are also sanctuaries for animals driven away from the lowland by human activities.

Mountains play a vital role in the water cycle. They absorb precipitation in the soil and vegetation and slowly release the water through small streams. These streams often join together and become rivers. Thus, the mountains act as reservoirs, storing water in the monsoon and releasing it during the dry season.

What is happening to the mountain ecosystems now?

Man is out to plunder the mountains too: roads have been laid, forests have been cleared, rivers have been dammed, hill stations have been built, and minerals have been mined. The resulting degradation has many effects.

The barren slopes get further eroded when rains wash away the valuable topsoil that ends up as sediment on rivers, reservoirs, and the ocean. The mountains can no longer hold the water and hence there are floods during the monsoon and no water in summer. The biodiversity, of course, disappears.

The International Centre for Integrated Mountain Development (ICIMOD) in Nepal works for the sustainable development of mountains.

Key Idea
Mountains provide vital ecosystem services, but they are facing severe degradation.

Ending on a Hopeful Note: Positive Story

In the lead story of this chapter, we saw how the unique Western Ghats ecosystem is being degraded. Now see Box 3.3 for a famous success story in the annals of the Indian environmental movement: the saving of one part of the Western Ghats.

BOX 3.3 HOPE: *The Story of Silent Valley—A Pristine Valley Saved?*

Situated in the Kundali Hills of the Western Ghats, in Kerala, the Silent Valley Forests are considered to be one of the last remaining virgin tropical evergreen forests in India, a climax ecosystem. Covering an area of 90 sq km, it has many rare plants and animals. The tree diversity here is very high and is comparable to some rain forests.

In the late 1970s, the Kerala Government decided to build a hydropower project in the area to generate 240 MW of power and irrigate 100,000 ha of land. The project would have, however, submerged 500 ha of the forest.

Several organizations like the Bombay Natural History Society (BNHS) and the Kerala Sastra Sahitya Parishad (KSSP) formed a 'Save Silent Valley' movement to urge the state government to abandon the project. International organizations like the World Wide Fund for Nature and the International Union for the Conservation of Nature supported the struggle.

The issue became highly politicized and the pro-dam groups came up with the slogan: 'Man or Monkey'. The reference was to the lion-tailed macaque that the conservationists were concerned about.

Finally, the continued agitation and the intervention of the then Prime Minister, Indira Gandhi, forced the state government to shelve the project. In 1984, the area was declared a national park. It is now part of the core area of the Nilgiris Biosphere Reserve. There is, however, the ever-present danger of new 'development' projects!

REVIEW: A SUMMARY OF THE KEY POINTS

- Terrestrial biomes are determined by temperature and precipitation.
- Forest ecosystems still cover a large area on land.
- Human beings have interfered in about 73% of land; even the Arctic has not escaped our attention.
- Tropical forests are the treasure chests of the world's biodiversity and they are being destroyed at a rapid pace.
- Deserts can be damaged easily and take very long to recover from any disturbance.
- Mountains are unique ecosystems providing valuable services.

EXERCISES

Objective-type questions

In each case below, choose the best answer out of the given set of choices:

1. Which of the following is **not** a biome?
   (a) Tundra
   (b) Tropical rain forest
   (c) Earth
   (d) Desert
2. Which of the following is **not** found in a tropical rain forest?
   (a) Desert area
   (b) Rich diversity of plants and animals
   (c) Acidic soil
   (d) Abundant rainfall
3. Which of the following statements is **not** true with regard to global forests?
   (a) Forests are adversely affected by acid rain.
   (b) Forests are submerged by reservoirs created when big dams are built.
   (c) Cutting down forests leads to landslides and floods.
   (d) Forests lead to water scarcity.
4. Which of the following statements is true with regard to deserts?
   (a) Deserts are affected by human activities.
   (b) Plants do not adapt to deserts.
   (c) Animals do not survive in deserts.
   (d) Days and nights are always hot in deserts.

Short-answer questions

1. How do desert organisms survive the heat and lack of water?
2. Why are tropical rain forests important to us?
3. What are the ecosystem services provided by mountains?

Long-answer questions

1. How do biomes vary based on the temperature and precipitation of the region?
2. Describe the human impact on the world's forests.
3. What lessons can we learn from the two cases described in this chapter: The Western Ghats and the Silent Valley?

Think critically: Deeper question for reflection and discussion

How does one use the forest without harming it? What can we learn from the tribal communities or the Native Americans in this regard?

ENJOY AND EDUCATE YOURSELF

1. Watch the film *Avatar* (2009) directed by James Cameron, who also made the movie *Titanic*. *Avatar* is a science-fiction film set in 2154, when humans have severely depleted earth's natural resources leading to a severe energy crisis. There is also a 2022 sequel called *Avatar: The Way of Water*.
2. Relax with *Where the Wild Things Are* (1963), written and illustrated by Maurice Sendak. Set in a forest, it is considered to be one of the best picture books ever written for children.

ACCESS THE OUP ONLINE RESOURCE CENTRE FOR MORE

- Additional text and other recommended references, websites, and films

4 Aquatic Ecosystems: Ocean, Rivers, Lakes, and Wetlands

For all at last return to the Sea—to Oceanus, the ocean river, like the ever-flowing stream of time, the beginning and the end.

Rachel Carson (1907–1964), American marine biologist and author of the famous book *Silent Spring*

MAIN QUESTIONS ADDRESSED

- What is the state of the global ocean as well as the coastal zone, coral reefs, and mangroves?
- How is the ocean governed?
- What is the state of freshwater ecosystems such as rivers and lakes?
- What is the importance of wetlands and how are they being conserved?

KEYWORDS AND PHRASES

abyssal zone, Antarctica, aquatic life zone, Aral Sea, bathyal zone, benthos, coastal zone, Common Heritage of Mankind, coral bleaching, coral reef, EEZ, estuary, euphotic zone, Gulf of Mannar, mangrove, Namami Gange, nekton, open ocean, phytoplankton, plankton, polyp, UNCLOS, wetland, zooplankton, zooxanthellae

LEAD STORY

THE STORY OF THE GULF OF MANNAR: UNIQUE AQUATIC ECOSYSTEM IN PERIL

The island of Kurusadai, near Rameswaram, is a biologist's paradise. Even today you can see its dense foliage, shallow coral reefs, plants, and aquatic life with an extraordinary diversity of form and colour. This is just one example of the marine life in the Gulf of Mannar, one of the world's richest marine biodiversity regions.

The Gulf of Mannar is located in the south-eastern tip of Tamil Nadu extending from Rameswaram to Kanyakumari. It covers an area of 10,500 sq km, includes 21 islands, and contains over 3,600 species of flora and fauna. They include mangroves, seagrass beds, algae, coral reefs, many fish species, marine turtles, dolphins, dugongs, and many migratory birds. Over 150,000 people in 90 villages and hamlets in the area depend on fishing for their livelihood.

By the end of the twentieth century, this biological paradise was in deep trouble. The habitat was getting degraded, the marine species were threatened, and the people's livelihood seriously affected. The three main threats to the ecosystem were the destruction of the marine resources by bottom trawling, the mining of corals, and the pollution from industries.

The fisherfolk faced serious issues: Over the years, the variety and catch of fish had been steadily going down. As a result, there was more indebtedness among the people. There were also conflicts between the trawler operators and the fisherfolk.

Illegal coral mining went on unchecked in the area. Several hundred boats mined huge quantities of coral every day using levers and dynamite to break up the reefs. The catch was sent to cement companies as raw material. Between 1988 and 1998, nearly 25 sq km of coral reef was lost. The loss of corals increased coastal erosion and as a result two of the islands disappeared.

Human activity was threatening many marine species. There was a drastic decline of turtle nesting sites. The dugongs were also dwindling in number.

Environmentalists and the government took notice of the degradation. The Gulf of Mannar Biosphere Reserve (GOMBR) was notified in 1989 and was brought under Man and the Biosphere Programme of UNESCO in 2001. The UN Global Environmental Facility (GEF) provided support to the biosphere reserve through the GOMBR Trust. This body is responsible for the coordination of a management plan for the biosphere reserve in cooperation with government agencies, private entrepreneurs, and local people's representatives. When the GEF Project ended in 2012, the Government of Tamil Nadu took over the GOMBR Trust.

The Trust has been working with the local people to create ecological awareness and to help the fisherfolk and others find alternative livelihood. The Trust has been able to reduce coral mining through joint patrolling initiatives by forest department, fisheries, coast guards, and local youth. It is said that coral reef cover in the area has increased from 37% to 43% between 2005 and 2009. In spite of such successes, the Biosphere Reserve is still in a critical condition.

In April 2022, GOMBR was designated as a Ramsar wetland site (See Table 4.3). There is now fresh hope that it will be conserved better.

1st fish: *What happened to the corals we had here?*
2nd fish: *Don't you know, they have been mined off.*

CLIMATE CHANGE AND ECOSYSTEMS

The biggest threat to our ocean's health is climate change, with its twin super-dangers of rising sea temperatures and acidification.

What do we learn from the Gulf of Mannar case?

It is once again a case of a unique natural environment, population pressure, people's livelihood issues, and local and international conservation efforts. The story tells us also how valuable the ocean is and how human impact is adversely affecting the ocean ecosystems.

How do Aquatic Ecosystems Differ from Terrestrial Ones?

Key Idea In aquatic life zones, the characteristics of water—salinity, light penetration, nutrient levels, waves, and currents—are the crucial factors.

Aquatic life zones, which include the ocean, rivers, lakes, and wetlands, differ in many respects from terrestrial biomes. Unlike the situation in terrestrial biomes, temperature and precipitation are not the factors that determine the types of organisms that thrive in an aquatic life zone. First, water itself tends to moderate temperature and second, any precipitation falling on water cannot obviously be a major influence.

In this chapter, we will learn about different categories of aquatic life zones and their components:

- Saltwater systems (ocean, inland seas)
- Coastal zone (estuaries, coastal wetlands, coral reefs, mangroves)
- Freshwater systems (rivers, streams, lakes, ponds, inland wetlands, etc.)

What kinds of organisms do we find in aquatic life zones?

There are three main types of organisms in aquatic life zones: plankton, nekton, and benthos. The free-floating plankton are microorganisms that cannot swim easily and are buffeted about by the waves and currents. Plankton again are of two types: phytoplankton and zooplankton.

Phytoplankton are the photosynthetic producers of the ocean and they form the basis of the ocean's food web. The tiny zooplankton are the primary consumers that feed on phytoplankton. They in turn become the food for newly-hatched fish and small organisms and the food chain continues up the trophic levels.

The nekton, which are strong swimmers, include all the larger organisms like fish, turtles, and whales. The benthos are bottom-dwellers adapted to living on the floor of the water body. Some fix themselves to one spot like sponges, oysters, and barnacles. Others burrow themselves into the sand like worms and clams. Some others move about on the floor, like crawfish and brittle stars.

How Large is the Ocean and How Important is It?

This planet should really be called ocean and not earth because the ocean covers 71% of the earth's surface. The ocean has an area of about 361 million sq km, an average depth of 3.7 km, and a total volume of 1,347,000 million cubic km.

Although we talk of different oceans in the world, there is just a single global ocean. For convenience, we have divided the ocean into the Pacific, Atlantic, Indian, Arctic, and Southern. The last one, the Southern Ocean, was created in 2000 by the International Hydrographic Organization and it completely surrounds Antarctica.

The largest geographical division is the Pacific Ocean that covers one-third of the earth's surface and contains more than 50% of its water. The Pacific also has the deepest part of the ocean, the Mariana Trench, with a maximum depth of 11,000 m, which is 2200 m more than the height of Mt Everest!

The global ocean is important to us in many ways. The biodiversity and resource-base of the ocean far exceeds that of the land. The ocean contains more than 250,000 species of plants and animals. This could well be an underestimate, since hardly 10–15% of the ocean has been explored and mapped in detail. Every day, we are discovering new wonders about the ocean—its behaviour, services, and products (Box 4.1).

BOX 4.1 STATE OF THE PLANET: ***Census of Marine Life***

The first global Census of Marine Life was conducted from 2000 to 2010 by 2700 scientists from more than 80 countries. The Census found a changing ocean, richer in diversity, more connected through distribution and movements, more impacted by humans, and yet less explored than what the scientists had known.

The major findings were the following:

- The Census encountered an unanticipated riot of species and found more than 6000 potentially new ones.
- The Census found living creatures everywhere it looked, even where heat would melt lead, sea water froze to ice, and light and oxygen were lacking. It found that in marine habitats, extreme is normal.
- The Census affirmed that by weight 90% of marine life is microbial and that we know less about the small than the large.
- After all its work, the Census still could not reliably estimate the total number of species in the ocean. There could be a million or more species and tens or even hundreds of millions of kinds of microbes.

- For more than 20% of the ocean's volume, the Census database still has no records at all, and for vast areas very few.
- The Census documented declining numbers and sizes of species, even within a human generation.

The ocean provides many ecosystem services like regulation of climate and rainfall, cycling of nutrients, absorption of carbon dioxide, waste treatment, being a nursery for many species, storage of biodiversity and genetic resources, and protection from storms. The economic benefits include food items (fish, sea weed, and other items), fishmeal, oil and gas, minerals, medicines, building materials, transportation, recreation, and employment.

How do We Divide the Ocean into Meaningful Zones?

The marine ecosystem of the world is divided into two major zones: the coastal zone and the open ocean. The coastal zone extends from the high tide mark on land to the edge of the continental shelf**,** which is the submerged part of the continent. At this point, there is a sharp increase in the depth of water and from here onwards it is the open ocean. The coastal zone is discussed in a later section.

Key Idea We have explored just a small part of the ocean. Yet we know that it provides us with a variety of vital ecosystem services.

The open ocean is divided into three zones by depth (Fig. 4.1). The euphotic zone is the upper part where there is enough light for the phytoplankton to carry out photosynthesis. Large fish like sharks and swordfish are found here. The bathyal zone lacks sunlight and hence contains no producers. Zooplankton and smaller fish that populate this zone have to move to the upper levels at night for feed.

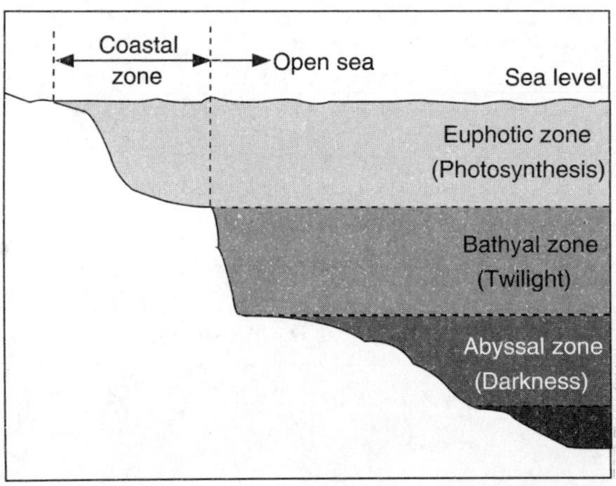

FIGURE 4.1 The Zones of the Ocean

The abyssal zone is the cold and dark zone at the bottom, reaching in places to a depth of 4,000 to 6,000 m. It is too dark for photosynthesis and yet there are producer organisms at this depth near hydrothermal vents. They are the bacteria that can withstand temperatures of 200°C and they produce food through a chemical reaction.

Before we move to the coastal zone and the freshwater life zones, let us look at a unique part of the ocean.

What is Special about Antarctica and the Southern Ocean?

Antarctica is an icy continent, surrounded by the Southern Ocean. It is a fragile ecosystem and is relatively unexploited. The Antarctic ice cap contains 70% of the world's fresh water. A thin layer on the ocean supports krill (very small shellfish), which is consumed by other fish, seals, penguins, and whales.

Antarctica is a sensitive indicator of environmental changes. Between 1947 and 2000, the mean temperature of the Antarctic Peninsula went up by 2.5°C in summer and 5.6°C in winter. The reason could be global warming from the burning of fossil fuels. With increasing temperature, huge pieces of the ice shelf have been breaking off. Over a period of time, this melting of ice could raise global sea levels.

Seals and whales were first hunted in Antarctica, leading to the near-extinction of the southern fur seal, elephant seal, and the blue whale. The pollution from the rest of the world has now reached Antarctica. Radioactive particles from atomic testing as well as DDT and other chemical residues have been found in these waters. Tourism that is being promoted now will also have ecological consequences.

No country owns Antarctica, though several countries have made claims on parts of it. In 1991, 41 countries (including India) signed the Antarctic Treaty. They agreed to ensure that Antarctica is used for peaceful purposes, for international cooperation in scientific research, and does not become the scene or object of international discord. The Treaty seeks to establish Antarctica as a zone free of nuclear tests and radioactive waste and includes agreed measures for the conservation of Antarctic flora and fauna.

Key Idea Antarctica is a sensitive indicator of the environment. Its ice shelves are breaking up due to global warming.

Several countries including India have been conducting scientific research and exploration for oil and minerals in Antarctica. The first Indian expedition to Antarctica was sent in 1981 and since then Indian scientists have established two research stations, *Dakshin Gangotri* and *Maitri*, on the continent. Joint teams representing a number of scientific organizations in the country have participated in a number of expeditions to the continent. Parliament passed a comprehensive Indian Antarctic Act in 2022 (Box 4.2).

BOX 4.2 ENVIRO FACT: ***The Indian Antarctic Act of 2022***

The Indian Antarctic Act of 2022 seeks to give effect to the Antarctic Treaty, the Convention on the Conservation of Antarctic Marine Living Resources, and the Protocol on Environmental Protection to the Antarctic Treaty. It also seeks to protect the Antarctic environment and regulate activities in the region. The key features of the Act are:

Applicability: The provisions of the Bill will apply to any person, vessel or aircraft that is a part of an Indian expedition to Antarctica under a permit issued under the Bill.

Central committee: The central government will establish a Committee on Antarctic Governance and Environmental Protection. The Committee will be chaired by the Secretary of the Ministry of Earth Sciences. It will include 10 officials from various Ministries and organisations such as defence, external affairs, National Centre for Polar and Ocean Research, and National Security Council Secretariat. In addition, two experts from Antarctic environment and geo-political fields will be nominated by the central government.

The functions of the Committee include: (i) granting permits for various activities, (ii) implementing and ensuring compliance of relevant international laws for protection of Antarctic environment, (iii) obtaining and reviewing relevant information provided by parties to the Treaty, Convention, and Protocol, and (iv) negotiating fees/charges with other parties for activities in Antarctica.

Need for permit: A permit by the Committee or written authorisation from another party to the Protocol (other than India) will be required for various activities such as: (i) an Indian expedition to enter or remain in Antarctica, (ii) a person to enter or remain in an Indian station in Antarctica, (iii) a vessel or aircraft registered in India to enter or remain in Antarctica, (iv) a person or vessel to drill, dredge or excavate for mineral resources, or collect samples of mineral resources, (v) activities which may harm native species, and (vi) waste disposal by a person, vessel or aircraft in Antarctica.

Before a permit is granted by the Committee, the applicant has to carry out an environmental impact assessment of the proposed activities. Moreover, a permit must not be granted unless a waste management plan has been prepared for the expedition by the Committee.

Prohibited activities: The Act prohibits certain activities in Antarctica including: (i) nuclear explosion or disposal of radioactive wastes, (ii) introduction of non-sterile soil, and (iii) discharge of garbage, plastic or other substance into the sea which is harmful to the marine environment.

Offences and penalties: The Act specifies penalties for contravention of its provisions.

What is the UN Decade of Ocean Science for Sustainable Development (2021–2030)?

The UN has proclaimed a Decade of Ocean Science for Sustainable Development (2021–2030) to support efforts to reverse the cycle of decline in ocean health and gather ocean stakeholders worldwide behind a common framework that will ensure ocean science can fully support countries in creating improved conditions for sustainable development of the Ocean.

The marine realm is the largest component of the Earth's system that stabilizes climate and support life on Earth and human well-being. However, the First World Ocean Assessment released in 2016 found that much of the ocean is now seriously degraded, with changes and losses in the structure, function and benefits from marine systems. In addition, the impact of multiple stressors on the ocean is projected to increase as the human population grows towards the expected 9 billion by 2050.

Adaptation strategies and science-informed policy responses to global change are urgently needed. Scientific understanding of the ocean's responses to pressures and management action is fundamental for sustainable development. Ocean observations and research are also essential to predict the consequences of change, design mitigation and guide adaptation.

The Intergovernmental Oceanographic Commission (IOC) of UNESCO will coordinate the Decade's preparatory process, inviting the global ocean community to plan for the next ten years in ocean science and technology to deliver "the ocean we need for the future we want".

The Decade will provide a 'once in a lifetime' opportunity to create a new foundation, across the science-policy interface, to strengthen the management of the ocean.

The Key Challenges and the expected outcomes identified for the Ocean Decade are given in Box 4.3.

BOX 4.3 ***The Key Challenges and the Expected Outcomes of the Ocean Decade***

***Challenge 1**: Understand and beat marine pollution*

Understand and map land and sea-based sources of pollutants and contaminants and their potential impacts on human health and ocean ecosystems and develop solutions to remove or mitigate them.

***Challenge 2**: Protect and restore ecosystems and biodiversity*

Understand the effects of multiple stressors on ocean ecosystems, and develop solutions to monitor, protect, manage and restore ecosystems and their biodiversity under changing environmental, social and climate conditions.

***Challenge 3**: Sustainably feed the global population*

Generate knowledge, support innovation, and develop solutions to optimise the role of the ocean in sustainably feeding the world's population under changing environmental, social and climate conditions.

***Challenge 4**: Develop a sustainable and equitable ocean economy*

Generate knowledge, support innovation, and develop solutions for equitable and sustainable development of the ocean economy under changing environmental, social and climate conditions.

***Challenge 5**: Unlock ocean-based solutions to climate change*

Enhance understanding of the ocean-climate nexus and generate knowledge and solutions to mitigate, adapt and build resilience to the effects of climate change across all geographies and at all scales, and to improve services including predictions for the ocean, climate and weather.

***Challenge 6**: Increase community resilience to ocean hazards*

Enhance multi-hazard early warning services for all geophysical, ecological, biological, weather, climate and anthropogenic related ocean and coastal hazards, and mainstream community preparedness and resilience.

***Challenge 7**: Expand the Global Ocean Observing System*

Ensure a sustainable ocean observing system across all ocean basins that delivers accessible, timely, and actionable data and information to all users.

***Challenge 8**: Create a digital representation of the Ocean*

Through multi-stakeholder collaboration, develop a comprehensive digital representation of the ocean, including a dynamic ocean map, which provides free and open access for exploring, discovering, and visualizing past, current, and future ocean conditions in a manner relevant to diverse stakeholders.

***Challenge 9**: Skills, knowledge and technology for all*

Ensure comprehensive capacity development and equitable access to data, information, knowledge and technology across all aspects of ocean science and for all stakeholders.

***Challenge 10**: Change humanity's relationship with the ocean*

Ensure that the multiple values and services of the ocean for human wellbeing, culture, and sustainable development are widely understood, and identify and overcome barriers to behaviour change required for a step change in humanity's relationship with the ocean.

The expected outcomes are:

- A clean ocean where sources of pollution are identified and reduced or removed.
- A healthy and resilient ocean where marine ecosystems are understood, protected, restored and managed.
- A productive ocean supporting sustainable food supply and a sustainable ocean economy.
- A predicted ocean where society understands and can respond to changing ocean conditions.
- A safe ocean where life and livelihoods are protected from ocean-related hazards.
- An accessible ocean with open and equitable access to data, information and technology, and innovation.
- An inspiring and engaging ocean where society understands and values the ocean in relation to human wellbeing and sustainable development.

What was the 2022 State of the Ocean Report?

In August 2022, the Intergovernmental Oceanographic Commission (IOC) of UNESCO released the pilot edition of the State of the Ocean Report 2022. The report is structured around the initial challenges of the UN Decade described above.

The attempt to create the Report led to a 'moment of truth': Although society is aware in principle of what is happening in the ocean, and what should be done about it, the quantitative description of the ocean is drastically incomplete and, as a result, current knowledge is insufficient to effectively inform solutions to the ocean issues that humanity is now facing.

Therefore, the Report concluded that the way forward was to:

- broadly communicate the findings on the continued lack of quantitative knowledge about the ocean;
- continue to promote and develop the UN Ocean Decade as the prime platform to transform ocean science, so that it can effectively contribute to sustainable development;
- act to create a theoretical basis for sustainable ocean planning and management, within and beyond areas of national jurisdiction, focusing on ocean economy, climate and biodiversity, and develop corresponding implementation plans in consultation with key stakeholders; and
- strengthen the ocean science-policy interface.

Who Controls the Ocean Activities?

For a long time the ocean area beyond the territorial limit was governed by the concept of the Freedom of the High Seas. This meant that any country or anyone could exploit the wealth of the ocean without any control. Now, however, that concept has been replaced by that of the Common Heritage of Mankind.

> **Key Idea** The UN Convention on the Law of the Sea governs the use of marine resources. The Convention considers the ocean as the Common Heritage of Mankind.

In a landmark agreement, many countries came together to draft the UN Convention on the Law of the Sea (UNCLOS), which came into force in November 1994. Apart from setting the territorial limit as 12 nautical miles (from the shoreline), this Convention establishes for every country an Exclusive Economic Zone (EEZ) up to a distance of 200 nautical miles from the shoreline (One nautical mile is equal to 1.85 km.). Every country has the exclusive right to exploit the resources of its EEZ. What is beyond the EEZ is the International Area of the Seabed.

According to the Convention the ocean has to be used only for peaceful purposes and should be managed in the interests of all, including future generations. To control the ocean resources and to resolve disputes, two bodies have been established: the International Tribunal for the Law of the

Sea, Hamburg, and the International Seabed Authority, Jamaica. The Seabed Authority controls the exploitation of resources in the International Area.

The International Seabed Authority is currently discussing the question of commercial seabed mining. Several countries have demanded a moratorium on such mining until further research on the environmental impact is carried out, and until regulations with strict environmental standards are in place.

India has a coastline of over 7000 km and an EEZ of 2 million sq km, which is two-third of our land area. The Seabed Authority has granted exclusive rights to India to explore 150,000 sq km in the central Indian Ocean.

Are Inland Seas Also Special?

Inland seas are large saltwater bodies and they occur on all continents. They include the Caspian Sea, Dead Sea, Black Sea, and Aral Sea. They are sensitive ecosystems and their environmental importance is only now becoming clear. Most of the large inland seas of the world are facing environmental degradation. They were once healthy waters used for fishing, transport, etc. Now, however, human activities like overfishing, pollution, and diversion of inflow are decimating many of these water bodies. (Read about the Aral Sea in Box 4.4.)

BOX 4.4 DISASTER: *The Story of the Aral Sea—Death of an Inland Sea*

The Aral Sea, on the border between Uzbekistan and Kazakhstan, was once the world's fourth largest freshwater body. It was spread over 68,000 sq km in 1960. Over the past forty years, however, it has lost over 75% of its volume and over 50% of its area. How did such degradation happen?

The Sea has no outflow other than evaporation and the inflow is from the rivers, Amu Darya and Syr Darya. In the 1950s, the erstwhile USSR decided to divert the water from these two rivers to irrigate the desert area around the lake for planting cotton. The Soviets also constructed the world's longest irrigation canal (over 1300 km long) to take the water into Turkmenistan.

Millions of hectares of cotton were planted and soon USSR became a net exporter of cotton. This success came with a cost to the Aral Sea. By the early 1980s, 95% of the inflow had been diverted and by then the Sea had shrunk to a considerable extent.

The fish catch used to be 44,000 tonnes per year, providing livelihood for 600,000 people. Today, most of the 24 fish species are gone and the fishing industry has collapsed. These are hard times for the 35 million people living in the watershed.

The shoreline has receded by an incredible 100 km! Abandoned boats dot the landscape. Toxic dust-salt mixture arises like a storm from the exposed seabed and gets deposited on the farmland, damaging crops. The dust also causes many illnesses including throat cancer and tuberculosis. The weather has changed for the worse, with summers getting warmer and the winters colder.

After the breakup of USSR, the five republics of the region established in 1994 a joint fund to prevent the complete disappearance of the Aral Sea. The World Bank and UNEP gave funds to save the Sea. Reviving the Sea is a hard task, however. Even if all the diversion of water for irrigation is stopped now, it will take 50 years for the lake to fill up! The dilemma is that, with the collapse of the fisheries, irrigation for agriculture has become even more important. Do we want water on the farm or water in the lake?

By 2007 the Aral Sea had declined to 10% of its original size, splitting into three lakes—the North Aral Sea and the South-eastern and Southwestern basins. By 2009, the South-eastern lake had disappeared and the Southwestern lake had become just a thin strip.

There is some good news, however. The North Aral Sea is making a recovery, due to the efforts of the Kazakh government, the World Bank, and scientists. A dam completed in 2005 raised water levels and decreased salinity, and increased the North Aral's span by 20%. Some native plants and migrating birds like pelicans, flamingos, ducks, and even freshwater fish are coming back.

What is the Coastal Zone?

The coastal zone (Fig. 4.2) is the area of interaction between land and ocean, but there is no clear definition of the zone. On the seaward side, it is commonly taken to extend up to the gently sloping, shallow edge of the continental shelf. On the landward side, we could define the limit of the zone as the high tide line or even up to the watershed. Thanks to the edge effect, this zone shows very high levels of biodiversity. 90% of all marine species are found in this zone.

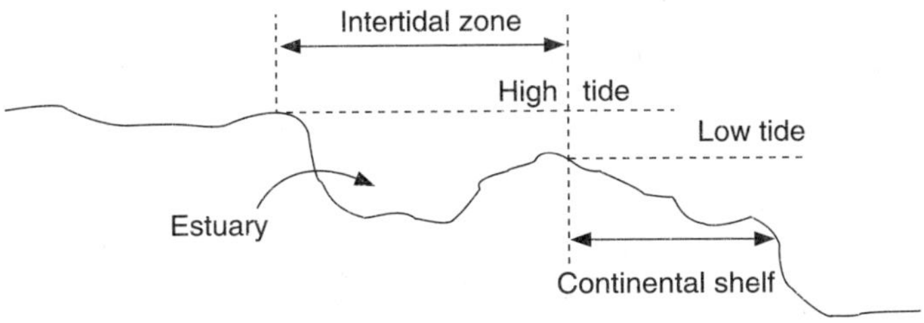

FIGURE 4.2 The Coastal Zone

The coastal zone is easily affected by human activities. A general trend in the world is for the population to move towards the coastal zone. One estimate is that 60% of the world population now lives within 60 km of the coast. This proportion is expected to increase to 75% by 2025. Even conservative estimates suggest that at least 40% of the population lives within 100 km of the coast. One undeniable fact is that the rate of increase of coastal population is higher than that of the general population.

> **Key Idea** The coastal zone with its diversity is ecologically important, but it is being degraded due to population pressure, urban expansion, infrastructure development, and pollution.

Most of the large cities of the world can be found on the coast. Twelve of the twenty most highly populated urban areas in the world are within 150 km of the coast and these include Mumbai and Kolkata. Coastal megacities have very large Ecological Footprints. In most cases, they dump enormous amounts of untreated sewage and industrial pollutants into the ocean.

What are Coral Reefs?

Coral reefs are one of the natural wonders of the ocean. On many beaches, these beautiful and colourful creations are on sale. Where do they come from and who makes them? Coral reefs are found in the shallow coastal zones of tropical and subtropical oceans, where light can penetrate. Apart being aesthetically appealing, they are also among the world's oldest, most diverse, and most productive ecosystems.

Corals are formed by huge colonies of tiny organisms called polyps. They secrete calcium carbonate (limestone) to form a protective crust around their soft bodies. When they die, their outer skeletons remain as a platform for others to continue building the coral. The intricate crevices and holes in the coral catacombs become the home for 25% of all marine species.

The colour of the corals comes from zooxanthellae, the tiny single-celled algae that live inside the tissues of the polyps. In return for the home provided by the polyps, zooxanthellae produce food and oxygen through photosynthesis.

Why are coral reefs important?

Coral reefs are complex ecosystems that perform many ecological services. When polyps form their shells, they absorb some carbon dioxide as part of the carbon cycle. Reefs help protect the coastal zone from the impact of waves and storms. They are the nurseries for hundreds of marine organisms. In their biodiversity and intricacy of relationships, they can be called the rain forests of the ocean.

On the economic side, they provide fish, shellfish, building materials, medicines, and employment to people. Through tourism, they bring in valuable foreign exchange and give us the pleasure of enjoying the world under the sea.

Like many other parts of nature, coral reefs are also in trouble. They are very vulnerable to damage because they grow very slowly, get disrupted easily, and are very sensitive to variations in temperature and salinity.

Coral bleaching is the biggest threat faced by all colonies. When a reef becomes stressed, it expels the zooxanthellae, loses its colour and food, and ultimately dies. An increase of even one degree in the water temperature can trigger bleaching. Sediment runoff from land that smothers the reef and prevents photosynthesis is another stress. Any pollution and disease could also lead to bleaching. Direct physical damage can also occur.

60% of the world's reefs are threatened by coastal development, pollution, overfishing and warmer temperatures. Of more than 100 countries with large coral formations, 90% are experiencing decline of the reefs. Southeast Asia with the most species of all coral reefs is the most threatened region. 300 reefs in 65 countries are protected as reserves and 600 more are under consideration. Protected reefs do recover, but the process is difficult and expensive.

What is the Importance of Mangroves?

Mangroves are unique salt-tolerant trees with interlacing roots that grow in shallow marine sediments. Often, they are found just inland of coral reefs. Mangroves provide valuable ecosystem services. Their roots are the breeding grounds and nurseries for many fish species like shrimp and sea trout. The branches are nesting sites for birds like pelicans, spoonbills, and egrets. They stabilize the soil, prevent erosion, and provide protection to the coast during cyclones. They are more effective than concrete barriers in absorbing wave action.

> **Key Idea** Coral reefs and mangroves provide invaluable ecosystem services (protection against storms, breeding grounds for fish, etc.), but they are in decline all over the world.

Mangroves occur all along the Indian coast covering 6,700 sq km, which is about 7% of the world's total mangrove area. Some of the important mangrove forests are found in Andaman and Nicobar Islands, Sundarbans (West Bengal), Bhitarkanika (Odisha), Pitchavaram (Tamil Nadu), and Goa.

In India and elsewhere, mangroves are fast disappearing due to coastal development, logging, and shrimp aquaculture. Between 1985 and 2000, the world lost half of its mangroves.

Why are Estuaries and Coastal Wetlands Important?

Estuaries and coastal wetlands include river mouths, bays, mangrove forests, and salt marshes. Here the sea water mixes with fresh water and nutrients from rivers, streams, and runoffs. These ecosystems experience, daily and seasonally, wide fluctuations in temperatures and salinity levels because of tidal rhythms, variations in fresh water inflow from land and river, and the impact of storms.

The organisms in these ecosystems have to adapt to changing conditions. Yet, these ecotones are among the most fertile ecosystems, often more productive than the adjacent ocean or river. The main reasons are flow of nutrients from land, removal of waste products by tidal action, and the availability of sunlight.

Coastal saltwater wetlands are the oceans nurseries, where many fish species spend the first part of their lives. These wetlands also protect coastlines from erosion and reduce damage from storms and cyclones. The flow of ground water through coastal marshes prevents saltwater intrusion that would otherwise contaminate the wells. Coastal wetlands are, however, in steep decline all over the world.

How do We Define Freshwater Life Zones?

Aquatic zones with less than 1% dissolved salts are freshwater life zones. They include flowing bodies like streams and rivers and standing bodies like lakes, ponds, and inland wetlands.

Freshwater ecosystems perform many services like climate moderation, nutrient recycling, flood control, waste treatment, groundwater recharge, providing a habitat for species, and preserving a pool of genetic resources and biodiversity. On the economic side, they provide food, drinking water, irrigation, hydropower, transportation, recreation, and employment.

Freshwater ecosystems are influenced by the local climate, soil, and resident communities as well as by the surrounding biomes. Anything that happens upstream will have an impact on them.

What are the General Characteristics of Rivers and Streams?

The nature of any flowing-water ecosystem like a stream or a river varies greatly between its source and its mouth (where it meets the ocean or flows into another water body like a lake). A river often begins as a stream high in the mountains in a forest, which absorbs the precipitation and releases it slowly. In other cases, the river begins with the melting of snow or a glacier.

The source or headwater stream flows downstream rapidly over rocks or becomes a waterfall. Once it reaches the plains, it slows down. Other tributaries may flow into the river. Finally, it reaches the delta, the low-lying plains at the mouth, before flowing into the ocean. The delta is fertile thanks to the sediments carried along by the river.

Human activities are taking a heavy toll on the world's rivers. About 60% of the 240 large rivers are strongly or moderately fragmented by dams, diversions, and canals.

What is the State of India's Rivers?

More than 70% of India's territory drains into the Bay of Bengal via the Ganges–Brahmaputra river system and a number of large and small peninsular rivers. The Indus basin (in North-western India) and a completely separate set of basins to the south (in Gujarat, Madhya Pradesh, Maharashtra) drain into the Arabian Sea.

The two most important west-flowing rivers of peninsular India are the Narmada and Tapti. The Narmada and its basin are undergoing large-scale, multipurpose development. The major rivers that drain into the Bay of Bengal are Mahanadi, Godavari, Krishna, and Kaveri.

Most Indian rivers are in crisis due to several causes:

- Obstruction of flows by dams, barrages, and hydroelectric projects
- Excessive withdrawal or diversion of waters (largely for irrigation, but also increasingly for industrial use)
- Excessive extraction of ground water affecting the base flow in rivers
- Drastic reduction of aquatic and riparian biodiversity (primarily the result of deteriorating river-health)
- Deterioration of catchments through human activity such as deforestation and destruction of water sources such as lakes and wetlands
- Reckless and unregulated mining of sand from the river-beds
- Enormous generation of waste and sewage by cities and its disposal into rivers
- Dumping of industrial effluents, chemical residues from agriculture, and other pollutants and contaminants

The question of interlinking Indian rivers is discussed in Chapter 5.

How can We Study Large Lakes?

Lakes are natural bodies of standing fresh water when precipitation, runoff, or groundwater seepage fills up depressions on land formed by geological changes. Lakes and their surrounding watersheds are unique and valuable ecosystems. Lakes store fresh water and give it to us in off-monsoon months. The water in lakes also recharges the ground water. More than 90% of all available surface fresh water is contained in lakes and reservoirs.

> **Key Idea** Lakes provide fresh water, recharge the ground water, and act as habitat for many aquatic species. But many lakes are shrinking in size, becoming polluted, and losing their fish populations.

Lakes provide habitat for bacteria, fungi, algae, plants, plankton, molluscs, crustaceans, insects, fish, amphibians, reptiles, birds, and mammals. They support large numbers of threatened and endemic species.

Human communities that surround lakes depend heavily on lake biodiversity and natural lake processes for their water, food, and way of life. Many of the world's poorest people depend on freshwater biodiversity for their protein needs.

There are about 500,000 lakes on earth, most of them located in North America (25%), Africa (30%), and Asia (20%). Although most lakes are relatively new to earth (in geological time), there are at least 14 lakes older than one million years. In many countries, lakes supply a large proportion of the drinking water.

Many of the world's lakes, however, are in crisis. Lake Chapala (Mexico), which has been shrinking dramatically due to water diversion for inefficient irrigation, is the main water source for 5 million people in Guadalajara, Mexico. Lake Victoria in east Africa lost most of its native fish due to the introduction of an alien predator, the Nile perch.

What about Indian lakes?

India had a very large number of lakes and ponds, constructed by kings of the past for storing water. The major and well-known Indian natural lakes include the Dal and Wular lakes in Jammu-Kashmir, Chilika Lake in Odisha, Loktak Lake in Manipur, Vembanad Lake in Kerala, Kodaikanal Lake in Tamil Nadu, and Nainital Lake in Uttarakhand.

Many of the Indian lakes are now polluted or have been drained and converted as cropland. Lakes in cities such as Bengaluru have become built-up areas (Box 4.5).

BOX 4.5 ECOSYSTEM: *The Story of Bengaluru's Lakes*

Bengaluru (or Bangalore), the capital of Karnataka, was known as the city of lakes. The city once had about 280 large lakes and hundreds of ponds, constructed by the kings and later by the British for drinking water, irrigation, and fishing. The water bodies were connected by canals so that the overflow from one would run into another one at a lower level. The lakes provided all the drinking water that the city needed and also recharged the ground water.

These water bodies also moderated the microclimate. They also drained all the excess rain water and the city never saw any flooding.

Over the years most of the water bodies have disappeared due to urbanization and encroachments. Lakebeds have become bus stands, golf courses, playgrounds, and residential colonies. Just 15 lakes exist today and even they are in a bad condition and toxic. The two largest existing lakes—Bellandur and Varthur—are both heavily polluted by sewage and effluents. The canals too have been polluted. Water tables have dropped to deep levels, drinking water for Bengaluru now comes from 100 km away, and the city gets flooded during every monsoon.

Thanks to a Public Interest case and a High Court decision, the Karnataka Government set up a Lake Development Authority (LDA) in 2002. The LDA identified 2800 large, medium, and small lakes within Bangalore Metropolitan Regional Development Authority (BMRDA) limits including 608 within the limits of Bangalore Development Authority (BDA) to take remedial and restoration measures. The LDA tried leasing out lakes to private companies, but these developers set up food courts and amusement parks and also restricted public access to the lakes. Protests and public interest cases followed and the High Court stopped the privatization. In 2012, the Court passed specific orders for the protection of lakes.

While citizen groups have taken up the conservation of specific lakes, LDA continues to be ineffective. Meanwhile, the Rockefeller Foundation has included Bengaluru among the 100 cities chosen for its Resilient Cities Programme. The focus will be on cleaning up the water system in the city.

In 2016, the state government set up the Karnataka Lake Conservation and Development Authority. This body has powers to identify and recover encroached lakebed and take steps to protect, conserve, and restore water bodies all over the state. The Authority, however, has been largely inactive and ineffective.

What Are Freshwater Wetlands And What Is Their Importance?

A wetland is an ecosystem that is flooded either permanently or seasonally. A scientific definition is that 'wetlands are lands transitional between terrestrial and aquatic eco-systems, where the water table is usually at or near the surface or the land is covered by shallow water.'

The Ramsar Convention (discussed below) defines wetlands as 'areas of marsh, fen, peatland, or water, whether natural or artificial, permanent or temporary, with water that is static or flowing, fresh, brackish, or salt, including areas of marine water, the depth of which at low tide does not exceed six metres.'

What is the importance of wetlands?

Wetlands are vital for the earth ecosystem for several reasons:

- Wetlands are among the most diverse and productive ecosystems, comparable to rainforests and coral reefs.
- Many wetlands contain an immense biodiversity, including a wide variety of microbes, plants, insects, amphibians, reptiles, birds, fish, and mammals.
- Wetlands provide enormous amounts of food for many organisms. As the plants break down in water, they become detritus (Chapter 2), which is food for many organisms.
- Wetlands are a carbon sink and they also help regulate the water, nitrogen, and sulphur cycles. They recharge groundwater aquifers.
- When wastewater flows through a wetland, a natural filtration process occurs. This function has been used by some city governments.
- Wetlands in and around a city act as a flood control mechanism by absorbing the excess water.
- Wetlands on the shores of lakes, rivers, and the ocean prevent erosion and act as buffers against river currents and waves.
- Wetlands are the source of fish, shellfish, blueberries, cranberries, timber, wild rice, and medicinal plants. They are also the habitats for fur-bearers like muskrat, beaver, mink, and reptiles such as alligators.
- Many wetlands are places of natural beauty, very attractive for recreation – hunting, fishing, hiking, photography, painting, etc.

To sum up, wetlands have been called the 'kidneys of the landscape' because they clean polluted waters, prevent floods, protect shorelines, and recharge aquifers. They've also been called 'biological supermarkets' because of their extensive food webs, rich biodiversity, and unique habitats.

What is happening to the wetlands of the world?

In India and elsewhere, wetlands are degraded and converted to other uses at an alarming rate:

- Wetlands in or near cities are being drained and filled up for the construction of housing colonies and industries.
- Wetlands are also converted for agricultural use.
- Many wetlands are getting polluted by industrial and domestic effluents, pesticide runoff, automobile, and factory exhaust, etc.
- Grazing and the introduction of alien species are affecting the vegetation in many wetlands.
- Many wetlands have been inundated by the construction of big dams.
- Direct deforestation also occurs in wetlands.

What is the Ramsar Convention on Wetlands?

The Ramsar Convention is the oldest of the modern global intergovernmental environmental agreements. The Treaty was negotiated by countries and NGOs concerned with the increasing loss and degradation of wetland habitat for migratory water birds. It was adopted in the Iranian city of Ramsar in 1971 and came into force in 1975. The Convention's mission is 'the conservation and wise use of all wetlands through local and national actions and international cooperation, as a contribution towards achieving sustainable development throughout the world.'

The Convention uses a broad definition of wetlands (given above). It includes all lakes and rivers, underground aquifers, swamps and marshes, wet grasslands, peatlands, oases, estuaries, deltas and tidal flats, mangroves and other coastal areas, coral reefs, and all human-made sites such as fishponds, rice paddies, reservoirs, and salt pans.

171 countries are parties to the Convention. Under the Convention, the countries commit to:

- work towards the wise use of all their wetlands;
- designate suitable wetlands for the list of Wetlands of International Importance (the 'Ramsar List') and ensure their effective management; and
- cooperate internationally on transboundary wetlands, shared wetland systems, and shared species.

The Convention defines wise use of wetlands as 'the maintenance of their ecological character, achieved through the implementation of ecosystem approaches, within the context of sustainable development.' Wise use can thus be seen as the conservation and sustainable use of wetlands and all the services they provide, for the benefit of people and nature.

What are Ramsar Sites or Wetlands of International Importance?

At the time of joining the Convention, each country undertakes to designate at least one wetland site for inclusion in the List of Wetlands of International Importance (called Ramsar Sites). Thereafter, countries should continue to designate suitable wetlands within their territory for the List, based on specified criteria.

Ramsar Sites are designated according to nine criteria. Eight of these are biodiversity criteria, emphasizing the importance the Convention places on sustaining this diversity by designating and restoring wetlands. A wetland is considered internationally important if it:

- contains a representative, rare, or unique example of a natural or near-natural wetland type found within the appropriate biogeographic region.
- supports vulnerable, endangered, or critically endangered species or threatened ecological communities.
- supports populations of plant and/or animal species important for maintaining the biological diversity of a particular biogeographic region

- regularly supports 20,000 or more water birds or supports 1% of the individuals in a population of one species or subspecies of water bird.

There are also criteria based on fish species and wetland-dependent non-avian animal species.

The inclusion of a site in the List embodies the government's commitment to take the steps necessary to ensure that its ecological character is maintained. Wetlands included in the list acquire a new national and international status: they are recognized as being of significant value not only for the country or the countries in which they are located, but for humanity.

The Convention has mechanisms to preserve the ecological character of the Sites and to enable countries to work together to manage wetlands extending across international borders. Ramsar Sites are often also listed under other international and national protection schemes such as the UNESCO World Heritage Convention and the UNESCO Biosphere Reserves.

The Ramsar sites together form the world's largest network of protected areas. There are over 2400 Ramsar Sites on the territories of the 171 parties across the world, covering more than 2.5 million sq km.

What is the Montreux Record?

The Montreux Record is the principal tool of the Ramsar Convention for highlighting those Sites, where an adverse change in ecological character has occurred, or is likely to occur as the result of technological developments, pollution, or other human interference, and which are therefore in need of priority conservation attention. If such a change occurs in a Site, the country should inform the Ramsar Secretariat of such changes.

Alternatively, the Convention Secretariat, on receipt of information on actual or possible adverse change from partner organizations, other international or national NGOs, or other interested bodies, may draw the attention of the country concerned to this information.

The Site may then be placed on the Montreux Record. This is a means of drawing attention to such Sites and it is subject to continuous review. The Convention Secretariat will help the country take conservation measures and if they succeed, the Site may be removed from the Montreux Record after a review and at the request of the country.

What were the key messages of the 2020 Global Wetland Outlook (Special Edition)?

The Global Wetland Outlook: Special Edition 2021 was prepared for the Convention's 50th anniversary. Drawing on more than 30 major global and regional assessments and other recent scientific findings, it describes the pandemic and its implications; trends in wetlands since 2018; lessons for wetland wise use and protection; and how the Convention on Wetlands can be leveraged to address challenges facing wetlands.

Key messages:

- The COVID-19 pandemic has changed the way we think about health and the environment, with more recognition of the importance of nature for health, including mental wellbeing. Meanwhile, water-borne diseases 'like infant diarrhoea' are increased by poor wetland management and cause millions of deaths every year.
- People's health and livelihoods depend on well-managed wetlands. Control of emergent zoonotic diseases is increasingly seen as dependent on maintenance of well-managed, intact ecosystems and native biodiversity.
- Wetlands are critical to delivering on global commitments relating to biodiversity, climate change and sustainable development.
- Deterioration of wetlands is widespread, but more wetlands are still reported as in 'good' rather than 'bad' ecological character.

- Climate change is occurring faster than previously anticipated, with thresholds crossed and major changes inevitable. Wetlands are particularly impacted by sea-level rise, coral bleaching and changing hydrology, with Arctic and montane wetlands especially at risk.
- Wetlands need to be part of delivering climate solutions. Adequate water provision is fundamental, and wetlands are critical for water security.
- Agriculture is a key driver of wetland degradation, but the future of sustainable food production is dependent on healthy wetlands and wise use.
- A confluence of international policy can drive positive change. Failure to meet the Aichi Targets and slow progress on the Sustainable Development Goals (SDGs), show that new approaches are needed.
- There are many examples of success - good site management, improvement in species conservation status, progress with ecosystem restoration, and benefits in terms of water security, adaptation, and mitigation outcomes. However, the world's wetlands are still being lost at alarming rates. Implementation of the Convention needs to be strengthened to fully realize its potential.

TABLE 4.1 Indian Wetlands by Category

No.	Category	Wetland Area (million ha)
1	Inland wetlands: Natural	6.60
2	Inland wetlands: Man-made	4.00
3	Coastal wetlands: Natural	3.70
4	Coastal wetlands: Man-made	0.44
5	Small wetlands (<2.5 ha)	0.56
	Total	**15.30**

What is the extent and distribution of wetlands in India?

In 2011, the Space Applications Centre, Ahmedabad, released a National Wetlands Atlas. The Atlas, mapped through Satellite Remote Sensing, was prepared under the National Wetland Inventory and Assessment Project. Some details of the distribution of wetlands are given in Tables 4.1 and 4.2.

Which are the Ramsar Sites in India?

The Ramsar Convention on Wetlands entered into force in India on February 1, 1982. By March 2023, India had designated 75 Ramsar Sites in India, covering 1,326,677 ha. The largest 10 Ramsar Sites are shown in Table 4.3. Access the ORC for the full list of Ramsar sites in India.

TABLE 4.2 Largest Indian Wetlands by State

Extent of Wetlands	State	Wetlands as % of Geog. Area of State
Highest extent	Lakshadweep	96
	Andaman & Nicobar Is.	19
	Daman & Diu	18
	Gujarat	18
Wetland-rich	Puducherry	13
	West Bengal	13
	Assam	10
	Tamil Nadu	7
	Goa	6
	Andhra Pradesh	5
	Uttar Pradesh	5

TABLE 4.3 Largest 10 Ramsar Wetland Sites in India (as of June 2023)

Rank	Name	State	Date	Area (ha)
1	Sundarbans Wetland	W. Bengal	30.1.2019	423000
2	Vembanad-Kol Wetland	Kerala	19.8.2002	151250
3	Chilika Lake	Odisha	1.10.1981	116500
4	Satkosia Gorge	Odisha	12.10.2021	98197
5	Kolleru Lake	A.P.	19.8.2002	90100
6	Hirakud Reservoir	Odisha	12.10.2021	65400
7	Bhitarkanika Mangroves	Odisha	19.8.2002	65000
8	Ashtamudi Wetland	Kerala	19.8.2002	61400
9	Gulf of Mannar Marine Biosphere Reserve	Tamil Nadu	8.4.2022	52672
10	Point Calimere Wildlife and Bird Sanctuary	Tamil Nadu	19.8.2002	38500

Are there Indian Ramsar Sites on the Montreux Record? Two Indian Sites are currently on the Montreux Record: Keoladeo National Park (since July 1990) and Loktak Lake (since June 1993). Chilika Lake was once placed on the Record and removed later, when conservation measures were implemented and succeeded.

How are the wetlands of India being conserved?

- The National Plan for Conservation of Aquatic Ecosystems (NPCA) provides the policy framework and support to State Governments for integrated management of wetlands.
- The Ministry has also initiated the process of revising the existing regulatory framework on wetlands to enable a greater role and ownership by State Governments in management of wetlands, particularly as water and land are State subjects. The State Wetland Authorities are to be entrusted the role of management and regulation of wetlands within their jurisdiction.
- In a strategic step towards increasing the capacity of wetland managers in integrated and holistic management, the existing Wetland Research and Training Centre of Chilika Development Authority at Barkul, Odisha, will be upgraded into the National Capacity Development Centre for Wetlands.

What are the Wetlands Rules of 2017?

In September 2017, MoEFCC notified the new Wetlands (Conservation and Management) Rules, 2017. The new Rules supersede the Wetlands (Conservation and Management) Rules, 2010.

The key provisions in the new rules are:

- The Rules decentralise wetlands management by giving states powers to not only identify and notify wetlands within their jurisdictions but also keep a watch on prohibited activities.
- They also indirectly widen the ambit of permitted activities by inserting the 'wise use' principle, giving powers to State Wetland Authorities to decide what can be allowed in larger interest.
- The Centre's role will be restricted to monitoring its implementation by states/UTs, recommending trans-boundary wetlands for notification, and reviewing integrated management of selected wetlands under the Ramsar Convention.

In 2020, MoEFCC released the Guidelines for Implementing the Wetlands (Conservation and Management) Rules, 2017. These guidelines have been drafted to support the States/UTs in the implementation of the Rules by providing guidance on:

- Preparing a list of wetlands in the State/UT
- Identifying wetlands for notification under 2017 Rules
- Delineating wetlands, wetlands complexes and zone of influence
- Preparation of Brief Document
- Determining 'wise use' and ecological character
- Developing a list of activities to be regulated and permitted
- Developing an Integrated Management Plan
- Constitution and operational matters of the Wetlands Authorities

Environmentalists have strongly reacted against the rules for the following reasons:

- The 2010 Rules itself have hardly been implemented and there was no need for a fresh set of rules now.
- The new rules essentially transfer the power to manage wetlands to the states. There are always strong local pressures to take over and 'develop' wetlands and, without central control, all the wetlands will disappear.
- The rules contain no ecological criteria for recognizing wetlands, such as biodiversity, reefs, mangroves, and wetland complexes.
- Sections on the protection of wetlands, and interpretation of harmful activities which require regulation, which were listed in the 2010 Rules have now been deleted.
- Prohibition on setting up new industries, storage/disposal of hazardous substances, solid waste dumping, discharge of untreated wastes, construction of permanent structures have all been removed from the list.
- The new rules will substantially weaken the conservation of wetlands by doing away with:
    - Central Wetlands Regulatory Authority
    - The elaborate list of activities that are prohibited or restricted.
    - The need for the environmental impact assessment before permitting such activities
    - Appeals to NGT against decisions made by local authorities.

What needs to be done about wetlands in India?

According to a study by the Indian Institute of Science and the Salim Ali Centre for Ornithology and Natural History, Coimbatore, a national wetland strategy should encompass the following:

- Protection: Legally protect all the existing wetlands.
- Planning, Managing, and Monitoring: Evolve a clear management plan involving the various stakeholders along with the local community and the corporate sector; monitor the wetland system.
- Comprehensive Inventory: For each wetland, make an inventory of the flora, fauna, and biodiversity along with wetland direct and indirect values.
- Legislation: Enact special laws to protect wetlands, including rules for Environment Impact Assessment of new projects.
- Coordinated Approach: Make their protection and management a common responsibility and set up an appropriate forum for resolving the conflict on wetland issues.
- Research: Conduct research on the dynamics of these ecosystems.
- Building Awareness: Create awareness among the public, students, and companies.

What should be done about conserving wetlands?

- The Rules of 2010 must be implemented first.
- A comprehensive law to protect wetlands must be promulgated to ensure efficient wetland conservation and management.
- The wetlands law must include provisions to reclaim lost wetlands.
- The law should also clearly specify prohibited activities and other activities that need permission. The states should be able to add activities to the list.
- Both the earlier rules and the new ones expose a basic issue: The government sees wetlands as waste land and not as a vital part of the ecosystem. This attitude must change.

Ending on a Hopeful Note: Positive Stories

Box 4.6 gives an account of some success achieved in restoring the Chilika Lake in Odisha. After many failed attempts, the cleaning of the Ganga has now received momentum under the Namami Ganga Programme (Box 4.7).

BOX 4.6 ECOSYSTEM: *The Story of Chilika Lake—New Life for an Old Lake?*

With an area of about 1,000 sq km, the Chilika Lake in coastal Odisha is the largest brackish water lagoon in Asia. Rich in fauna, it has been home to a variety of residential and migratory birds, many fish species, and the Irrawady dolphin.

It is one of the largest wintering grounds for migratory waterfowl from all over the world. From October to December every year, birds migrate here from places as far away as Siberia and Australia.

Chilika was recognized as a biodiversity hotspot and was designated as a Ramsar site in 1982. This refers to the Convention on Wetlands, an intergovernmental treaty adopted in 1971 in the Iranian city of Ramsar. There are more than 1,200 Ramsar sites in the world.

During the latter part of the twentieth century, Chilika was facing a number of ecological and social problems. Heavy siltation due to massive deforestation in the catchment area was reducing the lake area by 2 sq km every year. The blocking of its opening to the sea reduced the salinity level and many fish species were affected. The number of fish species dropped from 126 in 1930 to 69 in 1995. The poor drainage of water led to water logging in the agricultural lands around the lake.

200,000 fisherfolk and 800,000 people in the catchment area depend on the lake for their livelihood and the increasing population strained the resources further. The annual fish catch dropped from 8,800 tonnes to 1,600 tonnes during the decade of the 1990s. Illegal prawn culture has also been a problem.

In 1993, Chilika was placed on the Montreux Record, a list of Ramsar sites requiring priority conservation attention. By the end of the 1990s, the lake appeared to be dying, with no hope of restoration. Positive developments were, however, in the offing.

The Government of Odisha created the Chilika Development Authority (CDA) for the restoration of the lagoon. The CDA commissioned the National Institute of Oceanography (NIO), Goa and the Central Water and Power Research Station (CWPRS), Pune to study the problems and suggest solutions.

The consultants pinpointed the decrease in the salinity level as the major cause of the problems. Acting on their recommendation, the CDA opened an artificial mouth connecting the lake and the sea in 2000. This intervention seemed to have a positive effect, since the fish catch started going up—4,900 tonnes in 2000–2001 and 11,800 tonnes in 2001–2002. The Irrawady dolphin was seen again and the seagrass meadows reappeared.

The better exchange of water between the lagoon and the sea brought in more nutrients and flushed away the waste products. As a result, the productivity of the ecosystem increased. Thanks to the quicker drainage, the surrounding villages were not affected even in the unprecedented floods of 2001. The local people had been involved in the planning and implementation of the restoration work.

Impressed by the achievements, the Ramsar Bureau removed Chilika from the Montreux Record in 2002 and also conferred the Ramsar Wetland Conservation Award for 2002 on CDA for the successful restoration work involving the local community. In 2013, CDA was given powers under the Wildlife (Protection) Act of 1972.

A success story? Not quite, say some environmentalists. The increased salinity appears to have affected the migratory birds and their numbers are declining. In addition, large-scale poaching of the birds has also been reported. Illegal shrimp culture, overfishing, and the use of fine mesh nets are some of the other continuing problems.

BOX 4.7 *Namami Gange Programme*

The Namami Gange Programme is an Integrated Conservation Mission, approved as 'Flagship Programme' by the Union Government in June 2014, with budget outlay of ₹20,000 Crore to accomplish the objectives of effective abatement of pollution as well as the conservation and rejuvenation of National River Ganga.

Main activities of the Namami Gange Programme are:-

- Sewerage Treatment Infrastructure
- River-Front Development
- River-Surface Cleaning
- Biodiversity Conservation
- Afforestation
- Public Awareness
- Industrial Effluent Monitoring
- Ganga Gram

The plans and key achievements under Namami Gange programme are:

1. Creating Sewerage Treatment Capacity: 48 sewage management projects are under implementation and 99 sewage projects have been completed in the states of Uttarakhand, Uttar Pradesh, Bihar, Jharkhand, West Bengal, Delhi, Himachal Pradesh, Haryana, and Rajasthan. Work is under construction for creating a sewerage capacity of 5658.37 (MLD).
2. Creating River-Front Development: Construction of 71 Ghats and Crematoria and renovation of 270 others.
3. River Surface Cleaning: Collection of floating solid waste from the surface of the Ghats and River and its disposal at 11 locations.
4. Biodiversity Conservation: Restoring viable populations of all endemic and endangered biodiversity of the river.
5. Afforestation: Forestry interventions to enhance the productivity and diversity of the forests in head water areas and all along the river and its tributaries.
6. Public Awareness: A series of activities such as events, workshops, seminars and conferences were organized to make a strong pitch for public outreach and community participation in the programme. Various awareness activities through rallies, campaigns, exhibitions, shram daan, cleanliness drives, competitions, plantation drives and development and distribution of resource materials were also organized.
7. Industrial Effluent Monitoring: The number of Grossly Polluting Industries (GPIs) in April, 2019 were 1072. Regulation and enforcement through regular and surprise inspections of GPIs is carried out for compliance verification against stipulated environmental norms. The GPIs are also inspected on annual basis for compliance verification of the pollution norms and process modification. Out of 961 GPIs inspected in 2018, 636 are complying, 110 are non-complying and 215 are self-closed. Closure action has been taken against 110 non-complying GPIs. Online Continuous Effluent Monitoring Stations (OCEMS) have been connected to CPCB server in 885 out of 1072 GPIs.
8. Ganga Gram: Funds have been released for the construction of toilets in 1674 Gram Panchayats of 5 Ganga Basin States (Uttarakhand, Uttar Pradesh, Bihar, Jharkhand, and West Bengal). More than 8.5 lakh toilets have been built.
9. Consortium of seven IITs has been engaged in the preparation of Ganga River Basin Plan and 65 villages has been adopted by 13 IITs to develop as model villages. UNDP has been engaged as the executing agency for rural sanitation programme and to develop Jharkhand as a model State at an estimated cost of ₹127 Crore.

The Project has now been recognized as a UN Flagship Programme (Chapter 2).

REVIEW: A SUMMARY OF THE KEY POINTS

- Many large inland seas and freshwater lakes are facing severe environmental problems.
- The ocean is a treasure house of biodiversity and the provider of a whole range of ecological services.
- Coral reefs and mangroves are vital organisms that are under threat.
- The relatively unexploited Antarctica is now under pressure.
- The use of the ocean is now regulated by the UN Convention on the Law of the Sea.
- The coastal zone with its immense biodiversity is being degraded by development and population pressure.
- The importance of estuaries and wetlands are now being appreciated.

EXERCISES

Objective-type questions

In each case below, choose the best answer out of the given set of choices:

1. Which of the following factors **does not** determine the types of organisms that thrive in an aquatic life zone?
   (a) Salinity
   (b) Waves
   (c) Light penetration
   (d) Precipitation
2. Which of the following organisms is the 'producer' of the ocean?
   (a) Phytoplankton
   (b) Nekton
   (c) Benthos
   (d) Zooplankton
3. Which of the following statements is **not** true with regard to the ocean?
   (a) There is just a single ocean.
   (b) The ocean covers nearly three-fourths of the earth's surface.
   (c) The Indian Ocean has the deepest part of the ocean.
   (d) The biodiversity of the ocean far exceeds that of the land.
4. Which of the following statements is **not** true with regard to coral reefs?
   (a) Coral reefs are increasing in area everywhere.
   (b) Corals are formed by polyps.
   (c) Corals are the nurseries for hundreds of marine organisms.
   (d) Coral bleaching is the biggest threat faced by reefs.
5. Which of the following statements is **not** true with regard to mangroves?
   (a) Mangrove roots are the breeding grounds and nurseries for many fish species.
   (b) Mangrove branches are nesting sites for birds.
   (c) Mangroves stabilize the soil and prevent erosion.
   (d) Mangroves do not provide protection against cyclones.
6. Which international agreement governs the ocean?
   (a) UN Convention on the Law of the Sea
   (b) International Tribunal for the Law of the Sea
   (c) International Seabed Authority
   (d) Montreal Protocol

Short-answer questions

1. What are the factors that determine the types of organisms found in aquatic ecosystems?
2. List the main types of marine organisms. Who are the producers and consumers in the ocean?
3. Describe the main features of the UN Convention on the Law of the Sea (UNCLOS).
4. Explain why the following are important:
   (a) Coral reefs
   (b) Mangroves
   (c) Estuaries and coastal wetlands
   (d) Freshwater wetlands

Long-answer questions

1. Write essays on the importance of
   (a) the ocean and
   (b) the coastal zone
   with regard to economic and ecological services.
2. What are the general conclusions about the environmental problems of aquatic ecosystems you can draw from the cases described in this chapter?

Think critically: Deeper questions for reflection and discussion

There are still vast areas of ocean to be explored. How should we regulate exploration and exploitation of the ocean's resources?

ENJOY AND EDUCATE YOURSELF

1. Watch *The Perfect Storm* (2000), directed by Wolfgang Petersen, a disaster drama based on a true story.
2. Relax with the classic novel *The Old Man and the Sea* by Ernest Hemingway or watch its film version with Spencer Tracy playing the main role.

ACCESS THE OUP ONLINE RESOURCE CENTRE FOR MORE

- The story of Lake Victoria: Reap what you sow
- Full list of Ramsar sites in India
- Additional text and other recommended references, websites, and films

5 Water Resources

Water is the basis of life; it is a gift of nature;
it belongs to all living beings on earth.
Water is not private property.
It is a common resource for the sustenance of all.

Plachimada Declaration
World Water Conference, January 2004

MAIN QUESTIONS ADDRESSED

- What are renewable and non-renewable natural resources?
- How much water do we need and how much do we have?
- Why is there a worldwide water scarcity?
- What are the possible solutions to the water crisis?

KEYWORDS AND PHRASES

check dam, interlinking of rivers, Ken-Betwa project, non-renewable natural resource, rainwater harvesting, renewable natural resource, virtual water, water cycle, Water Footprint

LEAD STORY

THE STORY OF CHERRAPUNJI: THE WETTEST PLACE ON EARTH, YET NO WATER TO DRINK

When the monsoon comes to this place, it does not rain; it pours. It could pour continuously for over two months and you may not see the sun for 20–25 days at a stretch. With an average annual rainfall of 11.5 metres, Cherrapunji is listed in geography books as the wettest place on earth.

Some years, it rains much more than the average. In 1974 the place received 24.5 metres of rain and the record for one day is 1,563 mm. Yet, Cherrapunji, in the state of Meghalaya in Northeast India, faces severe drought the rest of the year!

How is it that not a drop of the 11.5 metres of rain remains to quench the thirst of the people? The answer lies in the destruction of forests. Once upon a time, the hills around Cherrapunji were full of dense forests. These forests soaked up the heavy rain and released it slowly the rest of the year. Over the years, however, the

Students talking: *Our book lists Cherrapunji as the Wettest land. I am confused! Why then do we have water scarcity?*

forests were cut down. The heavy rains washed away the topsoil, turning the slopes into deserts. It is now a mining town with most people making a living out of extraction of coal and chalk. The dusty air chokes the life out of people.

There is no reservoir to store the water. For over 20 years, the residents have depended on a piped water supply that comes from afar. That supply is always erratic and undependable.

Traditionally, the people of Cherrapunji celebrate the arrival of the rains every year with an elaborate festival. The rain gods do respond generously for four months. Yet the people do not have enough water for the next eight months!

To cap it all, Cherrapunji is no longer the wettest place on earth. The nearby village of Mawsynram now gets more rain than Cherrapunji! On June 17, 2022, Mawsynram recorded a rainfall of 1003.6 mm.

CLIMATE CHANGE AND WATER Climate change is already changing rainfall patterns and melting glaciers, thus causing too much water in some areas and too little water in others. Later this century, floods and droughts could become more common, and less fresh water will be available.

What does the story of Cherrapunji tell us?

The story shows how important it is to have forests that would slow down the flow of rain water and protect the topsoil, especially in the hills. Water is a unique resource and water scarcity is increasing in the world.

Before we learn more about water, however, it is important to understand the difference between renewable and non-renewable natural resources.

What is the Difference between Renewable and Non-renewable Natural Resources?

A natural resource is anything that we take from the environment to meet our needs. Solar energy, water, plants, petroleum, and minerals are examples. Some resources like water can be used straightaway, while others like petroleum need some processing before use.

A renewable resource is one that nature replenishes again and again over time through its own processes. One example is fresh water, which we get as rain every season, thanks to the global water cycle. Clean air, fresh topsoil, forests, and fish are other examples of renewable resources.

We must, however, give nature enough time to renew a resource. A forest that is cut down will grow back over the years, if the land is left undisturbed. If we continue to cut every new shoot that comes up or use the land for other purposes, the forest cannot grow again. Again, if we use the water in a well carefully, it will replenish itself every year. If, however, we draw water faster than the rate of replenishment, the well will go dry.

What about the sun and wind, which provide us with energy? These belong to a special case of renewable source—they are inexhaustible natural resources. They do not need replenishment.

A non-renewable natural resource is available as a finite amount on earth and does not replenish itself over human timescale. Petroleum, coal, and minerals are examples. They were formed over millions or billions of years, but we have been depleting them rapidly over the last two centuries or so. As a result, we will exhaust such resources at some time or other. If we use them carefully, however, they would be available to us for a long time to come.

Why is Water a Unique Resource?

Water is a prerequisite for the existence of life. Human beings, animals, and plants cannot survive without water and the human body itself is mostly water. We can go without food for even 30 days or more, but we cannot go without water even for a few days. When the water content in the body drops just by 1%, there is thirst. If it drops by 10%, there is a danger of death.

> **Key Idea** There is plenty of water on earth, but still millions face water scarcity.

Water is the most critical limiting factor for many aspects of life such as economic growth, environmental stability, biodiversity conservation, food security, and health care. In most cases of water use, there is no other substitute. In the case of energy, one source can often replace another, but water, as a resource, is mostly irreplaceable.

The good news about water is that we can reuse it many times. It may change its form, but we can always get it back. In fact, the molecules in the water we use now have been around for millions of years. The earth holds the same quantity of water as it did when it was formed.

The paradox of the water situation is that there is scarcity amidst plenty. As we shall see later, in this world there is a lot of water and yet there are millions of people facing acute water scarcity.

How Much Water do We Need?

We need water for personal use, agriculture, and industries. At home, water is necessary for drinking, cooking food, washing, cleaning, toilet use, and gardening (Box 5.1).

BOX 5.1 ENVIROFACT: *Urban Domestic Water Needs*

In India, the urban water supply systems are designed for a consumption of 135 litres per day per person (See the following table).

Use	Litres/day/person
Drinking	3
Cooking	4
Bathing	20
Flushing toilet	40
Washing clothes	25
Washing utensils	20
Gardening	23
Total	**135**

Many urban residents consume much more than this norm. Note how much water the flush toilet consumes! People in our villages manage with much less water.

In agriculture, we need water for growing food items such as rice, wheat, vegetables, fruits, coffee, tea, and sugarcane. Non-food items like cotton also use water. Factories, thermal and nuclear power plants, etc. require large amounts of water. Industries use water for cleaning, as a coolant, and as part of the manufacturing process.

Nature and the rest of the earth need water too! We often forget that animals need water to drink and to clean themselves. A cow, for example, must drink four litres of water to produce one litre of milk. Natural systems like wetlands, lakes, and deltas also need water.

The absolute minimum water requirement for domestic use is 50 litres per person per day, though 100–200 litres is often recommended. Adding the needs of agriculture, industry, and energy sectors, the recommended minimum annual per capita requirement is about 1,700 cu. m.

In addition to using water directly, we also consume water indirectly (Box 5.2).

BOX 5.2 CONCEPT: *Virtual Water and Water Footprint*

In addition to the direct use of water for our needs, there is also an indirect use of water in making many items that we eat, drink, or use. Every agricultural and industrial process uses up lots of water for producing items. This 'virtual' water is often hidden from us.

'Water Footprint' is an indicator that measures both direct and virtual water use of a consumer or producer. The concept is similar to that of Ecological Footprint (Chapter 1). The Water Footprint of a product is the volume of fresh water used up to produce the item, taking into account the volumes of water consumed and polluted in the different steps of the supply chain (See the following table).

Item and quantity	Water Footprint (litres)
Bottled water (1 litre)	3–6
Paper (1 A4 sheet)	10
Potato (100 g)	25
Cup of coffee (125 ml)	140
Milk (1 litre)	1000
Cane sugar (1 kg)	1800
Rice (1 kg)	2500
Beer (1 litre)	3000
Cotton T-shirt (500 g)	4100
Pair of shoes (bovine leather)	8000
Beef (1 kg)	16,000

The Water Footprint of an individual, community, or business is defined as the total volume of fresh water that is used to produce all the goods and services consumed by the individual or community or produced by the business.

The Water Footprint of a country = (Yearly amount of domestic water used to produce all goods and services consumed within the country) + (Yearly amount of virtual water in the goods and services imported into the country) – (Yearly amount of virtual water in the goods and services exported from the country). We get the per capita Water Footprint by dividing the total amount by the population (See the following table).

Country	Water Footprint cu. m per capita per year
US	2840
Germany	1430
Thailand	1410
Pakistan	1330
India	1090
China	1070
Global average	**1385**

China, India, and the US have the largest water footprints within their territories and together they account for 38% of the world's total water footprint.

How is the Available Water Used in the World?

Human beings use about 54% of all accessible freshwater supplies in the world. By 2025, this share will increase to 70%. This will have serious implications for all other forms of life, including plants. Table 5.1 shows the current pattern of water use in the world by humankind.

Key Idea Since the total water available is finite, greater consumption by one sector can only result in less supply for other sectors.

It is significant that domestic consumption accounts for only 8% and yet there is worldwide scarcity of drinking water. Agriculture continues to consume a major portion of the available fresh water. However, there is a clear difference in the water use between the developing countries and the industrialized countries. While agriculture takes the bulk of the supply in the former, industry consumes more than agriculture in the latter. This shows that there will be a severe problem in the developing countries once they industrialize to the level of the rich countries.

Now that we know how much water we need and how we use what we have, let us find out how much water there is in the world.

TABLE 5.1 Pattern of Water Use (Percentage of total water consumed by sector)

Sector	Global use %	% use in industrialized countries	% use in developing countries	% use in India
Agriculture	70	30	82	80
Industry	22	59	10	15
Domestic	8	11	8	5

How Much Water is There in This World?

We know that 97% of the world's water is in the ocean, too salty to drink. Of the remaining 3%, two-thirds are locked up in relatively inaccessible icecaps and glaciers. That leaves a mere 1% or 14 million cu. km. Again, half of this amount is ground water and most of it lies too far underground.

How do we get fresh water every year?

A key element of the water cycle (Chapter 2) helps us get a regular supply of fresh water. Annually, about 430,000 cu. km of water evaporates from ocean and only about 390,000 cu. km falls back over the ocean as precipitation. The remaining 40,000 cu. km moves from the ocean and falls on land as rain and snow. The first advantage is that we get this supply every year. Second, as the water evaporates from the ocean and falls on land, it loses its salt content and thus becomes potable.

Is the annual supply of fresh water enough for our needs?

There is indeed an annual fresh supply of 40,000 cu. km and this amounts to about 5,000 cu. m per person per year (for the current population of 8 billion). This appears to be plentiful, since the minimum annual needs of a person is only about 1,700 cu. m. By this token, we should be comfortable with regard to the water situation. Yet, there is worldwide water scarcity.

Key Idea The global water cycle provides us with fresh water every year.

The UN publishes every year World Water Development Report (WWDR) covering water and sanitation. WWDR 2023 paints a grim picture of the water situation (Box 5.3).

BOX 5.3 STATE OF THE PLANET: ***World Water Development Report 2023***

The main conclusions of WWDR 2023 were:

The world's water: demand, availability and quality

- Water use has been increasing globally by roughly 1% per year over the last 40 years and is expected to grow at a similar rate through to 2050, driven by a combination of population growth, socio-economic development and changing consumption patterns. The bulk of this increase is concentrated in middle- and lower-income countries, particularly in emerging economies.
- Water scarcity is becoming endemic as a result of the local impact of physical water stress, coupled with the acceleration and spreading of freshwater pollution.
- As a result of climate change, seasonal water scarcity will increase in regions where it is currently abundant – such as Central Africa, East Asia and parts of South America – and worsen in regions where water is already in short supply – such as the Middle East and the Sahel in Africa.
- On average, 10% of the global population lives in countries with high or critical water stress.
- Low-, middle- and high-income countries all show signs of risks related to water quality. Poor ambient water quality in low-income countries is often related to low levels of wastewater treatment, whereas in higher-income countries runoff from agriculture is a more serious problem.

Progress towards Sustainable Development Goal 6 Targets

- Half-way through the 2030 Agenda timeline, progress towards SDG 6 targets is only significantly reported for drinking water and sanitation, with some preliminary and rough indications of progress for water stress, water use efficiency, transboundary cooperation and Integrated Water Resources Management (IWRM), leaving 5 of the 11 target indicators without quantified information on progress.
- At current rates, progress towards all the targets of SDG 6 is off-track and in some areas the rate of implementation needs to quadruple, or more.
- According to the latest figures from 2020, 26% of the world's population (2 billion people) did not have access to safely managed drinking water services (SDG Target 6.1), and an estimated 46% (3.6 billion) lacked access to safely managed sanitation (SDG Target 6.2).

- Approximately 60% of the world's reported water bodies were categorized as having 'good' ambient water quality (SDG Target 6.3). However, the poorest 20 countries are grossly underrepresented in this global estimate.
- Globally, water use efficiency (SDG Target 6.4) rose by 9% from 2015 to 2018 (from 17.3 to 18.9 US$/m^3). Progress has been greatest in the industrial sector (15% increase), followed by the water supply and sanitation services and agricultural sectors (8% increase).
- While most countries have reported some progress, the global rate of progress on IWRM implementation (Target 6.5) needs to double to approach the target.
- The data required to track changes in the extent of water-related ecosystems over time (Target 6.6) are not yet refined enough to reveal discrete trends in recent years. However, available data show an 80% loss in the extent of natural wetland area since the pre-industrial era (1700).

How do We Measure Water Scarcity?

If a country has about 1,700 cu. m per person per year, it will experience only occasional or local water problems. If the availability falls below this threshold value, the country will begin to experience periodic or regular *water stress*. At the next stage, when the figure falls below 1,000 cu. m, the country will suffer from chronic *water scarcity*. Lack of water will then begin to adversely affect human health and well-being as well as economic development. If the annual per capita supply falls below 500 cu. m, the country will reach the stage of *absolute scarcity*.

Water scarcity already affects every continent. Around 1.2 billion people, or almost one-fifth of the world's population, live in areas of water scarcity, and 500 million people more are approaching this situation. Another 1.6 billion people, or almost one quarter of the world's population, face economic water shortage (where they lack the necessary infrastructure to take water from rivers and aquifers). By 2025, 1.8 billion people will be living in countries or regions with absolute water scarcity, and two-thirds of the world population could live under water stress.

Why is Water Becoming Scarce?

Even as the demand for water is soaring, the availability of fresh water is going down. The main reasons behind the increasing water scarcity are:

Increasing demand

Population growth, increasing irrigation needs (due to methods like the Green Revolution), rapid urbanization, industrialization, and increases in production and consumption are pushing up the demand for fresh water to unprecedented levels. Some examples are:

- Global water demand for manufacturing is predicted to increase by 400% from 2000 to 2050, which is much larger than any other sector. Most of this increase will be in emerging economies and developing countries.
- Freshwater withdrawals for energy production account for 15% of the world's total and are expected to increase by 20% through 2035.
- In general, city dwellers consume more water than rural citizens do. Many large cities of the world are already going farther or digging deeper to access water. By 2050, 66% of the world's population is projected to be urban and their water needs will be extremely high.

Overexploitation of ground water and surface water

- Ground water provides drinking water to at least 50% of the global population and accounts for 43% of all of the water used for irrigation. Worldwide, 2.5 billion people depend solely on groundwater resources to satisfy their basic daily water needs.

- An estimated 20% of the world's aquifers is being overexploited, leading to serious consequences such as land subsidence and saltwater intrusion.
- Water tables are falling rapidly, notably in India, China, and US (which together produce half the world's food).
- The agricultural sector accounts for roughly 70% of all freshwater withdrawals globally, and more than 90% in most of the world's least-developed countries. Current growth rates of agricultural demands on the world's freshwater resources are unsustainable.
- Inefficient use of water for crop production is depleting aquifers and reducing river flows. The major rivers of the world are drained dry before they reach the sea. The Yellow River in China, the Ganga in India, the Amu Darya in Central Asia, the Nile in Egypt, and the Colorado in US are examples.

Pollution of water sources

- The rapidly increasing pollution of rivers, lakes, as well as the ground water is reducing the usable supply. Pollution has made many water sources unfit for use. Incredibly small amounts of substances like oil can pollute huge amounts of water.
- Eutrophication of surface water and coastal zones is expected to increase almost everywhere. Globally, the number of lakes with harmful algal blooms will increase by at least 20% until 2050.

What Else are the Issues with Water Availability?

Distribution of the available water is also uneven over space and time. Some areas of the world get too much water while other places get too little. The transport of water over long distances is impractical.

Further, in some regions rainfall occurs over a short period in the year leading to floods in monsoon and drought in summer. The runoff, aided by deforestation, reaches the ocean quickly before it can be used. Much of the rain also falls in remote places that are inaccessible. Some of the rain is also needed to maintain special ecosystems like wetlands, lakes, and deltas. Climate change is now affecting rainfall patterns.

> **Key Idea** Even as the demand for water is rising sharply, the availability is going down.

In addition, there is a gross inequity in the allocation of water resources. In general, the richer groups corner more of the water supply. The urban areas again draw a great deal of water from the surrounding areas depriving the poorer rural people of their needs.

Why do Many Cities Face Severe Water Scarcity?

The megacities of the world, many of them in the poorer countries, need a lot of water and this water is often drawn from the neighbouring villages and far-off rivers and lakes. Even if a city gets good rain, the water is not retained in the area. Buildings, paving, and roads cover most of the land and the rain water does not percolate into the ground.

Megacities also pollute the water and release large amounts of waste water into the rivers and the ocean. Currently, less than 20% of urban waste water worldwide is treated. The increasing use of flush toilets also results in enormous wastage of potable water. Further, in many cities, more than half the available supply is lost through leaks and rotting pipelines.

Will There be Enough Water for Irrigation?

Today, irrigation takes away 70% of the usable water in the world. There was a five-fold increase in use of water for irrigation over the 20th century. The situation became worse since the adoption of the Green Revolution package. In many countries 50% or more of the food production comes from irrigated land. These include countries like India, China, Egypt, Indonesia, Israel, Japan, Korea, Pakistan, and Peru. By 2025, up to 4 billion people will live in countries that will lack water to produce their own food.

Even now, inefficient and outdated practices of irrigation continue, leading to wastage of water. Many fields are flooded and though some water gets to the root zone helping the growth of the plant, 50% is wasted as it percolates, evaporates, or runs off.

Most new land brought into agriculture uses ground water that is depleting fast. Meanwhile, available agricultural land is also lost due to salinization, reservoir siltation, shift of water use, etc. Salinization is often the result of raising water tables, which happens due to the flooding of the fields. As the water evaporates, it leaves behind salt on the topsoil. The siltation of reservoirs in big dams has often cut their lives to a mere 20 or 25 years. Cultivation is stopped in some places in favour of selling water to a nearby city. As a result of the loss of cropland, the total irrigated area may, in fact, be decreasing.

The farmers take 80% of the water and the fields are often over-irrigated. This is primarily because the farmers get free electricity and subsidized pumps and thus do not pay the real economic price of water.

The world over, there are second thoughts on the utility of large dams and canal systems due to spiralling costs, environmental concerns, and displacement of people. Protest movements in many places have stalled the construction of dams.

> **Key Idea** We cannot continue to meet the heavy and ever-increasing demand for irrigation water and this could affect our food security.

Globalization and industrialization increases demands for water from industry and urban areas in different parts of the world. The rapid increase in population also means that more water is needed for food and drinking purposes. All these facts seem to indicate that there is not much scope for increasing irrigation at the same rapid rate of the last century. It is also a sobering thought that all irrigation-based societies have failed in the past!

Why are There So Many Conflicts over Water?

Around the world, more than 200 water bodies are shared by two or more countries. Conflicts are brewing over the water available in many rivers and river basins.

Strife over water is erupting throughout the Middle East, from the watersheds of the Nile to the Tigris and Euphrates rivers. Likewise, there is a problem in the Ganga-Brahmaputra Basin, where Bangladesh, India, and Nepal dispute the use of water. India and Nepal want to exploit the basin's huge hydroelectric power-generating potential, whereas Bangladesh wants the water managed in such a way as to minimize flooding during monsoon months and water shortages during dry months.

Of equal concern are the water conflicts between states in India that share river basins, such as Karnataka and Tamil Nadu, which share the Cauvery river. Inequitable distribution and use of water resources, sometimes arising from development projects, leads to disputes.

The third category of conflicts is between industries and local communities on several issues—excessive water consumption by industry, resulting in reduced availability for irrigation; preferential treatment for industry in pricing; and pollution of ground water, rivers, and other local water bodies from the discharge of waste water.

Agitations and public interest litigation on water issues are increasing and more conflicts at all levels are expected in the future (Box 5.4).

BOX 5.4 INSPIRATION: *The Story of Plachimada—Who Owns the Water?*

If a soft drink industry owns a piece of land, can it exploit the ground water without any limit? This is the core issue in what has come to be known as the Plachimada case.

In January 2000, Hindustan Coca Cola Beverages began drawing ground water and producing cola in Plachimada, Kerala. The Panchayat received an annual income of about ₹600,000 in the deal. In addition, the plant provided employment for about 400 people.

By early 2002, the villagers started noticing changes in the water quality in the area. They felt that the plant was drawing too much water from the ground and this was affecting the harvest of rice and coconuts. In April 2002, the villagers started an agitation against the plant.

The panchayat cancelled the company's licence. The matter went to court, which ordered the plant not to draw water from the ground and to find alternate sources of water. The judge said that the company had no right to extract excessive natural wealth and the panchayat and the government were bound to prevent it. The ground water was a national resource, which belonged to the entire society and not to the company even though it owned the land.

On March 9, 2004, the company stopped operations. On January 15, 2005, which marked the 1000th day of protest, the activists declared that the company would not be allowed to resume operations at any cost.

In 2010, a government committee indicted the company for causing incalculable harm to the ecology and the people of Plachimada. The panel assessed the overall cost of the damage at ₹216 crores and recommended setting up of a tribunal with judicial powers to make Coca Cola pay individual claims. The bill passed by the state assembly to set up the tribunal has been stalled by the union government.

On November 4, 2022, the villagers of Plachimada wrote to the UN to remove Coca Cola as a sponsor of the COP27 climate talks. There was no response from the UN.

The Plachimada struggle is still going on and we do not know how the story will ultimately end. The case, however, has become the focal point for the debate on the people's right to water and a company's right to exploit the water under its land.

What is the State of the Global Bottled Water Industry?

In March 2023, the United Nations University released a report entitled "Global Bottled Water Industry: A Review of Impacts and Trends". The main conclusions were:

- Bottled water has developed into a major and essentially standalone economic sector in just around the past five decades. The global bottled water market is currently worth US$270 billion producing some 350 billion litres a year. This market is growing faster than any other food market, and is projected to reach and exceed US$500 billion by around 2025–2030.
- Bottled water sales and consumption are the highest in the Asia-Pacific region followed by North America and Europe.
- The largest market is the USA with total revenue of around US$64 billion, followed by China (almost US$45 billion) and Indonesia (US$22 billion). These three countries combined constitute almost half of the global bottled water market.
- In the Global North, bottled water is often perceived as a healthier and tastier product than tap water; it is, therefore, more a luxury good than a necessity since they have often reliable and good quality public drinking water supply. In the Global South, the bottled water market develops primarily due to the lack or absence of reliable public water supply along with increasing urbanization with associated limited infrastructure for water delivery.
- Marketing campaigns by the bottled water industry aim to promote the concept of bottled water "purity" and to discredit tap water for its poor quality. The perception that bottled water is safer than tap water needs to be challenged. Evidence clearly indicates that bottled water quality can be compromised either by the origin of water or by industrial processes that may potentially impact human health. There are hundreds of cases of inorganic, organic, and microbiological contamination of bottled water.
- Bottled water producers have, by and large, managed to avoid the kind of scrutiny imposed by government standards and regulations that public utilities must adhere to.
- Water withdrawals by the bottled water industry can lead or contribute to the depletion of groundwater resources in areas of water procurement for bottling

> **Key Idea** The global bottled water industry is worth US$270 billion and is growing rapidly. It depletes ground water and creates plastic waste. Many brands of bottled water have contaminants in them.

in many parts of the world. In certain cases, groundwater withdrawn for bottled water production may not even be replenishable.

- The world currently generates around 600 billion plastic bottles and containers, which converts to some 25 million tonnes of PET waste. Most of this waste is not recycled.
- Expansion of bottled water may adversely affect investments and the role of the state in long-term public water supply infrastructure development.
- Less than half of what the world pays for bottled water annually at present would pay to provide clean and long-term public water supply for hundreds of millions of people without it.

What is the Water Situation in India?

India and China are counted as water hotspots in the world primarily because of the large population that has to be provided with food and drinking water. Table 5.2 shows how the per capita availability has been going down in India.

In India, more than 60,000 villages exist without a single source of drinking water. Diarrhoea, brought on by contaminated water, claims the lives of 1 million children every year. In addition, 45 million people are affected annually by the poor quality of water.

Key Idea
Water conflicts are increasing at the local, national, and regional levels.

While increasing population is one cause of India's water crisis, the problem has been compounded by the steady deterioration, disuse, and disappearance of the traditional tanks and ponds. These water bodies were very effective in retaining the rain water and recharging the ground water. The local communities took care of these resources. Over the last 100 years or more, these tanks were neglected and many of them disappeared. Deforestation of the hills coupled with the absence of tanks has increased the runoff into the sea.

TABLE 5.2 Water availability in India

Year	Per capita availability (cu. m)
1951	5,000
2001	1,820
2011	1,545
2030	1,300 (estimate)

In recent years, the extraction of ground water using borewells operated by electric or diesel pumps has reached gigantic proportion. Free electricity and the Green Revolution package have sharply increased the water usage. One estimate is that the extraction is already twice the recharge rate. In many states, water tables have been dropping at alarming rates.

As India develops, industries need water more and more. The total available water is limited and hence any increase of supply to industries means taking water away from irrigation and domestic use.

What about urban water supply in India?

Our municipalities have to bring drinking water from outside the cities. For example, during summer, water for Chennai comes from many surrounding agricultural villages. The farmers find it more profitable to sell the water than cultivate the fields. Water for Chennai is also brought from the Krishna River, Mettur, and other faraway places. This clearly constitutes an unwelcome shift in water use that will ultimately threaten our food security.

Chennai, in fact, gets an average rainfall of 1290 mm per year, which is more than the national average. Yet, 90% of this rain is lost in runoff, evaporation, and flow into the sewage system.

Bengaluru gets its water from 90 km away and 500 m below its altitude. Apart from increasing the cost of supply of water, this practice also deprives the rural areas of much-needed water.

How much water do Indian industries consume?

We have no reliable figures on water consumption by the Indian industry, with the estimates ranging from 40 to 70 billion cu. m. We are sure, however, that the amount is increasing rapidly. It is estimated that the water demand of Indian industry will triple over the next 20 years.

In India, thermal power plants use about 87% of total industrial consumption of water. The efficiency of water use in the Indian industry is way behind international standards. Another important aspect of industrial use is the pollution of water bodies caused by wastewater discharge.

> **Key Idea** In India, the per capita availability of water is steadily going down, even as the needs of industry and agriculture are going up.

There is no incentive for Indian industry to reduce consumption, since it gets water at ridiculously low prices. In order to attract industrial units to an area, state governments often offer assured water supply at low rates. The pricing in most cases ignores the opportunity cost of water (that is, benefit from possible alternative use) as well as the damage caused by the pollution of supplies by the discharge of waste water.

In several parts of India, there are conflicts between industries and local communities over the use of water (Box 5.4).

What do the Optimists Say?

Even in this grim situation, there are optimists who believe in dramatic solutions that would solve the water problem once and for all. Such dreams include:

- Transport of water in huge bags by sea
- Towing of icebergs to needy places
- Discovery of new deep aquifers full of water
- Finding a new cheap energy source that will make desalination affordable
- Interlinking rivers (Box 5.5)

BOX 5.5 CONTROVERSY: *Interlinking Indian Rivers*

The idea of linking rivers has been around for a long time. However, in 2002, the Supreme Court of India, acting on a public interest petition, directed the government to interlink rivers within 10 years. In response, the government set up a task force to build national consensus, work out the detailed plans and complete the entire work by 2016.

Three major advantages were cited in favour of the scheme—droughts will never occur, there will be no more floods in rivers like the Ganga and the Brahmaputra, and an additional 30,000 MW of hydropower will be generated.

The budget for the project ranges from ₹5,600 to 10,000 billion. Even the lower estimate equals 25% of our GDP, 2.5 times our tax collection, and double our present foreign exchange reserves. Obviously, funds of this magnitude will have to be raised from international sources. Even if we succeed in raising the funds, the annual interest alone would amount to ₹200–300 billion. Water will have to be priced high to meet such a burden. Will the farmers and other users be ready to pay the charges?

It is doubtful if a political consensus can ever be achieved on the project. Would the states be willing to share freely all the river waters? Even the current interstate water problems have defied amicable solutions. It is not even clear that the rivers like the Ganga, the Brahmaputra, the Mahanadi, and the Godavari are water-surplus. The sources of such rivers are drying up and the rivers themselves are choked with silt.

The likely ecological consequences of building over 200 reservoirs and a network of crisscrossing canals cannot even be assessed now. Judging from the experience of Narmada Dam and other large projects, the consequences could be disastrous. Environmentalists and social activists fear large-scale submergence of habitats, forests, and fertile land, heavy destruction of wildlife habitats and biodiversity, displacement of large populations, and so on. In some places, enormous amounts of energy will have to be spent pumping water uphill.

In spite of the potential problems, the central government is moving ahead with the interlinking project. The Ken-Betwa link is the first major project (Box 5.6).

BOX 5.6 THE KEN-BETWA PROJECT

Launched in 2021, the Ken-Betwa River-Linking Project will transfer water from the Ken river to the Betwa river. Both the rivers are tributaries of river Yamuna, but Ken is supposed to have excess water, which would be fed to Betwa through dams, tunnels, canals, and barrages.

The Ken flows through Madhya Pradesh and Uttar Pradesh. The project is supposed to bring water to the drought-prone Bundelkhand region spread over both the states. The Union Jal Shakti Ministry claims that the project would provide annual irrigation of 10.62 lakh ha, supply drinking water to about 62 lakh people, generate 103 MW of hydropower, facilitate groundwater recharge, and reduce the occurrence of floods. The project cost estimate is ₹35,000 crore at 2017–18 prices, with the Centre contributing 90% of it. It will take eight years for completion.

The government appears to be ignoring the environmental and social costs of the project:

- 12,500 ha of land will be submerged by the project, of which more than 9000 ha are categorised as forest land.
- The submergence area will include an important section of the Panna Tiger Reserve. (This Reserve has been commended for the successful improvement of tiger and vulture populations.)
- 23 lakh trees with a girth of 20 cm or more will be cut down.
- Many wildlife species will be affected including tigers, endangered vultures, mahseer fish, and gharials in the Ken Gharial Sanctuary.
- Ten villages, including Daudhan, are expected to be submerged, displacing over 10,000 people.

The project must get clearance from the Central Empowered Committee of the Supreme Court, which had raised concerns about the project. Further, environmentalists and local groups also question the supposed benefits of the project:

- The claims of Ken having surplus water may be unrealistic as the river is not perennial. Sometimes it slows to a trickle.
- The Ken River flows 60-70 feet lower than the Betwa and at least 30% of the 103 MW power generated will be used for pumping the water up.

In spite of all such concerns, the union and state governments are going ahead with the project.

Is There a Way out of the Water Crisis?

Boxes 5.7 and 5.8 give a list of possible solutions to the water crisis in India and elsewhere.

BOX 5.7 WHAT WE CAN DO: *Some Solutions to the Water Crisis*

- Reduce demand
  - Educate people to use less water.
  - Install water-saving devices such as self-closing taps and dual-flush toilets.
  - Use decentralized wastewater-recycling systems in homes, apartment blocks, campuses, and industries, using natural methods like planted filters.
  - Adopt composting toilets to save water and also to minimize the sewage disposal problem. Adopt agriculture practices that require less water:
    - Replace water-hungry crops by those requiring less water
    - Promote crops that can tolerate salty water
    - Return to indigenous species that can withstand drought
    - Switch to organic and natural farming
    - Get more crop per drop—use drip irrigation, sprinkler method, etc.
  - Persuade people to change to a vegetarian diet that would require less water for production.
  - Reduce industrial consumption through recycling, reuse, and new water-efficient technologies.
- Catch the rain where it falls
  - Retain water on land as long as possible through check dams and contour bunds allowing it to percolate into the ground.
  - Implement rainwater harvesting in urban and rural areas (Box 5.8).
  - Restore traditional system of ponds and lakes.
- Adopt decentralized systems of water supply and sanitation
  - Plan many small local catchments in place of large ones.
  - Implement large number of small-scale schemes.
- Adopt fairer policies
  - Give control of water sources to the community.
  - Price water properly.
  - Remove inequities in access to water.

BOX 5.8 WHAT WE CAN DO: *Rainwater Harvesting*

There are two ways in which rain water can be harvested. One way is to slow down the flow of water on land through bunds and check dams. The longer the water remains on land, the more it percolates into the ground. In this way, it recharges the aquifers and wells. This method is best suited for rural areas.

The second way is to collect and store rain water. This is a very effective method for our cities. The rain water that falls on the roof can be collected, filtered, and stored. A surprisingly large amount of water can be collected in this way.

Suppose you live in Delhi. Your house has a terrace area of 100 sq m. How much of rain water can you collect in one year?

Average annual rainfall in Delhi = 910 mm
Amount of rain falling on

100 sq m area = Roof area × rainfall
= 100 sqm × 0.91m
= 91cu.m
= 91,000 litres

For a family of five, consuming 750 litres a day, this rain water will last for 120 days or one-third of the year!

Normally, rain water is good enough to drink. As a precaution, however, you could avoid using water from the first rain of the monsoon. Rainwater harvesting systems usually incorporate first rain separators. As long as the storage is completely closed, the water remains good for a long period.

Rooftop rain water can also be used to recharge ground water. We dig a few percolation pits around the house and fill it with gravel. Water from the roof is directly let into these pits. It percolates into the soil and recharges the ground water, if the soil is porous. After a while, the water levels in the area will go up and the wells will have enough water. Water from storm water drains can also be diverted into percolation pits.

Key Idea We can meet the water crisis only by reducing demand, harvesting rain water, implementing decentralized systems, and adopting fairer policies.

Ending on a Hopeful Note: Positive Stories

In recent times, a number of initiatives have been taken by individuals, communities, and NGOs to implement measures for water conservation and management (Box 5.9).

BOX 5.9 INSPIRATION: *Water Conservation in India*

In recent times, a number of initiatives have been taken by individuals, communities, NGOs, and even by government agencies to implement measures for water conservation and management. Some of the well-known cases are:

- Auroville: The spectacular efforts of this international community near Puducherry over the past 45 years in afforestation, water conservation, wastewater treatment, etc. are models to follow. Auroville also works with local communities and the government to rejuvenate the traditional ponds and get the control back to the people.
- Tarun Bharat Sangh, Alwar, Rajasthan: This NGO, founded by Rajendra Singh, built thousands of earthen check dams in villages with community participation. As a result, water tables rose, dead rivers came back to life, and farming improved. (Visit the ORC for this story.)
- Ralegaon Siddhi, Maharashtra: Through the efforts of Anna Hazare, the people have constructed sand percolation tanks and brought back the greenery.
- Gram Gaurav Pratishtan: In Maharashtra, the late Vilas Salunke introduced the idea of a Pani Panchayat for a fair sharing of water.
- Tamil Nadu: Rainwater harvesting was made compulsory in the state in 2003.

REVIEW: A SUMMARY OF THE KEY POINTS

- A renewable natural resource is one that nature replenishes again and again over time through its own processes.
- A non-renewable natural resource is available as a finite amount on earth and does not replenish itself over human timescale.
- Water is essential to life and is, in most cases, irreplaceable.
- The water cycle helps us get a regular annual supply of fresh water.
- There is only a finite amount of water in the world.
- The paradox of the water situation is that there is scarcity amidst plenty, primarily due to the impact of human activities.
- By the middle of the present century, most countries in the world (and cities in particular) will be facing water scarcity. India will face severe problems.
- Even places with heavy rainfall can experience water scarcity in other seasons, if water management is poor.
- The world's food security may be threatened due to shortage of irrigation water.
- The global bottled water industry is growing rapidly. It depletes ground water and creates plastic waste. Many brands of bottled water have contaminants in them.
- There could be future wars over water issues.
- There are effective ways of conserving and reusing water, which can be followed by anyone.
- There are many examples of successful water conservation efforts in India.
- The attempts to interlink Indian rivers will have financial, social, and ecological consequences.

EXERCISES

Objective-type questions

For each question below, choose the best answer out of the given choices:

1. What is the most important reason for water scarcity even in a high-rainfall place such as Cherrapunji?
   (a) Forests have been cut down.
   (b) Too much water is consumed.
   (c) Forests do not retain water.
   (d) There is no reservoir.
2. Why is water a unique resource?
   (a) There is a finite amount of water in the world.
   (b) Water is often polluted.
   (c) We cannot meet the demand.
   (d) Water has no substitute.
3. Which of the following statements is true with regard to water?
   (a) There is not enough water available per capita.
   (b) We cannot reuse water.
   (c) There is a lot of water and yet there is scarcity.
   (d) The total amount of water in the world is constantly decreasing in quantity.
4. Which of the following statements is true with regard to water use and sanitation in the world?
   (a) Human beings are using less water than before.
   (b) Water contamination is not the main cause of diseases.
   (c) 50% or more of the population lacks sanitation facilities.
   (d) People are never displaced due to water scarcity.
5. Which of the following items uses the maximum amount of water per kg during its production?
   (a) Rice
   (b) Beef
   (c) Potato
   (d) Sugar
6. Which of the following statements is true with regard to roof-top rainwater harvesting?
   (a) The water cannot be used at home.
   (b) The water is very expensive.
   (c) Large amounts of water can be collected even with small roof area.
   (d) Only the first rain must be collected.

7. Which of the following statements is **not** true with regard to rainwater harvesting?
   (a) With good rains, even small roofs can collect a lot of rain water.
   (b) Rain water can be harvested by building bunds and check dams.
   (c) Rooftop rain water can be used to recharge ground water.
   (d) Rooftop rain water is unfit for drinking.
8. Globally, which sector uses the maximum percentage of water?
   (a) Agriculture
   (b) Industry
   (c) Homes
   (d) Hotels
9. Which of the following statements is **not** true with regard to the water situation in India?
   (a) Thousands of villages have no source of drinking water.
   (b) Per capita availability of water is going down.
   (c) Millions of children die due to contaminated water.
   (d) Our cities have enough water supplies.
10. Which of the following is considered to be a non-renewable natural resource?
   (a) Petroleum that could replenish itself over millions of years.
   (b) Water that is replenished every year, thanks to the water cycle.
   (c) A mango tree, which gives fruits every year.
   (d) A forest that is cut down, but grows back in 20 years.

Short-answer questions

1. What is the natural process that provides us with fresh water every year? How does it work?
2. The annual per capita requirement of water is 1,700 cu. m, while the annual freshwater supply is at least three times more. Why then do we have water scarcity?
3. What are the levels of water availability that indicate water stress and water scarcity?
4. What are the special problems that big cities face on the water issue?
5. Describe the global pattern of water use across sectors. What are the main differences between the industrialized countries and the developing countries with regard to water use?
6. What is the implication of the statement 'Any increase of water supply to one user means taking it away from another user'?
7. What is the link between water scarcity and food security?
8. What are the main reasons for water scarcity in India?
9. How can we reduce the total demand for water?
10. What is the importance of rainwater harvesting?
11. What are the pros and cons of the plan to interlink Indian rivers?
12. Give two examples of successful Indian attempts in water conservation.
13. Distinguish between renewable and non-renewable natural resources.

Long-answer questions

1. What are the reasons for the worsening water situation in many countries? What is likely to happen in another 40 years or so?
2. What negative role do cities play in the water scene? How can this be corrected?
3. Why do conflicts occur over water?

Think critically: Deeper questions for reflection and discussion

1. There is very little control in India over the use of water by industry. Should the government impose stricter regulations on the use of water and the discharge of waste water? Should the government also ensure that the industry pays a fair price for the water? Will such control increase the costs for industry and push up the prices?
2. If more water is taken by industry, less water will be available for agriculture. If industry does not get enough water, economic growth will suffer; if agriculture is deprived of water, food security will be hit. What is the way out of this dilemma?
3. Should water be considered as a common resource or a private one? Do all citizens have a right to adequate access to water? Should water be privatized and fair prices charged for it?
4. Is it ethical to exploit the ground water on your land without any restriction? Remember that the ground water may have seeped in from the surrounding lands. A neighbour may take the trouble of recharging the ground water and the geology may be such that all that water collects under your land.

ENJOY AND EDUCATE YOURSELF

1. Watch the film *Paani* (2015), directed by Shekhar Kapur. Many years into the future, the earth's water supply has run out. The events and wars that follow are depicted in the film.
2. Watch the acclaimed Tamil feature film *Thanneer Thanneer (Water, Water)*, made by K. Balachandar in 1981. The film deals with water scarcity and political corruption.

ACCESS THE OUP ONLINE RESOURCE CENTRE FOR MORE

- Full text of the Plachimada Declaration adopted on January 23, 2004, at the World Water Conference held near Plachimada, attended by delegates from all over the world.
- The story of water conservation in Rajasthan by Rajendra Singh and Tarun Bharat Sangh.
- Additional text and other recommended references, websites, and films.

6 Forest Resources

The best time to plant a tree was twenty years ago.
The second best time is now.

Author unknown

MAIN QUESTIONS ADDRESSED

- What is the state of forest resources?
- What are the products and services we receive from forests?
- How are forests being destroyed and what are the attempts to conserve them?

KEYWORDS AND PHRASES

direct uses of forest, extractive reserve, joint forest management, non-direct uses of forest, old-growth forest, second-growth forest, social forestry, sustainable forest management

LEAD STORY

THE STORY OF THE ANDAMAN AND NICOBAR ISLANDS: LAST CHANCE OR LOST OPPORTUNITY?

It is a complex case involving a century of forest exploitation, the rights of indigenous people, inward migration, road development, and finally an intervention by the Supreme Court. Through it all, the plunder of the forests has continued unabated.

The Andaman and Nicobar Islands contain some of the finest tropical evergreen forests in the world. They are also rich in biodiversity with a variety of known and unknown species of flora and fauna.

The British established a forest department on the islands in 1883 and began the extraction of timber using convict labour. Even after Independence, however, logging has continued without a break. This has led to forest degradation. Further, the resulting soil erosion has resulted in heavy flow of sediments into the coastal waters that has smothered and killed a substantial amount of corals. Mangroves and corals have also been adversely affected by extraction. Species like the saltwater crocodile and the Andaman wild pig have become endangered.

Tribals requesting tourists: *"Please keep off this island. We have enough problems with development and the trunk road!"*

The indigenous communities have been seriously affected with their traditional occupations threatened and rights violated. Communities like the Great Andamanese, the Onge, the Jarawa, and the

Sentinelese have lived and flourished here for at least 20,000 years, but they could soon become extinct.

About 150 years ago, the population of the tribal communities was estimated to be at least 5000. Over the years, there has been a substantial government-supported migration of people from other parts of the country into the Islands. Today, in a total population of 380,000, the four indigenous communities put together account for a mere 550. The current total population, however, is much more than the size that the Islands can support. Already, there is a scarcity of drinking water.

A major factor affecting the forests and the communities is the 340-km-long Andaman Trunk Road (ATR). Originating in Port Blair in South Andaman, the ATR cuts across the islands to reach Diglipur in the north. In some places, it traverses through virgin tracts of forestland in the Jarawa Reserve. The ATR has increased the interaction between the Jarawas and the settlers as well as the tourists and eroded much of the natives' original way of life.

Responding to a public interest petition, the Supreme Court of India passed several orders in 2002: ban on the commercial exploitation of timber from the islands' forests, ban on the transport of timber to any other part of the country, removal of encroachments, restrictions on inward migration, phasing out of monoculture plantations, reducing of sand mining on the beach, and closure of the ATR in areas where it passes through the Jarawa Reserve.

One might think that it was a happy ending. The local administration, however, did not implement many of the orders. Several months after the passing of the court deadlines, they filed a petition asking for a review of the orders. Perhaps a great opportunity to implement a model conservation programme was lost.

Then came the tsunami of December 2004, which hit the Islands with devastating effect: over 3500 people dead or missing; nearly 8000 ha of fertile land rendered useless; nearly 1000 boats completely damaged; and more than 150,000 cattle lost. The tsunami also destroyed coral reefs, mangroves, and the coastal ecology. There have also been several earthquake warnings since then.

More than a decade after the Supreme Court judgement, the population influx continues, and the ATR still remains open for traffic. The ecology of the Islands and the fate of the tribes continue to be in the balance.

In 2021, the central government proposed large-scale projects in the islands to establish a port and trade zone ignoring tribal and ecological concerns.

CLIMATE CHANGE AND FORESTS

Forests both influence and are influenced by climate change. Deforestation releases carbon and contributes to climate change. On the other hand, climate change causes more forest fires and damages forests through extreme weather.

What does the case of Andaman and Nicobar islands tell us?

The case of Andaman and Nicobar Islands is typical of what is happening to the world's forests. Massive deforestation through the extraction of timber, opening up of forests through road-building, population pressures, problems of indigenous people, and similar issues plague forests everywhere.

What is the State of the World's Forests?

It is difficult to assess the extent of the world's forests. Data supplied by countries are often not reliable, though satellite imagery is being increasingly used to verify data from ground surveys. The definition of a forest also varies from one assessment to another.

The UN FAO regularly monitors the state of the world's forests and puts out two regular reports:

1. The Global Forest Resources Assessment (FRA): FAO produces this assessment every five years in an attempt to provide a consistent approach to describing the world's forests and how they are changing. The assessment is based on two primary sources of data:
   - Country Reports prepared by National Correspondents and
   - Remote sensing that is conducted by FAO together with national and regional partners.

   The 2020 FRA provides a picture of the current state of the world's forest resources and of the main changes that have occurred over the period 1990–2020.

2. The State of the World's Forests (SOFO): This report covers the status of forests, recent major policy and institutional developments, and key issues.

The key findings of 2020 FRA and 2022 SOFO are given in Boxes 6.1 and 6.2.

BOX 6.1 2020 UN FAO Global Forest Resources Assessment

Key Messages:

Forests cover nearly one-third of the land globally:

- This area is equivalent to 0.52 ha per person – although forests are not distributed equally among the world's peoples or geographically.

The world's forest area is decreasing, but the rate of loss has slowed:

- The rate of net forest loss decreased substantially over the period 1990–2020 due to a reduction in deforestation in some countries, plus increases in forest area in others through afforestation and the natural expansion of forests.
- Fires, insects, diseases, and severe weather events damage millions of ha of forests every year.

Area of planted forests is increasing:

- The area of naturally regenerating forests has decreased since 1990 (at a declining rate of loss), but the area of planted forests has been increasing.

More than 700 million ha of forest is in legally established protected areas:

- The area of forest in protected areas globally has increased by 191 million ha since 1990, but the rate of annual increase slowed in 2010–2020.
- More than 2 billion ha of forest has management plans.

Other points:

- The world's forests are mostly publicly owned, but the share of privately owned forests has increased since 1990.
- Total forest carbon stock is decreasing.
- About 30% of all forests is used primarily for production of wood and non-wood forest products.
- About 10% of the world's forests is allocated for biodiversity conservation.
- The area of forest designated primarily for soil and water protection is increasing.
- More than 180 million ha of forest is used mainly for social services such as recreation, tourism, education research and the conservation of cultural and spiritual sites and this area is increasing.

BOX 6.2 UN FAO 2022 State of the World's Forests (SOFO)

Key Messages:

- Trees, forests, and sustainable forestry can help the world recover from the COVID-19 pandemic and combat looming environmental crises such as climate change and biodiversity loss. But this requires societies to better recognize the considerable value of forests and their crucial roles in building inclusive, resilient, and sustainable economies.
- Three pathways involving forests and trees offer means by which societies, communities and individual landowners, users and managers can derive more tangible value from forests and trees while addressing environmental degradation, recovering from crises, preventing future pandemics, increasing resilience and transforming economies:
    1. *Halting deforestation and maintaining forests*
    2. *Restoring degraded lands and expanding agroforestry*
    3. *Sustainably using forests and building green value chains*
- The three pathways are mutually reinforcing. When synergies are maximized, the pathways can provide some of the highest returns in the form of climate and environmental benefits while also enhancing local sustainable development potential, adaptive capacity and resilience.
- Shifts in policies are needed to divert financial flows away from actions that harm forests and to incentivize investment in conservation, restoration and sustainable use. Finance for the three forest pathways needs to at least triple (to more than USD 200 billion per year for forest establishment and management alone) by 2030 to meet climate, biodiversity and land degradation neutrality targets.
- Smallholders, local communities and Indigenous Peoples own or manage nearly half – 4.35 billion ha – of the world's forest and farm landscapes and will be crucial for scaling up implementation of the pathways. According to one estimate, smallholders

on such lands generate a gross annual income of up to USD 1.29 trillion. More than 8.5 million producer organizations now exist to help local actors participate in and support a green recovery.

- Companies in forest-based value chains will be essential partners in the development of circular economies. Many are already expanding the range of forest products as substitutes for materials with higher greenhouse-gas emissions and increasing processing efficiency. Local forest growers and processors can obtain more benefit by strengthening links with buyers and developing capacity through producer organizations.
- Scaling up action on the three forest pathways carries risks, especially for smallholders, whose investments in them could fail in the absence of supportive policies and institutions. Risks associated with climate change, such as increased vulnerability to fire, pests and drought, also need to be managed.
- Starting points for moving swiftly along the pathways may include:
  1. Directing funding for recovery towards long-term policies aimed at creating sustainable and green jobs and further mobilizing private-sector investment;
  2. Empowering and incentivizing local actors, including women, youth and Indigenous Peoples, to take a leading role in the forest pathways;
  3. Engaging in awareness raising and policy dialogue on sustainable forest use as a means for simultaneously achieving economic and environmental goals; and maximizing synergies among the three forest pathways and between agricultural, forestry, environmental and other policies and minimizing trade-offs.

Key Idea The rate of deforestation in the world shows signs of decreasing, but is still alarmingly high.

What is the State of the Forests in India?

The Forest Survey of India (FSI) publishes every two years an assessment of India's forest cover. In January 2022, MoEFCC released the 'India State of Forest Report 2021'. The Report provides information on forest cover, tree cover, mangrove cover, growing stock, carbon stock in India's forests, forest fire monitoring, forest cover in tiger reserve areas, above ground estimates of biomass, and climate change hotspots in Indian forests.

Salient findings of the report

- The total forest and tree cover of the country is 80.9 million ha which is 24.62% of the geographical area of the country. As compared to the assessment of 2019, there is an increase of 2,261 sq km in the total forest and tree cover of the country. Out of this, the increase in the forest cover has been observed as 1,540 sq km and that in tree cover is 721 sq km.
- Increase in forest cover has been observed in open forest followed by very dense forest. Top three states showing increase in forest cover are Andhra Pradesh (647 sq km) followed by Telangana (632 sq km) and Odisha (537 sq km).
- Area-wise Madhya Pradesh has the largest forest cover in the country followed by Arunachal Pradesh, Chhattisgarh, Odisha, and Maharashtra. In terms of forest cover as percentage of total geographical area, the top five States are Mizoram (84.53%), Arunachal Pradesh (79.33%), Meghalaya (76.00%), Manipur (74.34%), and Nagaland (73.90%).
- 17 states/UT's have above 33% of the geographical area under forest cover. Out of these states and UT's, five states/UTs namely Lakshadweep, Mizoram, Andaman & Nicobar Islands, Arunachal Pradesh, and Meghalaya have more than 75% forest cover while 12 states/UTs namely Manipur, Nagaland, Tripura, Goa, Kerala, Sikkim, Uttarakhand, Chhattisgarh, Dadra & Nagar Haveli and Daman & Diu, Assam, Odisha, have forest cover between 33% to 75%.
- Total mangrove cover in the country is 4,992 sq km. An increase of 17 sq km in mangrove cover has been observed as compared to the previous assessment of 2019. Top three states showing mangrove cover increase are Odisha (8 sq km) followed by Maharashtra (4 sq km) and Karnataka (3 sq km).

- Total carbon stock in country's forest is estimated to be 7,204 million tonnes and there an increase of 79.4 million tonnes in the carbon stock of country as compared to the last assessment of 2019. The annual increase in the carbon stock is 39.7 million tonnes.

Environmentalists and voluntary organizations have been witnesses to unending deforestation in many parts of the country. They question the figures given in the official reports.

What are the Important Types of Forests in India?

About 80% of India's forests is spread over four types. Table 6.1 gives the distribution and the locations.

TABLE 6.1 Distribution of Indian Forests by Type

Key Idea
According to the Forest Survey of India, our forest and tree cover is 24.6% of the land area. However, environmental groups do not fully accept this claim.

Type	Percentage	Locations
Tropical moist deciduous	37	Andamans, Uttar Pradesh, Madhya Pradesh, Gujarat, Maharashtra, Karnataka, Kerala
Tropical dry deciduous	28	North-south strip from Himalayas to Kanyakumari
Tropical dry evergreen	8	Western Ghats, Assam, Andamans
Subtropical pine	7	Himalayas
Others	20	
	100	

How are Forests Classified from the Point of View of Exploitation as a Resource?

There are mainly three categories of forests: old-growth, second-growth, and plantations. Old-growth or frontier forests are uncut forests that have not been seriously disturbed by human activities or natural disasters for several hundred years or more.

Second-growth forests result from ecological succession (Chapter 2) that takes place when forests are cleared (by human activities or due to natural disasters) and then left undisturbed for long periods of time.

Plantations are managed forests of commercially valuable trees. They are created mostly by clearing old-growth or second-growth forests. Plantations promote monoculture, concentrating on one or a few species. Being less diverse than natural forests, they are more prone to diseases and other disturbances.

There is now an increasing reliance on plantations as the source of industrial wood. This is a new development and half of all the plantations of the world are less than 15 years old. More than 60% of plantations are in Asia, many owned by foreign companies.

What are the Kinds of Economic Benefits We Receive from Forests?

We can divide the economic benefits from forests into several categories:

Use values:

- Direct use values include economic benefits obtained from direct use of the forest and they can be extractive or non-extractive.
  - Extractive direct uses include timber, fuelwood, edible plants, game (animals hunted for food or sport), and medicinal plants.
  - Non-extractive direct uses include recreation and tourism.
- Indirect use values refer to environmental services provided by forests that are of indirect value, such as carbon absorption, the provision of habitat to protect biodiversity or various ecosystem protection services such as the ability to reduce soil erosion, and the siltation of rivers.

- Option value refers to the value people may place on maintaining the option to enjoy the direct or indirect use values at some time in the future, including preservation of a natural gene bank.

Key Idea Forests provide us with many economic benefits, which can be classified into use values and non-use values.

Non-use values:

- Bequest value refers to the desire to leave natural capital to future generations.
- Existence value refers to the benefit obtained simply from knowing that certain wilderness areas, or species, are being conserved. For example, many people will never have the opportunity to see the Amazon rainforest, yet are willing to pay for its preservation.

What are the Actual Products and Services Provided by Forests?

Forests provide us with material goods, ecosystem services, and other benefits:

Industrial wood and fuelwood

According to FRA 2010, reported wood removals amounted to 3.4 billion cu. m annually in the period 2003–2007. Considering that informally and illegally removed wood, especially fuelwood, is not usually recorded, the actual amount of wood removals is undoubtedly higher. Half of the wood removed is fuelwood, mostly produced and consumed in the developing countries. The remaining half is industrial wood, 80% of which comes from the industrialized countries.

Non-wood products

In many of the poorer countries, especially in Asia, non-wood forest products (NWFP) such as food, fibre, honey, and medicinal plants form an important source of income and a critical component of food security and well-being. Some forests are also sources of minerals.

Ecosystem services

Forests provide a range of ecological services like soil generation, soil and water conservation, purification of air and water, nutrient recycling, maintenance of biodiversity, providing habitat for animals, mitigation of climate change, and absorption of carbon. Forests contain about half of the world's biodiversity. Natural forests have the highest species diversity and endemism among all ecosystems.

Key Idea Forests provide a range of invaluable products and ecosystem services.

Other contributions

Forests provide employment and income, recreation, education, scientific study, protection of natural and cultural heritage, aesthetic pleasure, and spiritual solace.

What is the Impact of Human Activities and Natural Forces on the Forests of the World?

The major effects of human activities on forest ecosystems are the following:

- The clearing and burning of the forests for agriculture, cattle rearing, and lumber result in loss of biodiversity, extinction of species, soil erosion resulting in the loss of vital topsoil, and disturbance of the carbon cycle leading to global warming.
- The clear cutting and conversion of forest land on hilly areas for agriculture, plantations, and housing leads to landslides and floods that affect people in the forests and on the plains. It also increases siltation of rivers.

- Many forests have been affected by acid deposition originating from industries.
- The harvesting of old growth forests destroys crucial habitat for endangered species.
- Pesticide spraying to control insects in forest plantations leads to poisoning all the way up the food chain and unintended loss of predatory hawks, owls, and eagles; this could, in turn, lead to the increase of the pest population.
- Dams built in forest areas for hydropower and water drown huge areas, destroying species and depriving people of their lands; they could also induce earth tremors.
- In wilderness areas like the Arctic, oil exploration and military activities disrupt the ecosystem, contaminate areas, and lead to the decline of species.

Key Idea Human activities have had a very adverse impact on forests.

How Much of the Wood Goes into Making Paper?

Paper is the world's fastest growing use of wood. Worldwide, 40% of the wood is used for making paper and this figure is expected to reach 60% by 2050. The US alone accounts for 30% of the world's paper use, consuming 1 billion trees a year and releasing 100 million tonnes of toxins every year during processing.

India has about 600 paper mills with an annual capacity of 8.5 million tonnes. Of the raw material they use, 39% comes from wood and bamboo, 31% from agricultural residues, and 30% from waste paper. Even though waste paper is abundant in India, the industry imports annually about 1.2 tonnes of it costing US$ 116 million.

Reforestation has not kept pace with the world demand for paper. The amount of paper recycled has also been too small to make any difference. Some countries like the Netherlands and Germany recover over 70% of waste paper. India has a recovery rate of just 18%, mainly because we have a poor collection and segregation system.

In What Other Ways are Forests being Destroyed?

Commercial logging methods directly and indirectly lead to deforestation. In many places, for obtaining one cubic metre of logs, two cubic metres of standing trees are destroyed. New extractive technologies can cut trees very quickly. When some species are selected for logging, non-target species are also damaged.

Logging companies create infrastructure, especially roads, in forests to make their tasks easier. However, roads provide easier access to interior parts and encourage the entry of invasive species, hunters, poachers, tourists, plant collectors, and people in general. This, in turn, leads to further exploitation of the resources.

Another area of concern is the depletion of forest-based wildlife due to the commercial harvesting and trade of bushmeat. This practice of killing wild animals for meat is prevalent in Africa, where many primates and antelopes are threatened.

The construction of dams in forests invariably causes enormous damage. Dam reservoirs inundate and destroy forests and their biodiversity.

What is the Impact of Deforestation?

Deforestation exposes soils and shade species to wind, sunlight, evaporation, and erosion. Soil fertility goes down due to the rapid leaching of essential mineral nutrients. Topsoil is eroded and this accelerates siltation in dams, rivers, and the coastal zone. The increased sedimentation harms downstream fisheries.

When the forest disappears, there is no regulation of the flow into rivers. As a result, floods and droughts alternate in the affected areas.

Deforestation, degradation, and fragmentation of forests affect many species and lead to the extinction of some. In particular, migratory birds and butterflies suffer due to the loss of their habitat.

Studies have shown that about 97% of the water absorbed from the soil by the roots evaporates and falls back on land as precipitation. When a large forest is cut down, the regional rainfall pattern may be affected.

> **Key Idea**
> Deforestation has a series of adverse effects on the planet and the people.

Deforestation also leads to global warming by releasing carbon stored in the trees. If the trees burn, the carbon is released immediately. If the trees are cut and removed, half the carbon remains in the form of branches, twigs, etc. When they decompose, the carbon is slowly released.

Clearing of forests affects the local communities, who lose their sources of food, fuel, construction materials, medicines, and areas for livestock grazing. What is more, they lose their culture and way of living.

What is the Role of Forest Fires?

Wildfires, usually started by lightning, have an ecological role. The combustion frees the minerals locked up in the dry organic matter. The mineral-rich ashes are necessary for the growth of plants. The vegetation usually flourishes after a fire.

Fires remove plant cover and expose the soil, which stimulates the germination of certain types of seeds. They also help control pathogens and harmful insects. Occasional fires burn away some of the dry organic matter and prevent more destructive fires from occurring later on. For all these reasons, prevention of fires is not necessarily good for a forest.

Intentional or accidental human-induced fires do cause damage. Such fires have become a major problem in large forests, especially in countries like Canada and the US. In a number of developing countries, fires continue to be used for land-clearing with adverse consequences.

What is the Relationship between Forests and Climate Change?

Forests play a major role in climate change:

- Forests hold more than 50% of the carbon that is stored in terrestrial vegetation and soil organic matter. Hence, deforestation contributes significantly to net emissions of carbon dioxide into the atmosphere.
- Forests react sensitively to a changing climate. If the predicted global warming occurs, the impact on forests is likely to be regionally varied, dramatic, and long-lasting. Even now, we can see how any extreme weather has great impact on forests. For example, the 1999 storms in Europe caused heavy damage to forests and also to trees outside forest areas.
- Climate change also causes more forest fires than usual. In many countries, there was an increase in wildfires during the 1990s compared to the previous decades, possibly due to climate change.
- When managed sustainably, forests produce fuelwood as a benign alternative to fossil fuels.
- Forests have the potential to absorb about one-tenth of global carbon emissions projected for the first half of this century into their biomass, soils, and products and store them—in principle in perpetuity.

What are the Global Initiatives in Forest Conservation?

Sustainable forest management was first discussed at the international level at the Earth Summit in 1992. There were major differences between the industrialized countries and the developing countries, and the Summit could only come up with a set of non-binding principles.

The International Tropical Timber Organization (ITTO) was set up in 1983 under the UN Commission for Trade and Development (UNCTAD). ITTO brings together the producer and consumer countries and is a major platform for issues concerning sustainable forest management. In 1985, FAO, UNDP, World Bank, and World Resources Institute came up with the Tropical Forestry Action Plan, later revamped and renamed as the National Forest Action Programme.

The Convention to Combat Desertification (Chapter 7) and the Convention on Biological Diversity (Chapter 10) are two of the international agreements that have a bearing on forests.

Declaring forests as protected areas or as biosphere reserves is a measure adopted by most countries. This is also supported by initiatives like the UNESCO Man and the Biosphere Programme. The protected area approach will be discussed in Chapter 10 under biodiversity conservation.

The UN Forum on Forests (UNFF), created in October 2000, is a permanent high-level intergovernmental body with universal membership. In 2007, the UN General Assembly adopted the Non-Legally Binding Instrument on All Types of Forests negotiated by the UNFF earlier that year. The purpose of this instrument is to:

- strengthen political commitment and action at all levels to implement effectively sustainable management of all types of forests and to achieve the shared global objectives on forests
- enhance the contribution of forests to the achievement of the internationally agreed development goals, including the Millennium Development Goals, in particular with respect to poverty eradication and environmental sustainability
- provide a framework for national action and international cooperation.

What is Sustainable Forest Management?

The UN FAO defines sustainable forest management (SFM) as the stewardship and use of forests and forest lands in a way, and at a rate, that maintains their biodiversity, productivity, regeneration capacity, vitality, and their potential to fulfil, now and in the future, relevant ecological, economic, and social functions, at local, national, and global levels, and that does not cause damage to other ecosystems.

In simpler terms, SFM seeks to achieve a balance between society's increasing demands for forest products and benefits, and the preservation of forest health and diversity. This balance is critical to the survival of forests, and to the prosperity of forest-dependent communities.

SFM is the use of the world's forests in such a way that that they continue to provide resources now without depriving future generations of their needs. One of the principles of SFM is to involve the local communities fully in forest management. Implementing this principle is, however, difficult since forest departments are usually very reluctant to lose their control over forest resources.

There has been mixed progress toward SFM. While many trends remained alarming, there were also many positive developments over the last 20 years. However, all regions and sub-regions displayed a mixture of positive and negative trends, which made it difficult to say anything definite about the level of progress towards SFM.

A Report from UN FAO noted the following:

> **Key Idea** Many steps have been taken for forest conservation at national and international levels with mixed results.

- Significant progress has been made in further developing an enabling framework for SFM.
- A large number of forest policies and laws have been created or updated.
- National forest programmes now cover close to 75% of the world's forests.
- An estimated 52% of the total forest area had been designated as permanent forest estate or its equivalent.

Certification of timber as coming from sustainable forests is another approach to SFM (Box 6.3).

BOX 6.3 SOLUTION: *Forest Certification*

How can we halt deforestation and save the remaining forests? One way is to act as a responsible consumer and buy wood only from companies that follow sustainable practices. How do we locate such companies? Forest certification is meant to help us.

Certification is a voluntary market-based approach that enables us to identify forest products backed by high environmental standards. It focuses on the quality of forest management rather than on that of forest products.

The two main certification bodies are:

- Forest Stewardship Council (FSC): Producers have to meet certain principles and standards for good forest stewardship. They can then use the FSC trade- mark for product labelling. By 2022, FSC had certified as well as managed more than 195 million ha globally. Certification is based on sustainability of timber resources, socio-economic benefits provided to local people, and forest ecosystem health including preservation of wildlife habitat and water-shed stability.
- Programme for the Endorsement of Forest Certification (PEFC): This international NGO promotes SFM through independent third-party certification. PEFC is an umbrella organization. It works by endorsing national forest certification systems developed through multi-stakeholder processes and tailored to local priorities and conditions. It seeks to ensure that timber and non-timber forest products are produced with respect for the highest ecological, social, and ethical standards. Thanks to its eco-label customers and consumers are able to identify products from sustainably managed forests. With 48 endorsed national certification systems and more than 280 million ha of certified forests, PEFC claims to be the world's largest forest certification system.

Certification is also possible through the Pan-European Forest Council (PEFC), Canadian Standards Association (CSA), Sustainable Forest Initiative (SFI), ISO 14001 Standards, etc. Most of the certified area is found in Europe, Canada, and the US. India has also begun the process.

There is a growing demand for certified wood. Environment-conscious consumers have welcomed certification, though some producers consider it a restrictive practice.

How can Local Communities be Involved in Forest Conservation?

Many local communities have lived in or near forests and used them in a sustainable manner. In the twentieth century, however, there were two developments in this regard. Due to increase in population and poverty, new groups migrated into the forest areas and began overexploiting the resources. When governments began protecting forests and declaring them as protected areas, they viewed the local people as enemies of the forests and tried to prevent them even from entering the area. The result was an increase in illegal use of the resources and conflicts.

It is now increasingly being realized that local people should be seen as partners in conservation. Most programmes now involve the local communities in planning, decision- making, and implementation. In return for controlled access to the forests, the locals can provide labour and help in conservation. They can become excellent guides in ecotourism.

What are extractive reserves?

Extractive reserves are protected forests, in which local communities are allowed to harvest products like fruits, nuts, rubber, oil, fibres, and medicines in ways that do not harm the forest. The objective is to improve the lives of the people, while conserving the biodiversity.

The approach believes that the local people would have a greater stake in conservation if they get the benefits they were earlier enjoying. It recognizes the fact that, in many instances, we have to use land and forest in order to preserve them.

How are Communities Involved in Forest Conservation in India?

In India and some other countries, communities living in or near the forests are being involved in conservation through *joint forest management* and *social forestry*.

What is joint forest management?

During the 1980s, the Government of India came to recognize the important role of local communities in forest conservation. They introduced the concept of joint forest management (JFM) for working closely with the local user communities in the protection and management of forest resources.

In JFM, the local communities are involved in the planning of the conservation programme. They are allowed controlled access to the forest areas and permitted to harvest the resources in a sustainable manner. In return, they become the guardians of the forest.

What is social forestry?

Social forestry refers to the planting of trees, often with the involvement of local communities, in unused and fallow land, degraded government forest areas, in and around agricultural fields, along railway lines, roadsides, river and canal banks, in village common land, government wasteland, and panchayat land.

The term 'social forestry' was first used in India in 1976 and the idea has been adopted in many Asian countries. A major controversy has been the planting of eucalyptus trees under social forestry. Eucalyptus was chosen for the majority of social forestry projects because it survives on difficult sites and outperforms indigenous species in growth, producing wood very rapidly. However, it has some adverse ecological impacts on soil nutrients, water hydrology, biodiversity, and wildlife.

> **Key Idea**
> The importance of involving local communities in forest management is now well-recognized.

Apart from JFM and social forestry, the traditional sacred groves of India have played an important role in community participation and conservation of biodiversity (See Chapter 16, Box 16.3).

How can Wood be Used More Efficiently?

Currently, enormous quantities of wood are wasted, primarily in countries like the US in many ways: inefficient use as construction material, excessive packaging, excessive junk mail, inadequate paper recycling, not reusing wooden shipping containers, etc. There is great scope to reduce such wastage.

Tree-free paper can be made from natural fibres and agricultural residues from wheat, rice, and sugarcane. China plans to make 60% of its paper from tree-free pulp. A number of publishers in the world now use paper from forest-friendly sources.

What should We Do to Save the World's Forests?

The summary recommendations of the World Commission on Forests and Sustainable Development (WCFSD) were:

- Stop the destruction of the earth's forests; their material products and ecological services are severely threatened.
- Use the world's rich forest resources to improve life for poor people and for the benefit of forest-dependent communities.
- Put the public interest first and involve people in decisions about forest use.
- Get the price of forests right, to reflect their full ecological and social values, and to stop harmful subsidies to lumber companies.
- Apply SFM approaches so we may use forests without abusing them.
- Develop new ways of measuring forest capital so that we know whether the situation is improving or worsening.
- Plan for the use and protection of whole landscapes, not the forest in isolation.
- Make better use of knowledge about forests, and greatly expand this information base.
- Accelerate research and training so that SFM can become a reality quickly.

- Take bold political decisions and develop new civil society institutions to improve governance and accountability regarding forest use.

There is no sign, however, of these recommendations being implemented seriously.

Ending on a Hopeful Note: Positive Stories

There are remarkable stories from all over the world of individuals and groups going to great lengths to save or plant trees. Some examples are:

- *Chipko*, the people's movement to save the forests of Tehri Garhwal (Box 6.4)
- The planting of roadside avenue trees in Karnataka by Thimmakka and Chikkanna (Box 6.5)

Visit the ORC for two more positive stories.

BOX 6.4 INSPIRATION: *The Story of Chipko—The Women Who Saved the Trees*

On March 26, 1974, a group of men arrived stealthily in the forest next to Reni Village in the Garhwal District of Himalayas. They had been sent by a contractor to begin cutting down 2500 trees in the forest. Anticipating resistance from the villagers, the contractor had ensured that all the men were away on that day.

Word of the arrival of the axe-men spread in the village and the women came out of their houses. About 25 of them, led by Gaura Devi, confronted the contractor's men. They pleaded with the men not to start the felling operations, but the men responded with threats and abuses. As the confrontation continued, more women joined the protest. Ultimately, the men were forced to leave, since the women did not budge.

This small event was a milestone in the *Chipko* Movement, which became known all over the world as a symbol of people's action in preventing the destruction of the environment. *Chipko* means 'to cling' or 'to hug hard'. The vision of women hugging the trees and successfully confronting the loggers fired the spirit of environmentalists the world over.

The *Chipko* Movement spread rapidly across the Himalayan Region in the 1970s led by dedicated activists like Sunderlal Bahuguna and Chandi Prasad Bhat. The contract system allowed rich contractors from the plains to make huge profits from cutting trees on the hills. The Movement was a response of the hill communities to the unfair and destructive nature of this system. The government had to abolish the contract system and stop the indiscriminate felling of trees, at least for some years.

The *Chipko* Movement brought unprecedented energy and direction to environmental preservation in India. It remains one of the celebrated environmental movements of the world.

BOX 6.5 INSPIRATION: *The Story of Thimmakka—Trees as Children*

There is something special about the 300 towering avenue trees on a 4-km stretch of the road from Kudur and Hulikal in Karnataka. All of them were planted and cared for by an elderly couple, Thimmakka and Chikkanna.

Thimmakka was born about 80 years ago in the town of Gubbi and was married off at an early age to Chikkanna of Hulikal Village. They were landless labourers working on farmlands. Thimmakka could not have children and the couple were often lonely in the evenings.

About 60 years ago, they decided to plant trees on the main road to Kudur. The couple thought that the trees would provide shade for the villagers, who had to walk often on the hot and dusty road.

They chose the peepul tree (*Ficus religiosa*), created a small nursery, and began planting the saplings. They built thorn guards around the saplings, watered them daily until they took root. They tended each tree until it was 10 years old.

Every year they planted 15 to 20 trees, until they had covered the entire stretch of 4 km. They took care of the trees as if they were their children. In fact, Chikkanna quit working so that he could devote himself full time to this task. The trees grew tall and have been providing shade for the road users, shelter for many birds and animals, and biomass for the fields.

Chikkanna died in 1990. Since 1995, many honours have come Thimmakka's way: National Citizen's Award, Priyadarshini Vrikshamitra Award, etc.

REVIEW: A SUMMARY OF THE KEY POINTS

- Forests provide us with invaluable products and services.
- Forests are facing rapid and uncontrolled destruction all over the world with serious consequences for the environment and the local communities.
- Forests both influence and are influenced by climate change.
- In order to conserve forests, we have to reconcile the conflicting interests of the environmentalists, government officials, and local communities.
- A number of national and international measures have been introduced for sustainable forest management, but implementation has been poor.
- Local communities are increasingly being involved in forest conservation.

EXERCISES

Objective-type questions

For each question below, choose the best answer out of the given choices:

1. Which of the following statements describes best the status of global forests?
   (a) The definition of a forest varies from one assessment to another.
   (b) The rate of deforestation shows signs of decreasing, but is still alarmingly high.
   (c) The forest cover has stabilized since 1999.
   (d) Asia continues to have the largest net loss of forest.
2. What are plantation forests?
   (a) They are old-growth forests.
   (b) They are second-growth forests.
   (c) They are more diverse than natural forests.
   (d) They are managed forests.
3. Which of the following items is **not** provided by natural forests?
   (a) Fuelwood
   (b) Honey
   (c) Medicinal plants
   (d) Monoculture
4. Which of the following statements is true with regard to deforestation?
   (a) It adversely affects local communities.
   (b) It does not lead to global warming, since trees absorb carbon dioxide.
   (c) It does not affect rainfall pattern.
   (d) It does not lead to the loss of topsoil.
5. Which of the following statements is true with regard to forest certification?
   (a) It is carried out only by the UN Forum on Forests.
   (b) It is now compulsory.
   (c) It enables the consumer to make responsible choices.
   (d) India's reserve forests are all covered by certification.
6. Which of the following statements is **not** true with regard to joint forest management?
   (a) It recognizes the important role of local communities in forest conservation.
   (b) The local people are allowed controlled access to the forest areas.
   (c) The local people are not permitted to harvest the resources, since the forest belongs to the government.
   (d) The local people act as the guardians of the forest.
7. What did the word *Chipko* become famous for?
   (a) It is the name of the people's movement to save the forests in the Himalayas.
   (b) It means 'hugging trees'.
   (c) It is a song of the hill communities.
   (d) It happened only in Reni village.

Short-answer questions

1. Describe the efforts of any two individuals who have worked for the conservation of trees or forests.
2. Explain in your own words the problems facing the forests of Andaman and Nicobar Islands.

3. What is the state of the world's forests according to global assessments?
4. What is the difference between old-growth and second-growth forests?
5. What are the ecosystem services provided by forests?
6. What is the impact of deforestation on the environment?
7. Are natural fires good or bad for the forests? Explain.
8. How can local communities be involved in forest conservation?
9. How can we save the remaining forests of the world?

Long-answer questions

1. Study the full report of the World Commission on Forests and Sustainable Development and write a critical review.
2. Write an essay on the international initiatives in forest conservation.

Think critically: Deeper questions for reflection and discussion

1. There are three conflicting aspects of forest resources: conservation measures, developmental activities, and lives of local communities. How can we balance these conflicting interests?
2. How would you react to the destruction of tropical forests, if you were:
   (a) a poor landless farmer in Brazil
   (b) owner of a biotechnology company
   (c) an environmentalist

ENJOY AND EDUCATE YOURSELF

1. Watch the animated short film *The Man Who Planted Trees* (1987), made by Frederic Back, based on the book by Jean Giono. It is a remarkable story of a shepherd's long, single-handed, and successful effort to reforest a desolate valley.
2. Relax with the novel *The Last Wave* by Pankaj Sekhsaria. Set in the Andaman and Nicobar Islands at the turn of the new millennium, it is a story of love, longing, and loss woven around tumultuous happenings in and around the Jarawa Reserve.

ACCESS THE OUP ONLINE RESOURCE CENTRE FOR MORE

- The story of Wangari Mathaai of Kenya, who was given the Nobel Peace Prize for promoting the largescale planting of trees by Kenyan women
- The story of Julia Butterfly Hill, who stayed high up on a tree in California, US, for two years to prevent the logging of redwood trees in the area
- Additional text and other recommended references, websites, and films

7 Land, Soil, and Mineral Resources

Only after the last tree has been cut down,
only after the last river has been poisoned,
only after the last fish has been caught,
only then will you find that money cannot be eaten.

Native American Prophecy

MAIN QUESTIONS ADDRESSED

- What is the state of the world's land surface and soil?
- What is the scale of desertification?
- What is the state of global agriculture and food production?

KEYWORDS AND PHRASES

Aravalli Hills, Bt Brinjal, Cuba, desertification, food security, Genetic Modification, Global Hunger Index, Green Revolution, Land Degradation Neutrality, mining, Nammalvar, natural farming, organic farming, overfishing, Punjab, soil erosion, UNCCD, wasteland reclamation, waterlogging

LEAD STORY

THE STORY OF PUNJAB: POVERTY OF PLENTY?

Punjab has been known as India's granary and a success story of the Green Revolution. Today, however, it is a story of degraded soil, depleted water tables, reduced productivity, and farmer suicides. How did things change so quickly?

Approximately in the mid-1960s, a whole new package was developed by the agricultural university in Ludhiana and implemented throughout Punjab with unprecedented energy. It consisted of a high yielding dwarf wheat seed, a regimen of chemical fertilizer and pesticide use, and most importantly, an irresistible bait of a guaranteed lucrative support price. The subsistence farmers were initially suspicious of the chemicals but the package as a whole was offered on the basis of 'take it or leave it'.

Birds calling out: *Help!!*

The yields, however, were high and the farmers began to prosper. As the farmers' income rose, they began to stretch the land area under wheat and rice to the limits. As cultivation became more intensive and gap between crops narrowed, the farmers felt the need to buy tractors and other machinery.

As their cash income grew, more machinery and chemicals followed.

Soon, with higher incomes, the farmers' lifestyle too began to change; large and small brick houses began to replace traditional mud structures; modern gadgets such as refrigerators and motorized two-wheelers as well as cars came into fashion. Clothes became fancier and people more sedentary. Now, almost all Punjab farmers use labour from Bihar, some entirely depend on them. Many more young men and women seek college education than 20 years ago. Food habits have changed. The list is endless. Under these circumstances, even if the farmers want to stop producing the lucrative cereal crops, they cannot.

There is, however, another side to this story of prosperity. The soil has now lost its natural capacity to nourish the crops and the farmers have to keep adding more and more fertilizers. Naturally, the cost of production is going up. It was not a good idea to grow two heavy crops of cereals on the same land year after year. The water table is also going down. The farmers are now caught in the vice-like grip of high-input cultivation, many are in deep debt, and some have committed suicide.

Another disturbing fact is the extraordinary number of cancer cases in Punjab, particularly in the fertile Malwa belt. It is widely believed that this is due to the excessive use of pesticides and other agricultural chemicals, which have directly affected the farmers and also polluted the ground water.

Some farmers are also concerned about the long-term effects of the poisons they spray on the crops and the soil. For example, they notice the effect on birds. One old farmer says, 'The birds are more or less gone. There are no vultures to eat the dead animals. In fact, one does not see or hear any birds except an occasional crow, dove, or egret. I think this is a bad omen, but most people do not seem to care.'

What does the future hold for this state?

CLIMATE CHANGE, LAND, AND FOOD

Agriculture and fisheries are among the most climate-sensitive sectors. Extreme weather will have immediate adverse impacts on food production and on livelihood assets, thus worsening the living conditions of farmers and fishers who are already vulnerable and food-insecure. Hunger and malnutrition will increase.

What does the Punjab crisis tell us?

Indeed, things have changed in Punjab. But problems like soil degradation, falling water tables, and increasing use of chemicals are not unique to Punjab. Such environmental problems are now common in many parts of India and the world. In this chapter, we will examine the reasons for the crisis.

What is the Importance of Land as a Natural Resource?

The land area of the earth, about 140 million sq km, occupies less than a third of the surface. Yet, it is vital for our existence since it is land that:

- preserves terrestrial biodiversity and the genetic pool,
- regulates the water and carbon cycles,
- acts as the store of basic resources like ground water, minerals, and fossil fuels,
- becomes a dump for solid and liquid waste, and
- forms the basis for human settlements and transport activities.

What is the condition of the world's land surface?

UN studies estimate that 23% of all usable land (excluding mountains and deserts, for example) has been degraded to such an extent that its productivity is affected. The main causes are deforestation, fuelwood consumption, overgrazing, agricultural mismanagement (planting unsuitable crops, poor crop rotation, poor soil and water management, excessive input of chemicals, frequent use of heavy machinery like tractors, etc.), establishment of industries, and urbanization.

What is the Importance of Soil?

Soil is a complex mixture of rock particles, minerals, organic matter, water, air, and billions of microorganisms. Soil forms when rocks break down into particles due to physical, chemical, and biological processes.

Soil is the foundation for agriculture and the medium in which nearly all food-producing plants grow. In fact, it is estimated that 95% of our food is directly or indirectly produced on our soil. The topsoil, just a few centimetres in thickness, supports all plant growth and is hence the life support system for all organisms, including humankind. Soil also supports other vegetation that is cultivated for animal feed, fibre, fuel, and medicinal products.

Healthy soil supplies the essential nutrients, water, oxygen, and root support that plants need to grow and flourish. A shortage of any one of the 15 nutrients required for plant growth can limit crop yield.

Soils on earth also:

- support our planet's biodiversity and host a quarter of the total.
- help us in combating and adapting to climate change by playing a key role in the carbon cycle.
- store and filter water, improving our resilience to floods and droughts.
- serve as a buffer to protect delicate plant roots from drastic fluctuations in temperature.

Soil, however, is a finite resource, meaning its loss and degradation is not recoverable within a human lifespan. It can take up to 1000 years to form 1 cm of soil. Thus, its preservation is essential for food security and our sustainable future.

Our soils are in danger because of expanding cities, deforestation, unsustainable land use and management practices, pollution, overgrazing, and climate change. The current rate of soil degradation threatens the capacity to meet the needs of future generations. The promotion of sustainable soil and land management is central to ensuring a productive food system, improved rural livelihood, and a healthy environment.

What is the state of soil in India?

There are more than 20 types and subtypes of soil in India. The main types are alluvial, laterite, black, red, mountain, and desert soils. In most parts of India, the soil has been degraded due to the factors listed in the previous section.

What is the Scale of Desertification and What is being Done about It?

Desertification is land degradation in arid and semi-arid areas caused by human activities and climatic changes. It occurs slowly, as different areas of degraded land spread and merge together, rather than through advancing desert. It is a slowly but clearly progressing 'skin disease' over the planet. The desertification problem remains poorly understood, but estimates suggest that a third of all agricultural land is either highly or moderately degraded. Further, 12 million ha of productive land become barren every year due to desertification and drought alone.

Land degradation is a problem that affects all regions, not only the drylands and developing countries. Drylands are more vulnerable to natural and human destruction due to the small water containment in soil.

One-fifth of the world's population is threatened by the impacts of global desertification. Its effects can be seen all over the world, in Asia, the African Sahel, Latin America, throughout North America, and along the Mediterranean. Cultivable land per person is shrinking throughout the world, threatening food security, particularly in poor rural areas, and triggering humanitarian and economic crises.

Fertile topsoil takes centuries to form, but it can be washed or blown away in a few seasons. Human activities such as over-cultivation, deforestation, and poor irrigation practices, combined with climate change, are turning once fertile soils into barren patches of land. When large barren patches merge together, a desert comes up.

The international community has long recognized that desertification is a major economic, social, and environmental problem of concern to many countries in all regions of the world. The Earth Summit in 1992 supported a new, integrated approach to the problem, emphasizing action to promote sustainable development at the community level. The UN Convention to Combat Desertification (UNCCD) was adopted in 1994 and entered into force in 1996. Over 190 countries are now parties to the Convention. UNCCD is the international legal framework for tackling desertification, land degradation, and drought. Box 7.1 gives the touching introduction given in a 2014 Report of UNCCD.

BOX 7.1 STATE OF THE PLANET: *Desertification—The Invisible Frontline*

In 2014, UN Convention to Combat Desertification (UNCCD) released a new edition of its report *Desertification: The Invisible Frontline.* Here is the introduction to the Report:

To fight or to flee? These are the stark choices Maria, a single mother from the Bangalala midlands of Tanzania, faces repeatedly. Her choice, along with those of families like hers, is felt all over the world.

After the rains failed for a few years, some neighbours claimed our trees were drawing too much water from the ground. We cut them down. Our harvests fell. My mother closed her stall at the local market. That is when my father and I moved from the midlands to the Ruvu Mferejini river valley..... But where we moved to, my crop also failed last year. That is why early this year I moved yet again, but I left my father behind. I hope to farm here much longer, as I am sure the people I left behind with my father will have to move too. But when will this moving end? I cannot afford it anymore.

This is not an isolated case. Maria is in the same situation that women in Darfur, Mali, Chad, or Afghanistan were in before local conflicts over water or land turned into civil wars, sexual violence, or genocide. Nor is this situation unique to sub-Saharan Africa, where a majority lives off the land and desertification is a constant threat to their livelihood.

More than 1.5 billion people in the world depend on degrading land, and 74% of them, like Maria, are poor. More than 160 countries have declared they are affected by desertification.

Desertification is a silent, invisible crisis that is destabilizing communities on a global scale. As the effects of climate change undermine livelihood, interethnic clashes are breaking out within and across states and fragile states are turning to militarization to control the situation. The effects of desertification are increasingly felt globally as victims turn into refugees, internally displaced people, and forced migrants or they turn to radicalization, extremism, or resource-driven wars for survival.

Changing weather events are threatening the livelihood of more and more people, survival options are declining, and state capacities are overburdened. More should be done to combat desertification, reverse land degradation, and mitigate the effects of drought. Otherwise, many small-scale farmers and poor, land-dependent communities face just two choices: fight or flight.

In 2022, UNCCD released the Global Land Outlook (Second Edition). The key messages of the report are given in Box 7.2.

BOX 7.2 2022 UNCCD Global Land Outlook

Key Messages:

- The world is facing a confluence of unprecedented crises: the COVID-19 pandemic merged with the ongoing and relentless global changes to our climate, land, and biodiversity.

- Land resources – soil, water, and biodiversity – provide the foundation for the wealth of our societies and economies.
- Humans have already transformed more than 70% of the Earth's land area from its natural state, causing unparalleled environmental degradation and contributing significantly to global warming.
- Poor rural communities, smallholder farmers, women, youth, indigenous peoples, and other at-risk groups are disproportionately affected by desertification, land degradation, and drought.
- Roughly US$ 44 trillion of economic output – more than half of global annual GDP – is moderately or highly reliant on natural capital. Yet governments, markets, and societies rarely account for the true value of all nature's services that underpin human and environmental health.
- Globally, food systems are responsible for 80% of deforestation, 70% of freshwater use, and are the single greatest cause of terrestrial biodiversity loss. At the same time, soil health and biodiversity below ground – the source of almost all our food calories – has been largely neglected by the industrial agricultural revolution of the last century.
- Land is the operative link between biodiversity loss and climate change, and therefore must be the primary focus of any meaningful intervention to tackle these intertwined crises.
- Land restoration is about creating sustainable livelihood opportunities for people – small-scale farmers, indigenous peoples and local communities, businesses and entrepreneurs, women and youth – to boost incomes, secure food and water supplies, and make individuals and communities less vulnerable.
- Redirecting public spending towards regenerative land management solutions offers a significant opportunity to align private sector investment with longer-term societal goals.
- Restoration is a proven and cost-effective solution to help reverse climate change and biodiversity loss caused by the rapid depletion of our finite natural capital stocks.
- The land restoration agenda is a multiple benefits strategy that reverses past land and ecosystem degradation while creating opportunities that improve livelihoods and prepare us for future challenges.
- The stark implications of the business-as-usual scenario means that decisive action at all levels and from all actors is needed to realize the promise of the restoration scenarios. Ambitious land restoration targets must be backed by clear action plans and sustained financing.
- The international community has pledged to restore one billion hectares of degraded land by 2030. This is only the start.

How Serious are Waterlogging and Soil Salinity?

When irrigation is not accompanied by proper drainage, waterlogging occurs. This in turn brings salt to the surface, where it collects at the roots of plants or as a thin crust on the land surface. Rapid evaporation of ground water also adds salt to the soil.

Key Idea Erosion, waterlogging, salinization, and desertification are some of the ways in which land has been degraded in many parts of the world.

Pakistan, Egypt, India, and the US are some of the countries worst affected by salinization and waterlogging. In Egypt, 90% of all farmland suffers from waterlogging. In Pakistan, two-thirds of all irrigated land is salinized. In India, 12–25% of land is waterlogged or salinized.

What are the Measures being Taken to Prevent Desertification and Restore Degraded Land?

Among the practical measures undertaken to prevent and restore degraded land are prevention of soil erosion; improved early warning system and water resource management; sustainable pasture, forest, and livestock management; aero-seeding over shifting sand dunes; narrow strip planting, windbreaks, and shelterbelts of live plants; agroforestry ecosystems; afforestation and reforestation; introduction of new species and varieties with a capacity to tolerate salinity and/or aridity; and environmentally sound human settlements. You can get more information from the UNCCD Secretariat.

What is wasteland reclamation?

Wasteland is land, which is deteriorating due to natural causes or due to the lack of appropriate water and soil management. Such land is left uncultivated or under-utilized. We have in India about 70 million ha of wasteland. Wasteland reclamation is the process by which such lands are brought again under vegetative cover and made productive.

Some steps that could be taken for wasteland reclamation are:

- Soil conservation through contour bunds and water conservation through rainwater harvesting.
- Identification of pioneer species, which can grow fast even in poor soil, grow lots of biomass in a short time, fix nitrogen, and withstand both drought and flood. They should also be of some economic value and be unpalatable to cattle.

After the pioneer species grow well, secondary species of indigenous trees are planted. These could be fruit, oilseed, or timber trees. Over a few years, the soil health may improve and regular cultivation could be started. This kind of wasteland reclamation has been successfully carried out in the international community called Auroville, near Puducherry.

What is the Impact of Urbanization and Industrialization on Land?

More than 50% of the world's population now lives in urban areas and this figure is expected to go up. Urban areas constantly need more land for settlements, infrastructure, industries, leisure activities, and the like and hence increase pressures on land. More and more agricultural land gets converted into urban colonies. Larger cities affect even larger areas outside them, thanks to their widening Ecological Footprint (Chapter 1).

We see solid waste piled up on many urban streets. Outside the city, there are large dumps of waste brought from the city It is estimated that about 2 million ha of land have been degraded due to waste disposal and landfills.

Urban agriculture has been expanding globally over the past 25 years. In Sao Paulo in Brazil and Havana in Cuba, for example, urban home gardens have been very successful. While urban agriculture provides locally grown food and helps recycle organic matter, it can also cause pollution of water and soil if chemicals are used.

What is the Future of land as a Resource?

With increasing world population, there will be intense pressure on land, particularly in Africa and Asia. More intensive land use will be needed to feed the people. More land will also be brought into agriculture by converting forests and grasslands. Climate change will only worsen the situation.

What is Land Degradation Neutrality?

Land degradation is the result of human-induced actions which exploit land, causing its utility, biodiversity, soil fertility, and overall health to decline. Land is being degraded rapidly worldwide. Ensuring food security for a growing global population requires healthy land resources and flourishing ecosystems. Yet our current agricultural practices are causing soils worldwide to be eroded up to 100 times faster than natural processes replenish them.

We have already altered 70% of all ice-free land, impacting over 3.2 billion people. At current rates, 90% of land will bear our imprint by 2050. The impacts of land degradation will be felt by most of the world's population. Land degradation also changes and disrupts rainfall patterns, exacerbates extreme weather like droughts or floods, and drives further climate change. It results in social and political instability, which drives poverty, conflict, and migration.

The UNCCD's goal of land degradation neutrality (LDN) can halt, and then reverse, this alarming picture of the future. UNCCD defines LDN as "a state whereby the amount and quality of land resources necessary to support ecosystem functions and services to enhance food security remain stable, or increase, within specified temporal and spatial scales and ecosystems."

UNCCD is already helping 129 of the world's 196 countries that have pledged (or are aiming) to arrest land degradation by 2030. More than 100 countries participate in the Changwon Initiative, which supports national voluntary target setting processes to achieve land degradation neutrality (LDN).

Achieving LDN requires three concurrent actions:

- Avoiding new degradation of land by maintaining existing healthy land;
- Reducing existing degradation by adopting sustainable land management practices that can slow degradation while increasing biodiversity, soil health, and food production; and
- Ramping up efforts to restore and return degraded lands to a natural or more productive state.

The UNCCD's objectives for LDN include:

- Maintaining or improving the sustainable delivery of ecosystem services
- Maintaining or improving land productivity to enhance global food security
- Increasing the resilience of land and the populations dependent on it
- Seeking synergies with other social, economic, and environmental objectives
- Reinforcing and promoting responsible and inclusive land governance

Where does the World's Food Come from?

Food comes from three sources:

- Croplands that provide 76% of the total, mostly grains
- Rangelands that produce meat mostly from grazing livestock, accounting for about 17% of the total food
- Fisheries that supply the remaining 7%.

What is the Global Food Availability?

The key messages of the UN FAO 2022 Report on the State of Food Security and Nutrition in the World are given in Box 7.3.

BOX 7.3 UN FAO 2022 Report: *State of Food Security and Nutrition in the World*

Key Messages:

- Despite hopes that the world would emerge from the COVID-19 pandemic in 2021 and food security would begin to improve, world hunger rose further in 2021. The increase in global hunger in 2021 reflects exacerbated inequalities across and within countries due to an unequal pattern of economic recovery among countries and unrecovered income losses among those most affected by the COVID-19 pandemic.
- Between 702 and 828 million people were affected by hunger in 2021. The number has grown by about 150 million since the outbreak of the COVID-19 pandemic – 103 million more people between 2019 and 2020 and 46 million more in 2021.

- Projections are that nearly 670 million people will still be facing hunger in 2030, that is, 8% of the world population.
- Around 2.3 billion people in the world were moderately or severely food insecure in 2021, and 11.7% of the global population faced food insecurity at severe levels.
- Globally in 2020, an estimated 22% of children under five years of age were stunted, 6.7% were wasted, and 5.7% were overweight.
- Globally in 2019, nearly one in three women aged 15 to 49 years (571 million) were affected by anaemia, with no progress since 2012. Anaemia affects more women in rural settings, in poorer households and who have received no formal education.
- Almost 3.1 billion people could not afford a healthy diet in 2020. This is 112 million more than in 2019, reflecting the inflation in consumer food prices stemming from the economic impacts of the COVID-19 pandemic and the measures put in place to contain it.
- The recent setbacks indicate that policies are no longer delivering increasing marginal returns in reducing hunger, food insecurity and malnutrition in all its forms. Governments where the economy is fragile are also facing fiscal constraints to transform agrifood systems. This is the time for governments to start examining their current support to food and agriculture.
- Worldwide support to food and agriculture accounted for almost USD 630 billion per year on average over 2013–2018. The lion share of it is targeted to farmers individually, through trade and market policies and fiscal subsidies largely tied to production or unconstrained use of variable production inputs. Not only is much of this support market-distorting, but it is not reaching many farmers, hurts the environment and does not promote the production of nutritious foods.

What is the State of Food Production and Hunger in India?

Indian agriculture is considered a success story. Despite uncertain weather and price shocks in the past few years, it has done remarkably well in terms of output growth. India now produces annually 250–260 million tonnes of food grains, 5 million tonnes of meat products, and 9.6 million tonnes of fish. The increase in grain production since the 1960s is ascribed to the Green Revolution.

While the production has been high, the availability has been a different story. Between 1972 and 1991, the average per capita net availability of food grains went on increasing every five-year period. Since 1991, however, it declined in every five-year period without exception.

Hunger in India is widespread and the causes are different across various sections of the society and across the country. The 2022 Global Hunger Index (GHI) ranked India at 107 out of 121 countries. GHI scores are based on the values of four component indicators - undernourishment, child stunting, child wasting and child mortality. India ranked below Sri Lanka (64), Nepal (81), Bangladesh (84), and Pakistan (99).

What is Meant by the Green Revolution and What has been Its Impact?

The Green Revolution (See also Chapter 9) refers to the rapid increase in world food production, especially in the developing countries, during the second half of the twentieth century, primarily through the use of lab-engineered high-yielding varieties of seeds. It was hailed as a success story of agricultural science and technology. It is now clear, however, that it has brought in its wake many problems too.

In the middle of the last century, there were severe food shortages in many developing countries. With growing populations, countries like India had to import food. The answer to this problem came from Mexico.

In the early 1940s, Mexico's wheat yields were low and the country was importing 50% of its food. Under a research programme set up to increase the production of grains, the American agricultural scientist, Norman E. Borlaug developed a high-yielding variety of wheat through new

Key Idea While the Green Revolution increased yields dramatically, it is a high-input system that has degraded the soil, lowered water tables, reduced biodiversity, and impoverished the small farmer.

concepts in plant breeding. It was a variety that could respond to high inputs of fertilizer and irrigation. Between 1950 and 1965, Mexican wheat yields increased 400% and a Green Revolution was born.

By mid-1960s, the Green Revolution was fully adopted in India too. The new high-yielding varieties (HYVs) increased the production and made multi-cropping possible. Ultimately, India achieved self-sufficiency in food.

The Green Revolution, however, was a clear shift from traditional agriculture. It came as a package of HYVs along with high inputs of chemical fertilizer, pesticide, water, and agricultural machinery like tractors. It was an energy-intensive method: apart from the energy that went into the making of the inputs, energy was again needed to run the machinery and to pump water.

Governments had to subsidize many of the inputs to keep the farming going. The Green Revolution also made the developing countries dependent on foreign technology.

The farmers found that they had to buy the seeds every year and that, year after year, the inputs had to be increased to maintain the productivity levels. On the whole, the Green Revolution has benefited large landowners and not the subsistence farmers. (Recall the story of Punjab.)

A large number of traditional varieties have disappeared. Currently, just 12 HYVs provide most of the world's food and they are more prone to diseases and pest attacks compared to the traditional varieties. The soil has also been getting degraded and drained of its nutrients through the excessive use of chemicals. Large-scale use of pesticides has also affected the health of human beings and many other organisms.

By 2050, agricultural production must increase by 60% globally—and by almost 100% in developing countries—in order to meet food demand alone. Further, such an increase will have to come from the same amount of land we now have and by using less water and other inputs. Climate change is also affecting the environment in which crops are grown, presenting farmers with new challenges.

What is the Way out for Agriculture?

The Punjab crisis and similar stories elsewhere in India and other countries show beyond any doubt that the present system of chemical agriculture with constantly increasing inputs of fertilizers, pesticides, and water is unsustainable.

One way out of the crisis is the gradual shift from chemical agriculture to organic farming. Organic farming does not use chemical fertilizers and chemical pesticides. It is in fact a return to the traditional methods like crop rotation, use of animal and green manures, and some forms of biological control of pests.

Organic farming is based on the following principles:

- Nature is the best role model for farming since it uses neither chemicals nor poisons and does not demand excessive water.
- Soil is a living system and not an inert bowl for dumping chemicals.
- Soil's living populations of microbes and other organisms are significant contributors to its fertility on a sustained basis and must be protected and nurtured at all costs.
- The total environment of the soil—from soil structure to soil cover—is more important than any nutrients we may wish to pump into it.

Organic farming can, over a period of time, reverse soil degradation and improve soil health. Conversion to organic farming will mean initial problems and economic losses as the soil recovers, but it will be a better option in the long term. Worldwide, there is an active movement towards organic farming and farmers can get advice and support from many groups.

Organic farming is used as a general label for the following systems of agriculture:

- Reliance on the soil's natural fertility enhanced through composting and vermiculture: While simple composting is the natural conversion of organic matter into manure, vermiculture uses earthworms to speed up the process.
- Natural farming: No-tillage, no-chemicals, and no-weeding method of farming, pioneered by Masanobu Fukuoka of Japan.
- Biodynamic farming: Exploiting bio- and solar rhythms in farming, based on the ideas of Rudolf Steiner.
- Bio-intensive farming: Intensive garden cultivation using deep-dug beds.
- Permaculture: An approach that goes beyond organic farming, developed by Bill Mollison and David Holmgren in Australia.
- LEISA: Low External Input Sustainable Agriculture developed by Dutch farmers and scientists committed to organic farming.

Key Idea Organic farming is a way out of the agricultural crisis.

What are Genetically Modified Crops?

Genetic Modification (GM) or Genetic Engineering of crops has been proposed as the ultimate answer to the problems of food and agriculture. GM is a modern branch of biotechnology, which can be defined as any technological application that uses biological systems or living organisms to make or modify products or processes for specific use. Biotechnology includes plant breeding and animal husbandry, practised by farmers since ages. Such natural processes took many years of cross breeding.

GM, however, is the direct modification of the genetic makeup of an organism through a process that would not occur naturally. It is usually done in a laboratory by introducing foreign genes into the gene pool of the organism. All life is composed of cells that contain genes, and genes are made of molecules called DNA. The DNA molecule of an organism contains information about its characteristics and behaviour.

GM manipulates the genes in an organism to change its characteristics. It can move a favourable gene from one organism to another. Thus, GM can make a plant resistant to specific pests or diseases. Bt Cotton and Bt Brinjal are examples. Bt stands for the bacterium *Bacillus thuringiensis*, which acts as a microbial pesticide. Each strain of this bacterium specifically kills one or a few related species of insect larvae. Scientists introduce the Bt gene into the plant's own genetic material. Then the plant manufactures the substance that destroys the pest.

GM can also produce new varieties of plants with some desired characteristics, such as herbicide tolerance, virus tolerance, and resistance to drought and salinity However, there are strong opinions in favour of and against the introduction of GM crops.

Those who support GM crops give arguments such as:

- GM is the only way to produce enough to feed the increasing world population.
- Plants will be resistant to pests, droughts, water salinity, and even climate change.
- There will be a reduction in the use of fertilizers and pesticides.

Those who oppose GM raise questions such as:

- How do we know the unintended consequences of GM foods, such as long-term effects on humans and other organisms?

- We know that a GM crop contaminates the non-GM varieties grown nearby. What would be the effects of such contamination on biological diversity?
- Can the farmer grow seeds for the next planting or is he perpetually dependent on the seed company? Would GM lead to domination of agriculture by a few large companies?
- Is it ethical and safe to introduce animal genes into plants and vice versa?

Key Idea While GM crops are hailed as the ultimate solution to the agricultural crisis, questions remain about their safety and efficacy.

Bt Cotton is a GM crop currently cultivated in India in large areas. However, the results of using Bt Cotton have been mixed. Meanwhile, Bt Brinjal created a major controversy (Box 7.4). Both these GM crops have been developed jointly by the giant US Corporation Monsanto and the Indian firm Mahyco.

BOX 7.4 CONTROVERSY: *The Story of Bt Brinjal—Ban It or Plant It?*

Bt Brinjal is a genetically modified brinjal created by inserting a gene from the soil bacterium *Bacillus thuringiensis* into the plant. The objective is to give the brinjal plant resistance against certain insects.

Bt Brinjal created a controversy in India. The proponents say that Bt Brinjal would be beneficial to small farmers because it is insect-resistant and increases yields. The opponents have concerns about its possible adverse impact on human health and biosafety, livelihood, and biodiversity.

The Genetic Engineering Approval Committee (GEAC) of the Ministry of Environment and Forests (MoEFCC) recommended the release of Bt Brinjal in India. However, faced with opposition from several citizens' groups, Jairam Ramesh, the then Minister for Environment and Forests, arranged public consultations across the country before taking a final decision on this issue.

At the end of the consultations in February 2010, the Minister imposed 'a moratorium on the release of Bt Brinjal till such time studies establish the safety of the product from the point of view of its long-term impact on human health and environment, including the rich genetic wealth existing in brinjal in our country, to the satisfaction of both the public and professionals'.

Sharad Pawar, the then Agriculture Minister, disagreed with the ban. He said that the ban would 'set the clock back', demoralize Indian scientists, and jeopardize R&D crucial to food security. The then PM, Manmohan Singh, then decided that MoEFCC should not take such decisions unilaterally.

After Bt Brinjal, there are many more GM food crops awaiting GEAC's approval—25 kinds of rice, 23 kinds of tomatoes, many types of groundnut, pigeon peas, potato, mustard, sugarcane, soy, and okra. In July 2014, GEAC cleared the field trials of GM rice, mustard, cotton, chickpea, and brinjal.

In 2020, the Modi government approved the field trials of Bt Brinjal, but this step was questioned by farmers' unions such as the Bhartiya Kisan Sangh. In 2021, the government announced that scientific field trials of GM crops, including Bt brinjal, would not be taken up for consideration by the GEAC without recommendations from states/union territories where the trials are proposed to be undertaken.

As we await the final verdict, we could ask, 'If Bt Brinjal is approved, what will happen to the 2500 indigenous brinjal varieties?'

While agriculture is going through a crisis, fisheries, the other major source of food, has its share of problems too.

How Important is Fish as a Food Source and Where does Fish Come from?

About 2 million people, mostly in the developing countries, depend on fish as their main source of food. 55% of the fish comes from the ocean, 33% from aquaculture, and 12% from inland freshwater fishing in rivers, lakes, reservoirs, and ponds. Aquaculture is the artificial production of fish in ponds and underwater cages. A third of the world's fish harvest is used as animal feed, fishmeal, and oils.

It is a wrong notion that the vast open sea holds unlimited amount of fish. 80–90% of global commercial fish catch comes from coastal waters within 300 km of the shoreline.

Is There a Fisheries Crisis?

The world's fisheries are in fact in deep crisis. An environmental and social catastrophe is in the making, but most consumers of fish do not perceive it.

A massive increase in global fishing began in the 1950s and 1960s with the rapid induction of new technology: factory trawlers, satellite positioning, acoustic fish finders, spotter planes, huge nets, etc. Industrial fishing technology employed in the modern trawlers operating in all the seas began locating and catching the last remnants of all varieties of fish stocks. Soon, the rate of harvest exceeded the rate of fish population growth.

The first sign of problem was the collapse of the world's largest fishery, the Peruvian anchovy in 1972. The decline in the North Atlantic started in the mid-1970s and over the next two decades, most of the cod stocks in New England and Eastern Canada collapsed. Centuries of fishing tradition came to an end.

80% of the marine fish stocks are now fully exploited, overexploited, or in a state of depletion. Large-scale fisheries are very likely to collapse within a few decades in most areas.

> **Key Idea** Global fisheries have nearly collapsed.

We are now fishing down the food web. Once the larger fish are exhausted, the fleets start catching the smaller fish. These being often the prey of the larger fish, there is further decline of the latter. Meanwhile, we are also removing the species living on the ocean floor through bottom trawling, which is like clear cutting a forest. This removes the species at the base of the food web.

The tragedy is that the massive harvesting of fish was not driven by nutritional needs, but by the demand for luxury foods or livestock feed. The rich countries actively encouraged the unsustainable exploitation through heavy subsidies to their fishers. Apart from overexploitation, fisheries are threatened by pollution of water bodies, destruction of mangroves and coral reefs, and undoubtedly climate change.

What is the State of India's Fisheries?

The current annual fish production is about 9.6 million tonnes, with roughly equal share from marine and inland fisheries. About 500,000 tonnes of fish are exported. Ten million people depend directly or indirectly on fishing for their livelihood.

The catch per vessel has been going down in all the coastal states. This is because there are about 35,000 small mechanized boats and 2 million artisanal crafts competing for the fish.

To add to the problems, the government announced a new deep sea fishing policy in 1991, opening up Indian seas to foreign vessels in the name of joint ventures. When industrial fleets have depleted the huge fisheries of the Atlantic and the Pacific, how long will Indian stocks last?

India has about 1000 freshwater fish species, but this diversity is under threat. Overharvesting, competition from newly-introduced exotic species, and pollution are taking their toll.

What is the Way out for Global Fisheries?

Some recommendations given by experts to save global fisheries are:

- Adopt an ecosystem-based approach by considering the food needs of the key fish species
- Eliminate any fishing gear that destroys the ocean floor or catches non-target species as bycatch
- Establish marine reserves as no-fishing zones to help populations recover

- Move away from the notion that the ocean will always give us all that we demand
- Employ traditional aquaculture integrated with agriculture (for example, raising fish in paddy fields at appropriate seasons)

Let us now turn to mining, which is a major activity in human exploitation of natural resources.

What are Minerals and Mining?

A mineral is any substance that is naturally present in the earth's crust and is not formed from animal or vegetable matter. The earth's geological processes have formed these minerals over millions or billions of years and hence they are non-renewable.

Mining is the process of extracting and processing minerals. Over 100 minerals are mined and these include metals like gold, iron, copper, and aluminium and non-metals like stone, sand, and salt. Apart from minerals, coal is the major material that is mined from the earth.

What are the environmental and social impacts of mining?

Underground mining has little direct effect on the environment, but it can cause long-term problems like subsidence and pollution of aquifers. In underground mines, the workers are at great risk. Accidents like flooding and collapse are common and the work itself causes severe health problems like respiratory illnesses.

Surface or open cast mining destroys all vegetation in the area and pollutes the landscape with the dust that is thrown up. Once the available material is mined out, large craters are left behind. When hills that act as watersheds are mined away, the water tables go down.

The processing of the mined material, often done on site, using in many cases, mercury, cyanide, and large quantities of water, pollutes rivers and other water bodies. The waste material like slag is often far greater in quantity than the usable part and is left behind as unsightly, unstable, and dangerous heaps.

Mining has huge social impacts. Mining-induced displacement and resettlement leads to the following problems for the communities:

- Loss of land and livelihood: The displaced communities lose their lands as well as their traditional occupations.
- Increased health risks due to contamination of natural resources such as land and water: Resettled populations often do not have access to safe water and sanitation.
- Changes in population dynamics: Since trained manpower is usually not available locally, the workers come from outside.

What is the Status of Mines and Minerals in India?

Here are some facts about mining in India:

- India produces as many as 86 metals and minerals.
- 80% of mining in India is for coal.
- India has over 3500 legal mines.
- Illegal mining is a major problem and thousands of cases of illegal mining have been registered across the country.
- Over 1 million people are employed in the industry.
- Mining has adversely affected biodiversity, ecosystems, local cultures, and communities.

Key Idea Mining is necessary, since we need metals and minerals. But it has serious environmental and social impacts.

- About 10 million people have been displaced from mining areas and 75% of them have not received proper compensation. The tribal communities are the worst affected.

The case of the Aravalli Hills in Rajasthan is typical of the Indian mining scene (Box 7.5).

BOX 7.5 ECOSYSTEM: ***The Story of the Aravalli Hills—Mining vs Jal, Jangal, Jameen***

The Rajasamand Lake in Rajasthan had not dried up for at least 300 years. It did so in 2001. The likely reason: a decade of marble mining in Rajnagar area.

The Aravalli Hills, spread across Haryana, Rajasthan, and Gujarat, are the lifeline of the three states as they control the climate and drainage system. The hills act as the watershed for the region. Unfortunately, however, the hills are also repositories of immense mineral wealth including talc, marble, and granite.

The mining and related industries employ about 175,000 workers and 600,000 others are indirectly dependent on the mining operations. In Rajasthan alone, 9,700 industrial units are connected with mining.

Forest cover has been depleted by 90% over the past 20 years since large-scale mining began. When the mines reach below the underground water level, a cone of depression is formed that sucks water from the surrounding areas, drying up wells and affecting agriculture. Several studies have pointed out that the natural drainage system and the water table of the entire region have been badly affected over the years. Pollution levels have also increased.

Studies have shown that the labourers are not provided with any healthcare. Lung diseases like tuberculosis and silicosis are common, making the labourers invalids or killing them by the time they are forty. Child labour constitutes 10–15% of the workforce and women workers 30–40%, and their condition is the worst.

Environmentalists have charged that owners generally mine in much larger areas than are legally allocated to them. They fear that all the minerals in Rajasthan will be exhausted within 50 years, if the mining goes on at the current rate. According to them, mining affected water, forest, and land. While mining led to the depletion of water in wells, mining waste destroyed fertile land.

In 2002, the Supreme Court of India imposed a blanket ban on mining activities in the Aravallis. The basic premise for the ban was the argument that the Aravallis came under the category of forestland. Later, the Court constituted a high-level monitoring committee to suggest ways and means for the overall ecological restoration of the hills and give environment clearance for all mines seeking renewal of their leases.

In February 2010, the Supreme Court directed the cancellation of 157 mining leases operating in the Aravalli Hills and asked the Forest Survey of India to carry out satellite imagery of the entire 50,000 sq km range spread across 15 districts of the State to assess the extent of ecological damage.

Ending on a Hopeful Note: Positive Stories

The success of Cuba in shifting to organic farming is a classic case (Box 7.6). Organic farmers like Nammalvar have been leading major movements to promote sustainable agriculture in India (Box 7.7).

BOX 7.6 INSPIRATION: ***The Story of Cuba—From Crisis to a Success Story***

Imagine a country that suddenly finds itself with no fertilizer or pesticide for its fields and all imports of meat, grains, and processed foods gone. Most countries would not be able to recover from such a crisis, but this is the story of one country that did.

The small island of Cuba has been for long under severe economic sanctions by its neighbour, the US. It had depended on the Soviet Union and the Eastern Bloc for exchanging its sugar for fertilizers, oil, and grains. When the Soviet Union collapsed in 1989, Cuba's economy and food security were seriously threatened. The people were facing starvation.

The Cuban government's answer was a major shift to organic farming. The strategy was to transform derelict city plots into well-funded vegetable gardens under the supervision of organic farming associations. Thousands of gardens across Cuba began producing organic vegetables and many other crops. Organic farming on small family plots currently provides employment to 326,000 people out of a population of 12 million.

The gardens use organic compost and mulch instead of chemical fertilizers, biological pest control methods instead of chemical pesticides, and other environment-friendly techniques. Giant greenhouses produce vegetables in all seasons. Organic sugar and coffee are now being produced.

The organic gardening associations bring together farmers, farm managers, field experts, researchers, and government officials to develop and promote organic farming methods. Its aim is to convince Cuban farmers and policy-makers that the country's previous high-input farming model was too import-dependent and environmentally damaging to be sustainable, and that the organic alternative has the potential to achieve equally good yields.

The Cuban success in shifting to organic farming points the way to the rest of the world.

BOX 7.7 INSPIRATION: *Nammalvar—Crusader of Organic Farming*

On December 30, 2013, Govindasamy Nammalvar died at the age of 75. He was then on a peaceful march in Thanjavur district of Tamil Nadu, where he was leading a campaign against the methane exploration project for which the state government had granted a licence to an American multinational company.

Not many in India would have heard about him, but he was well known among the environmentalists of Tamil Nadu, even as the government and the media generally ignored him. He was considered to be the father of the organic farming movement in Tamil Nadu.

Many years ago, as an agricultural graduate, he was asked to wean away farmers from traditional agriculture to the methods of the Green Revolution. Soon, he realized the folly of chemical farming, quit his job, and joined an organization called Islands of Peace, founded by the Nobel Peace Laureate, Dominique Pire. There he worked on improving standard of living of farmers and workers in Tirunelveli district. In 1990, he helped found the movement called Low-External Input Sustainable Agriculture (LEISA).

He became a farmer himself to experiment with organic farming. His large farm, called Vanagam, is today a living example of sustainable farming carried out through traditional and organic methods. He also set up the Nammalvar Ecological Foundation, which has been creating awareness among the public on traditional farming methods, including the use of organic manure and herbal pest repellents, backyard and terrace gardening, soil preservation, vermiculture, and multi-cropping. During his lifetime, Nammalvar was instrumental in founding, guiding, or inspiring many movements including Kudumbam, LEISA Network, Millet Network of India, and Save Our Rice campaign.

Nammalvar will always be remembered as a wise and gentle pioneer of organic farming, who inspired thousands of farmers and activists.

REVIEW: A SUMMARY OF THE KEY POINTS

- The world's land surface is continuously degrading, soil is becoming unhealthy, and desertification is increasing.
- One-fifth of the world's population is threatened by the impacts of global desertification.
- There is enough food available in the world to feed everyone, but poverty keeps one-eighth of the population hungry.
- While the Green Revolution increased crop production dramatically, it has led to many problems in the long term, leading to a crisis even in states like Punjab.

- India has 25% of the total undernourished population in the world.
- The wise option for agriculture seems to be to shift gradually to organic farming, minimizing or altogether avoiding chemical fertilizers and chemical pesticides.
- There are many examples of successful adoption of organic farming.
- There are strong opinions in favour of and against the introduction of genetically modified (GM) crops.
- There is a global fisheries crisis with most fish stocks in collapse or decline.
- Mining has become more intense and widespread and causes many environmental and social problems.

EXERCISES

Objective-type questions

In each question below, choose the best answer out of the given choices:

1. Which is the most important support for all plant growth and all life?
   (a) Topsoil
   (b) Fertilizer
   (c) Farming
   (d) Pesticide
2. Which of the following is **not** a problem associated with land?
   (a) Waterlogging
   (b) Salinization
   (c) Desertification
   (d) Climate change
3. Which of the following statements is **not** true?
   (a) Soil supports our planet's biodiversity.
   (b) Soil helps us in combating and adapting to climate change.
   (c) Soil stores and filters water.
   (d) Soil is a quickly renewable natural resource.
4. Which of the following statements is true with regard to food on this planet?
   (a) There is unlimited amount of fish.
   (b) There is enough food to feed every person.
   (c) Every person is able to buy food.
   (d) Green Revolution has solved the problem of hunger.
5. Which of the following statements is **not** true with regard to the Green Revolution?
   (a) It increased crop yields.
   (b) It needs fertilizers and pesticides.
   (c) It requires decreasing inputs over time.
   (d) It uses high-yielding varieties of seeds.
6. Which of the following statements is true with regard to organic farming?
   (a) It uses chemical fertilizers.
   (b) Over time, it makes the soil healthier.
   (c) It uses chemical pesticides.
   (d) It does not use animal or green manure.
7. Which of the following statements is **not** true with regard to GM crops?
   (a) They could have greater resistance to pests.
   (b) They are proven to be completely safe.
   (c) They could resist drought or salinity.
   (d) They could reduce the amount of fertilizer needed.
8. Which of the following statements is **not** true with regard to global fisheries?
   (a) Most of the marine fish stocks are now fully exploited or overexploited.
   (b) We are now fishing down the food web.
   (c) The demand for luxury foods and livestock feed has led to overexploitation.
   (d) The rate of fish population growth exceeds the rate of harvest.
9. Which of the following statements is **not** true with regard to communities in mining areas?
   (a) They often lose their land and livelihood.
   (b) All of them get employed in the mines.
   (c) They often do not have access to fresh water and sanitation.
   (d) They are displaced from their land.
10. Which of the following statements is **not** true?
   (a) Desertification happens only in drylands.
   (b) More than 160 countries are affected by desertification.
   (c) Desertification is a silent, invisible crisis.
   (d) Desertification leads to a refugee crisis.

Short-answer questions

1. In what ways is the world's land surface getting degraded?
2. What are the sources of our food and is there enough food in the world for all?
3. Explain in brief the basic principles of organic farming.
4. Why is there a global fisheries crisis?
5. What are the environmental and social impacts of mining?

Long-answer question

Write an essay on the Green Revolution answering questions such as: When and why was it introduced? What benefits did it bring? What are the problems now being faced by the farmers who have adopted the Green Revolution package? What is the likely long-term impact of the Green Revolution on the environment?

Think critically: Deeper question for reflection and discussion

If India has excess food stocks that are rotting, why are millions still going hungry? Why can't we implement a 'Food for Work' programme and distribute the excess food?

ENJOY AND EDUCATE YOURSELF

1. Watch the movie *The Milagro Beanfield War* (1988), directed by Robert Redford. The film is about one man's struggle as he defends his small beanfield and his community against big business and state political interests.
2. Watch the film *Peepli Live* (2010), written and directed by Anusha Rizvi and produced by Aamir Khan. It is a satirical comedy that explores the topic of farmer suicide and the subsequent media and political response.

ACCESS THE OUP ONLINE RESOURCE CENTRE FOR MORE

- The story of Permaculture: Designing sustainable human settlements
- The story of Ramesh Dagar: Small, organic, and profitable!
- Additional text and other recommended references, websites, and films

8 Energy Resources

My father rode a camel.
I drive a car.
My son flies a jet-plane.
His son will ride a camel.

An Arab saying

MAIN QUESTIONS ADDRESSED

- What are our major energy needs?
- What are our primary sources of renewable and non-renewable energy?
- What are the problems with regard to the use of fossil fuels as well as renewable sources?
- What is the way out of the energy crisis?

KEYWORDS AND PHRASES

Bioenergy, biofuel, biogas, Chernobyl, fossil fuel, fuel cell, fuelwood scarcity, Fukushima, geothermal energy, Hubbert Curve, hydro power, hydrogen, net energy yield, nuclear power, OPEC, OTEC, Peak Oil, photovoltaic cell, primary energy, renewable energy, solar energy, tidal energy, tight oil, tar sands, wave energy, wind energy

LEAD STORY

THE STORY OF WOMEN HEADLOADERS: NOMADS WITH HOMES?

Basumati Tirkey, a 35-year-old resident of Bangamunda village in Orissa, walks 9 km every day, carrying a load of 35 kg of fuelwood, to earn ₹15. And she has spent a lifetime doing so.

Basumati is just one of the 11 million desperate women in India who eke out a living collecting and selling fuelwood. 70% of women living in and around forest areas are engaged in this work. It is estimated that, in an average village in a semi-arid region, a woman walks more than 1000 km a year to collect firewood alone. No wonder they are called 'nomads with homes'.

The UN Food and Agricultural Organization estimates that the fuelwood business in India has a turnover of US$60 billion. It must be the most valuable non-timber forest activity and yet it is the last resort of the poorest of the poor. It is generally regarded as being a threat to the forests and an illegal activity. In fact, a substantial part of the huge turnover ends up as payments to the forest guards or profit for the middlemen.

Forest guard to headloader: *'You are anti-environment. Pay me something'*

Fuelwood is still the most preferred (and often the only available) energy source in the rural areas and a major source for the urban poor too. It is estimated that 47% of the total energy consumed by households in India is from firewood, 17% from animal dung, and 12% from crop residues. This leaves just 24% for commercial energy.

While many millions like Basumati make their living by collecting and selling fuelwood, millions more collect wood just for their daily energy needs. Because of low incomes, these poor people are unable to shift to commercial fuels like kerosene. All this collection of wood puts tremendous pressure on the environment and leads to deforestation and loss of green cover.

CLIMATE CHANGE AND ENERGY

Our reckless extraction and burning of fossil fuels has resulted in unprecedented levels of emissions, leading to severe climate change. Well before we run out of fossil fuels, we will be facing the enormous and widespread negative impacts of climate change on human and natural systems.

What does the story of Basumati and others mean?

With increasing population, the demand for fuelwood keeps going up, even as the availability is going down. The challenge is to provide sufficient energy for the poor without degrading the environment.

Is There a Global Energy Crisis?

Different groups have different perceptions on the question of an energy crisis. This is because of the huge disparity in the needs, availability, and consumption of energy between the rich and the poor of the world.

Key Idea There is a huge disparity in energy needs, availability, and consumption between the rich and the poor of the world.

1.2 billion people worldwide lack access to electricity even for lighting, while 2.8 billion people rely on wood, coal, charcoal, or animal waste for cooking and heating. In industrialized countries, the energy problem is one of waste and pollution, not shortage.

In countries like the US, any hint of shortage of oil supplies or even a small increase in the price of oil is considered a crisis. In poorer countries like India, the shortage or increasing price of fuelwood in a village could be a crisis. An urban resident in India faces frequent power cuts, especially in summer, and thus experiences an energy crisis.

Why is It Difficult to Study Energy as a Topic?

Unlike water, energy sources and energy itself come in many different forms. There are complex interactions among these forms and other aspects of the energy scene. Economic, political, environmental, and social factors add further complexity in any study of energy.

We should also note here that statistics about energy availability, supply, and consumption are notoriously unreliable. For political and economic reasons, countries, agencies, and companies often provide false figures. For the same parameter being measured, different agencies give different figures. Sometimes, the inconsistencies may be just due to uncertainty in knowledge.

There are widely varying forecasts about energy reserves. Some believe that there will be enough energy for a long time to come; many others are sure that a severe shortage is only a few years away.

What are the Sources of Energy in the World?

We cannot create new energy. We can only use the energy that was created when the universe formed approximately 14 billion years ago. The amount of energy in the universe is huge, but only a small part is available for our use. There are, however, many energy resources we can tap into.

99% of our energy comes from the sun. The commercial energy we pay for is just 1% of the energy we use. Without the sun, life on earth would not exist, since the average temperature would go down to –240°C. It is this solar energy that gets stored in plants as biomass. Plants use the energy for photosynthesis that produces food.

Primary energy is an energy form found in nature that has not been subjected to any conversion or transformation process. The main primary energy sources include the sun, the wind, potential and kinetic energy stored in water (rivers, lakes, tides, and ocean), fossil fuels (coal, oil, and natural gas), biomass, the earth's heat (geothermal energy), and radioactive minerals.

Sometimes, we use a primary source directly. For example, we can burn wood or heat water by keeping it under the sun. Most of the time, we convert primary energy into a secondary, easily usable, form of energy, called an energy carrier. For example, we convert crude oil into petrol, solar energy into electricity, and so on.

The primary sources of energy are of two types—non-renewable and renewable. Non-renewable sources are limited in supply and get depleted by use. Oil, coal, and natural gas are examples. Nuclear energy is again non-renewable since it requires material like uranium, which is limited in supply.

Renewables are replenished by natural processes at the same rate as their rate of consumption by humans. The sun and the wind are special sources of renewable and inexhaustible energy. What about biomass? It can be either renewable or non-renewable. Once upon a time, traditional biomass or fuelwood was clearly a renewable source, since people cut only dead trees and branches for burning. Now, in many areas, the rate at which people cut down trees and plants for fuel is much faster than their natural rate of regeneration. Such biomass is obviously non-renewable.

The world's primary energy comes mostly from fossil fuels like oil, coal, and natural gas. It is difficult to get precise data on supply by source, but Table 8.1 gives a rough idea.

TABLE 8.1 Global Primary Energy Supply by Source

Energy Source	% of Total Energy
Oil	31
Coal	27
Natural gas	23
Nuclear	5
Biomass (Mainly wood)	9
Solar, wind, hydro, and geothermal power	5

Which are Our Major Energy Needs?

There are three major energy end-use sectors:

Industrial sector

We use a major part of global energy for making our vehicles, appliances, clothes, and so on and also for constructing buildings. We need energy to make an item (embodied energy), to use it during its life (operation and maintenance), and to dispose it of when it is no longer useful (waste management).

Transportation sector

This is the world's fastest growing form of energy use, largely due to the rise of the private car. There are more than 600 million cars on the road now and 40–50 million more are added every year. Around the world, we are taking more trips and travelling greater distances.

Residential and commercial sector

This sector includes energy use in buildings, commerce, public services, agriculture, and fishing.

The electrical power generation sector also consumes energy. The electricity produced by this sector is consumed by other end-use sectors. There are also losses in electricity generation, transmission, and distribution of energy. The electricity consumed by the three major energy end-use sectors and electricity losses can be apportioned to the end-use sectors to calculate their total energy use.

TABLE 8.2 Global Energy Consumption by Sector

Sector	% Share of Total Energy Use
Industrial	40
Transportation	24
Residential and commercial	30
Others including agriculture	6

What is the Global Energy Consumption Pattern?

Table 8.2 gives the percentage of global energy consumed by each of the sectors (including the losses). About 39% of the primary energy goes into the production of electrical power, which in turn is used by the three sectors.

Why do we often hear about energy consumption in the US?

With just 4.6% of the world's population, the US consumes 17.8% of the total primary energy supply. China (with 20% of the world population) consumes about 22.4%, while India (with 16% of the population) accounts for just 4.7% of the total energy.

A comparison of the per capita consumption of energy for transportation shows stark differences among countries. For every 100 units of energy consumed by a US citizen for transportation, a Danish citizen uses 45 units, a Japanese 30 units, and an Indian just two units. 76% of Americans get to work by driving alone in a car, while just 5% use public transportation.

Now, many countries including India and China are striving to reach the level of prosperity of the US. If all of us start consuming energy at the same rate as US citizens, the world will experience an energy crisis!

> **Key Idea** While the US and other industrialized countries consume disproportionately large amounts of energy, countries like India and China wish to catch up with them.

What is Special about the Energy that We Produce?

The key point about energy is this: It takes energy to produce energy. For example, consider how we transform crude oil into petrol and make it available at the bunk. Every step in this process—exploring, drilling, extracting, refining, transporting, and so on—uses energy, often derived from the oil itself. Also, because of the Second Law of Thermodynamics, some energy is lost at every step.

What counts is the net energy yield**,** the usable amount of high-quality energy that we get from an energy source. The net energy yield is different for different energy sources. For example, the yield is medium-to-high for coal, medium for conventional oil, and low for nuclear power.

What Exactly are Fossil Fuels and Why are They Non-renewable?

Fossil fuels (coal, oil, and natural gas) are the remains of organisms that lived 200–500 million years ago. During that stage of the earth's evolution, large amounts of dead organic matter had collected. Over millions of years, this matter was buried under layers of sediment and was converted by heat and pressure into coal, oil, and natural gas.

Once we discovered them, we began consuming them faster and faster. From 1859 to 1969, the total production was 227 billion barrels. (In the oil industry, the barrel is the preferred unit and one barrel contains 159 litres.) 50% of this total was produced during the first 100 years, while the next 50% was extracted in just 10 years!

Today, our consumption rate is extremely high. We consume in one day what the earth took 1000 years to form! Fossil fuels continue to be formed, but at an extremely slow pace. That is why fossil fuels are non-renewable.

> **Key Idea** Our rate of oil consumption is very high and the reserves are finite.

Where does all the oil go?

The millions of cars, trucks, and buses whizzing along the world's highways consume enormous amounts of processed oil. Oil is easy to carry and hence it is the preferred fuel for transport. Petroleum is also needed for making fertilizers, pesticides, plastics, and thousands of other products.

What is the difference between conventional and unconventional oil?

Conventional oil is a category of oil that includes crude oil and natural gas liquids. Unconventional oil consists of a wider variety of liquid sources including oil sands and shale. In general, conventional oil is easier and cheaper to extract than unconventional oil. Also, the extraction of unconventional oil is environmentally very destructive.

Unconventional oil includes shale oil and oil from tar sands. Shale oil (or more correctly 'tight oil') is crude oil stored in a rock formation called shale and requires modern drilling and recovery techniques (such as horizontal drilling and hydraulic fracturing or 'fracking') to get it out. Tight oil is found in large amounts in the US and Russia.

Tar sands are a combination of clay, sand, water, and bitumen. Tar sands can be mined and processed to extract the oil-rich bitumen, which is then refined into oil. The largest deposits of tar sands are found in Canada and Venezuela.

The production of both tar-sand oil and tight oil is more complex and costlier than the refining of conventional crude oil. Further, the processing is environmentally very destructive.

What is Peak Oil?

The extraction of conventional crude oil from the earth is not a simple process. When a new oil field is tapped, oil gushes out, but not for long. We have to wait for the oil to seep slowly into the well from the surrounding rocks. For this and other reasons, the maximum annual production cannot exceed 10% of the remaining reserves. Oil production is thus subject to the phenomenon of peaking (Box 8.1).

BOX 8.1 CONCEPT: *Peak Oil*

The production of conventional oil is governed by the Hubbert Curve (Fig. 8.1), proposed by the geophysicist M. King Hubbert. In any oil field, the annual production increases until about 50% of the reserve has been extracted. The production peaks at this point and thereafter declines because it becomes increasingly more difficult and expensive to extract the remaining oil. At some point, the field is abandoned.

The Hubbert Curve is applicable also to countries and regions. The production of conventional oil in the US peaked as early as 1970 and ever since it has been declining. Most probably, the world production of conventional oil has also peaked.

'Oil peak' does not mean 'running out of oil'. There will still be half the oil left, but it will need more effort and expense to get it out.

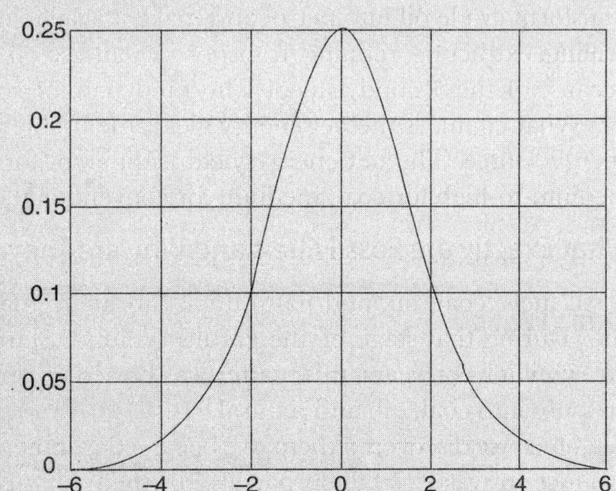

FIGURE 8.1 The Hubbert Curve for Oil Production For applications, the X and Y scales are represented by time and production scales.

Did oil production peak, as predicted by Hubbert?

The production of conventional oil did peak in the US around 1970 as predicted by Hubbert. It was also expected that at some stage, world oil production would peak, leading to massive rise in oil prices.

> **Key Idea** The term Peak Oil refers to the maximum rate of the production of conventional oil in any area under consideration, recognizing that it is a finite natural resource, subject to depletion.

A surprising thing happened, however, in recent years. The US oil production started rising again in 2009. This increase is mainly due to advancement in oil-field technology, making it possible to produce tight oil from shale. Though tight oil is costly to produce, it became economically feasible due to rising oil prices.

Many oil-industry experts now think that we are limited not by the amount of oil in the ground, but by how inventive we are about reaching new sources of fuel and how much we are willing to pay to get at it.

It is now clear that severe climate change will hit us much more and earlier than oil scarcity will. We must have the wisdom to mitigate the impact of climate change by voluntarily letting some oil stay in the ground. As of now, however, such wisdom is hard to find among governments, international agencies, and oil companies.

> **Key Idea** Climate change will hit us well before real oil scarcity arrives. The wise option is to voluntarily reduce oil extraction and use, thus reducing dangerous emissions.

Thus, the question 'How much oil do we have on earth?' has lost its significance. The more important question is 'How do we control emissions (and the resulting climate change) through policies that discourage excessive extraction and use of oil?'

Besides Climate Change, What are the Environmental Costs of Oil?

The environmental costs of oil include air pollution and damage to ecosystems in the extraction areas. Major and minor oil spills have caused untold damage to the ocean, coastal zones, and marine life. In addition, the ballast water from the oil tankers has carried deadly organisms and toxic substances to far-off lands.

What are the Factors that Determine Oil Prices?

Since we are so dependent on oil for our energy needs, any increase in oil prices affects millions of people. Transportation costs, commodity prices, and general cost of living go up.

The price of crude oil in the world market depends on a complex set of factors including supply, demand, oil reserves, political conditions (especially in the oil-producing countries), speculation, and the policies of the Organization of the Petroleum Exporting Countries (OPEC). This group currently consists of Algeria, Angola, Congo, Equatorial Guinea, Gabon, Iran, Iraq, Kuwait, Libya, Nigeria, Saudi Arabia, United Arab Emirates, and Venezuela.

Let us now turn to coal, the other major fossil fuel.

Don't We Have Huge Amounts of Coal?

At current rates of use, the world's coal reserves will probably last for another 200 years. There are, however, many problems with coal use. Coal has to be mined from underground or from the surface. Underground mines, besides being dangerous, also cause lung disease among the miners.

Among the fossil fuels, coal is most harmful to the environment. The mines create major land disturbances and the burning of coal causes severe air pollution. Coal is currently responsible for 30% of carbon dioxide emissions in the world. In addition, it releases huge amounts of radioactive particles into the atmosphere, more than a properly operating nuclear power plant. Every year, air pollution from coal kills thousands of people and causes respiratory diseases in thousands more.

Is Natural Gas a Good Option?

Natural gas, a mixture of methane, butane, ethane, and propane, is found above most oil reserves. While propane and butane are liquefied and removed as liquefied petroleum gas (LPG), methane is cleaned and pumped into pipelines.

About 40% of the total natural gas is in Russia and Kazakhstan. The available reserves are expected to last 200–300 years. Its abundance, low production cost, and low pollution make it the ideal fuel during the transition from fossil fuels to renewable sources.

Methane, however, is a deadly greenhouse gas, 20 times more potent than carbon dioxide. There is a lot of methane leakage from the natural gas systems. The long pipelines needed to carry natural gas cause leakage and accidents.

What are the Pros and Cons of Nuclear Power?

In a nuclear reactor, neutrons split the nuclei of elements such as uranium and plutonium and in the process, release energy as heat. This high-temperature heat is used to produce steam, which runs the electric turbine.

In 1953, the US President Eisenhower announced that nuclear power would be 'too cheap to meter'. At that time, it was predicted that, by the end of the century, nuclear power would be generating most of the world's electricity. This source seemed the ideal answer to the energy problem. The fuel supply seemed unlimited, the environmental impact was thought to be very low, and safety appeared to be assured. Things, however, turned out to be very different.

What went wrong with nuclear power?

The plants cost much more than the estimates, the operating costs were high, the technical problems were more intractable than expected, and the economic feasibility came to be doubted. But worse was to come.

The plants generate large amounts of deadly radioactive waste. The low-level waste must be stored safely for 100–500 years, while the high-level waste remains radioactive for a mind-boggling 240,000 years! Sixty years after the advent of nuclear power, we have no satisfactory way of storing the dangerous waste. Meanwhile more wastes are piling up in the plants. In addition, plutonium (a by-product of certain nuclear reactions) removed from old nuclear warheads has to be also stored somewhere.

Nuclear power plants as well as nuclear weapons testing have created thousands of contaminated sites, particularly in the US and the former USSR. The cost of cleaning them up will run into millions of dollars. Similarly, decommissioning an old plant costs more than the original construction!

The biggest problem, however, has been the loss of public confidence over the safety of the plants. Several minor accidents were followed by the major one in Chernobyl, which released radioactive dust over thousands of square kilometres and may ultimately cause between 100,000 and 475,000 cancer deaths. Again, in 2011, a tsunami and an earthquake hit the Fukushima Nuclear Power Complex in Japan, causing the meltdown of three out of six nuclear reactors. 100,000 residents were evacuated from the area. Ten reactors in Fukushima were permanently closed and 43 other nuclear plants in Japan stopped generating power. Clean-up operations continue in Fukushima, but radioactive leaks continued to occur.

What is the state of nuclear power?

The nuclear industry has been in decline since 2002. Nuclear power's contribution to global electricity supply has fallen from a peak of 17.5% in 1996 to 10.1% in 2020. The ageing of the world's reactor fleet is a huge problem for the nuclear industry, as is the ageing of its workforce. Every year, there are more closures than start-ups. The number of countries phasing out nuclear power is steadily growing and now includes Germany, Belgium, Taiwan, Spain, Switzerland, and South Korea.

> **Key Idea** Coal, natural gas, and nuclear power have associated problems and cannot easily replace oil.

In spite of its drawbacks, nuclear power is favoured even by some environmentalists. They feel that climate change caused by fossil fuels is a much bigger problem and, until we move away from oil and coal, nuclear power may well be our best option now.

Why can't We Move to Safer Renewable Sources?

An estimated US$200–250 billion is invested in energy-related infrastructure every year and another US$1.5 trillion is spent on energy consumption, with nearly all of this investment going to conventional energy. Thus, the world has been locked into indefinite dependence on unhealthy, unsustainable, and insecure energy structures. However, things are improving now, with rapidly increasing investments in renewables like solar and wind power.

What Kind of Energy do We Get from the Sun?

We receive from the sun a pure, non-polluting, and inexhaustible form of energy. Solar energy comes from the thermonuclear fusion reaction constantly taking place in the sun. All the radioactive and polluting by-products of the reaction are safely left behind in the sun, 150 million km away.

An enormous amount of solar energy falls on this tiny planet Earth. What we get from the sun in one month is more than the energy stored in all the fossil fuels we have. Also, using this vast amount of energy does not pollute the biosphere in any way.

Why then are we not using solar energy for all our needs?

There are difficulties in using solar energy. It is a diffuse source falling evenly over a vast area and the first problem is to collect it efficiently. The second problem is to convert it into a usable form like electricity.

You can guess what the third problem is—What do we do when it is cloudy and the sun does not shine? We must have an efficient way of storing the energy. All research in solar energy is about finding cost-effective ways of collection, conversion, and storage.

How do we convert solar energy directly into electricity?

This conversion is done by a photovoltaic cell (or PV cell), which consists of two layers of silicon. The lower layer has electrons that are easily lost and the upper one readily gains electrons. When light energy strikes the cell, it dislodges electrons from the lower layer. This sets up an electric current through the circuit carrying the electrons to the upper layer. Each cell generates only a small amount of power, but many cells, placed together on a panel, create enough power to run an appliance.

The power from a solar panel is usually stored in a battery, to which we connect the appliance. Thus, the energy is generated and stored when the sun shines on the panel and is used whenever needed. The direct current from the battery can be converted into alternating current through an inverter. You can then run normal appliances like a fan or a television.

The cost of solar energy has been dropping sharply over the last decade.

How has the solar water heater become so popular in some Indian cities?

The water heater is a simple and successful use of solar energy. It absorbs solar radiation as heat and transfers the heat to the water. An efficient design of heater uses evacuated tube collectors. The collectors are made of parallel rows of transparent glass tubes, each of which has inner and outer tubes. The vacuum in the space between the two tubes minimizes conductive and convective heat loss.

The collector is placed at a suitable angle to catch the sun's radiation. Cold water moves through a smaller pipe in the inner tube, gets heated, and collects in a tank. An electric heater element is also provided in the tank as backup for cloudy days.

Since electric water geysers are energy-guzzlers, solar heaters are a very good option. They pay back their capital cost in reasonable time. Soft bank loans are also available for buying such heaters. Some cities in India have made it mandatory for all new houses to install solar water heaters.

Why can't we directly focus the sun's rays on the material we want to heat?

Make a parabolic reflector, something like a dish antenna and place a bowl with rice at the focal point. You will soon have your lunch ready. In fact, solar cookers of this type are available in India and some hotels and community kitchens use them.

In the international community of Auroville near Pondicherry, there is a large solar bowl, 15 m in diameter. It concentrates the sun's energy on to a tube that carries a special liquid. The hot liquid in turn heats water to produce steam, which is used for cooking. The solar kitchen serves 2000 meals every day.

For home needs, there are small box-type solar cookers. Food cooked this way saves fuel, tastes better, and is good for the health. Put it out in the sun facing in the right direction and food will be ready in an hour or two, depending on the food and the intensity of sunlight.

> **Key Idea** Solar energy is renewable and non-polluting, but the challenge is to find cost-effective ways of collection, conversion, and storage of energy. Such ways are now becoming available.

What about Tapping Wind Energy?

If you travel from Nagercoil to Kanyakumari in South India, you will see hundreds of sleek-looking windmills slowly rotating and generating electricity. India is now a leading player in the wind energy scene. Our installed wind energy capacity increased from 11 GW in 2009 to 42 GW in 2022. China's capacity is 328 GW.

Wind energy produces electricity at low cost, the capital costs are also moderate, and there are no emissions. Wind farms can be quickly set up and easily expanded.

Where is the catch?

Obviously, you need steady winds of a certain velocity and not every place is suitable. You will also need some form of backup for windless days. It is a case of high land use, though attempts have been made to use the space below the windmills for agriculture or grazing. There is some noise pollution and the monotonous view of hundreds of windmills is visual pollution. In addition, there is a fear that windmills could interfere with the flight of migratory birds.

Is Hydropower a Good Alternative?

20% of the world's electricity comes from hydropower. In order to get sizable amount of power, we need a high dam on a river with a large reservoir. The potential energy of the water falling from a height runs the turbine.

Hydropower has several advantages. The cost of generation is low and there are no emissions. The reservoir can provide water for irrigation round the year and can also be used for fishing and recreation. It also gives drinking water to towns and cities.

What is the bad news about hydropower?

Dams cost a lot of money and take years to build. Most of the suitable rivers of the world have already been dammed and it is now difficult to find new spots. The reservoir drowns large areas of farmland, wildlife habitats, and places of historical and cultural importance. An example is Tehri town, which disappeared under the waters of a dam.

Large dams also cause large-scale displacement of local (often tribal) communities. The people lose their lands and become environmental refugees. Often, compensation for the lost land is meagre (and not even paid on time) and resettlement is never satisfactory. Dams impede the migration of fish along the river and reduce the silt flowing downstream. In fact, the sediments pile up against the dam and reduce its useful life. There is a worldwide movement against the building of large dams. We will return to this issue in Chapter 17.

> **Key Idea**
> Hydropower depends on dams, which cause ecological damage and displacement of people.

Micro hydropower, or small-scale hydropower, is a viable alternative where flowing water is available. We can generate power by diverting the flow into a turbine. Micro hydropower systems usually generate up to 100 KW of electricity. Micro hydropower is eco-friendly because unlike large-scale hydropower, it does not attempt to interfere significantly with river flows. In some hilly areas in India where electricity does not reach, micro hydropower has been tried.

What about Hydrogen as a Fuel?

Many experts believe that, as we run out of fossil fuels, we will move towards using the element hydrogen as the main fuel to run the world's economy. When hydrogen burns and gives us energy, it combines with oxygen to produce water vapour. In this process, there is no air pollution or emission of carbon dioxide.

This is good news again! What are we waiting for?

There is some bad news too. Hydrogen is not available in a free state: it is locked up in water and in compounds like petrol and methane. We need energy and an effective method to get the hydrogen out. We can split water by heat or by a process called electrolysis to get hydrogen. We can also get it from fuels like petrol, natural gas, and methanol. Thus, the first problem is one of collection.

As in the case of solar energy, we have the problem of storage too. Hydrogen is highly explosive and if it is stored as compressed gas, the tank will be large, heavy, and costly. Only large buses and trucks can hold the tanks. If we store it as a liquid, we need very low temperatures and this will require energy. Another method being tried out is storage as solid metal hydride. Here again, energy is needed to release the hydrogen when we want it.

What about fuel cells that are often in the news?

A fuel cell is so called because it is an electrochemical unit like a battery. The fuel cell electrochemically generates electricity from hydrogen and oxygen. In the process, hydrogen combines with oxygen to produce water vapour. Thus there is no pollution and it runs continuously as long as there is input.

Unlike a battery, the fuel cell draws its input (hydrogen and oxygen) from outside. Again, a battery requires recharging, but the fuel cell does not. Finally, there is no toxic output when a fuel cell is discarded.

Fuel cells were developed as far back as 1960 for space applications. The progress since then has, however, been slow. There are now experimental buses and cars running on fuel cells, but they are very expensive. Automobile companies like Daimler-Chrysler, Honda, and General Motors have made prototype fuel-cell cars and buses.

What are the problems with using hydrogen?

> **Key Idea**
> Renewable sources such as solar energy, wind power, hydrogen, and hydropower all have limitations.

First, it takes energy to produce hydrogen. Energy produced from a fuel cell is always less than the energy used to produce hydrogen. Thus, hydrogen can only be thought of as an energy carrier or a means of storage useful in some applications.

Second, if this input energy comes from fossil fuels, there will be environmental effects. Third, the situation is even worse, if we produce the hydrogen from fossil fuels themselves. Finally, we have not fully solved the problem of storing hydrogen.

Where is the hydrogen fuel then?

We must find first cost-effective ways of producing hydrogen from water using renewable energy like solar energy. We should solve all the storage problems too. In the best scenario, we would be using electrical and thermal energy produced by renewable sources like solar and incorporate hydrogen as the fuel for transport.

What is Bioenergy?

Bioenergy is energy extracted from biomass, which is organic matter formed using solar energy. The oldest, and still the most common, form of bioenergy is that obtained by burning fuelwood or firewood. Now, however, we derive energy from other forms of biomass:

- Plants
- Residues from agriculture or forestry
- Municipal and industrial waste

Biofuels: Biofuels are obtained by converting biomass into liquid fuels for transportation:

- Bio-Diesel: This is produced from oils or fats using a chemical process. The raw material includes animal fats, vegetable oils, soy, rapeseed, jatropha, mahua, mustard, flax, sunflower, palm oil, hemp, *Pongamia pinnata,* and algae. When burned, bio-diesel produces very little emission.
- Bio-Ethanol: This is the most common biofuel and is produced by fermentation of sugars derived from wheat, corn, sugar beets, sugar cane, molasses, and any sugar or starch that alcoholic beverages are made from. Ethanol can be used in petrol engines as a replacement for petrol.

Biogas: This is produced by the process of anaerobic digestion of organic material such as cow dung and vegetable waste. Biogas is primarily a mixture of methane (60%–80%) and carbon dioxide (40%–20%). The solid by-product can be used as a biofuel or a fertilizer.

Bioproducts: Converting biomass into chemicals for making products, which are typically made from petroleum.

Bioenergy has the following advantages:

- Biomass is renewable since nature keeps on producing biomass.
- It is plentiful wherever there are agricultural crops and forestry;
- It converts waste into useful and valuable energy.
- Burning biomass can be taken to have zero net emissions, since the carbon dioxide given off during combustion is absorbed by the growth of the next crop of biomass. Thus, biofuels provide an alternative to less sustainable fuels.
- Wasteland can be used to grow crops for biomass.
- Unlike wind, wave, and solar energy, biomass can be easily stored, transported, and utilized at any time.
- It is a decentralized form of energy and helps the local economy.
- Biofuels significantly reduce or eliminate air pollution.
- It can help to stabilize soils, improve soil fertility, and reduce erosion.

Bioenergy has also some drawbacks:

- There is concern about shifting land from food crops to biofuel plants. Many people believe that land and water resources used for biomass crops would be better dedicated to food production.
- Bioenergy is generally a more expensive energy source compared to fossil fuels because it requires more fuel to produce the same amount of energy. There is also the cost of harvesting, extracting, transporting, and handling biomass.

- Bioenergy uses a lot of wood from natural forests which can lead to deforestation, and if wood is not fully burnt it can release soot-like particles that may cause widespread air pollution.
- Environmentalists believe that industrial-scale bioenergy production would increase greenhouse gas emissions.

How Can We Harness Energy from Ocean Waves?

Wave energy systems use the up-and-down motion of waves to generate electricity. The energy in waves comes from the movement of the ocean and the changing heights and speed of the swells. An enormous amount of kinetic energy is contained in waves.

Solar energy creates winds, which in turn gives its energy to waves. Waves gather, store, and transmit this energy thousands of kilometres with little loss. Generally, extreme latitudes and west coasts of continents are suitable places for tapping wave energy.

Some of the experimental methods for converting wave energy into electricity:

- Float or buoy systems that use the rise and fall of ocean swells to drive hydraulic pumps.
- Oscillating water column devices in which, a column fills with water as the wave rises and empties as it descends. In the process, air inside the column is compressed and heats up, creating energy the way a piston does.

On the positive side, wave energy:

- will be available as long the sun exists.
- varies in intensity but is available all the time.
- contains roughly 1000 times the kinetic energy of wind. Compared to wind farms, wave energy systems can produce the same power in much smaller space and with smaller equipment.
- does not create any pollution.

The technologies, however, are complex, not fully proven, and are also expensive. Experimental installations have been set up in many countries including Scotland, Portugal, Norway, US, China, Japan, and Australia. An Indian experiment off the coast of Kerala failed.

What is Tidal Energy?

Tidal energy is produced by the surge of ocean waters during the rise and fall of tides. This is possible only in areas where there is a significant difference in height between high tide and low tide.

There are currently three different ways to get tidal energy:

- Tidal stream: A tidal stream is a fast-flowing body of water created by tides. Turbines, placed in the tidal streams, generate electricity.
- Barrage: A barrage is a low dam constructed across the tidal flow of water. The water spills over the top of the barrage and creates a reservoir. Then the water is released through turbines, which generate power. The process is like that of generating hydropower, but the scale is small.
- Tidal lagoon: A tidal lagoon is a body of ocean water that is partly enclosed by a natural or manmade barrier. Tidal lagoons might also be estuaries and have freshwater emptying into them. The turbines work as the lagoon fills up and empties out. The process is like that of the barrage, but tidal lagoons can be constructed along the natural coastline. A tidal lagoon power plant could also generate continuous power.

The technology of tidal power is yet to develop. There are very few commercial tidal power plants in the world.

What is Ocean Thermal Energy Conversion (OTEC)?

OTEC uses the difference in temperature between the ocean surface water and the colder deep ocean water. Power plants can be built that use this difference in temperature to make energy. A difference of at least 30 degrees Celsius is needed between the warmer surface water and the colder deep ocean water. The cold ocean water can also be used to cooling buildings, and desalinated water is often a by-product.

What is Geothermal Energy?

Geothermal energy is the heat contained within the earth. The term 'geothermal energy' is used nowadays to refer to that part of the earth's heat that can be recovered by us. Since ancient times, people knew from volcanoes and hot water springs that there was heat below the ground. Science now tells us that there is immense heat inside the earth. We can tap the thermal energy contained in the rock and fluid (that fills the fractures and pores within the rock) in the earth's crust.

There are three ways of using geothermal energy:

- Power generation: The steam that comes out of the well drives a turbine that generates electricity.
- Direct use for heating: The heat in the water is used directly (without a heat pump or power plant) for heating buildings, industrial processes, greenhouses, aquaculture, and resorts.
- Heat pumps: Water is circulated in a closed system installed horizontally or vertically in the ground adjacent to or even beneath a building. In winter, the water picks up the geothermal heat and transfers it to the building. In summer, the process is reversed, and the water carries the heat from the building to the ground.

In 2020, the global geothermal capacity was 14 GW spread over 26 countries. There are plans to increase the capacity to 26 GW. The top five countries in geothermal power operating capacity in 2020 were the US, Indonesia, the Philippines, Turkey, New Zealand, and Mexico.

Advantages of geothermal power stations:

- Pollution free: Few chemicals and pollutants feature in geothermal electricity production.
- Highly Efficient.
- Cost Effective: Geothermal power stations are relatively small, less complex, and hence highly cost effective.
- Perennial source: Geothermal activity in a particular area is likely to be available for anywhere between 5000 and 1,000,000 years.
- Always available: The energy source can provide continuous electricity production whatever the weather.
- Very quiet operation.

Disadvantages of geothermal power stations:

- Limited availability: The availability of geothermal energy that can feed geothermal power stations is limited. This intense energy source is only available in countries where geothermal activity is at its peak, mainly tectonic/volcanic regions such as Iceland.
- Initial high investment: Geological surveys and transporting equipment to places of sufficient geothermal activity cost money.
- Potential for harmful gas: Geothermal power stations could release toxic gases that exist deep beneath the ground.
- Localised supply: We cannot extract, store, and transport this energy source to other places as we do with fossil fuels. We can only generate electricity and supply it to the grid.

- Stoppage of steam: Geothermal power stations have the potential to cool the rocks beneath them buried deep under the ground. If the rocks are cooled via too much water flowing into the well, they will no longer be able to produce the steam required to turn a generator.

Given All the Limits and Difficulties, are We Using Energy Efficiently?

Increasing the efficiency of energy use will be equivalent to finding free sources of energy. There is tremendous scope for increasing energy efficiency in all our activities.

The internal combustion engine (I.C. Engine) that runs our automobiles is another device that wastes 80% of the input energy. Driven by the first oil crisis, the fuel efficiency of American cars gradually increased between 1973 and 1985. Since then, however, it has levelled off primarily because of the consumer craze for the so-called sport utility vehicle (SUV), minivan, etc. and because of the availability of cheap oil.

Makers like Toyota and Honda have introduced hybrid electric cars with much higher fuel efficiency. They run on petrol and a battery. The battery is kept charged by the petrol engine and an electric motor provides energy for acceleration and hill climbing. When brakes are applied, part of the heat generated is used to charge the battery. Fully electric cars are now being produced in a big way. Tesla is a company that produces only electric cars.

Whenever we use energy, some waste is inevitable. However, there is a large amount of avoidable waste in energy use. One estimate is that we waste more than 40% of commercial energy we buy. Examples are vehicles and furnaces that waste fuel and poorly designed buildings that use up huge amounts of energy for heating and cooling. There is also the huge inefficiency of power stations and big transmission losses.

Key Idea Our first task is to use energy very efficiently.

Technology helps in increasing the efficiency of most appliances by 50% or more. As the demand for energy-efficient appliances increase, the prices will also come down. We must always consider the lifecycle cost of devices, that is, the total of the initial cost and the operating costs over the lifetime of the device. Such an approach will make us take better decisions that will save cost and energy.

How is the Energy Scene in India?

India is the fourth largest energy consumer in the world after China, the US, and Russia. However, our per capita energy consumption is 615 units (kg of oil equivalent), compared to 6800 units in the US and 2030 units in China.

TABLE 8.3 Total Energy Consumption in India by Source (2021)

Energy source	%
Coal	57.0
Oil	27.0
Natural gas	6.3
Hydropower	4.3
Nuclear	1.1
Wind	1.8
Solar	1.8
Other renewables	1.4

Coal is India's primary source of energy. The country is the third largest global consumer of coal and has the fifth largest coal reserves in the world. We have very little oil and hence we import 83% of our crude oil needs. We are the world's fourth largest oil importer after China, Japan, and the US. Our annual oil import cost is of the order of US$140 billion. The government is forced to subsidize the price of energy products, but is also trying to reduce such subsidies. Table 8.3 gives India's total energy consumption by source.

In India, about one-third of the energy comes from non-commercial sources. The rural population depends heavily on fuelwood, dung, and animal waste. In the urban areas, there are large numbers of non-motorized vehicles like bicycles, rickshaws, handcarts, and animal carts.

About 25% of the population (over 300 million people) lack basic access to electricity, while electrified areas suffer from constant electricity blackouts.

We have major programmes for renewable energy. The government is promoting wind farms, solar energy, hydropower, as well as waste-to-energy projects.

Several wind farms have been set up in South India. Solar pumps, water-heaters, and lighting systems are widely available, and their costs are coming down rapidly.

Are we trying to conserve energy?

It is clear that we must conserve energy by improving efficiency at each of the stages: production, transmission, and utilization. According to estimates, we can save up to 40% of energy in India through conservation. The Energy Conservation Act (2001) specifies energy standards and promotes energy audits.

The Bureau of Energy Efficiency (BEE) is the agency that implements the Act. Among other activities, BEE awards star ratings to brands of appliances such as fluorescent lamps, refrigerators, and air conditioners. Each tested brand gets a rating of one star (least energy efficient) to five stars (most energy efficient). The voluntary scheme will be made compulsory later.

What does It All Amount to?

We are unlikely to find some magical source of energy that would let us keep increasing our energy use or even maintain the current usage levels indefinitely. Once again, we face the same hurdle: There is a natural limit to the amount of resources on this planet. When we overstep that limit, we will inevitably face an insurmountable hurdle. We can survive only if we use energy much more efficiently and reduce our consumption levels. As of now, there is no sign of this happening.

Meanwhile, our intensive energy use is leading to global warming and climate change. We will discuss these topics in Chapters 14 and 15.

The challenge is to provide sustainable energy for all—energy that is accessible, clean, and more efficient. The UN General Assembly has declared the period 2014–2024 as the Decade of Sustainable Energy for All, underscoring the importance of energy issues for sustainable development (Box 8.2).

BOX 8.2 *UN Decade of Sustainable Energy for All (2014–2024)*

The UN invites everyone to join the Sustainable Energy for All effort. The Decade of Sustainable Energy offers a unique opportunity to

- take action and seek new projects and partnerships. The number of possibilities in the field of sustainable energy is limitless. The Decade can be your incentive to explore these possibilities and come together with new partners and create new opportunities for yourself and others.
- showcase success stories, best practices, lessons learned, commitments, and achievements. There is no lack of current initiatives, projects, and transformations that have the potential to inspire others to follow suit.
- help shape the Decade to be as effective as possible—by adding your perspective, you can bring in some good ideas that should be explored during the Decade. Sustainable energy has connections to themes as important as gender equality, health, water, and food, as well as many other development enablers.
- spread the word on the importance of Sustainable Energy for All and the Decade. You may be responsible for an upcoming event or network where highlighting of the Decade would fit in nicely. Let people know about the importance of sustainable energy for all, the challenges that exist, and not least the opportunities it entails.

Ending on a Hopeful Note: Positive Stories

- An Indian initiative to bring solar lanterns to the poor people in several countries (Box 8.3)
- A remarkably simple idea for providing free lighting in the dark slums of the world (Box 8.4)

BOX 8.3 INSPIRATION: *The Story of a Solar Campaign—Lighting a Billion Lives*

The Energy and Resources Institute (TERI), New Delhi, has launched an initiative called 'Lighting a Billion Lives' (LaBL)—a campaign to promote the use of solar lighting devices by the poor.

Over 1.6 billion people in the world lack access to electricity and roughly 25% of them are in India. These people are forced to light their homes with kerosene lamps, dung cakes, firewood, and crop residue. While the consequent indoor pollution causes severe health problems and even death, poor lighting has an impact on children's education and general safety.

The LaBL campaign plans to bring solar light into the lives of one billion rural people. The distribution and servicing of solar lanterns is done by local entrepreneurs trained by TERI in association with its grassroots level (government and NGO) partners. These local entrepreneurs are village youth, women, elders, or teachers. The lanterns are supplied by product partners.

The rural entrepreneurs are selected and trained to manage and run central solar lantern charging/distribution centres from where people rent the lanterns for a reasonable fee. The entrepreneurs are responsible for generating awareness, finding customers, maintaining the solar lanterns, and operating the charging stations. Thus apart from providing reliable and ensured lighting to households at an affordable rate, the campaign also facilitates entrepreneurial development among rural communities.

The campaign is being implemented according to a necessity index that has been developed for each state in India. Funds to the tune of ₹230 billion need to be raised for providing lanterns to 65 million rural households in India. But this amount is less than half of the total implied subsidy on kerosene consumption in the country. Further, each solar lantern saves 40–60 litres of kerosene per year, leading to a total saving of ₹100 billion burned each year in kerosene and wick lamps. And, of course, indoor pollution is avoided and children study better.

Thousands of lanterns are already in use in a number of states in India. The campaign is also spreading its light across Africa, South Asia, and Southeast Asia. Besides providing solar lighting to villages in African countries, the LaBL campaign is also expanding through local partnerships, beginning with two solar charging stations in Sierra Leone. Also, under the Asian Development Bank's Lighting for All initiative, LaBL is poised to bring modern lighting to 50 million people in Asia-Pacific.

BOX 8.4 INSPIRATION: *Litre of Light—Lighting the Slums with Zero Energy*

Millions of plastic bottles are thrown away every day in the world. Millions of people live in dark homes in the slums of the world. The global Liter of Light project uses discarded bottles to bring natural light into poor homes.

Take a discarded 1.5 litre bottle and fill it up with water and a little bleach. Push the bottle through a steel sheet that serves as a metal lock to prevent it from slipping. Then embed the unit into a corrugated iron roof. Leave a small part of the bottle outside and let the rest of it protrude into the house. Put a sealant around the hole made in the roof to keep it weather-proof. When the sun is out, the bottle lights up the whole room.

The refractive properties of water ensure that the light from the sun that reaches the inside of the bottle becomes omni-directional, mimicking an electric light bulb and emitting the same amount of light as a 40–60 W incandescent bulb, depending on the amount of solar radiation falling on the roof. Adding bleach to the water prevents it from turning green with algae and ensures a high quality light keeping the water clear for a longer time. Once installed, the bottle will last about five years before being replaced.

The use of plastic bottles to provide indoor lighting from daylight was developed by Alfredo Moser of Brazil and Suryaan Nadeen of New Zealand. Illac Diaz developed the idea as a social enterprise in the Philippines under the My Shelter Foundation in April 2011. The bottle bulbs were assembled and installed by local people, who earned a small income for their work. Within months, 15,000 solar bottle bulbs were installed in 20 cities and provinces around the Philippines.

MyShelter Foundation also established a training centre that conducts workshops with youth, business companies, and other groups who are interested in volunteering their time to build lights in their communities. The idea spread to 18 countries and, in less than a year, over 200,000 bottle bulbs were installed in communities around the world. Liter of Light has a goal to light up one million homes by the end of 2015.

The simple bottle bulb has many positive environmental and social impacts: It reuses thousands of discarded bottles, avoids the use of fossil fuels like kerosene and gas, and reduces emissions, while providing much-needed light as well as employment for the poor.

REVIEW: A SUMMARY OF THE KEY POINTS

- The many forms of energy and energy sources, their complex interactions, as well as economic, political, environmental, and social factors make it difficult to study the topic of energy.
- We need energy for the industrial, transport, residential, and commercial sectors.
- There are renewable and non-renewable sources of primary energy.
- There is a huge disparity in energy needs, availability, and consumption between the rich and the poor of the world.
- It takes energy to produce energy and what counts is the net energy yield.
- Our rate of oil consumption is very high and the reserves are finite.
- Peak Oil refers to the maximum rate of the production of conventional oil in any area under consideration, recognizing that it is a finite natural resource.
- Climate change will hit us well before real oil scarcity arrives and we must cut oil consumption and reduce emissions.
- Almost all sources of energy have their limits and problems.
- We must use the most sustainable, least polluting energy sources with high efficiency.

EXERCISES

Objective-type questions

For each question below, choose the best answer out of the given choices:

1. Which source provides the maximum percentage of energy to the people of India?
   (a) Fuelwood or firewood
   (b) LPG
   (c) Animal dung
   (d) Electricity
2. Which of the following statements is true with regard to global energy?
   (a) We know clearly how much of reserve energy we have.
   (b) Industrialized countries consume a huge part of the total energy.
   (c) Energy supply is evenly distributed across all countries and within countries.
   (d) Fuelwood is easily available for the poor people in the developing countries.
3. Which is the world's fastest growing form of energy use?
   (a) Manufacturing
   (b) Buildings
   (c) Transport
   (d) Home consumption
4. Which of the following statements is **not true** with regard to fossil fuels?
   (a) We consume as much fossil fuel in one day as what the earth took one thousand years to form.
   (b) Fossil fuels are non-renewable sources of energy.
   (c) The burning of fossil fuels causes environmental damage.
   (d) Fossil fuels continue to be formed at a rapid pace.
5. Which of the following is a renewable energy source?
   (a) Natural gas
   (b) Coal
   (c) Wind
   (d) Uranium
6. Which of the following is **not** a problem with regard to solar energy?
   (a) Efficient collection of energy
   (b) Conversion of energy into electricity
   (c) Availability as a renewable source
   (d) Storage of energy

7. Which of the following is **not** a problem with regard to hydropower?
   (a) It is a renewable source.
   (b) People have to move to other places.
   (c) Dams submerge large areas.
   (d) Dams get silted up.
8. What is the main problem in using hydrogen as fuel?
   (a) The burning of hydrogen produces no emissions.
   (b) The burning of hydrogen produces water.
   (c) Hydrogen can be produced from water.
   (d) It takes energy to produce hydrogen.

Short-answer questions

1. What is the main source of energy for this planet and how does it give us the energy?
2. Solar energy and fuelwood are both renewables. But what is the essential difference between them as energy sources?
3. List the various forms of primary energy and give the proportion of each in the total supply.
4. Why are fossil fuels non-renewable?
5. Explain the Hubbert Curve and the concept of peaking of oil.
6. What is the difference between conventional and unconventional oil?
7. Compare the advantages and disadvantages of oil, coal, and natural gas as energy sources.
8. What are the special problems of nuclear power?
9. How is solar energy converted to electrical power and what are the problems in this regard?
10. What are the prospects of getting more hydropower?
11. What are the hurdles in using hydrogen as a fuel?
12. How can we improve energy efficiency?
13. Describe the energy scene in India about demand and supply.
14. Give a short account of each of the following renewable energy sources: Bioenergy, geothermal energy, OTEC, tidal energy, wave energy, wind energy.

Long-answer questions

1. Describe the fuelwood situation in the developing countries, emphasizing the relationship between poverty and environment.
2. Describe the different scenarios with respect to the availability of oil. Which scenario appears reasonable to you and why?
3. Explain how almost every source of energy has its limits.
4. Consider the statement—It takes energy to produce energy. Why is it correct and what does it mean to us?

Think critically: Deeper question for reflection and discussion

Given that almost every source of energy has its limits and problems, what should be our attitude to using energy in this world?

ENJOY AND EDUCATE YOURSELF

1. Watch the movie *Syriana* (2005), starring George Clooney and Christopher Plummer. The film explains in an entertaining manner how things really are when it comes to oil, the Middle East, and the US policy.
2. Relax with the novel *Oil Dusk: A Peak Oil Story* by John M. Cape and Laura Buckner.

ACCESS THE OUP ONLINE RESOURCE CENTRE FOR MORE

- The stories of focus on renewable energy in Denmark and Iceland.
- Additional text and other recommended references, websites, and films.

UNIT 3

Biodiversity and Its Conservation

9 Introduction to Biodiversity

Different I am, so unusual my life,
my death too will surprise you
like untimely rain.

Krishna Kalamb,
Poet-farmer of Maharashtra,
whose debts drove him to commit suicide

MAIN QUESTIONS ADDRESSED

- What is the meaning of biological diversity?
- What are the services provided to us by ecosystems and their biodiversity?
- What is the state of global biodiversity?
- What are the causes and impacts of the severe loss of biodiversity?

KEYWORDS AND PHRASES

background extinction, biological diversity, biological extinction, ecological extinction, ecosystem diversity, endangered species, farmer suicide, genetic diversity, habitat fragmentation, indicator species, keystone species, mass extinction, sentinel species, species diversity, threatened species, vulnerable species

LEAD STORY

THE STORY OF THE INDIAN SMALL FARMER: SEEDS OF PLENTY OR SEEDS OF SUICIDE?

Krishna Kalamb, Gosavi Pawar, Mahendra Reddy, Adinarayana—The names of just a few of the 300,000 Indian farmers who committed suicide since 1995. In most cases, an intolerable debt burden drove them to take their lives. They had all borrowed money for the inputs in their farming—seeds, fertilizers, and pesticides.

Until about the middle of the twentieth century, such small farmers in India needed very little input from outside. They grew a variety of crops and kept aside some part of the harvest as seeds for the next year. They used organic manure and natural pesticides. Even if one crop failed, there were others to save the farmer from ruin.

Life was not easy, but the farmers were not in deep crisis either. However, India's population was growing and food was being imported.

Man 1: *"Let us go! I have given him our bank's final notice for the repayment of the loan he took."*

This was also the problem with many poor countries of the world.

The solution came in the form of the Green Revolution with the promise of plenty. The key element was new seeds called high-yielding varieties (HYVs). Developed first in Mexico and then taken to many countries, the new seeds increased the yield per hectare to very high levels.

It was certainly a revolution in agriculture, but it came as a whole package. The HYVs needed large inputs of fertilizers, pesticides, and water. Further, the small number of laboratory-developed HYVs replaced the very large number of traditional varieties cultivated by farmers.

With the active encouragement of the government and international agencies, the Green Revolution was enthusiastically adopted in India. Food production increased and the country became self-sufficient.

The Green Revolution, however, changed the traditional agricultural practices. The farmers had to buy every year new seeds, fertilizers, and pesticides. Soon, the traditional varieties disappeared, leaving just a few HYVs. In other words, diversity gave place to uniformity. The seeds, however, came from the National Seeds Corporation or other certified government agencies.

From about 1998, another major change occurred with the entry into India of the international seed companies. They need mass markets and they aggressively promote the use of a small number of varieties.

The small farmer is now in the clutches of a new breed of entrepreneurs. They provide all the inputs (seeds, fertilizers, and pesticides) at high prices, give credit at very high interest rates, and buy the crops at low prices. A crop failure due to spurious or low quality seeds, pest attack, or drought is often the last straw. The farmer is perpetually in debt and often the only escape is through suicide.

CLIMATE CHANGE AND BIODIVERSITY

Biodiversity is affected by climate change, but biodiversity, through the ecosystem services it supports, also makes an important contribution to both climate-change mitigation and adaptation.

What is the basic cause of the farmers' problems?

The Green Revolution increased the yields, but created problems like soil degradation, falling productivity over time, increasing use of fertilizers, greater proneness to diseases, and scarcity of water. It has also reduced drastically the diversity of plants being grown. In fact, due to government policies, the farmer has lost control over what seeds to plant and how to get them.

In Chapter 7, we discussed the crisis on food and agriculture. In this chapter and the next, we will cover the importance of biological diversity for the health of the planet and our well-being.

What is Biodiversity?

Biodiversity or biological diversity refers to the numbers, variety, and variability of living organisms and ecosystems. The term includes all the terrestrial, marine, and other aquatic organisms. It also covers diversity within species, between species, as well as the variation among ecosystems. It is concerned also with their complex ecological interrelationships.

What are the important types of biodiversity?

Species diversity refers to the number of plant and animal species present in a community or an ecosystem. It varies a great deal between ecosystems. For example, species diversity is very high in tropical rainforests and coral reefs and low in isolated islands. You will find a large number of different plants and animals in an ecosystem with high diversity.

Key Idea
Biodiversity is the earth's primary life support system and is a precondition for human survival.

Genetic diversity is the variety in the genetic makeup among individuals within a species. Ecosystem diversity is the variety of habitats found in an area. It is the variety of forests, deserts, grasslands, aquatic ecosystems, etc. that occur in the area.

The following factors determine the degree of diversity in an ecosystem or community:

- Habitat stress: Diversity is low in habitats under any stress like harsh climate or pollution.
- Geographical isolation: Diversity is less in isolated regions like an island. If a species in an island disappears due to random events, it cannot be easily replaced. Organisms from the mainland have difficulties in reaching and colonizing the island.
- Dominance by one species: The dominant species consumes a disproportionate share of the resources. This does not allow many species to evolve and flourish.
- Availability of ecological niches: A complex community offers a greater variety of niches than a simple community and promotes greater diversity.
- Edge Effect: We saw in Chapter 2 how there is always greater diversity in ecotones or transition areas between ecosystems.
- Geological history: Old and stable ecosystems like rain forests that have not experienced many changes have high diversity. An ecosystem like the Arctic has undergone many changes and this does not allow many species to establish themselves.

What is the Value of Biodiversity and Ecosystems in General?

Biodiversity is an integral part of the larger ecosystems of the earth. These ecosystems provide us with services that are of immense value (Chapter 2). Life on earth, including that of human beings, would be impossible without these services. We are just beginning to appreciate their importance.

Can we at all put a monetary value on life and nature?

We saw in Chapter 2 that the ecosystem services were worth more than US$36 trillion per year. Some critics feel that placing a monetary value on ecosystem services is misleading and dangerous. They are infinitely valuable, since they are irreplaceable. Just being close to nature gives many of us enjoyment and spiritual solace. Writers, poets, artists, and composers derive inspiration from nature for their creative work.

Consider the rainbow in the sky, the sun rising from the ocean, the dance of whales, the grace of the deer, the shimmering oasis in the desert, or the snows on the mountain. What price can you put on these?

Finally, we can consider that biodiversity has an intrinsic or ethical value. In this view, every species has a value and role in nature. It has a right to exist, whether or not it is known to be useful to humans. In fact, since humans have so much power over nature, they should perhaps conserve all species. The final ethical argument is that all life is sacred and must be protected.

How Many Species are There in This World?

We do not know exactly how many species inhabit this earth. Estimates range from 4 million to 100 million. The best guess is 10–14 million. Most of the species in the world are insects and microorganisms not visible to the naked eye.

How many species have been identified and named?

So far about 1.8 million species (not including bacteria) have been identified, named, and catalogued. These include 270,000 plant species, 45,000 vertebrates, and 950,000 insects. Roughly 10,000 new species are identified every year.

Overall, our knowledge of species, biomes, and ecosystems is poor. Even out of the identified (1.8 million) species, only a third have been studied and described to some level. Species are considered 'described' when they have been given a two-part Latin name and have had a description published in a scientific journal. Even among the described species, we understand the exact roles and interactions of just a small number of species.

Indigenous knowledge of biodiversity is increasingly recognized as being very important. What was dismissed as primitive knowledge and quackery is now seen as a valuable storehouse of biodiversity knowledge. In agriculture, farmers have experimented over hundreds of years to develop local crop varieties and animal breeds best suited to the local conditions.

In medicine, local communities and medicine men in the villages possess a tremendous amount of knowledge about the uses of herbs and other plants in curing illnesses. In many cases, indigenous knowledge is far ahead of what scientists know. There are initiatives now to use such knowledge and compensate the community (Chapter 10, Box 10.1).

Key Idea Our knowledge of biodiversity is extremely limited.

TABLE 9.1 The 19 Megadiversity Countries of the World

1. Australia	8. Ethiopia	15. Peru
2. Brazil	9. India	16. Philippines
3. Cameroon	10. Indonesia	17. South Africa
4. China	11. Madagascar	18. Venezuela
5. Colombia	12. Malaysia	19. Zaire
6. Costa Rica	13. Mexico	
7. Ecuador	14. Myanmar	

TABLE 9.2 Origins of Food Plants

Plant	Place of origin
Potato	Andes, South America
Wheat	Turkey and Afghanistan
Bean	Central America
Coffee	Ethiopia
Soya, cucumber, orange	China
Rice	India

Where is All the Biodiversity?

The vast majority of all species are in the developing countries. 50–75% of all species are to be found in the tropical moist forests that account for just 6% of the land area. A handful of soil in a tropical forest contains hundreds of species and more than a million individual organisms.

In the tropics and the sub-tropics, where we also find most of the developing countries, there was always evolutionary activity giving rise to a rich biodiversity. Biodiversity is less in the colder Northern regions because the recurrent ice ages there slowed down the proliferation of life forms.

The 19 most biodiverse nations of the world are listed in Table 9.1.

Almost all the plants eaten today in Europe originated in the developing countries (Table 9.2). The genetic diversity needed to maintain the world agricultural system is mainly in these places. Most of the medicinal plants too are also found only in the developing countries.

What about Aquatic Biodiversity?

We know very little about aquatic biodiversity, since we have explored and mapped less than 5% of the ocean. Corals reefs, estuaries, and the deep-ocean floor contain enormous amount of biodiversity. The deep ocean species are mostly microbes living under the sea floor in a dark world without oxygen. Biodiversity is high near the coasts too, thanks to a variety of producers, habitats, and nursery areas.

What is Meant by the Extinction of Species?

By extinction, we mean the complete disappearance of a species, that is, not a single member of the extinct species is found on earth. It is an irreversible loss and is called biological extinction.

Before a species goes biologically extinct, it goes through stages of local and ecological extinction. Local extinction means that the species is no longer found in the area it once inhabited. It is, however, present elsewhere in the world. Ecological extinction means that so few members are left that the species can no longer play its normal ecological role in the community.

Extinction is the ultimate fate of all species. Since multi-cellular organisms evolved on earth 570 million years ago, about 30 billion species have lived on this planet. Today, there are only about 14 million of them. This means that 99.9% of all species that ever lived are extinct!

Over the life of the earth, environmental conditions have been changing, gradually or rapidly. Large-scale movement of the continents and climate change are examples. When such changes occur, the affected species must adapt itself, move to a more favourable area, or become extinct.

There are mainly two ways in which species become biologically extinct. Background extinction refers to the gradual disappearance of species due to changes in local environmental conditions. Thus, a process of natural and low-level extinction goes on continuously.

> **Key Idea** 99.9% of all species that ever lived are now extinct.

The rate of background extinction has been generally uniform over long geological periods. On occasions, however, a second type, called a mass extinction, has occurred on earth.

What is meant by mass extinction?

Mass extinction is characterized by a rate of disappearance significantly higher than the background extinction. It is often a global, catastrophic event, with more than 65% of all species becoming extinct over some millions of years. This is a brief period in geological terms, compared to 4.6 billion years the earth has existed.

Scientists believe that there have been five mass extinctions over the past 500 million years. In each case, the character of ecological communities changed dramatically. After each such extinction, it took 20 to 100 million years for the global biodiversity to recover.

The most severe extinction occurred about 225 million years ago when 95% of marine species vanished. The most famous (and the last) mass extinction, however, took place about 65 million years ago when the giant dinosaurs, which had ruled the world for 140 million years, were wiped out.

Why did the mass extinctions occur?

Both biological and environmental factors would have led to mass extinctions. The suggested causes include global cooling, falling sea levels, predation, and competition. A more recent theory with considerable supportive evidence is that a giant comet or asteroid hit the earth. This event created huge clouds of dust that blocked out sunlight for so long that the majority of species died.

What is Happening Now to the World's Species?

Before humankind became very active, the world was losing annually one out of every million species. In early twentieth century, we were perhaps losing one species a year. Now, we are losing one to hundred species a day and soon the rate of extinction is likely to be one thousand each day. These are estimates, but it is definite that we are losing species rapidly.

Over the next 50 to 100 years, as population and resource use grow exponentially, the rate of biodiversity loss will also increase sharply. Biologists estimate that 20% of the current species will be gone by 2030 and 50% by the end of the century. Distinguished scientists like Edward O. Wilson, Richard Leakey, and Norman Myers are convinced that the sixth mass extinction is under way. The effects of human-induced extinction of species will persist for thousands of generations to come.

What do Studies on Global Biodiversity Tell Us?

In 2010, UN FAO released the Second Report on the State of the World's Plant Genetic Resources for Food and Agriculture (PGRFA), which made the following points:

- Plant genetic resources are essential raw materials for helping farmers respond to climate change.

- Loss of plant genetic resources has reduced options for the agricultural sector. The major causes of genetic erosion are land clearing, population pressures, overgrazing, environmental degradation, and changing agricultural practices.
- Local plant diversity found in farmers' fields is still largely inadequately documented and managed.

The Third PGRFA Report will be released in 2023.

What is the Living Planet Report?

The Living Planet Report is the world's leading, science-based analysis on the health of our planet and the impact of human activity. It is published every two years by WWF, one of the largest conservation organizations in the world. WWF works in 100 countries.

The Report includes the Living Planet Index, which acts as an early warning indicator by tracking trends in the abundance of mammals, fish, reptiles, birds, and amphibians around the world. Such indicators help us to build up a picture of both the speed and scale of change in biodiversity around the world, and the impacts of this change.

The Living Planet Report 2022 provides the scientific evidence to back what nature has been demonstrating repeatedly: unsustainable human activity is pushing the planet's natural systems that support life on Earth to the edge. The report calls on world leaders to come together to build a more sustainable, resilient, and healthy post-COVID-19 world for people and nature. The key messages of the Living Planet Report 2022 are given in Box 9.1.

BOX 9.1 STATE OF THE PLANET: *The Living Planet Report 2022*

The Key Messages:

- We know that the health of our planet is declining, and we know why.
- We are living through climate and biodiversity crises; these are not separate from each other but are two sides of the same coin.
- We also know that we have the knowledge and means to address climate change and biodiversity loss.
- Land-use change is still the most important driver of biodiversity loss.
- The cascading impacts of climate change are already affecting the natural world. Unless we limit warming to 1.5°C, climate change is likely to become the dominant cause of biodiversity loss in the coming decades.
- The 2022 global Living Planet Index shows an average 69% decrease in monitored wildlife populations between 1970 and 2018.
- Latin America shows the greatest regional decline in average population abundance (94%).
- Population trends for monitored freshwater species are also falling steeply (83%).
- The landmark recognition in July 2022 by the UN General Assembly of the human right to a healthy environment cements our understanding that climate breakdown, nature loss, pollution and pandemics are human rights crises.
- We know that transformational change – game-changing shifts – will be essential to bring theory into practice.
- There must be system-wide changes in how we produce and consume, the technology we use, and our economic and financial systems.
- Linking international trade to its impacts on nature is a key part of bending the curve of biodiversity loss at scale.
- In addressing these complex, interlinked challenges there is no one-size-fits-all solution.

What is the IUCN Red List?

IUCN stands for the International Union for Conservation of Nature (IUCN), the world's oldest and largest global environmental organization, with more than 1200 government and NGO members and almost 11,000 volunteer experts in some 160 countries. IUCN tries to find solutions to our most pressing environmental and development challenges. IUCN supports scientific research, manages field projects all over the world, and brings governments, NGOs, the UN, and companies together to develop policy, laws, and best practices.

> **Key Idea** Human activities are leading to the rapid extinction of many species.

The IUCN Red List, updated regularly, is the world's most comprehensive information source on the global conservation status of wild species and their links to livelihood. The latest version, released in November 2022, evaluated more than 150,000 species including 60,000 vertebrates. Table 9.3 shows the state of vertebrate species – globally and in India.

TABLE 9.3 Threatened Vertebrate Species (2022)

Vertebrate Group	No. of Threatened Species	Best Estimate of % Threatened Species	No. of Threatened Species in India
Mammals	1340	27	99
Birds	1400	13	91
Reptiles	1842	21	106
Amphibians	2606	41	83
Fishes	3561	Not available	292

What are keystone species?

Keystone species play roles affecting many other organisms in an ecosystem. They determine the ability of a large number of other species to survive. When a keystone species becomes extinct, it could result in a cascade of extinctions of other species.

An example of keystone species is a top predator like the grey wolf. If wolves go locally extinct (say, due to hunting) in an ecosystem, the populations of deer and other herbivores increase exponentially. The grazing pressure then drives many plants to extinction. Next, the small animals and insects that depend on the plants disappear.

What are indicator or sentinel species?

They are very sensitive indicators of environmental problems. They give us early warning of problems that could potentially affect other species. Frogs and other amphibians are examples (Box 9.2).

BOX 9.2 ECOSYSTEM: ***The Story of Disappearing Frogs—Early Warning from a Sentinel Species***

Scientists are puzzled and concerned at two events concerning frogs occurring in recent times: first, the sharp worldwide decline in frog populations and second, the large-scale occurrence of deformities among frogs in some places.

Why should we worry about mere frogs? Frogs and other amphibians are sentinel species, that is, they are very sensitive indicators of environmental problems. They give us early warning of problems that could potentially affect other species.

Amphibians are organisms that can live both on land and in water and include frogs, toads, and salamanders. There are 5100 known species of amphibians from small frogs to big salamanders. Since frog species live in small, specialized habitats, they are indicators of the environmental conditions in a variety of places.

Frogs breathe through moist, absorptive, and permeable skins that are sensitive to pollutants in the environment. They lay gelatinous and unprotected eggs in ponds and these are very vulnerable to radiation and pollution.

Hundreds of amphibian species are vanishing or declining everywhere. According to IUCN, 25% of all known species are extinct, endangered, or vulnerable. In the US, 92 of the 242 native amphibian species are in decline. Worldwide, 32 species have become extinct in the last few decades and more than 200 species are in decline.

The decline is not restricted to areas where there is a clear degradation of the environment or high levels of pollution. It is happening even in remote areas in pristine environments and also in protected parks and reserves.

In 1995, a group of school children in Minnesota, US, discovered a large number of deformed frogs in a pond. In fact, 50% of the leopard frogs in the pond were deformed, while the normal deformity rate is just 1%. Soon, there were similar reports from most other parts of the US. Deformed frogs die early, before they can reproduce, thus leading to a decline in numbers.

Scientists believe that a number of reasons together are causing the problems with frog species. Agricultural pesticides in the water, increase in ultraviolet radiation in the atmosphere, infectious diseases, parasites, habitat loss, alien predators, and other such factors could be acting together on the amphibian populations. They have survived climate changes before, but the current changes are accelerating too rapidly for frog species to keep pace.

The rapid disappearance of the tough, but sensitive, amphibians indicates a general deterioration of the global environmental health conditions. Further, the adult amphibians play an important role in ecosystems. For example, they eat more insects than birds do. If they die of pesticide poisoning, then many organisms like reptiles and birds that eat them will also be affected.

What are Threatened Species and How are They Classified Further?

For a species to survive and flourish, enough numbers must be present in the habitat to make reproduction possible. If density and population size fall below threshold values, the numbers start going down.

Threatened species are those that are facing threats to their survival, and may be at risk of extinction. IUCN classifies threatened species into different categories, depending on their relative risk of extinction:

- *Vulnerable:* A species considered to be facing a high risk of extinction in the wild. Hippopotamus is an example. A vulnerable species is still found in reasonable size in its natural habitat, but the numbers are declining. Unless conservation measures are taken, it is likely to move down into the next category, that is, the endangered list.
- *Endangered:* A species considered to be facing a very high risk of extinction in the wild. The peregrine falcon is in the endangered category. The number of survivors of an endangered species is so small that it could soon become extinct over all or most of its habitat. Unless it is protected, the species will move down into the critically endangered category.
- *Critically endangered:* A species facing an extremely high risk of extinction in the wild. Mountain gorilla and orangutan are examples.

Thanks to conservation measures, a threatened species could also move up into the 'near threatened' or 'least concern' category.

What is a Biodiversity Hotspot?

If an area is unusually rich in biodiversity (mostly endemic) and its flora and fauna are under a constant threat of overexploitation, it is called a biodiversity hotspot. There are about 25 such hotspots in the world, mostly in the tropical forests.

The biodiversity hotspots together cover just 1.4% of land and yet hold about 60% of the world's biodiversity. One third of known species of the world are endemic to these hotspots.

A major reason why the hotspots are under great threat is that more than a billion poor people live near these areas. What is more, the rate of population growth in many of these areas is greater than the world average.

What are the Causes of Biodiversity Loss?

The major causes for the decline in biodiversity are the following:

- Loss, degradation, and fragmentation of natural habitats, which includes deforestation and takeover of land for agriculture, industries, and human settlements
- Overexploitation of biological resources including overfishing and the commercial hunting and poaching of wildlife
- Pollution, in particular the build-up of nutrients such as nitrogen and phosphorus on land and water
- Impacts of invasive alien species on ecosystems
- Climate change and acidification of the ocean

These causes of biodiversity loss are interconnected and they are, in turn, the result of the rapid increases in global economic activity, global population and consumption, urbanization, and so on—in other words, the increasing levels of human activities.

Habitat loss, degradation, and fragmentation

For any species to survive, a minimum extent of area is required in the ecosystem. For example, large animals like elephants and lions require large areas to move about and get their food and water. A bird species requires a minimum number of trees.

Due to constant expansion of human settlements and migration, many large and continuous areas of habitat are being reduced in extent or divided into patchwork of isolated fragments. This has many effects:

- Species become divided into smaller populations that cannot sustain themselves.
- Smaller fragments mean more edge area and this makes the species more vulnerable to predators and competitors as well as to wind and fire.
- Fragmentation creates barriers that limit the ability of the species to disperse and colonize new areas.
- Migratory birds face the loss of their seasonal habitats.

Commercial hunting, poaching, and man–wildlife conflicts

The illegal world trade in rare and endangered species of plants, birds, and animals is estimated to be US$8 billion per year, second only to arms smuggling. In this market, a live mountain gorilla fetches US$150,000 and a panda pelt US$100,000.

More than 37,000 plant and animal species are affected and these include rhinoceros, tiger, leopard, gorilla, butterfly, frog, tortoise, orchid, cactus, mahogany, etc. In addition, exotic pets and decorative plants are sold to collectors.

The poachers, mostly poor people in developing countries, depend on this trade for their livelihood. They collect specimens indiscriminately, killing young and old, male and female, often using very cruel methods. On an average, for each animal captured alive, 50 others are killed. What is worse, most of the live animals that are captured die in transit.

The tragedy is that the poacher finally gets very little, most of the money going to the middlemen. The country of origin also does not get any benefit, since no taxes or duties are paid. The country only loses its biodiversity for nothing.

Mass killing of animals for sport or for commercial purposes has driven some species like the blue whale into the endangered category (Read Box 9.3).

BOX 9.3 DISASTER: *The Story of the Blue Whale—Hunted to Extinction*

It is the world's largest animal. When fully grown, it could be 30 m long and weigh the equivalent of 25 elephants. Its heart is the size of a small car and a child can swim through its artery. Today, it is an endangered species.

The blue whale is a remarkable animal. For eight months, it is in the Antarctic, eating millions of krill (very small fish) by filtering them from sea water. Then it moves to warmer waters, where its young are born.

There were 200,000 blue whales before commercial whaling began. Today, the numbers are down to 3000–4000. It has been hunted to near extinction for its oil, meat, and bone. A blue whale matures sexually only when it is 25 and even then, it produces an offspring only every two to five years. Conservationists think that the number left is too few for the population to recover and avoid extinction.

Blue whales were caught in large numbers when they were in groups feeding in the Antarctic. Even otherwise, just due to their size, they are easy to spot and kill. An additional threat is the declining krill population in the Antarctic due to the melting of polar ice.

Whales in general have been under threat. Between 1925 and 1975, 1.5 million whales were killed, placing the many species on the road to extinction. The International Whaling Commission (IWC) was set up in 1946 to fix annual hunting quotas to countries. The IWC, however, has no powers to enforce the quotas.

In 1986, the IWC finally declared a moratorium on whale hunting. There was a sharp decline in the numbers killed. Japan and Norway continued to hunt and Iceland resumed the practice in 2002. These countries want the IWC ban on hunting and the CITES (Chapter 10, Box 10.2) ban on trading to be lifted citing large figures for current populations.

Conservationists question the IWC figures and argue that any relaxation will lead to overharvesting of all the species. They feel that these peaceful, intelligent, and social animals should be protected for ecological and ethical reasons.

In 2014, International Court of Justice (ICJ) declared that Japan's Southern Ocean whale hunt was illegal under international law. Following this judgment, the IWC has placed stricter regulations on 'scientific whaling.' Japan, however, resumed whaling in 2019. While Norway continues to hunt whales in large numbers, Iceland has announced that it would stop whaling by 2024.

The future of whales remains a question mark.

Introduction of non-native species or biological invasion

When a non-native species is introduced in an ecosystem and it has no predators, competitors, parasites, or pathogens to control its numbers, it can reduce or wipe out many local species. Hundreds of non-native species have been accidentally or intentionally introduced in coastal waters, lakes, and wetlands. Unintentional introduction occurs as stowaways in aircraft, through the ballast water of oil tankers and cargo ships, or as 'hitchhikers' on imported products like wooden packing crates.

In some cases, non-native species are deliberately introduced for getting some benefits. Initially, they may even be useful, but cause problems later by proliferating at the expense of local species.

In 1859, rabbits were introduced in Australia for sport shooting. Since the environment was favourable to them and there were no predators, their population exploded. They destroyed vast areas of rangeland, native wildlife, and sheep ranching. Finally, a disease virus was deliberately introduced to check their growth. We do not know what else the virus did!

Many species are affected by a combination of these reasons. An example is the decline of birds (Box 9.4).

BOX 9.4 ECOSYSTEM: *The Story of Disappearing Birds—Bleak Future for Winged Wonders*

If you like to watch the beauty of an eagle's flight, to listen to the song of a nightingale, or to enjoy the chatter of a parrot, savour the nice feelings now. Soon you may not have this pleasure.

1200 bird species, out of 9800 known ones, are likely to become extinct within this century. Over 900 species are already either endangered or critically endangered. About 128 species have vanished over the last 500 years and 103 of them since 1800.

Birds perform valuable ecosystem services like seed dispersal, insect and rodent control, scavenging, and pollination. Many birds are sentinel species that warn us of impending or current problems. They could indicate high acidity levels in water, chemical contamination, arrival of new diseases, and effects of global warming.

Colombia, which has more than 1800 species, is the most bird-diverse country. India, with about 1250 species, ranks among the top 10 bird-diverse countries of the world.

The major threats to birds are:

- Habitat loss and fragmentation
- Introduction of non-native species: bird-eating snakes, rats, cats, mongooses, etc.; insects and pathogens
- Hunting and capture
- Collection for pet trade
- Longline fishing: Thousands of sea birds are caught in hooks and drown.
- Oil spills
- Pesticides and herbicides
- Skyscrapers, towers, and power lines kill millions of migratory birds.

Bird-lovers and bird-watchers all over the world are trying to save the winged wonders. The future, however, looks bleak for birds everywhere.

What is the Level of Biodiversity in India?

Recall that India is one of the 19 mega-biodiversity countries. So far, about 70% of the total area has been surveyed for biodiversity assessment. 45,000 wild species of plants and 81,000 wild species of animals have been identified here. Together they represent 6.5% of the world's biodiversity.

The actual numbers must be much higher since many biologically rich areas like the Northeast have not been fully explored. The rich biodiversity is attributed to the presence of a variety of ecosystems and climates.

Key Idea India is one of the 19 mega-biodiversity countries.

18% of all plants found in India (including many flowering plants) are endemic. An endemic species is one that is only found in a given region or location and nowhere else in the world (according to current knowledge).

At least 166 crop species and 320 species of wild relatives of crops originated in India. We also had a large variety of domesticated species. For example, the number of rice varieties alone ranged from 30,000 to 60,000.

What is the Biogeographic Classification of India?

India can be divided into 10 biogeographic zones:

- *Trans-Himalayan:* Extension of the Tibetan Plateau including the high-altitude cold desert in Ladakh and Lahaul-Spiti
- *Himalayas:* The entire mountain chain, diverse biotic provinces, and biomes
- *Gangetic* Plain: Ganga River system
- *North-eastern zone:* Plains and non-Himalayan hill ranges
- *Desert:* Arid area west of the Aravalli high range, salty desert of Gujarat, and sand desert of Rajasthan
- *Semi-arid zone:* Area between the desert and the Deccan Plateau including the Aravalli range
- *Western Ghats:* Hill ranges and plains running along the western coastline
- *Deccan Peninsula:* South and south-central plateau, south of the Tapti River
- *Islands:* Andaman and Nicobar Islands
- *Coasts and Lakshadweep Islands*

Each zone contains distinct species of flora and fauna.

Is the Biodiversity of India under Threat?

At least 10% of India's plant species and a larger percentage of its animal species are threatened. The Asiatic cheetah and the pink-headed duck are amongst the well-known species that have become extinct in our country. More than 150 medicinal plants have disappeared in recent decades. 10% of flowering plants, 20% of mammals, and 5% of birds are threatened. Hundreds of crop varieties have disappeared and even their genes have not been preserved.

The biodiversity hotspots in India are the Eastern Himalayas and the Western Ghats. Both contain a large number of endemic species, which are now under threat.

What is the status of plant biodiversity in India?

> **Key Idea** India's biodiversity is now under serious threat.

India had tremendous diversity of wild plants and to this farmers had added a large variety of crop species. As we saw in the beginning of the chapter, the Green Revolution encouraged farmers to plant the new HYVs replacing the indigenous varieties. Over the years, the traditional species have disappeared. In place of 30,000 varieties of rice, Indian farmers now plant just 12 HYVs.

What will be the Impact of Biodiversity Loss in India and Elsewhere?

The poor people in the developing countries, who are dependent on biodiversity for their daily survival, will feel the impact first. Soon, however, the industrialized countries will also start experiencing the effects. Most of their food crops, medicines, textiles, spices, dyes, and paper originate from plants in the developing countries. The destruction of the rain forests means that less carbon will be absorbed and natural climate-control mechanisms are lost. This will have a major impact on the world's climate.

Why should we care?

Many scientists and environmentalists believe that the mass extinction that is now underway could be the biggest of our environmental problems. Almost all the other problems are potentially reversible. The loss of biodiversity is not.

The conservationist Norman Myers said, 'We could push back the deserts, restore the topsoil, and allow the ozone layer to be repaired in a century or so. We could restore climate stability in the wake of global warming within a thousand years. But once a species is gone, it is gone for good.'

We will see in the next chapter what the world is doing to conserve biodiversity.

REVIEW: A SUMMARY OF THE KEY POINTS

- The earth's biodiversity is its primary life support system and vital to our survival.
- Ecosystems provide invaluable services to us. They include economic, ecological, and cultural services.
- Our knowledge of the world's biodiversity is extremely limited.
- Most of the biodiversity exists in the tropical developing countries and India is one of the mega-diversity countries of the world.
- Biological extinction goes on all the time and most of the species that ever lived are now extinct.
- Five mass extinctions have occurred so far and the sixth one is under way due to several human-induced reasons.
- A large number of species are in the threatened category and need urgent conservation.

EXERCISES

Objective-type questions

In each case below, choose the best answer out of the given set of choices:

1. Which of the following statements is **not** true with regard to biodiversity?
   (a) Biodiversity refers to the numbers, variety, and variability of living organisms and ecosystems.
   (b) Biodiversity covers diversity within species and between species.
   (c) Biodiversity is not necessary for human survival.
   (d) Biodiversity covers variation among ecosystems.
2. When we visit a forest and enjoy its beauty, which kind of value are we placing on biodiversity?
   (a) Aesthetic value
   (b) Economic value
   (c) Ecological value
   (d) Ethical value
3. Which of the following statements is **not** true with regard to the species of the world?
   (a) Most of the species in the world are insects and microorganisms not visible to the naked eye.
   (b) We do not know exactly how many species inhabit this earth.
   (c) We have identified most of the species on earth.
   (d) Every year, we identify about 10,000 new species.
4. Where do we find the vast majority of species?
   (a) In the poorer countries
   (b) In the richer countries
   (c) In Europe
   (d) In the US
5. Which is the first stage in the process of a species becoming irreversibly extinct?
   (a) Ecological extinction
   (b) Mass extinction
   (c) Local extinction
   (d) Biological extinction
6. What is the estimated number of species that we are now losing every year?
   (a) One out of every million
   (b) 350 to 35,000
   (c) 350,000
   (d) One million

Short-answer questions

1. A witty person said that, 'To a first approximation, all species are extinct today'. Is this statement correct? If not, what is the correct situation about the extinction of species?
2. What are the suggested reasons for the five mass extinctions that have occurred so far?
3. How did the Green Revolution affect the diversity of food plants?
4. What are the factors that determine the level of biodiversity in an ecosystem?
5. List the important ecological and economic services provided by ecosystems and biodiversity. What is the estimated value of these services?
6. Distinguish between background extinction and mass extinction.
7. What are the human-induced causes of biodiversity loss?
8. What is the difference between threatened species and endangered ones?

Long-answer questions

1. Describe the different types of extinctions and explain how the coming sixth extinction is different.
2. Extinction is the ultimate fate of all species. Why then are we concerned about the decline of biodiversity?

Think critically: Deeper questions for reflection and discussion

1. Can you think of a situation in which human-induced extinction of a species would be morally justified?
2. Should we allow the patenting of life forms?

ENJOY AND EDUCATE YOURSELF

1. Watch the movie *Whale Rider* (2002): A young Maori would be in line to become the next chief—if it weren't for the fact that the person is a female. This movie is much more about humans than whales, but there are some great shots of these animals.

2. Relax with the delightful books of Gerald Durrell, who was a naturalist, zookeeper, and author. His most famous book is *My Family and Other Animals,* an autobiographical work written with humour. His other books include *Birds, Beasts, and Relatives* and *The Garden of the Gods.*

ACCESS THE OUP ONLINE RESOURCE CENTRE FOR MORE

- 2010 Global Study of Plants, Global Biodiversity Outlook, and other such reports
- The value of ecosystem services: The case of New York city
- The story of the passenger pigeon: Billions today, extinct tomorrow
- Additional text and other recommended references, websites, and films

10 Biodiversity Conservation

If all mankind were to disappear,
the world would regenerate back to
the rich state of equilibrium
that existed ten thousand years ago.
If insects were to vanish,
the environment would collapse into chaos.

Edward O. Wilson
(1929–)
American biologist, conservationist, and author

MAIN QUESTIONS ADDRESSED

- How can we conserve biodiversity?
- What are in-situ and ex-situ methods of conservation?
- What are the international efforts in biodiversity conservation?

KEYWORDS AND PHRASES

CITES, Convention on Biological Diversity, ex-situ conservation, in-situ conservation, Kanis, National Biodiversity Strategy and Action Plan, Olive Ridley turtle, Project Tiger, seed bank

LEAD STORY

THE STORY OF OLIVE RIDLEY TURTLES: AN ANNUAL DANCE OF DEATH?

Every year, they visit us in thousands. After travelling thousands of kilometres in the sea to reach the Indian coast, they lay millions of eggs. Thousands of them, however, die gory deaths and are washed ashore. This is the tragic story of the Olive Ridley turtles and their annual migration to the Gahirmatha coast of Odisha.

The Olive Ridley is a small, hard-shelled marine turtle. The most dramatic aspect of its life history is the habit of forming great nesting aggregations, called 'arribadas'. These nesting concentrations occur in Mexico, Costa Rica, Nicaragua, Panama, and India.

It is a threatened or endangered species throughout its range and there is a ban on all Olive Ridley products under the Convention on International Trade in Endangered Animal and Plant Species (Box 10.2). In India, the killing or capture of the turtle is punishable under the Wildlife Protection Act, 1972.

Olive Ridley Turtles calling out: *"Help us! We are dying in this plastic and oil."*

The turtles face many threats as they move long distances to their nesting sites. In areas where recreational boating and ship traffic is intense, propeller and collision injuries are common. Turtles develop problems with their respiration, skin, blood chemistry, salt gland, and other functions due to a variety of reasons:

- Consumption of marine debris such as plastic bags, plastic and Styrofoam pieces, tar balls, balloons, and raw plastic pellets. (Often, such items also contain toxic chemicals.)
- Movement through oil spills.
- Ingestion of pesticides, heavy metals, and other toxic chemicals from various sources on land and sea.

Odisha is one of the Olive Ridley mass nesting sites hosting as much as 50% of the world's population. Gahirmatha Beach supports perhaps the largest nesting population with an average of 400,000 females nesting in a given year.

The turtles start congregating off the coast by October–November every year. The couples mate in the sea and the females climb on to the sandy beaches to lay their eggs between January and March. A turtle nests up to three times per season, typically producing 100-110 eggs on each occasion.

After the females depart, it takes about 40 days for the eggs to hatch. During this period, the eggs are in danger. Some are washed away, others dry up in the sun, and yet others are eaten by birds and animals. The hatchlings again have a high mortality rate and it is a miracle that many of them make their way to the sea without their mothers to guide them.

The biggest threat to the turtles in Odisha is the mechanized fishing trawler. The turtles are either cut open by the rotary blades of the trawlers or suffocate in the fishing nets. More than 100,000 Olive Ridleys have been killed this way along the Odisha coast during the past 10 years. Most of the trawlers operate illegally and they do not also care to use in their nets the turtle exclusion device (TED), which would allow the animals to escape.

There are attempts to save the turtles by the Forest Department as well as environmental organizations. They lack, however, the manpower and infrastructure facilities to monitor 280 km of the coastline. Gahirmatha itself is a marine sanctuary. But that does not seem to help the turtles.

The case of the Olive Ridley shows how difficult it is to conserve biodiversity, but there is hope. On March 25, 2022, a record number of around 2,45,000 turtles came ashore for mass nesting at the islands of Gahirmatha marine sanctuary!

What is the Status of Global Biodiversity?

Let us review what we learnt about biodiversity in the previous chapter:

The biosphere is an extremely complex system with millions of known and unknown species—plants, animals, birds, bacteria, and viruses. Thousands of interactions take place every moment among these organisms and every link in this web is important for keeping the whole system stable.

Humankind has been interfering with the system far too much. They have cut many of the links in the web by destroying species with unknown consequences. Even if we are overestimating biodiversity loss, it is clear that the rate of extinction has gone up sharply due to human activities. We are losing more species than ever before. Instead of arguing over numbers or waiting to get reliable data, we must take precautionary steps to prevent further loss.

What is Meant by Biodiversity Conservation?

In biodiversity conservation, we study how human activities affect the diversity of plants and animals and develop ways of protecting that diversity. Conservation ranges from protecting the population of a specific species to preserving entire ecosystems.

Key Idea While in-situ conservation protects species where they are, ex-situ conservation protects species in a place away from their natural habitat.

There are two main types of conservation. In-situ (on-site) conservation tries to protect species where they are, that is, in their natural habitat. Ex-situ (off-site) conservation attempts to preserve and protect the species in a place away from their natural habitat. In general, in-situ conservation is more cost-effective. In many cases, however, the ex-situ approach may be the only feasible one.

How is Conservation Done In-situ?

In-situ conservation requires the identification and protection of natural areas that have high biodiversity. This includes the establishment of national parks and reserves. Over the past few decades, there has been an increase in the number of reserves and the area covered.

The main objective is to preserve large areas of undeveloped land so that the ecosystems and the biodiversity can continue to flourish and evolve. Large animals like elephants need big reserves. Large reserves are also less vulnerable to disturbances, since their edge length is short relative to the area covered. If a reserve is split into patches, then corridors are provided to enable movement of the animals.

In-situ conservation through reserves has its limitations. Many reserves do not receive the level of protection and management they need. Widespread encroachment by poachers, settlers, and others continue in many parks. Flora, fauna, as well as resources like wood and minerals continue to be exploited.

> **Key Idea**
> In-situ conservation primarily involves the setting up national parks and reserves.

The local people living near the reserve are often seen as adversaries and are not involved in the conservation process. The chances of success are higher if the local people are consulted in the planning and design of the reserve. Ideally, the locals must be made partners in conservation. They should be allowed to use part of the reserve or a buffer zone for grazing, timber cutting, agriculture, fishing, etc. They could also be trained as guides and wildlife experts to restore degraded areas.

What is on-farm conservation?

A special case of in-situ approach is on-farm conservation, which is a method farmers had been following all along. Faced with the problems of gene banks as well as in-situ methods, we have rediscovered the important role of the farmer in biodiversity conservation. In this approach, there is a farmer–scientist partnership to collect, maintain, and improve the traditional plant varieties.

It is impossible to preserve all biodiversity in-situ. Given the population and other pressures, we cannot set aside the required huge land area. Ex-situ conservation is equally important. In some cases, where the population of a species has dwindled to extremely low levels, ex-situ conservation may be the only way out.

How is Ex-situ Conservation Practised?

In this approach, we conserve biodiversity in an artificial setting. This includes the storage of seeds in banks, breeding of captive animal species in zoos, and setting up of botanical gardens, aquariums, and research institutes.

How do seed banks work?

There are more than 1700 seed banks (big and small) in the world and they hold more than 4 million seeds maintained at low temperatures and low humidity levels. The majority of the banks are in the industrialized countries or indirectly controlled by them.

The banks store a very large amount of plant genetic material in a small space. The seeds are supposed to be safe from habitat destruction, climate changes, and general destruction. They can even help reintroduce extinct species.

There are, however, many problems with seed banks. Seeds get dried out before storage and some seeds cannot tolerate being stored. No seed remains alive indefinitely and every seed must be periodically germinated and new seeds collected for storage. This is an expensive and difficult process. It is said that a very large number of seeds in banks have not been germinated or tested for long and many may be dead by now.

Fire accidents or power failures can permanently damage the seeds. One safeguard against such events is to subdivide the sample and store them in different banks. A more intractable problem is that the seeds in a bank have not been evolving in relationship to outer circumstances. When they are later reintroduced into the field, they may be less fit for survival.

Most of the seed banks concentrate on about 100 plants that give 90% of our food. There is a need for many more banks to store many more species, particularly in the developing countries. In spite of the problems and limitations, however, seed banks remain an important method of preserving biodiversity for the future. If they are not managed properly, however, they may be giving us a false reassurance that we are conserving biodiversity.

What is the role of zoos in biodiversity conservation?

Along with many other animals, zoos often preserve a few individuals of critically endangered species. If an animal breeds in captivity, the zoo may ultimately reintroduce the species into protected reserves.

Zoos need large spaces and huge funds. Only a small percentage of endangered species can be protected in zoos. The public tends to support the saving of large or popular species like the tiger, elephant, and panda. There is not much interest in protecting smaller or less attractive species, even if they are known to be very important for the ecosystem.

What about botanical gardens?

There are over 1600 botanical gardens in the world, holding 4 million plants. They cover about 80,000 species or 30% of all known species. The largest one is Kew Gardens in England, which has 25,000 species. When Britain was an imperial power, large numbers of plant species were taken from the colonies to the Kew Gardens.

Key Idea
Ex-situ conservation is attempted by establishing seed banks, zoos, botanical gardens, aquariums, and research institutes.

Botanical gardens have a significant educational value for scientists and students. Like zoos, botanical gardens too face the problems of funds and space. They increasingly focus on rare and endangered species.

Table 10.1 compares in-situ and ex-situ methods of conservation.

TABLE 10.1 Comparison of in-situ and ex-situ conservation methods

Aspect	In-situ conservation	Ex-situ conservation
Approach	Conservation of species in their natural habitats	Preservation of components of biodiversity outside their natural habitats
Applicability	Areas of high biodiversity	Selected species (e.g., endangered ones)
Methods	National parks Reserves Sanctuaries Wildlife refuges	Gene banks Plant tissue collections Captive breeding of animals Collecting living organisms for zoos, aquaria, botanical gardens, research institutes
Needs	Large area Some funds	Infrastructure Continuous funds
Cost	Cost-effective	Expensive
Feasibility	Not feasible in all cases	Cannot save all species
Problems	Relationship with local communities Encroachment by settlers and developers Poaching and exploitation of resources	Maintenance issues (drying and death of seeds, difficulties in captive breeding of animals, etc.)

How can We Use Indigenous Knowledge to Conserve Biodiversity?

The best approach is to:

- involve local communities in the conservation process as partners,
- make use of their traditional knowledge (especially in medicine) for documenting the value of diverse organisms and for developing new products, and
- compensate the communities for the knowledge they have shared (Read about the Kani-TBGRI case in Box 10.1).

BOX 10.1 HOPE: *The Story of the Kanis—Compensating Indigenous Knowledge*

In December 1987, a team of scientists were on a botanical expedition in the Western Ghats in Kerala. They had taken with them a few members of the Kani tribe as their guides. The scientists noticed that the guides were eating a fruit that seemed to keep them energetic even during tough treks. When the scientists tried it, they too felt a 'sudden flush of energy and strength'.

Initially, the Kanis were reluctant to reveal any information about the plant, saying that it was a sacred tribal secret not to be revealed to outsiders. After considerable persuasion, the tribals showed the team the plant *Aarogyapacha* as the source of the fruit.

The scientists, who were from the Tropical Botanic Garden and Research Institute (TBGRI), secured specimens of the plant and conducted investigations. They found anti-stress and other beneficial properties in the plant's active ingredients. Using *Aarogyappacha* and three other medicinal plants, they formulated a drug and gave it the name *Jeevani.*

TBGRI gave the right to manufacture the drug to a private company, Arya Vaidya Pharmacy (AVP), for a licence fee of ₹10 lakh and a royalty of 2%. The Kanis were to receive half the fee and half the royalty as compensation for sharing their knowledge of the plant and its properties. The Kanis formed a trust, which would use the money for promoting the welfare of the community, preparing a biodiversity register to document their knowledge, and promoting conservation of biodiversity.

This was the first and hopeful case of an indigenous community receiving compensation in exchange for their traditional knowledge of plants and their uses. However, soon after the pharmacy started production in 1996, disputes erupted over raw material and ownership of the resources. It had been envisaged that the Kanis would collect and sell *Arogyapacha* leaves to the pharmacy. But TBGRI had not taken the forest department into confidence. As per laws, the tribals could collect only minor forest produce and *Arogyapacha* was not one.

Meanwhile, traders started smuggling large quantities of the plant. The forest department then included the plant in the list of endangered species. The Kanis faced criminal cases for trying to sell the plant. The resulting shortage of raw material compounded by differences within the Kani community, lack of political will, and patent issues led to the demise of the whole project.

This failed (but a landmark) attempt to ensure that indigenous communities got benefits from sharing their knowledge of biodiversity was perhaps a learning experience for all. More sustainable methods may emerge in the future.

There is an international movement to conserve biodiversity through measures like documenting indigenous knowledge, assisting local communities to grow medicinal plants, make medicines, and market them, saving and propagating traditional seeds, and reintroducing traditional food items through restaurants. 'Seeds for Change' in the US and the Kokopelli Association in France are examples.

What is being Done to Protect Wildlife?

Many countries have declared certain areas as reserves and restricted human activities in those areas. There are several thousands of national parks, sanctuaries, wildlife refuges, and wilderness areas in the world. They are partially or fully protected and they cover about 1 billion ha.

Many of the reserves are too small to sustain large species or they are too poorly protected. The developing countries have the maximum biodiversity, but they do not have enough funds and, in many cases, the expertise needed to manage protected areas well. Most reserves in the poorer countries suffer encroachment by land grabbers, loggers, miners, and poachers.

Why is It Difficult to Protect Marine Biodiversity?

We continue to view the sea as a huge natural resource that can absorb unlimited amounts of waste and pollution. Unfortunately, the damage to marine biodiversity is not visible to most people. At the same time, there is a tremendous pressure to expand human activities on the coast (Chapter 4).

What are the International Efforts in Biodiversity Conservation?

In 1980, three organizations—United Nations Environment Programme (UNEP), International Union for Conservation of Nature (IUCN), and WWF International—together prepared a World Conservation Strategy. It was a plan to conserve biodiversity, preserve vital ecosystem processes on which all life depends for survival, and develop sustainable uses of organisms and ecosystems. In 1991, they published a new version of this document entitled *Caring for the Earth*.

Following the publication of the World Conservation Strategy and the holding of conferences like the 1992 Earth Summit, several international agreements and global initiatives have focussed on biodiversity conservation. The major ones are discussed below.

Convention on International Trade in Endangered Species of Wild Fauna and Flora (CITES)

This Convention has been in force since 1975 and 175 countries have signed it. Even though enforcement is difficult, CITES has helped reduce trade in many threatened species including elephants, crocodiles, and chimpanzees (Box 10.2).

BOX 10.2 HOPE: ***The Story of CITES—Stop the Trade, Save the Species***

In 1989, the African elephant was declared an endangered species. The elephants were disappearing primarily due to ivory trade. By 2000, however, the elephant population had recovered in Namibia, Botswana, and Zimbabwe. This is one of the success stories of CITES.

The Convention bans the hunting, capturing, and selling of endangered or threatened species. It lists over 900 species that cannot be traded as live specimens or wildlife products. It restricts the international trade of 29,000 other species that are potentially threatened.

CITES now has 184 member-countries. Under the Convention, each country is bound to pass laws according to the CITES guidelines and many countries have done so. Enforcement of the laws is, however, lax in many countries, and even when a violator is caught, the penalties are mild. Further, a member country can exempt itself from protecting any of the listed species. Trade in endangered species still goes on, especially in countries that have not joined CITES.

Returning to the African elephant case, the recovery of the population is also causing a problem. In some places, the area is not enough for the large herds. They uproot many small trees, which in turn affect many other species. The local people want to hunt some of the elephants to keep the numbers down and to get economic benefits. In 1997, CITES moved the African elephant to a less restrictive, but a potentially threatened list, allowing the sale of stockpiled ivory to Japan.

In March 2023, CITES completed 50 years of existence. The event was marked by the coming into force of regulatory measures for hundreds of additional species.

Any ban on hunting and trading can only be a short-term measure. The better way is to educate consumers to stop buying the illegal products. If the prices and the market decline, the illegal trade will also stop.

UN Convention on the Law of the Sea (UNCLOS)

Thanks to UNCLOS (discussed in Chapter 4), countries now have jurisdiction over their territorial seas as well as their exclusive economic zones. In effect, 36% of the ocean surface area and 90% of the fish stocks come under the control of individual countries. This provides a great opportunity for each country to protect its marine biodiversity (or to overexploit it!).

International Convention for the Control and Management of Ships' Ballast Water and Sediments

When a ship unloads at a port, its hull must be filled with water to maintain the ship's stability. As the ship then moves to another port, thousands of organisms travel with the water. When the ship takes in a new load at its destination, the ballast water and the organisms are released into the local waters. We saw in Chapter 9 how non-native species can destroy many local species.

The objective of the Convention on Ballast Water, adopted by 74 countries in 2004, is to prevent, minimize, and ultimately eliminate the transfer of harmful aquatic organisms and pathogens through the control and management of ships' ballast water and sediments. Under the Convention, ships must have facilities to treat the ballast water before releasing it in foreign waters.

Convention Concerning the Protection of the World Cultural and Natural Heritage

Adopted by UNESCO in 1972, this Convention seeks to encourage the identification, protection, and preservation of cultural and natural heritage around the world considered to be of outstanding value to humanity. A number of the sites in the Heritage list are nature parks and reserves that conserve biodiversity.

UNESCO Man and the Biosphere Programme (MAB)

This is a major effort in biodiversity conservation. MAB is an intergovernmental scientific programme that aims to establish a scientific basis for the improvement of relationships between people and their environments. MAB combines the natural and social sciences, economics, and education to improve human livelihood and the equitable sharing of benefits, and to safeguard natural and managed ecosystems, thus promoting innovative approaches to economic development that are socially and culturally appropriate, and environmentally sustainable. Its World Network of Biosphere Reserves currently counts 738 sites in 134 countries all over the world, including 22 transboundary sites.

Other treaties that promote biodiversity conservation are the Ramsar Convention on Wetlands (Chapter 4) and the Convention on the Conservation of Migratory Species of Wild Animals.

What is being Done to Protect Marine Biodiversity?

UNEP has initiated many regional agreements to protect large marine areas shared by countries. Many of the designated reserves under the UNESCO MAB are coastal or marine habitats. In addition, IUCN supports 1300 marine protected areas covering about 0.2% of the ocean area.

All the steps described above led finally to the Convention on Biological Diversity (CBD).

What is the Convention on Biological Diversity?

After five years of international negotiations, the CBD was approved in 1992 at the Earth Summit in Rio de Janeiro and came into force in 1993. As of May 2023, there are 196 parties to the Convention. India ratified it in 1994. The US signed the Convention in 1993, but has not ratified it.

The Convention has three main goals:

- Conservation of biodiversity.
- Sustainable use of the components of biodiversity.
- Sharing the benefits arising from the commercial and other utilization of genetic resources in a fair and equitable way.

Under the Convention, governments undertake to conserve and sustainably use biodiversity. They are required to develop national biodiversity strategies and action plans, and to integrate these into broader national plans for environment and development.

Other treaty commitments include:

- Identifying and monitoring the important components of biological diversity that need to be conserved and used sustainably.
- Establishing protected areas to conserve biological diversity while promoting environmentally sound development around these areas.
- Rehabilitating and restoring degraded ecosystems and promoting the recovery of threatened species in collaboration with local residents.
- Respecting, preserving, and maintaining traditional knowledge of the sustainable use of biological diversity with the involvement of indigenous people and local communities.
- Preventing the introduction of, controlling, and eradicating alien species that could threaten ecosystems, habitats, or species.
- Controlling the risks posed by organisms modified by biotechnology.
- Promoting public participation, particularly when it comes to assessing the environmental impacts of development projects that threaten biological diversity.
- Educating people and raising awareness about the importance of biological diversity and the need to conserve it.
- Reporting on how each country is meeting its biodiversity goals.

While CBD is a step forward, it has some drawbacks and implementation problems:

- It excludes the existing gene bank collections. Thus, 4 million seeds, which are also of high commercial value, are outside the control of CBD.
- It encourages bilateral agreements, even though many biodiversity issues are regional or global. This has led to some poor countries signing agreements with rich countries or big corporations giving away the rights over their biodiversity.
- As with many international agreements, the implementation of CBD has also been slow and poor. The Convention does not provide for severe penalties for violations, nor does it have an enforcement mechanism.

> **Key Idea**
> The Convention on Biological Diversity is the main international agreement for conserving global biodiversity.

What is the 2022 Kunming-Montreal Global Biodiversity Framework?

The Kunming-Montreal Global Biodiversity Framework (GBF) was adopted during the fifteenth meeting of the Conference of the Parties (COP 15) of CBD following a four year consultation and negotiation process. This historic Framework, which supports the achievement of the Sustainable Development Goals and builds on the Convention's previous Strategic Plans, sets out an ambitious pathway to reach the global vision of a world living in harmony with nature by 2050.

The implementation of the Kunming-Montreal Global Biodiversity Framework will be guided and supported through a comprehensive package of decisions also adopted at COP 15. This package includes a monitoring framework for the GBF, an enhanced mechanism for planning, monitoring, reporting and reviewing implementation, the necessary financial resources for implementation, strategic frameworks for capacity development and technical and scientific cooperation, as well as an agreement on digital sequence information on genetic resources. In adopting the Kunming-Montreal Global Biodiversity Framework, all Parties committed to setting national targets to implement it.

GBF includes four Goals and 23 Targets to be achieved by 2030. The four goals are:

GOAL A

- The integrity, connectivity, and resilience of all ecosystems are maintained, enhanced, or restored, substantially increasing the area of natural ecosystems by 2050;
- Human induced extinction of known threatened species is halted, and, by 2050, extinction rate and risk of all species are reduced tenfold, and the abundance of native wild species is increased to healthy and resilient levels;
- The genetic diversity within populations of wild and domesticated species is maintained, safeguarding their adaptive potential.

GOAL B

- Biodiversity is sustainably used and managed and nature's contributions to people, including ecosystem functions and services, are valued, maintained and enhanced, with those currently in decline being restored, supporting the achievement of sustainable development, for the benefit of present and future generations by 2050.

GOAL C

- The monetary and non-monetary benefits from the utilization of genetic resources, and digital sequence information on genetic resources, and of traditional knowledge associated with genetic resources, as applicable, are shared fairly and equitably, including, as appropriate with indigenous peoples and local communities, and substantially increased by 2050, while ensuring traditional knowledge associated with genetic resources is appropriately protected, thereby contributing to the conservation and sustainable use of biodiversity, in accordance with internationally agreed access and benefit-sharing instruments.

GOAL D

- Adequate means of implementation, including financial resources, capacity-building, technical and scientific cooperation, and access to and transfer of technology to fully implement the Kunming-Montreal global biodiversity framework are secured and equitably accessible to all Parties, especially developing countries, in particular the least developed countries and small island developing States, as well as countries with economies in transition, progressively closing the biodiversity finance gap of $700 billion per year, and aligning financial flows with the Kunming-Montreal Global Biodiversity Framework and the 2050 Vision for Biodiversity.

The 23 Targets cover the following aspects:

1. Reducing threats to biodiversity (8 Targets)
2. Meeting people's needs through sustainable use and benefit-sharing (5 Targets)
3. Tools and solutions for implementation and mainstreaming (10 Targets)

(See ORC for the full list of Targets)

What Actions have We Taken to Conserve India's Biodiversity?

The first protected area in the country was the Corbett National Park, established in 1936. Currently, there are more than 90 national parks, 350 wildlife sanctuaries, and 15 biospheres covering about 5% of the land. In addition, there are several reserve forests.

In the national parks, habitations and private ownership of land are not permitted. Traditional activities like grazing and fuel wood collection are also prohibited. On the other hand, in sanctuaries some activities are permitted.

A biosphere belongs to the third category of protected areas. Here the wild flora and fauna are protected, but the people are allowed to live in the area and carry on their traditional activities.

Of the 18 biosphere reserves of India, the largest three are the Rann of Kuchch (12,500 sq km), Gulf of Mannar (10,500 sq km), and the Sundarbans (9600 sq km). In addition, there are special projects to protect certain animal species like the tiger and the elephant. For example, Project Tiger attempts to conserve the tiger population (Box 10.3).

BOX 10.3 HOPE: ***The Story of Project Tiger—Good News from Census?***

In September 2004, the Wildlife Institute of India, Dehradun, sent a group of its students to the Sariska Tiger Reserve for training. The students trekked through 860 sq km of the reserve, but could not see a single tiger.

The Sariska Tiger Reserve in Rajasthan is one of the 40 tiger reserves under Project Tiger. This Project was established in 1973 by the Government of India to conserve this endangered species and now there are 47 reserves in 18 states. More than half the world tiger population is found in India.

When the news of the missing tigers came out, the reserve authorities made frantic searches. The Rajasthan government continued to insist that there was evidence of tigers inside the reserve. Yet, a survey carried out by WWF said that there was no evidence of any tigers in Sariska.

The then PM, Dr Manmohan Singh, wanted immediate action by both the central government and state authorities. He called it the 'biggest crisis in the management of our wildlife' since the launch of Project Tiger and suggested immediate measures.

Meanwhile, tigers were reported missing in other reserves like Rathnambore, Simlipal, and Panna. The Central Bureau of Investigation began an inquiry. A gang of poachers were arrested in Jabalpur. The PM set up a Tiger Task Force.

The Task Force Report said that Sariska was just one example of the total collapse of the tiger conservation system. The report emphasized the close connection between the animals and the forest people. It wanted the forest-dwellers to be relocated wherever possible to relieve the pressure on the forests and tigers. Against this approach, however, there is another view that relocation of people is not feasible in all places and that the forest must be shared between the people and the tigers, so that both can coexist.

Why do tigers disappear? The Wildlife Protection Society of India says: 'The illicit demand for bones from wild tigers for use in traditional oriental medicine, coupled with the international trade in tiger skins, continues to be the main reason for the unrelenting poaching pressure on tigers in India. There is virtually no demand for either bones or skins of tigers within India.'

In 2006, the government set up the National Tiger Conservation Authority (NTCA), which now administers 53 tiger reserves. NTCA conducts a periodical tiger census, According to NTCA reports, the number of tigers increased from 1411 in 2006 to 3167 in 2022. The government declared it as a huge success story, which demonstrated that the strategy of creating reserves staffed by specialists was working.

The substantial increase in numbers over eight years seems to be too good to be true. NGOs and scientists have, in fact, questioned the methodology used in the census. They say that the assessment may be inaccurate and that the tiger population in India may not be recovering as fast as it is made out to be.

Key Idea We have established a large number of national parks, sanctuaries, and biospheres in India for protecting biodiversity.

What about ex-situ conservation in India?

There are 35 botanical gardens and 275 zoos, deer parks, safari parks, and aquaria. Two institutions engaged in conservation are the National Bureau of Plant Genetic Resources, New Delhi and the National Bureau of Animal Genetic Resources, Karnal.

How is indigenous knowledge being used to conserve biodiversity?

Many local communities and voluntary organizations are now promoting conservation and sustainable use of biodiversity.

In 1996, the village of Pattuvam in Kerala created history by declaring its absolute ownership over all the genetic materials currently growing within its jurisdiction. The villagers had earlier prepared a detailed register of all the species found within the village. The village also set up a Forum for the Protection of People's Biodiversity, which would henceforth have to be consulted by any person or company who seeks access to the register and the genetic material it lists.

There are efforts all over India to document local biodiversity and indigenous knowledge. Some of the organizations involved in such work are the Foundation for the Revitalisation of Local Health Traditions and Green Foundation in Bengaluru, Centre for Indian Knowledge Systems in Chennai, Beej Bachao Andolan in Tehri Garhwal, and Navdanya in Dehradun. Annadana (in Auroville near Puducherry) is the base of the South Asian Network of Soil and Seed Savers, established with the help of Kokopelli Association of France.

What has India Done under the Convention on Biological Diversity?

In May 1994, India became a party to the Convention. In January 2000, the government released the National Policy and Action Strategy on Biodiversity. This document seeks to consolidate the on-going efforts of conservation and sustainable use of biodiversity and to establish a policy and programme regime for the purpose.

The Indian Parliament passed the Biodiversity Act in December 2002. The main intent of this legislation is to protect India's rich biodiversity and associated knowledge. It seeks to check biopiracy and to prevent the use of our biodiversity by foreign individuals and organizations without sharing the benefits with us. One thrust area is the conservation of medicinal plants. The National Biodiversity Authority (NBA) was established in 2003 to implement the Act. As required by the CBD, the government also prepared a National Biodiversity Strategy and Action Plan (Box 10.4).

BOX 10.4 ENVIRO FACT: *National Biodiversity Strategy and Action Plan*

As required by the CBD, a National Biodiversity Strategy and Action Plan (NBSAP) for India was finalized in 2004. The NBSAP process was carried out by the then Ministry of Environment and Forests (MoEF). In a unique arrangement, Kalpavriksh, a non-governmental organization, undertook its technical coordination.

Based in Delhi and Pune, Kalpavriksh is an action group working on environmental education, research, campaigns, and direct action since 1979. Kalpavriksh has been working on a number of local, national, and global issues.

The NBSAP process involved consultations and planning with thousands of people across the country, including tribal *(adivasi)* and other local communities, NGOs, government agencies, academics and scientists, corporate houses, students, armed forces, and other sections of society.

In order to reverse the erosion of biodiversity in India, the action plan focuses on three basic goals: conservation of biodiversity, sustainable use of biological resources, and equity in conservation and use. Some important measures suggested in the plan are:

- Restoration and regeneration of degraded eco-systems
- Recognition of community rights
- Development of alternative intellectual rights systems appropriate for indigenous knowledge
- Balancing of local, national, and international interests related to biodiversity
- Respect for cultural diversity
- Preventing deprivation of indigenous people from natural resources
- Preparation of People's Biodiversity Registers at the local level

Unfortunately, the original NBSAP was replaced with a new and diluted version in 2008. Even that has not been implemented seriously by the states. People are yet to benefit from the biodiversity around them because building awareness at the grassroots has just begun.

There is, however, an increased interest in biodiversity in the villages, thanks to the People's Biodiversity Registers that are being prepared. Farmers are realizing the importance of traditional crop varieties and agricultural biodiversity. This could lead to people's action to conserve biodiversity.

NBSAP has been updated over the years. Further, India submitted its Fifth National Report to CBD in 2014.

What are the Basic Issues in Protecting Wild Flora and Fauna?

There is often a conflict between conservation efforts and the livelihood issues of local communities. People capture or kill endangered animals often because of two related reasons: the poverty of the people combined with the willingness of rich to pay huge money for the products. What choice does the poor person have?

Should We Try to Protect All the Threatened Species?

From an ethical point of view, all life is sacred and must be protected. From a practical point of view, we are forced to decide which species we want to save. Money, scientific information, and trained personnel to do the job—all are in short supply. Clearly, we will be able to save only a limited number of species.

How do we choose the species we would try to save?

We need some criteria on which to base our choice. From a human point of view, we could choose those species that give us benefits now or are likely to be useful in the future. The problem is that we do not have enough knowledge about the possible uses of thousands of species.

From nature's point of view, we could select those that are of most value to the ecosystem, that is, the keystone species (Chapter 9). This may turn out to be good for the humans too. Another way is to simply choose species that have the best chance of survival. Given our constraints, it may be better to concentrate on a few strong species instead of many weak ones.

How does Gender Inequality Impact Conservation?

Here are some points on gender and conservation made in a report by the global NGO WWF:

- Despite women's critical roles in communities in many rural areas of developing countries. women are consistently underrepresented and face barriers to participating in natural resource management and climate adaptation decision-making from local to global levels.
- Discriminatory gender norms can lead to unequal gender representation in positions of power and decision-making spaces. This imbalance can lead to a vicious cycle that continues to deprive women of access to formal education, financial resources, and political power, perpetuating their low social status and creating barriers to participate in decision-making for the very natural resources they disproportionately rely on for their livelihoods and wellbeing.
- By empowering women we can reduce environmental damage, especially when women are engaged in natural resource management and conservation leadership positions.
- Countries with higher levels of gender inequality tend to have lower environmental wellbeing and vice versa.

There are at least two ways to transform gender inequality in conservation:

- Giving women access to the knowledge, tools, and training they need to claim their rights to participate in and lead in natural resource governance
- Engaging men as advocates for women's equality in environmental and other sectors.

Ending on a Hopeful Note: Positive Stories

1. Bhutan has taken very positive steps to conserve its rich biodiversity.
2. One dedicated individual, Romulus Whitaker, has taken extraordinary efforts to protect snakes and crocodiles from becoming extinct (Box 10.5).

BOX 10.5 INSPIRATION: *The Story of Romulus Whitaker—Conserving Snakes and Crocodiles*

The Irulas in Tamil Nadu are expert snake catchers. For long, they were catching hundreds of snakes and selling them to the flourishing skin trade. When the trade in snakeskin was banned, they lost their livelihood.

At that point, Romulus Whitaker entered their lives. He helped them set up the Irula Cooperative Society for extracting snake venom and selling it to the institutes that make life saving anti-venom. It was a win-win formula, since the killing of snakes stopped and the Irulas had a profitable occupation.

Romulus Whitaker came to India from the US when he was seven. From his childhood, he had a natural affinity for snakes and in fact for all wildlife. When he was a school student in Kodaikanal, he used to wander in the Palani Hills and picked up the observation skills needed for dealing with wildlife. Later, he learnt snake catching from Irulas and crocodile catching from the natives of Papua New Guinea.

In 1972, Whitaker and some friends set up the Madras Snake Park in Chennai. Most of the snake-keepers in the park are Irula tribals. The park has 31 species of Indian snakes, all the three species of Indian crocodiles, four species of exotic crocodiles, and three species of Indian turtles.

Many species of reptiles including endangered species like the Indian python have been bred in captivity in the snake park. The offspring have been either released into the wild or made available for exchange with other zoos.

Whitaker next established the Crocodile Bank, also in Chennai. In the early 1970s, crocodiles were facing extinction in the country. The Crocodile Bank supplied breeding populace for restarting the species in Tamil Nadu as well as in other parts of the country. Later, it became an international Crocodile Bank, gathering species, which were endangered in other countries as well.

The bank now has crocodiles from all over the world and has become a gene pool for all species. At the same time it is also a vibrant educational institution because over 500,000 visitors come here every year. For the first time, they encounter crocodiles as a non-menacing, interesting, and potentially viable animal, in terms of their ecological diversity.

Whitaker's life and work show that a single individual can make enormous contribution to biodiversity conservation through passion and dedication.

REVIEW: A SUMMARY OF THE KEY POINTS

- We can protect species in their habitat or away from their habitat and each method has its place.
- While there has been an increase in the number and area covered by the world's reserves, the management of many of the reserves is not satisfactory.
- Seed banks, zoos, and botanical gardens are important for biodiversity conservation, but they are beset with many difficulties.
- There are a range of international conventions and agreements to promote biodiversity conservation, the most important being the Convention on Biological Diversity (CBD).
- Under CBD, India has prepared a National Biodiversity Strategy and Action Plan.
- India has taken measures like the creation of biosphere reserves, protected areas, zoos, and botanical gardens for conserving biodiversity.

EXERCISES

Objective-type questions

In each case below, choose the best answer out of the given set of choices:

1. Which of the following methods is **not** in-situ conservation?
   (a) Setting up a national park
   (b) Establishing a reserve forest
   (c) Setting up a biosphere reserve
   (d) Building a seed bank
2. Which of the following methods is **not** ex-situ conservation?
   (a) Breeding animals in a zoo
   (b) Setting up a botanical garden
   (c) Establishing a national park
   (d) Setting up an aquarium
3. Which is the most important international agreement for conserving all biodiversity?
   (a) Convention on Biological Diversity
   (b) CITES
   (c) UNCLOS
   (d) Convention on Ballast Water
4. Which of the following measures is **not** a part of India's National Biodiversity Strategy and Action Plan?
   (a) Restoration and regeneration of degraded ecosystems
   (b) Recognition of community rights
   (c) Preventing deprivation of indigenous people from natural resources
   (d) Allowing free export of medicinal plant species

Short-answer questions

1. Distinguish between in-situ and ex-situ methods of conservation. Explain the advantages and disadvantages of each approach.
2. What are the threats faced by the Olive Ridley turtles on the Odisha coast? What are the difficulties in saving them from being killed?
3. What are the main provisions of the Convention on Biological Diversity?

Long-answer questions

1. Describe the major international efforts to save biodiversity. What has been the role of India in these efforts?
2. Describe the measures taken by India to save its biodiversity.

Think critically: Deeper questions for reflection and discussion

1. Diversity is not just about plants and animals. There is also human cultural diversity. The communities of this world differ in their agricultural practices, food habits, religion, spirituality, beliefs, medical systems, languages, literature, art, music, etc. This cultural diversity is also being threatened. Languages are becoming extinct, traditional knowledge of plants and their medicinal uses are being forgotten, and indigenous seeds are disappearing. Should this cultural diversity be conserved and if so, how can we do it?
2. Can we at all conserve all species? If that is not possible, how do we choose the species we should protect?

ENJOY AND EDUCATE YOURSELF

Watch the documentary *The Elephant Whisperers*, which shows how Bomman and Bellie, a couple in south India, devoted their lives to caring for an orphaned baby elephant named Raghu, forging a family like no other. The film, made by Kartiki Gonsalves, won the Oscar Award in 2023.

ACCESS THE OUP ONLINE RESOURCE CENTRE FOR MORE

- Discussion on biotechnology, genetic engineering, etc.
- The story of biodiversity conservation in Bhutan
- The story of UNESCO Man and the Biosphere Programme
- The full list of Goals and Targets under the Kunming-Montreal Global Biodiversity Framework
- Additional text and other recommended references, websites, and films

UNIT 4

Environmental Pollution

11 Solid Waste and Soil Pollution

Oh Beautiful for smoggy skies, for insecticided grain.
For strip-mined mountain's majesty above the asphalt plain.
America, America, man sheds his waste on thee,
And hides the pines with billboard signs, from sea to oily sea.

George Carlin
(1937–2008)
American comedian and social critic

MAIN QUESTIONS ADDRESSED

- What is waste and why does it require management?
- What is the state of municipal waste generation in the world?
- How can solid and liquid waste be properly managed?
- How does soil pollution occur and how can it be addressed?

KEYWORDS AND PHRASES

3Rs, Alang, biomedical waste, common effluent treatment plant, e-waste, landfill, municipal solid waste, plastic waste, sanitary landfill, ship-breaking, soil pollution, Swachh Bharat Abhiyan, waste segregation

LEAD STORY

THE STORY OF ALANG: TOXIC SHIPS, HAZARDOUS WASTE

There is a constant clang of metal. Dust and toxic fumes are everywhere. Huge metal monsters are ripped apart and become mountains of scrap. Welcome to Alang, the famous ship-breaking yard!

Alang is located in the Gulf of Kambhat on the Gujarat coast, 56 km south of Bhavnagar city. The unique geographical features of high tidal range and wide continental shelf, coupled with a mud-free coast, allow very heavy ships to reach the coast easily during high tide. It is an ideal place for ship-breaking.

The necklace-shaped Alang ship-breaking yard is said to be the largest in the world. With 184 shipbreaking plots, it dismantles about 300 ships every year and has a turnover of ₹6,000 crores. The yard employs 40,000 people directly and 100,000 more indirectly.

Seller to buyer: *This ship is now yours!*

The workers, mostly migrants from Orissa, Uttar Pradesh, and Bihar, toil under extremely hazardous conditions in a toxic atmosphere. Given the nature of the job, lack of training, and the absence of protective gear, accidents are common. The workers have no medical facilities, sanitation, housing, or safe drinking water. Accidents and related deaths are common.

Among the workers in Alang, there is a grim but popular saying: *Alang se Palang* (from Alang to the death bed). In fact, on June 28, 2014 five workers were killed in a gas explosion. From 1983 to 2013 there were 470 deaths in the yard, according to official records.

They reside in rented shanties in different villages around the yard in relative poverty. The huge influx of migrant labourers, with languages and cultures very different from the local ones, has also created social tensions in the area.

Most of the ships that come to Alang carry toxic waste, which cause environmental and health problems. In addition, the cost of clean-up falls on the Gujarat government.

Greenpeace and other organizations have been campaigning for the adoption of an environmentally safe approach to ship-breaking and for improving the conditions in the ship-breaking yards. Thanks to the directives issued by the Supreme Court and the Greenpeace campaign, some improvements are supposed to have been made in the working conditions at Alang. However, a 2014 study by the Tata Institute of Social Sciences, Mumbai, found that working conditions had hardly improved despite official claims to the contrary.

In early 2015, Japan offered help to Alang in areas of worker safety and environment protection. The project would make Alang fully capable of handling all the hazardous waste that comes from vessels brought for dismantling. But the condition was that India should ratify and implement the 2009 Hong Kong International Convention for the Safe and Environmentally Sound Recycling of Ships. This Convention is aimed at ensuring that ships, when being recycled after reaching the end of their operational lives, do not pose any unnecessary risks to human health, safety, and to the environment. India ratified the Convention in 2019. Japan has sanctioned US$ 76 million to Gujarat for improving the conditions of Alang.

We have to wait and see whether better days dawn for Alang and its workers.

CLIMATE CHANGE AND WASTE

Globally, the waste management sector contributes just 3–5% of total emissions caused by human activities. However, the waste sector can indirectly become a major saver of emissions. The prevention and recovery of wastes (as secondary materials or energy) will reduce emissions in all other sectors of the economy.

What is the message that the story of Alang carries for us?

Building huge ships may be a technological feat. The bigger problem, however, arises when their lives are over. How do we dispose of the solid waste, the huge hulk of metal with tonnes of toxic stuff inside? The Alang case shows the complex nature of hazardous waste disposal.

Solid waste is the source of pollution for air, soil, fresh water, and ocean. Though the title of this chapter is 'solid waste management', we will be considering liquid waste too.

What is Waste and Why does It Require Management?

Waste is any material that is not needed by the owner, producer, or processor. Humans, animals, other organisms, and all processes of production and consumption produce waste. It has always been a part of the earth's ecosystem, but its nature and scale were such that the ecosystem could use waste in its many cycles. In fact, there is no real waste in nature. The apparent waste from one process becomes input to another.

It is the exponential growth (Chapter 1) of human activities that has made waste a problem to be managed. We are simply producing much more waste than the amount nature can handle.

It is far better to prevent generation of waste than to produce waste and then try to 'manage' it. We cannot simply throw away waste. 'There is no away in throw away' What we throw away often comes back to us in a different form. What we dispose of remains in the ecosystem and causes some form of pollution. This pollution can have an impact far away from the point of generation and far removed in time too.

The composition, quantity, and disposal of waste determine the environmental problems it creates. To minimize the adverse effects of any waste, it has to be recycled, isolated permanently in storage, allowed to decompose and degrade into a harmless state, or treated to remove any toxicity it may have.

Gaseous waste, which is caused mainly by emissions from vehicles and other sources and carries fine particles of matter, leads to air pollution and smog (Chapter 13). When gaseous waste is deposited on land as acid rain, it pollutes the soil and water.

Most disposable wastes are in the form of solids, liquids, or slurries. The main categories of such wastes are the following:

Domestic waste: Sewage, waste water contaminated by detergents, dirt, or grease, household garbage, and bulky waste including packaging material, appliances, furniture, office equipment, and used cars.

Factory waste: Solids and effluents from factories of all types. The worst polluters are slaughterhouses, breweries, tanneries, textile, paper and steel mills, and most chemical industries; power plants discharge heated coolant water causing thermal pollution.

Waste from the oil industry: Oil spills, oil leaks, water used for cleaning tankers, etc.

Construction waste: Materials from buildings that are demolished or renovated and materials discarded after completing a building.

Waste from the extractive industries: Mining, quarrying, and dredging create solid waste (during extraction) and slurries (during processing).

Plastic waste: Thousands of different goods made of plastic (including the carry bag), thrown away after use, are everywhere on land and sea (Box 11.1).

BOX 11.1 ENVIROFACT: *Pollution by Plastic*

'Plastic' is a general term for a wide range of synthetic materials that are malleable and can be moulded into solid objects of diverse shapes. Developed in the 1860s, plastic is now one of the most useful and important materials in modern society. Thousands of products have plastic in them.

Plastic preserves and protects food and medicine. It is used to make electronic devices like computers and smartphones. It helps make transport more fuel efficient through its use in vehicles. It is more versatile and less expensive than many alternative materials.

About 280 million tonnes of plastic is produced globally each year and only a very small percentage is recycled. Plastic manufacturing processes use non-renewable resources, such as oil (4% of global oil production) and release greenhouse gases into the atmosphere contributing to climate change.

Toys, athletic goods, and durable household goods are heavy users of plastic. The soft drinks, personal products, and pharmaceutical sectors are among the most intensive users of plastic in packaging.

Longevity is plastic's useful characteristic, but this very quality has also become a major problem. It is the non-biodegradable nature of plastic that is causing a massive environmental problem. It simply does not 'go away' after use.

Plastic bags and bottles are found discarded everywhere. They now form an increasing proportion of municipal waste and cause many environmental problems. They clog sewage lines and canals and litter public places, gardens, wildlife reserves, and forests. Animals, birds, and marine organisms consume plastic items and even die as a result. Microscopic particles of plastic transfer toxins into the food chain. Chemical additives used in plastic goods are hazardous to human health. A good part of the plastic that we throw away ends up in the ocean with terrible consequences (Chapter 12, Box 12.4).

Globally, between 20% and 43% of plastic waste is disposed of in landfills. Such landfill sites affect the lives and health of local communities. If plastic is mixed with other materials, sorting the waste to collect useful materials becomes more complex, costly, and dangerous. Disposing of plastic by burning only creates more toxic fumes.

The worst offender is the thin carry bag that easily gets airborne when thrown away. The plastic carry bag has become a common item all over the world, both in the poor and rich countries. Globally, about 2 million plastic bags are used every single minute!

Certain plastics can be recycled. Many household articles like water containers and buckets are made of recycled plastic. Non-reusable items include carry bags, cups, plates, and magazine wrappers. Even in these cases, ecofriendly plastics are available as options.

There are strong views for and against plastic. The plastics industry cites the advantages of convenience, low cost, employment potential, recycling possibilities, etc. Environmentalists point out the problems listed above and also add the difficulty of separating the recyclable plastic items in landfills.

Some countries have banned plastic bags. In India, several states and local bodies have enforced various degrees of banning, mostly on thin bags. The Government of India has banned carrybags made of plastic films of thickness less than 40 microns. But this rule is not being implemented seriously.

Agricultural waste: Mostly organic waste from plants and animals; irrigation water from farms containing fertilizers and pesticides.
Waste from food processing: Organic solid and liquid waste from discarded food material.
Biomedical waste: Originates mainly from hospitals and clinics and includes blood, diseased organs, poisonous medicines, etc.
E-waste: A more recent form of waste from discarded electronic equipment (Box 11.2).

BOX 11.2 ENVIROFACT: *E-waste–Constant Obsolescence and Mounting Waste*

E-waste is a term used to cover items of all types of electrical and electronic equipment and their parts that have been discarded by the owner as waste without the intention of reuse. E-waste includes almost any household or business item containing circuitry or electrical components with either power or battery supply—items such as TV appliances, computers, laptops, tablets, mobile phones, white goods (fridges, washing machines, dryers, etc.), home entertainment and stereo systems, toys, toasters, and kettles.

The industries that make such products thrive on obsolescence. New gadgets and new models appear almost daily, prices keep dropping, and consumption is soaring. The older models are discarded as junk, even when they are in working condition. All this has resulted in e-waste becoming one of the fastest growing waste streams globally. From 19.5 m tonnes in 1990 global e-waste grew to 57.4 m tonnes in 2010 and is set to reach 75 m tonnes by 2030.

E-waste contains many hazardous materials like lead, copper, zinc, and aluminium, flame retardants, plastic casings, cables, etc. If e-waste is disposed in landfills, burned outdoors, or recycled in other inappropriate ways, the toxic substances can contaminate the air, water, and soil, affecting all living creatures.

In India, most e-waste ends in the informal or the unorganized sector. In addition to local waste, there is also e-waste imported from the industrialized countries. In the lanes of Delhi and other towns, a large number of poor people, including women and small children, break open these gadgets to recover valuable parts and materials. With no protective equipment and poor working conditions, these workers are exposed to a cocktail of toxic chemicals and suffer physical injuries, chronic ailments like asthma, skin and eye diseases, and even life-threatening diseases.

Responding to the problem, the Indian Government introduced the E-waste Management and Handling Rules in 2012. Most recently they were amended in November 2022. Consumers are now responsible for the proper disposal of e-waste generated by them and must hand over their used gadgets to authorized collectors, dismantlers, or recyclers. They can also give it back to the companies who sold the items. The producers are required to ensure collection and recycling of e-waste. They have to set up 'take-back' systems across the country.

While the regulation is welcome, environmentalists feel that the rules are weak and the implementation has been poor. Proper collection systems have not been put in place. There is no incentive either for consumers to deliver waste to collectors or for the small recyclers and scrap merchants to change their ways.

Nuclear waste: Radioactive waste from nuclear power plants and the manufacture of nuclear weapons; remains active and dangerous for thousands of years.

Apart from these regular sources, waste also comes from special events:

Waste from natural disasters: Rubble from earthquakes, slag and ash from volcanoes, wastes left behind by floods, cyclones, and typhoons.

Waste from wars and conflicts: Apart from dead bodies and destroyed buildings, wars leave behind exploded and live shells, landmines, etc. In some cases, deadly war material has effects lasting decades. Agent Orange, an herbicide, used the in Vietnam war, and depleted uranium in the 1991 Gulf War are examples.

> **Key Idea** There are many kinds of waste with known and unknown impact on health and environment.

It is very difficult to assess the effects of all the types of waste on the environment. We do not know the total amounts, composition, and dispersal of waste. Nor do we have enough scientific knowledge of the long-term impact of most substances that form part of waste. What is considered non-hazardous today may be declared dangerous tomorrow. In fact, environmentalists feel that we must follow the precautionary principle and treat every chemical or waste as being potentially harmful unless proved otherwise.

What is the State of Municipal Waste Generation in the World?

The Report *What a Waste 2.0* published by the World Bank in 2018 had these messages:

- The world generates 2 billion tonnes of municipal solid waste annually and at least 33% of that waste is not managed in an environmentally safe manner.
- Worldwide, waste generated per person per day averages 0.74 kilogram but ranges widely, from 0.11 to 4.54 kilograms.
- Though they only account for 16% of the world's population, high-income countries generate about 34%, or 683 million tonnes, of the world's waste.
- Global waste is expected to grow to 3.40 billion tonnes by 2050. Daily per capita waste generation in high-income countries is projected to increase by 19 % by 2050, compared to low- and middle-income countries where it is anticipated to increase by approximately 40% or more. The total quantity of waste generated in low-income countries is expected to increase by more than three times by 2050.
- Globally, most waste is currently dumped or disposed of in some form of a landfill. Some 37% of waste is disposed of in some form of a landfill, 8% of which is disposed of in sanitary landfills with landfill gas collection systems. Open dumping accounts for about 33% of waste, 19% is recovered through recycling and composting, and 11% is incinerated for final disposal.
- Based on the volume of waste generated, its composition, and how it is managed, it is estimated that 1.6 billion tonnes of CO_2-equivalent greenhouse gas emissions were generated from solid waste treatment and disposal in 2016, driven primarily by open dumping and disposal in landfills without landfill gas capture systems. This is about 5% of global emissions. Solid waste–related emissions are anticipated to increase to 2.6 billion tonnes of CO_2-equivalent per year by 2050, if no improvements are made in the sector.

> **Key Idea** Waste reduction must come before waste management; we should follow the four R's: Refuse, Reduce, Reuse, and Recycle.

How should we deal with municipal solid waste?

The first step is to reduce the generation of waste that goes out of our place and this is an urgent task for all of us. Even with our best efforts to reduce waste, however, some will be generated and this must be managed well. We should separate the different types at source, recover what is useful in the waste, and then handle the remaining amount without harming people or the environment.

How are Municipal Wastes Managed?

Separation of waste at source is the key to proper waste management.

In the industrialized countries, waste is sorted at the source (household, office, shop, or wherever) into categories like organic material, paper, glass, other containers, sanitary napkins, batteries, etc. The waste is collected in different bins, properly coloured and labelled. This source separation makes it easy for the municipal agency to handle each category of waste appropriately, leading to a high rate of recovery and recycling. In many cities in the developing countries, all the waste is collected together. Subsequent separation is difficult and hence the recycling rate is low. Now, some cities in the developing countries are trying to persuade the public to separate the waste.

Where does the collected waste go? In some places, central sorting is done to improve recovery and recycling. In most cities, however, the simplest and most common method is to dump the waste in a landfill. These landfills are located just outside the city. There are now thousands of landfills in the world with huge piles of waste. In the industrialized countries, you can also see separate mountains of used cars and tyres. Many countries and cities have run out of space for landfills. Other methods used include incineration and producing energy from waste.

In the poorer countries, rag pickers sift through the waste, collect the reusable and recyclable material, and sell it to the scrap traders. They, in turn, take the material to the recycling units. The rag pickers, the majority of whom are women and children, work under extremely unhygienic conditions and yet provide a great ecological service by manually separating thousands of tonnes of recyclable waste from the garbage dumps.

Often, the waste in a landfill is burnt away. While this reduces the volume of the garbage, it releases deadly dioxins. Proper incineration of waste needs modern technology and proper management.

What is a Sanitary Landfill?

Sanitary landfills are sites where waste is isolated from the environment until it is safe. Waste is deposited in thin layers (up to 1 m thick) and immediately compacted by heavy machinery. Several such layers are placed and compacted on top of each other to form a refuse cell (up to 3 m thick). At the end of each day the refuse cell is covered with a layer of compacted soil to prevent odours and windblown debris.

There are several requirements for a proper sanitary landfill:

- It should be located above the water table.
- The area should not be geologically active.
- It should not be very near residential communities.
- The land must be inexpensive to make the cost of operating the landfill worthwhile.
- It must be accessible to roads so that garbage can is delivered easily.
- Trained staff should be based at the landfill to supervise site preparation and construction, the depositing of waste and the regular operation and maintenance.

As the matter inside the sanitary landfill breaks down, it generates gases including methane. Some landfills simply vent these gases, while others collect and use them as fuel. Often, sanitary landfills are reclaimed once they are full. The area on top is used to make sports fields, parks, office parks, and so forth.

> **Key Idea**
> Dumping waste on open landfills is very common. Setting up safer sanitary landfills is uncommon and difficult.

How is liquid waste managed?

Sewage and industrial effluents are in most cases released directly into water bodies—rivers, lakes, or the ocean. Very often they are not treated before release.

The 1972 London Convention (Chapter 12) prohibits the ocean dumping of hazardous waste. The ocean, however, is still not safe, since all the countries do not observe the Convention. Further, thousands of tonnes of toxic substances (including nuclear waste), dumped into the ocean before the Convention came into force, are still present in the ocean and silently polluting the marine environment.

With increasing amounts being generated, management of waste is becoming difficult and expensive. The industrialized countries have found an easier and less expensive method: export the waste to other countries!

Why are Hazardous and Toxic Wastes Exported?

Many of the industrialized countries have a waste management problem. Since their economies are based on constant growth, development, and consumption, wastes are mounting up and they are running out of suitable space for landfills or dump yards. At the same time, these countries have strict environmental regulations that make waste management expensive.

The most attractive option for the industrialized countries is to export the waste to developing countries, where disposal is cheap and environmental regulations are lax. The latter needs the money and the former wants to get rid of the waste. Developing countries do have more space for disposal, but their tropical ecosystems are more vulnerable to the damaging effects of the waste. There are many cases of environmental damage caused in the developing countries due to improper management of imported toxic waste.

At any time, there are a number of ships carrying toxic waste prowling on the high seas, ready to dump the waste on an unsuspecting poor country. Alternately, they just dump the cargo somewhere in the middle of the vast ocean (Visit the ORC for one such story).

> **Key Idea** Industrialized countries often export their hazardous waste to other countries legally and illegally.

Waste management has become an international industry and even some industrialized countries like the UK import waste and make money on it. 90% of the hazardous waste generated in the US is exported to Canada.

The 1989 Basel Convention (Chapter 12) aims to minimize the creation of hazardous wastes, reduce transboundary movements of such wastes, and prohibit their shipment to countries lacking the capacity to dispose them off in an environmentally sound manner.

How is Municipal Waste Handled in Indian Cities and Towns?

It is difficult to estimate the amount of municipal solid waste (MSW) produced in Indian cities. The daily per capita generation of MSW in India ranges from 200 g to 870 g depending upon the region's lifestyle and the size of the city. The per capita waste generation is increasing by about 1.3% per year. The total amount of solid waste generated annually in Indian cities is about 62 million tonnes. The recyclable content is said to be 13–20% and waste collection efficiency ranges from 50% to 90%.

It is clear that the amount of solid waste is growing faster than the population. For example, during 1981–1991, Mumbai's population increased from 8.2 to 12.3 million (49%), while the daily municipal waste generation grew from 3,200 to 5,355 tonnes a day (67%). Now, Mumbai generates over 7,000 tonnes every day and this is expected to reach 10,000 tonnes by 2025.

> **Key Idea** Our cities are drowning in increasing mounds of waste and there is no easy solution.

70% of Indian cities do not have adequate waste transportation facilities. Out of the total municipal waste collected, on an average 94% is dumped on land and 5% is composted. As a result, streets are full of garbage, storm water drains are choked, and urban canals are covered with filth. The garbage that is transported in polluting old trucks is just dumped on sites in low-lying areas on the outskirts of cities. The choice of the site is more a matter of availability than suitability.

In most cities, the solid wastes lie unattended in the dumpsites and attract birds, rodents, insects, and other organisms. As the waste decays, it releases odour and airborne pathogens. Further, the practice of burning the waste creates toxic fumes and spreads the hazardous substances in the air.

A key issue is the lack of segregation of degradable and non-degradable waste at source. Even though some corporations require such segregation, citizens do not cooperate and officials are not ready to implement their own orders.

Villagers living near landfills protest against and even stop the dumping of waste in their area. As cities expand, corporations have to go farther and farther to find landfill sites. Citizen apathy, political and bureaucratic corruption, and the power of contractor mafias have made it impossible for municipalities to keep our cities clean.

A dangerous practice is disposing off biomedical waste (from hospitals and clinics) along with municipal waste in dumpsites. The biomedical waste could turn the entire yard infectious. Further, biomedical waste also contains sharp objects like scalpels, needles, broken ampoules, etc., which could injure or infect rag pickers and municipal workers. Though we have the Bio-Medical Waste (Management and Handling) Rules, 1998, many hospitals do not follow them.

Zero-waste systems are being attempted in some Indian cities (Box 11.3). Sanitary landfills are also coming up, near Delhi for example. In 2014, the Government of India launched the Swachh Bharat Abhiyan, a campaign to clean up the whole country (Box 11.4).

BOX 11.3 INSPIRATION: ***The Story of Vellore Srinivasan—Waste to Gold***

C. Srinivasan, a concerned citizen of Vellore, had first initiated a project to green the barren hills surrounding his town. Through this work, he came face to face with the environmental problems of the town. A major problem was that of garbage. There was almost no open space left in the town where waste could be dumped. As a result, garbage was being burnt or left to rot in the open all over town.

With the support of UNICEF and the NGO Exnora Green Cross, Srinivasan started a Community Composting Project, in which waste from five neighbourhoods was recycled and successfully processed. Later, Srinivasan turned the Vellore Fish Market into a clean and bustling place by collecting all the biodegradable waste from there and composting it at another location. Many more such projects followed and, even as Srinivasan refined his approaches, his work also came to be recognized.

Through his work, Srinivasan has evolved a Zero Waste Management (ZWM) model, which has been implementing in many places. The features of ZWM are:

- Separation of garbage at the source, be it at households, farms, villages, wards, municipalities, educational institutions, hospitals, jails, or temples.
- Separate collection (where possible) of each kind of waste—kitchen waste, toilet waste, cattle waste, temple waste, hotel and shop waste, plastics, metal, tyres, hair, etc.
- Segregation of waste into different categories and selling the recyclable items to appropriate buyers. Paper is sorted into categories like newspaper, cardboard, and wet paper and sent to third-party recycling facilities. Glass is dealt with in a similar manner. Hair is sold to wig companies.
- Composting of organic waste using cow dung and earthworms and selling the compost.
- Involvement of the community in all activities.
- Livelihood for the local poor through selling recyclable items and making and selling compost.

ZWM is financed by user fees and by the sales it makes by selling waste to recyclers. Each month, each household pays a nominal fee for joining the refuse collection program. ZWM also helps society by providing employment. The disabled or aged help sort garbage, while the young collect and transport waste.

Srinivasan now advises many cities and organizations on dealing with waste in the ZWM way.

BOX 11.4 HOPE: ***Swachh Bharat Abhiyan—Toward a Clean India***

On October 2, 2014, Prime Minister Narendra Modi launched the Swachh Bharat Abhiyan (SBA), a national campaign to achieve the goal of Clean India. The objective was to reach the goal in five years, by the 150th birth anniversary of Mahatma Gandhi. SBA was intended to make progress towards Sustainable Development Goal 6.2, which aims for adequate and equitable sanitation access for all, especially for women and girls.

The campaign objectives were:

- Elimination of open defecation
- Conversion of insanitary toilets to pour flush toilets
- Eradication of manual scavenging
- 100% collection and scientific processing, disposal, reuse, or recycling of municipal solid waste
- A behavioural change in people regarding healthy sanitation practices
- Generation of awareness among citizens about sanitation and its linkages with public health
- Supporting urban local bodies in designing, executing, and operating waste disposal systems
- Facilitating private-sector participation in capital expenditure and operation and maintenance costs for sanitary facilities

By 2019, through approaches such as people's participation, the campaign constructed over 100 million household toilets, benefitting 500 million people across 630,000 villages. It also paved the way for SBA Phase II since 2020.

The Mission's model is now being emulated by other national campaigns and has influenced equivalent policies in countries such as Nigeria, Indonesia and Ethiopia.

A more fundamental question remains: How will we resolve the contradiction between our mantra of rapid economic growth and the objectives of Swachh Bharat Abhiyan? Unrestrained growth will only increase consumption and waste generation.

(See also Chapter 12, Box 12.2 for more on SBA.)

Which are the Major Polluting Industries of India?

Here are some examples of polluting industries in India and the possible measures to mitigate the problems:

- 2500 tanneries discharge about 24 million cubic metres of waste water containing high levels of dissolved solids and 400,000 tonnes of hazardous solid wastes per year.
- About 300 distilleries discharge 26 million kilolitres of spent wash per year containing many pollutants.
- Thermal power plants discharge 100 million tonnes of fly ash and this figure is expected to reach 175 million soon. Fly ash contains silicon, aluminium, iron, and calcium oxides and is said to cause silicosis, fibrosis of the lungs, cancer, and bronchitis. Fly ash, however, is being utilized in many ways: making bricks, blending with cement, building roads and embankments, adding micronutrients to soil, etc.

India continues to produce several pesticides banned or restricted in other countries. Examples are DDT, Malathion, and Endosulfan. One-sixth of the total pesticides used in India are those banned elsewhere. The bulk of the production is from small units that have no technology to treat the toxic and non-biodegradable pollutants generated during the manufacturing process. 50% of the pesticides used in India are for cotton.

Industrialized states like Gujarat, Maharashtra, Tamil Nadu, and Andhra Pradesh face major problems of toxic and hazardous waste disposal. For example, the Ahmedabad–Vadodara–Surat industrial belt houses 2000 industrial units and more than 63,000 small scale units manufacturing chemicals like soda ash, dyes, yarns, and fertilizers. Most of the units dump their wastes in low-lying areas within a radius of 2 km. A major illegal dump yard has sprung up on the banks of the river Daman Ganga. During the monsoon, the hazardous substances are washed into the river. There are many such cases across the country.

MoEFCC estimates that 7.2 million tonnes of hazardous waste is generated annually in India. In addition, industries discharge about 150 million tonnes of high volume—low hazard wastes every year, which is mostly dumped on open, low-lying land.

Are Hazardous Wastes from Other Countries Dumped in India?

Huge amounts of wastes, particularly scrap metal, are imported into India. According to the Basel Convention as well as India's Hazardous Wastes (Management and Handling) Amendment Rules, scrap metal is hazardous. Import of such waste is not banned in India, but prior permission is needed from the respective state pollution control boards and the Ministry of Environment and Forests.

Customs authorities do not have the required personnel and the equipment needed to check each consignment of imported waste for explosive material or toxics. They only check if the seals are okay.

Another major concern is the hazardous waste that is released and generated during ship-breaking.

What are the Environmental Consequences of Ship-breaking?

Ship-breaking has become a big industry today. The huge vessels, which have served their lives and have been decommissioned, are sent to yards for recycling the parts to the extent possible. India, Taiwan, China, and Bangladesh have large ship-breaking facilities.

Most of the ships sent to the yards contain hazardous material such as asbestos, toxic paints, and fuel residues. However, as we saw in the case of Alang yard at the beginning of this chapter, ship-breaking is not just a solid waste problem. It has many dimensions: the export of hazardous waste to the developing countries, the environmental problems of handling toxic waste, the safety and health issues of the workers, the social tensions the enterprise creates, the role of the government, and so on.

Ship-breaking results in the following kinds of pollution:

- Discharge of oil into the ocean damages marine organisms and birds, and destroys their natural habitats.
- Wastes like blasting residue and paint chips contaminate the soil and surface water.
- Improper storage and disposal of scrap metal and other wastes cause lead contamination.
- Cutting the metal parts with a blowtorch generates smoke, hazardous fumes, and particulates of manganese nickel, chromium, iron, asbestos, and lead.

Responding to a public interest petition, the Supreme Court of India issued a number of directives in 2003 with regard to the ship-breaking industry. Some of the important directives are:

- The owners should properly decontaminate the ship before the breaking operation. They should also submit a complete inventory of hazardous waste on board.
- The Maritime Board and the Pollution Control Board of the concerned state should monitor all ship-breaking operations.
- The industry should be allowed to operate only if it has facilities for disposal of waste in an environmentally sound manner.
- Waste generated during the process should be classified into hazardous and non-hazardous categories and the details made know to the State Maritime Board.

From October 2004, decommissioned ships are also covered under the Basel Convention. Consequently, countries exporting ships for recycling should seek the informed prior consent of the importing countries. This decision would encourage the industrialized countries to set up domestic ship recycling facilities. Alternately, they would have to carry out some level of decontamination of ships before sending them abroad for recycling.

> **Key Idea**
> Ship-breaking is big business in India, but it is also a very dirty business, since the ships often contain toxic waste.

The Hong Kong International Convention for the Safe and Environmentally Sound Recycling of Ships, adopted in 2009 (recall the Alang story) intends to address all the issues around ship recycling, including the fact that ships sold for scrapping may contain environmentally hazardous substances such as asbestos, heavy metals, hydrocarbons, ozone-depleting substances, and others. It also addresses concerns raised about the working and environmental conditions at many of the world's ship recycling locations.

What are Common Effluent Treatment Plants?

A small-scale industry cannot afford to clean up all its effluents. One solution to this problem is to collect the waste of several units from an industrial estate and treat it in a common location. The state pollution control boards in India are now compelling specific polluting industries in an area to set up common effluent treatment plants (CETPs).

CETPs are cost-effective, perhaps the ideal, solution to control pollution. Half the cost is met by the industries and a quarter each by the state and central governments. Each unit also contributes towards the running of the plant.

The first CETPs were set up to treat tannery wastes in Tamil Nadu, textile wastes in Rajasthan, and industrial waste in Andhra Pradesh. There are more than 100 CETPs in the country.

CETPs have run into many problems. In many cases, reliable information is not available on the amounts and types of waste expected to reach the CETP. As a result, the design may not be the appropriate one. Further, a cocktail of different chemicals can be far more toxic than the individual chemicals themselves.

There are also problems in fixing the charges and getting the users to pay them. Questions also remain about the management and proper functioning of the CETPs. For example, who should be held responsible if the treatment is poor and the CETP itself becomes a polluter?

How can Solid Waste be Recycled?

A good way of dealing with the solid waste problem is recycling, which is the processing of a used item or any waste into a usable form. There is a large recycling industry in the world. In India, we have a thriving, unorganized recycling industry, thanks to the itinerant collector, who buys your old newspaper, bottles, used clothes, utensils, scrap, motor oil, etc.

Recycling brings multiple benefits:

- By taking away some of the waste, it reduces environmental degradation.
- As against expenditure incurred on disposing off the waste, we now make money out of the waste material.
- We save energy that would have gone into waste handling and the making of products.

Some specific examples of savings through recycling are:

- When aluminium is re-smelted, there is considerable savings in cost. The recycling process, however, is energy-intensive.
- Making paper from waste pulp rather than virgin pulp saves 50% energy
- Every ton of recycled glass saves energy equal to 100 litres of oil.

Safe and profitable technologies for recycling paper, glass, metals, and some forms of plastic are available. Biogas can be produced from landfill waste. Paper factories can certainly recycle their waste.

Recycling is not a solution for all waste material. In many cases, the technologies are not available or unsafe. In other cases, the cost of recycling is too high.

How does Soil Become Polluted?

We have discussed the importance of soil and the current massive degradation of soil in Chapter 7.

Soil pollution is any physical or chemical change in the soil conditions that may adversely affect the growth of plants and other organisms living in or on it. Soil pollution and water pollution are closely connected. Acid rain and excessive use of chemical fertilizers result in the soil becoming unable to hold nutrients. This, in turn, allows toxic pesticides or atmospheric fallout seep rapidly into ground water or runoff into rivers and coastal waters. Some of the persistent pollutants remain in the soil and degrade it.

Most soil pollutants are agricultural chemicals, primarily fertilizers and pesticides. It is now known that these chemicals attach themselves to soil particles and persist for long, continuously releasing contaminants into the surface water, ground water, and the topsoil. Dumping of waste including garbage, untreated sewage, industrial effluents, nuclear waste, and mining waste pollute the soil by leaking the dangerous substances.

Salts tend to accumulate in the soils of arid and semi-arid regions. The little precipitation that falls evaporates quickly leaving the salts behind. Salinization can also occur in any region due to continued application of irrigation water containing some salts.

Why are plants unable to tolerate saline soil?

Water always moves from an area of higher concentration to one of lower concentration. Normally, plants have a lower concentration than the surrounding soil and water flows into the plants. Saline soil, however, has often a lower concentration of water than plants. Consequently, water starts flowing out of the plant into the soil.

How can soil condition be restored?

Dilution is one way of removing pollutants from the soil. It involves running large quantities of water through the soil to leach out the pollutants. This works only if the soil has good drainage properties. Even then, disposing of the water carrying the pollutants poses a problem. The method also requires lots of water.

In vapour extraction, air is injected into the soil to remove organic compounds that evaporate quickly. Bioremediation uses bacteria and other microorganisms to clean up the soil. In phytoremediation, we use plants, whose roots absorb pollutants and store them in their stems and leaves.

From water and soil, we now move to marine pollution.

What is the Way out of the Waste Problem?

We have to move from waste management to waste prevention. That is, we should design clean production technologies or zero-discharge systems that use minimum amounts of raw materials, energy, and water and do not generate any wastes.

The life cycle of a product should be such that at no stage is any natural ecosystem adversely affected. This should apply to raw material extraction, design, manufacture, material transport, actual use, and disposal. Clean production technologies do exist and they will be cost-effective if the true environmental costs are taken into account.

Even as we move to clean technologies, there is another way out of the industrial waste problem. If the industries in an area cooperate, they could design a system in which the waste from one industry becomes the input for one or more industries in the neighbourhood.

What is the concept of 3R?

The concept of 3R refers to Reduce, Reuse, and Recycle:

- Reduce: Decrease the amount of wasteful stuff we buy and discard quickly.
- Reuse: Find new use from old things. For example, small grocery stores use old newspaper to pack groceries. We can donate old clothes to NGOs that accept them, repair, and clean them and give them away to poor people.
- Recycle: Send plastics and other recyclable materials such as metals to proper recycling facilities.

> **Key Idea** Waste prevention is far better than waste management.

Often, a fourth action 'Refuse' is also added to this approach. Just refuse to accept any item that becomes a waste. For example, you can carry your own cloth bags to the markets and refuse plastic bags. Or you can refuse to buy new clothes for every festival.

Ending on a Hopeful Note: Positive Stories

The inspiring work in waste management being done by Vellore Srinivasan (Box 11.3) and the government programme Swachh Bharat Abhiyan (11.4) are positive stories. Also, many apartment blocks in cities are now managing their waste well.

REVIEW: A SUMMARY OF THE KEY POINTS

- Waste has always been a part of the earth's ecosystem, but human activities now generate so much waste that it needs proper 'management'.
- Human activities generate many categories of wastes, each with its own characteristics and disposal problems.
- The amount of municipal solid waste is increasing rapidly.
- Hazardous and toxic wastes generated in the industrialized countries are often exported for disposal in the developing countries, where environmental regulations are lax.
- Hazardous wastes are imported into India and cause many problems.
- Disposing off decommissioned ships is a complex task, since it involves handling large amounts of toxic waste.
- Tanneries, distilleries, and thermal power plants are some of the polluting industries in India.
- The widespread use of plastics is a problem because many plastics are non-degradable, persist for long, and cause many environmental problems.
- E-waste is becoming a major issue in the world.
- Indian cities face huge problems in managing municipal waste and sewage, though some amount of recycling is done.
- The world's soil is becoming polluted with agricultural chemicals and hence getting degraded.
- The only way out of the waste problem is to prevent or minimize the generation of waste by following the four R's.

EXERCISES

Objective-type questions

For each question below, choose the best answer out of the given choices.

1. Which of the following statements is true with regard to waste and its management?
   (a) There is no real waste in nature.
   (b) Waste can always be fully reused.
   (c) Nature can handle our waste.
   (d) We can always handle waste by throwing it away.
2. What is the most serious issue with ship-breaking?
   (a) Lack of facilities for workers
   (b) Toxic content of ships
   (c) Marine pollution
   (d) Air pollution
3. Which of the following is the most dangerous and long-lasting?
   (a) Biomedical waste
   (b) Ash from volcano
   (c) Mining waste
   (d) Nuclear waste
4. What is the precautionary principle?
   (a) We can assess the effects of all types of waste on the environment.
   (b) We must take precautions while managing waste.
   (c) Any waste is potentially harmful unless proved otherwise.
   (d) We do not know the long-term effect of waste.
5. Which of the following statements is **not** true with regard to landfills?
   (a) Finding space for landfills is not difficult.
   (b) Rag-pickers work on landfills.
   (c) Waste in a landfill is often burnt.
   (d) Landfills are often outside the city.
6. What is the best way of managing hazardous waste?
   (a) Export it to another country.
   (b) Burn it away.
   (c) Import it and make money.
   (d) Dispose it off in an environmentally sound manner.
7. Which of the following statements is **not** true with regard to normal plastic waste?
   (a) It lasts long.
   (b) It clogs sewage pipes.
   (c) It can be composted.
   (d) Burning it produces toxic fumes.
8. Which of the following statements is **not** true with regard to recycling waste?
   (a) Recycling is a solution for all waste material.
   (b) Paper can be recycled.
   (c) Recycling brings in money.
   (d) Recycling saves energy.
9. What is the Basel Convention concerned with?
   (a) Hazardous waste
   (b) E-waste
   (c) Biomedical waste
   (d) Municipal solid waste
10. What is meant by upcycling?
    (a) Recovering useful material from waste
    (b) Composting biodegradable waste
    (c) Separating waste into categories
    (d) Turning waste into products of higher quality

Short-answer questions

1. What is ship-breaking and why is it a complex task?
2. Why has waste become a major problem in the world?
3. List any five categories of waste and give their sources.
4. What are the ways of managing waste?
5. List the major polluting industries in India and describe the scale of their pollution.
6. What are the effects of plastic waste?
7. What are common effluent treatment plants?
8. How are Indian cities handling the increasing amounts of municipal wastes?
9. How can solid waste be recycled?
10. What is e-waste and why is it a major problem?
11. Explain the concept of 3Rs.
12. Describe the programme Swachh Bharat Abhiyan. Why was it successful to a great extent?

Long-answer question

Write an essay on the export of hazardous and toxic wastes from one country to another? Why are the wastes exported? What are the environmental and social issues involved? Which international agreements cover the case of such movement and disposal of waste? What are the recent developments in this regard?

Think critically: Deeper question for reflection and discussion

Can a country shift its environmental problems to another country? Should the export of hazardous wastes be banned? What then will be the consequences in the developing countries, where thousands of people are employed in handling foreign waste (as in Alang, for example)?

ENJOY AND EDUCATE YOURSELF

1. Watch the Academy Award-winner *WALL-E* (2008), an animated feature film that tells the story of a small waste-collecting robot who inadvertently embarks on a space journey that will ultimately decide the fate of mankind. It is a cautionary tale, foretelling what might be if mankind's unsustainable habits are allowed to continue unabated.
2. Relax with *Ship Breaker* (2010), a novel by Paolo Bacigalupi. In a post-apocalyptic future, the polar ice caps have melted and New Orleans is buried underwater. On the Gulf Coast nearby, as humanity has reverted to survival mode, a small economy has grown from the scavenging of washed up oil tankers for bits of copper and other valuable things ... and the story goes on.

ACCESS THE OUP ONLINE RESOURCE CENTRE FOR MORE

- The story of Kalundborg: Zero waste, more profits!
- The story of *Khian Sea*: Around the world in 16 years
- Additional text and other recommended references, websites, and films

12 Water and Marine Pollution

The sea, the great unifier, is man's only hope.
Now, as never before, the old phrase has a literal meaning:
We are all in the same boat.

Jacques Cousteau (1910–1997)
French marine conservationist and underwater explorer

MAIN QUESTIONS ADDRESSED

- How do water sources and the ocean get polluted and what is the scale of such pollution in India and the world?
- How can we handle water and pollution?
- Why is sanitation a worldwide problem and what is the solution?
- What are the international initiatives to control marine pollution?

KEYWORDS AND PHRASES

Biological Oxygen Demand, biomagnification, bioremediation, ecological sanitation, eutrophication, fluorosis, Great Pacific Garbage Patch, Persistent Organic Pollutants, reverse osmosis, sludge, thermal pollution

LEAD STORY

THE STORY OF FLUORIDE CONTAMINATION: CANNOT LIVE, CANNOT DIE!

In Jharana Khurd village, 20 km from Jaipur, Rajasthan, there are no youth. All the 1200 inhabitants, irrespective of age, look old. Their shoulders, hips, and ankles are swollen and ache all the time. All have cracked teeth.

The people of Jharana Khurd are not alone. The story is similar in Baroli Aheer in Uttar Pradesh, Chukru in Jharkand, Kachariadih in Bihar, Annaparti in Andhra Pradesh, and thousands of other villages across the country. The people of all these villages suffer from fluorosis, caused by an excess of fluoride in water.

Excess intake of fluoride leads to fluorosis: dental, skeletal, or non-skeletal. Dental fluorosis results in blackened, mottled, or cracked teeth. Skeletal fluorosis means permanent and severe bone and joint deformities. Non-skeletal fluorosis leads to gastrointestinal and neurological problems. There seems to be no cure for fluorosis.

No youth in the village?

High fluoride concentration in ground water occurs naturally in a number of countries. While fluorosis is most severe and widespread in India and China, it is endemic in at least 25 countries affecting millions of people. The Indian geology is such that the bedrock contains minerals with high fluoride content. When the bedrock weathers, the fluoride leaches into the water and soil.

In India, fluorosis has wiped out the economy of whole villages by disabling most of the inhabitants. To women, the disease brings social stigma. Normally, the disease does not lead to death, but to extreme suffering. As someone put it, 'It neither allows a person to live nor to die.'

Why has fluorosis become a problem in recent years? Excessive extraction of ground water has led to deeper and deeper borewells, which draw water from aquifers containing high fluoride concentrations. There is no fluoride problem if one drinks water from an open well or pond.

Fluorosis is endemic in 19 Indian states, directly affecting 25 million people (including 6 million children) with another 66 million 'at risk'. At least 60,000 villages have high fluoride levels. As India digs deeper and deeper to get water, the fluoride problem will become more widespread and more acute.

Until now, state- and national-level initiatives to combat fluorosis have been weak. There is no regular monitoring and testing of ground water. Technologies are available for defluoridation, but the plants are expensive and involve significant maintenance costs.

UNICEF (UN Children's Fund) has introduced domestic de-fluoridation filter units, which can be used in homes to remove excess fluoride from drinking water. This easy-to-use device, where contaminated water poured into the upper chamber gets filtered and collects in the lower one, reduces the fluoride content to acceptable levels. Another solution is to use rain water in place of the contaminated water (Box 12.5).

CLIMATE CHANGE AND WATER QUALITY

Climate change, reflected as higher water temperatures and changes in the timing, intensity, and duration of rainfall, can affect water quality. Higher air temperatures, earlier snowmelt, and potential decreases in summer rainfall could increase the risk of drought as well as floods. In addition, sea-level rise may affect freshwater quality by increasing the salinity of coastal rivers and causing saltwater intrusion in coastal regions.

What do we learn from the Fluorosis story?

Under normal use of water resources, the fluoride problem would not have become such a widespread issue. Fluoride contamination began only when we went deeper and deeper into the ground to extract increasing amounts of water. It is once again a case of exceeding the limits of nature to satisfy our needs and paying a heavy price for it.

In this chapter, we will consider water and marine pollution.

What is Water Pollution and What is the Scale of Water Pollution in the World?

Water pollution is the contamination of water sources including ponds, lakes, rivers, ground water, and the ocean. Water pollution occurs when pollutants are discharged directly or indirectly into water bodies without removing harmful compounds. Water pollution affects plants and organisms living in these bodies of water as well as human communities that use the polluted water.

Here are some points and facts about water pollution from the website of UN Water:

- As populations grow and natural environments become degraded, ensuring everyone has safe and sufficient water supplies is becoming increasingly challenging. A major part of the solution is to produce less pollution and improve the way we manage wastewater.

- Water pollution is increasing throughout the water cycle. Due to population growth, accelerated urbanization and economic development, the quantity of wastewater being generated and its overall pollution load are increasing globally.
- A more circular, sustainable economy means reducing contamination of ecosystems, and increasing the treatment, recycling and safe reuse of wastewater as a source of water, energy and nutrients.
- Industry and agriculture are often big water polluters. Increased usage of chemical fertilizers and pesticides, and untreated wastewater in irrigation, pollutes groundwater and surface water. Industry in many areas still discharges waste directly into water courses.
- Wastewater management is being seriously neglected. Across the world, safely reused wastewater is grossly undervalued as a potentially affordable and sustainable source of water, energy, nutrients and other recoverable materials.
- Untreated wastewater in cities is a major issue. In poorer urban areas, a large proportion of wastewater is discharged untreated directly into the closest drainage channel or water body. Household effluent, human waste, toxic chemicals and medical waste are exposed to the air, contaminating the environment in often densely-populated residential zones.
- Globally, about 40% of household wastewater is not safely treated.
- 60% of water bodies assessed in 89 countries have good ambient water quality.
- Water quality data are not collected routinely in a majority of countries. This means that over 3 billion people are at risk because the health of their freshwater ecosystems is unknown.
- Of the 89 countries with water quality data, only 52 have information about groundwater, which is problematic because groundwater often represents the largest share of freshwater in a country.
- Several water-related diseases, including cholera and schistosomiasis, remain widespread across many developing countries, where only a very small fraction (in some cases less than 5%) of domestic and urban wastewater is treated prior to its release into the environment.
- The greatest increases in exposure to pollutants are expected to occur in low- and lower-middle income countries, primarily because of higher population and economic growth in these countries, especially those in Africa, and the lack of wastewater management systems.

Which are the Pollutants of Fresh Water and What are the Effects?

Most of the freshwater sources in the world like rivers, lakes, and ground water are already polluted. This is true even of remote places like the polar regions. Most of the pollution that ultimately reaches the ocean contaminates freshwater sources on the way.

The main categories of water pollutants and their effects are:

Sediments: Excessive amounts of soil particles carried by flowing water, when there is severe soil erosion. Sediments cloud the water and reduce photosynthesis, clog reservoirs and channels, smother coral reefs, destroy feeding grounds of fish, and disrupt aquatic food webs.

Oxygen-demanding wastes: Organic waste such as animal manure and plant debris that are decomposed by bacteria, from sewage, animal feedlots, paper mills, and food processing facilities. Bacteria that decompose these wastes deplete the oxygen and cause the death of fish and other aquatic organisms.

Infectious microorganisms: Parasitic worms, viruses, and bacteria from infected organisms as well as human and animal wastes. They are responsible for water-borne diseases that kill thousands of adults and children, primarily in the developing countries.

Organic compounds: Synthetic chemicals containing carbon from industrial effluents, surface runoff, and cleaning agents. These chemicals cause many health problems for humans and harm fish and wildlife.

Inorganic nutrients: Substances like nitrogen and phosphorus from animal waste, plant residues, and fertilizer runoff. The nutrients can cause eutrophication (explained below) and can affect infants and unborn babies.

Inorganic chemicals: Acids, salts, and heavy metals like lead and mercury from industrial effluents, surface runoff, and household cleaning agents. They make water unfit for drinking or irrigation, harm fish and other aquatic organisms, cause many health problems for humans, and lower crop yields.

> **Key Idea** Many kinds of pollutants, mostly from human activities, contaminate water sources and cause adverse effects.

Radioactive substances: Wastes from nuclear power plants, nuclear weapons production, and mining and refining uranium and other ores. Such substances cause cancers, birth defects, miscarriages, etc.

Thermal pollution: Hot water from industrial processes. The heat lowers oxygen levels and makes aquatic organisms more vulnerable to disease, parasites, and toxic chemicals. When the hot water is let in, the sudden increase in temperature produces thermal shock in aquatic organisms (discussed later).

Where do the Water Pollutants Come from?

Water pollutants come from point sources and nonpoint sources. Specific places like sewage treatment plants and factories are point *sources* that discharge pollutants through pipes, sewers, or ditches. Point sources can be regulated through laws and rules.

Pollution from nonpoint sources occurs when pollutants enter the water over large areas than at a single point. This is the case when rain water flows along the soil, picks up pollutants, and carries them into the water bodies. Nonpoint sources include rainfall or melted snow moving over and through the ground, mining wastes, municipal wastes, construction sediments, acid rain, and soil erosion. Nonpoint sources are difficult to control.

What is Eutrophication of Lakes?

A lake or a pond that has clear water contains minimal levels of nutrients and supports small populations of aquatic organisms. *Eutrophication* is the enrichment of such a standing water body by nutrients such as phosphorus and nitrogen. It occurs when sewage and fertilizer runoff bring large amounts of nutrients to the water body.

In eutrophic lakes, there is increased photosynthetic activity. This results in cloudy water covered by a slimy and smelly mat of algae and cyanobacteria. When the excessive numbers of algae die, they fall to the bottom of the lake and get decomposed. Since this process uses up a lot of the dissolved oxygen, some fish species die. They are replaced by other species that can tolerate lesser amounts of oxygen.

Eutrophication is not desirable, since it changes the species mix and also covers the surface. Reducing phosphorus and nitrogen input is the best way of controlling eutrophication.

How does Ground Water Get Polluted?

About 2 billion people, approximately one-third of the world's population, depend on ground water for their daily needs. About 600 to 700 cubic km of ground water is withdrawn every year, mostly from shallow aquifers.

It was believed for long that water that slowly seeps or infiltrates into the ground would be thoroughly filtered by the soil and hence ground water would be free of pollutants. We know now that this is not necessarily true. The filtering capacity of soil varies greatly from place to place. Further, there is also a limit to the amount of pollutants the soil can filter.

Excessive extraction leads to the natural pollution of ground water. Examples are the fluoride concentration described at the beginning of this chapter and the arsenic contamination discussed in Box 12.1. In coastal areas, when water tables drop due to excessive extraction, there is intrusion of salt water and this is often an irreversible process.

BOX 12.1 DISASTER: ***The Story of Arsenic Poisoning***

Arsenic is naturally present at high levels in the ground water of a number of countries and it is highly toxic in its inorganic form. Arsenic-contaminated water used for drinking, food preparation, and irrigation of food crops poses the greatest threat to public health.

The effect of arsenic in the body starts showing after 2–5 years of consuming the contaminated water. The skin develops spots, then hard nodules, leading later to gangrene and cancer. It also brings many other complications like blindness, liver and heart problems, diabetes, and goitre.

The contamination of ground water with arsenic was first reported in 1983 from the 24-Parganas District of West Bengal. Later, it was found that almost the whole of Bangladesh was affected by this problem. Arsenic-affected countries include Vietnam, Thailand, Argentina, Chile, Mexico, China, and the US.

Arsenic contamination has been worsening steadily in West Bengal, Bihar, and Bangladesh. About 60 million people in the two countries drink contaminated water. In Bangladesh, 1.5 million tubewells are heavily contaminated with arsenic. Globally, about 100 million people are exposed to the toxic water.

Some scientists believe that all this is only the tip of the iceberg. Many future generations could be at grave risk from this poisoning. This is perhaps the largest mass poisoning in history.

Where does the arsenic come from? One theory is that it originated in the Himalayan headwaters of the Ganga and the Brahmaputra and had been below the deltas of the region for thousands of years. Over a long period this arsenic has contaminated the deep wells.

The other theory is that arsenic deposits are present in aquifers. When the rate of groundwater extraction is very high, the water level goes below the deposits, and arsenic is released. When the aquifer gets recharged, the arsenic contaminates the water.

Until now national and international initiatives to tackle the problem have been tentative and ineffective. Testing for arsenic is a complex, difficult, and expensive process. There is also lack of basic knowledge about the movement of ground water and the location of arsenic in the water sources.

Scientists are working on methods to affordably and effectively remove arsenic from drinking water. The most important action that affected communities can take is the prevention of further exposure to arsenic by provision of a safe water supply.

Ground water receives pollutants from septic tanks, landfills, hazardous waste dumps, and underground tanks containing petrol, oil, chemicals, etc. Substances like paint thinners and motor oil that we pour on the ground ultimately reaches the ground water.

Key Idea The world's ground water, on which millions of people depend, are now polluted in many places.

Ground water pollution is long lasting because it does not get flushed or decomposed away. The flow of ground water is very slow, decomposing bacteria are few in number, and the cold temperatures slow down the decomposing process. As a result, even degradable waste stays in the water for hundreds to thousands of years. In any case, nondegradable waste like lead, arsenic, and fluoride remain in ground water permanently.

What is Thermal Pollution of Water?

Thermal pollution is defined as sudden increase or decrease in temperature of any natural body of water, which is caused by human activity. This normally occurs when a plant or facility takes in water from a natural resource and puts it back with an altered temperature. Most often, water is used as a coolant and hence the discharged water is at a higher temperature.

Thermal pollution also occurs due to other causes. Here are some examples:

- Deforestation, which exposes water bodies to direct sunlight.
- Run-off from hot surfaces such as roads falling into water bodies.
- Volcanoes and geothermal activity under the ocean that trigger warm lava to raise the temperature of water.

What is the impact of thermal pollution?

Thermal pollution has negative effects such as the following:

- Decrease in the levels of dissolved oxygen in water, which can suffocate species. An example is the mass fish kills seen in some water bodies.
- Loss of biodiversity because some species cannot tolerate the higher water temperatures—their reproductive systems are affected and they migrate to other areas.
- Alien species could migrate into the area.

What is Biomagnification?

Biomagnification is the increase in concentration of a substance, such as the pesticide, that occurs in a food chain. The pollutant enters the first organism in a food chain. When the second organism in the chain consumes the first one, the pollutant too moves into the second organism.

We know that, as we go up the levels of the ecological pyramid (Chapter 2), there is energy loss. Hence, at each succeeding level, the predator consumes more of the prey. As a result, the organisms at higher levels have greater concentrations of the pollutant. This is called biomagnification.

For example, mercury is only present in small amounts in sea water. It is absorbed by algae. Plankton consume a lot of algae and get higher doses of mercury. Through biomagnification, mercury level increases in each further link of the food chain: small fish and then larger fish.

Anything, which eats these fish, also consumes the higher level of mercury the fish have accumulated. Hence, swordfish, sharks, and birds like osprey and eagles have high concentrations of mercury in their bodies. We also take in high levels of mercury when we eat fish.

Let us now look at some aspects of water pollution in India.

What do We Know about Water Pollution in India?

It is estimated that almost 70% of India's surface water resources and many of its groundwater reserves are already contaminated by a variety of pollutants. In many cases, these water sources have been rendered unsafe for human consumption as well as for other activities such as irrigation and industrial needs. This has reduced the supply of fresh water.

What is the state of rivers in India?

While the major rivers retain their pristine quality at the headwaters stage, they become polluted once they reach the plains. Agricultural runoff, industrial effluents, and domestic sewage find their way into most rivers. The rivers are stressed in the middle stretches where both extraction rates and pollution levels are high.

Tests of the river waters near or in cities show that in most cases the water is unfit for drinking. This is the case with the Yamuna near Delhi, Sabarmati in Ahmedabad, Gomti in Lucknow, Adyar in Chennai, Vaigai at Madurai, and Sutlej near Ludhiana.

How Severe is Pesticide Contamination of Fresh Water in India?

Since the beginning of the Green Revolution, large amounts of pesticide have been used (and continue to be used) in agriculture and other sectors. It is not surprising that pesticide residues have contaminated many water sources.

> **Key Idea** Water pollution is severe in India and many of our rivers are polluted and unsafe for use.

We have reached the stage where we cannot be sure of the quality of any water source in the country. Even bottled water samples have shown the presence of pesticide residues. This is also the case with soft drinks, which use the same sources of water. (The state of the bottled water industry was discussed in Chapter 4.)

How do We Measure Water Quality?

Here are some ways in which water quality is measured:

Biological Oxygen Demand (BOD): This parameter measures the degree of water pollution from oxygen-demanding wastes and plant nutrients. BOD is the amount of dissolved oxygen needed by the decomposers to break down the organic material in specified conditions. It is measured in parts per million or ppm. Table 12.1 shows the connection between BOD level and water quality.

Total Dissolved Solids (TDS): This is a measure of the combined content of all inorganic and organic substances contained in a liquid. TDS is measured for freshwater systems such as streams, rivers, and lakes. TDS is not generally considered a primary pollutant, but it is used as an overall indicator of the presence of a broad array of chemical contaminants. TDS is also measured in ppm.

Presence of disease-causing organisms: The number of colonies of coliform bacteria present in a 100 millilitre (ml) sample of water is one measure. There should be no coliform colonies in drinking water, while water in a swimming pool could have up to 200 colonies per 100 ml.

Chemical analysis: The presence of chemicals like pesticides can be measured by analysis.

TABLE 12.1 BOD and Water Quality

BOD level (ppm)	Water quality	Description
1–2	Very good	Not much organic waste present
3–5	Moderately clean	
6–9	Somewhat polluted	Bacteria decomposing organic matter present
100 or greater	Very polluted	

How are Polluted Water and Sewage Treated?

The first step in freshwater purification is to use a chemical to make the suspended particles settle down. The water is then filtered and disinfected. The most common disinfectant is chlorine, though there is concern about the hazard of consuming low doses of chlorine over long periods.

Waste water, including sewage, goes through several stages of treatment. The *primary treatment* removes suspended particles by screening and settling. The *secondary treatment* uses microorganisms to decompose the organic material in the waste water. After several hours, the particles and the bacteria are allowed to settle down as secondary sludge. The *tertiary treatment* is a complex biological and chemical process that removes the remaining pollutants like minerals, metals, organic compounds, and viruses.

> **Key Idea** We can treat waste water, but we end up with toxic sludge at the end.

The major problem with sewage and wastewater treatment is the disposal of the sludge. The sludge is often toxic, since people tend to dump all kinds of waste into drains. Treating the sludge is a costly and time-consuming process. Cities in industrialized countries do not know how to get rid of the sludge and so they export it to the developing countries (Recall the discussion on this issue in Chapter 11).

What can be Done about Industrial Pollution of Fresh Water?

Every litre of waste water discharged by an industry pollutes on an average eight litres of fresh water. The total amount of water polluted in this manner is more than all the water in the largest river basins.

There are ways of reducing industrial pollution of fresh water:

- Improving process technology to reduce water demand
- Using the same water in series for two or more successive stages in the process
- Recirculating process water indefinitely, making up only for unavoidable losses
- Rainwater harvesting to meet as many of the requirements as possible

Governments could take the following steps to regulate the use of water by industries:

- Ensure that they withdraw water from downstream of their own discharge, forcing them to clean their discharges
- Establish specific and total load-based effluent standards
- Fix a quota for total freshwater withdrawal for each industry in a watershed
- Specify mandatory recycling percentage
- Restrict groundwater withdrawal where levels are low
- Make rainwater harvesting compulsory
- Price the water properly: charge high for an industry that can reuse water, charge for groundwater use, and increase unit price with increasing use
- Introduce pollution charges, high enough to be an incentive to reduce pollution
- Impose stiff penalties for non-compliance of regulations.

What are the Methods of Purifying Water?

Some of the purification methods are described below:

Reverse Osmosis (RO) method: This process was discovered in the late 1950s and was slow to catch on but now it enjoys patronage worldwide. In the RO method, water is forced through a semi-permeable membrane. This filters unwanted substances, producing clear, fresh-tasting drinking water. RO uses no chemicals and can also be used to desalinate sea water. The membranes, however, need to be manufactured and later disposed of.

The UV method: Ultraviolet radiation is directed through clear, pre-filtered, particle-free water. The UV light is extremely effective in killing and eliminating bacteria, viruses, fungi, and certain harmful organisms. It is mainly used in industry and hospitals to treat water. The method must be used in conjunction with sediment and carbon filters.

Distillation method: Water is boiled to create steam and when this steam cools, it condenses to form water droplets, which in turn are deposited in a container. The residual water contains the contaminants and is discarded. The resultant is pure mineral free water. When used in conjunction with other filter mediums such as carbon you can get very pure water.

Planted filter method: This can be used even to purify sewage water. The waste water first goes through a septic tank and a baffle reactor, in which all the particulate and organic matter are removed. Next, the water is sent through an open horizontal planted gravel filter containing pebbles with plants like reeds, which absorb many of the impurities. Finally, the water moves through an open polishing pond. The output is good enough for gardening and irrigation.

Water supply and sanitation are closely connected and it is time to review the global sanitation crisis.

What is the Status of the World's Sanitation?

According to WHO, sanitation generally refers to the provision of facilities and services for the safe disposal of human urine and faeces. Inadequate sanitation is a major cause of disease worldwide and improving sanitation is known to have a significant beneficial impact on health both in households and across communities. The word 'sanitation' also refers to the maintenance of hygienic conditions, through services such as garbage collection and wastewater disposal.

WHO defines an improved sanitation facility as 'one that hygienically separates human excreta from human contact'. This includes the following types of sanitation facilities:

- Flush toilet
- Piped sewer system
- Septic tank
- Flush/pour flush to pit latrine
- Ventilated improved pit latrine (VIP)
- Pit latrine with slab
- Composting toilet

Key facts on global sanitation from WHO:

1. In 2020, 54% of the global population (4.2 billion people) used a safely managed sanitation service.
2. Over 1.7 billion people still do not have basic sanitation services, such as private toilets or latrines.
3. Of these, 494 million still defecate in the open, for example in street gutters, behind bushes or into open bodies of water.
4. In 2020, 45% of the household wastewater generated globally was discharged without safe treatment.
5. At least 10% of the world's population is thought to consume food irrigated by wastewater.
6. Poor sanitation reduces human well-being, social and economic development due to impacts such as anxiety, risk of sexual assault, and lost opportunities for education and work.
7. Poor sanitation is linked to transmission of diarrhoeal diseases such as cholera and dysentery, as well as typhoid, intestinal worm infections and polio. It exacerbates stunting and contributes to the spread of antimicrobial resistance.

What is the state of sanitation in India?

The World Bank reported in 2000 that nearly 75% of India's population was practicing open defecation. In 2020, that number fell to under 15%. This dramatic change was the outcome of the Swachh Bharat Abhiyan (Box 12.2).

BOX 12.2 Success of Swachh Bharat Abhiyan

Parameswaran Iyer, the Secretary to the Government of India, who led SBA from 2014 to 2019, made the following points in a talk:

In 2019, states began self-reporting their ODF status, which showed the production of millions of new toilets, as well as over 600,000 villages, 700 districts, and 36 states declaring ODF. The self-reporting process included incentives to discourage local leaders from providing false data and checks to verify the ODF data published by states, including a "Sustainability Verification" performed by an external agency months after the state declared ODF.

The Department of Drinking Water and Sanitation also launched the National Annual Rural Sanitation Survey (NARSS). The survey covered 100,000 households in every state, as well as examined sanitation practices in schools, and rural childcare centres. The survey data showed that the percentage of rural households with access to toilets increased from 77% in 2017–2018 to 94% in 2019–2020.

SBA addressed four challenges:

1. Scale

In 2015, 550 million people reported defecating in the open in India, the world's second most populated country. Adequately addressing this public health crisis required a large network of dedicated players. The mission was able to recruit 120 million school students, 1 million masons—55,000 of whom were women—to build low-cost toilets. 650,000 Swachhagrahis (village motivators), 250 Sarpanches (local decision-makers), 700 district collectors, 500 Zila Preraks (young professional workers), and a team of brand ambassadors and communicators were also enlisted to help to expand sanitation awareness across the country.

2. Speed

There was a five-year timeline to define success for SBA. The Team tackled the "low-hanging fruit" first, including the states of Kerala, Himachal Pradesh, and Haryana. These "easy wins," where rates of open defecation were lower already, acted as inspiration to others to continue their mission.

3. Stigmas

The Team needed to destigmatize emptying toilet pits in households, which were viewed as being unclean. Broadcasting messages over the radio, a medium in nearly 100% of homes, to debunk common myths proved to be effective, as was adopting new media, such as social media. Lastly, SBA used the popularity of Bollywood films and popular culture campaigns to create the commercially successful movie, *Toilet: A Love Story*, to promote the mission and adoption of in-home toilet use.

4. Sustainability

The key challenge, after states and districts implemented strategies to discourage open defecation and promote the use of toilets, was sustaining the success of the program, while also broadening the definition of sanitation. This is the task of SBA's Phase 2.

SBA's success was due to several key factors:

- Political leadership was critical to garner public support– the backing from Prime Minister Modi played a major role in their success;
- The government backed this program with ₹1,700 Billion.
- The mission engaged with development partners including NGOs, private sector, civil society and media.
- The government inspired the people to take collective action and pride in their villages becoming ODF.

(See Chapter 11, Box 11.4 for more on SBA)

What is Ecological Sanitation?

Ecological sanitation (EcoSan) represents a shift in thinking about and acting upon human excreta. The faeces are composted close to the place of excretion, and the composted organic matter is applied to the soil to improve its structure, water-holding capacity, and fertility.

EcoSan is a sustainable closed-loop system and its main features are:

- It regards human excreta as a resource to be recycled rather than as a waste to be disposed of.
- It uses dry composting toilets, which is a practical, hygienic, and cost-effective solution to human waste disposal.
- It separates urine from faecal matter and uses it as fertilizer.
- Recycling of human waste prevents direct pollution caused by sewage, returns it as nutrients to soil and plants, and reduces the need for chemical fertilizers.
- It does not use water to carry away the solid waste. It is thus very appropriate for areas with water shortages or irregular water supplies.
- It is applicable for rural and urban areas, and for rich and poor alike.

Hundreds of EcoSan toilets have been built in Kerala, Tamil Nadu, Sri Lanka, and elsewhere. Read Box 12.3 for an account of the EcoSan toilet.

BOX 12.3 HOPE: ***The Story of EcoSan—The Sweet Smell of Compost***

It is now an almost dry, crumbly, black stuff that smells light, pleasant, and earthy. Six months ago, however, it was fresh human waste. Sounds unbelievable? This is the magic of ecological sanitation or EcoSan, for short.

Paul Calvert, a British engineer and a pioneer in ecological sanitation, has set up EcoSan toilets in numerous homes in rural Kerala. These are dry, composting toilets. One model consists of a slab constructed over two vaults. The slab has a hole over each vault for the faeces to drop in and a funnel for the urine to collect. While one hole is used, the other is kept closed. Washing is done separately so that wash water does not mix with the solid waste.

Before use, the vault is covered with straw to facilitate decomposition. After each use some ash or saw dust is sprinkled on the faeces. The urine is collected separately, diluted, and used as fertilizer. After six months, the first hole is closed and the second one is put into use. The faecal matter in the first hole begins to decompose and in six more months the fertilizer is ready for collection.

Calvert identifies three basic benefits of EcoSan:

- It prevents diseases by removing pathogen-rich excreta from the immediate environment.
- It does not contaminate ground water or use up scarce water resources.
- It creates a valuable resource that can be recycled back into the environment.

Calvert spends much of his time demonstrating and promoting the ecological sanitation approach among communities, government and non-government organisations. He has also designed EcoSan toilets for urban areas. He says, 'If everyone harvested rain water, used an ecological toilet, planted a tree, and helped their neighbour, India would surely be a land of plenty.'

Key Idea There is a world crisis in sanitation and we are unable to cover even for half the deprived population. Given this fact and the water scarcity, ecological sanitation seems to be a way out.

How does Marine Pollution Occur?

Since the ocean forms 71% of the earth's surface, most of the pollutants in the atmosphere fall on it. In recent decades, however, there is in addition a huge amount of direct marine pollution caused by human activities.

Industrial discharges and agricultural run-off (about 70 trillion litres a year) containing pesticides, fertilizers, and various toxic chemicals find their way to the ocean. Treated and untreated human and other domestic waste (about 6 million tonnes a year) end up in the ocean with all their contaminants. In fact, sewage remains the largest source of contamination of the coastal and marine environment. Further, the oil industry contributes deadly pollution through leaks, spills, and cleaning of tankers.

Nitrogen input into the ocean has been rapidly increasing due to agricultural runoff, atmospheric deposition, and loss of natural interceptors like coastal wetlands, coral reefs, and mangroves. The result is greater marine and coastal eutrophication. Blooms of toxic or otherwise undesirable phytoplankton are increasing in frequency, intensity, and geographic distribution. Such blooms or red tides greatly affect fisheries, aquaculture, and tourism.

Persistent Organic Pollutants (POPs), which spread through the atmosphere, are found everywhere in the ocean. POPs cause reproductive, immunological, and neurological problems in marine organisms and possibly in humans. Another concern is the increasing amounts of non-biodegradable waste like plastic articles and nets that float in the ocean. Large numbers of birds, turtles, and mammals are killed by entanglement in or ingestion of such waste.

Human activities have changed sediment flows into coasts and the ocean. Areas like deltas that need sediments do not get enough, whereas coral reefs are smothered by them.

How much Plastic is Present in the Ocean?

Large areas of the ocean are now littered with plastic debris. One such area is known as the Great Pacific Garbage Patch (Box 12.4)

BOX 12.4 DISASTER: *The Great Pacific Garbage Patch*

Charles Moore, the captain of a racing boat, was sailing in the Pacific in 2003 and this is what he saw:

Yet as I gazed from the deck at the surface of what ought to have been a pristine ocean, I was confronted, as far as the eye could see, with the sight of plastic. It seemed unbelievable, but I never found a clear spot. In the week it took to cross the subtropical high, no matter what time of day I looked, plastic debris was floating everywhere: bottles, bottle caps, wrappers, fragments.

What Capt. Moore discovered has come to be known as the Great Pacific Garbage Patch. The name, however, is a misnomer. While it evokes the picture of a giant island of solid garbage floating in the Pacific, the reality is that there is no island of trash forming in the middle of the ocean nor a blanket of trash that can be seen with satellite or aerial photographs. Instead, there are millions of small and microscopic pieces of plastic floating over a roughly 5000 sq km area of the Pacific. This amount has increased significantly over the past 40 years. The sheer amount of plastic is an alarming fact.

A lot of the plastic that we throw away reaches the ocean though the rivers, beaches, and ships that transport garbage. The ocean currents are such that the plastic litter gets concentrated in patches. There are several such patches in the Pacific as well as the other oceans.

Not much research has been conducted on marine debris in many such areas and hence we do not know how large these areas are, especially since they move and change, sometimes daily. No accurate estimate exists of how much debris is out there.

Regardless of the exact size, mass, and location of these areas of concentration, the plastic litter is a serious problem. Birds like the albatross mistake plastic for plankton, fish eggs, or other food. On remote Midway Atoll, albatross chicks die of starvation and dehydration because their parents have unwittingly fed them bottle caps and cigarette lighters, which they can't digest. The trash also threatens endangered species like Hawaiian monk seals, green sea turtles, and some fish species that eat them and slowly starve to death.

If the current trends continue, there will be more plastic than fish in the ocean. And with that plastic will come more invasive species. This could alter the open ocean forever—and destroy all the native life there that has kept the ocean healthy for thousands of years.

Can we clean it up? It is certainly not cost-effective to skim the surface of the entire ocean or even just the patches. There are other reasons why we cannot clean them up:

- The concentration areas are typically very large and they also move and change throughout the year.
- The marine debris is not distributed evenly within these areas.
- Most of the marine debris found in these areas is small bits of plastic, too small to sift through.
- In some areas where marine debris concentrates, so does marine life and this makes simple skimming the debris risky—more harm than good may be caused.

A recent study analysed data on plastic pollution at the ocean surface level from nearly 12,000 stations across six marine regions (North Atlantic, South Atlantic, North Pacific, South Pacific, Indian, and Mediterranean). The main findings were:

- Plastic pollution of the ocean is much more severe than estimated before.
- Trillions of small bits of plastic are floating on the world's oceans due to a rapid and unprecedented increase in the last two decades.
- The total amount would weigh between 1.1 million tons and 4.9 million tons.
- The rate of plastic entering the oceans could accelerate 2.6 times by 2040 if left without widespread policy changes.
- A lack of adequate plastic recycling worldwide has resulted in a flood of plastic products and packaging that remain as mismanaged waste in the receiving country.
- Another factor is an increased amount of plastic waste from large fishing fleets and artisanal fisheries.

Industry bodies, businesses, governments, civil society, and international institutions are recognizing the magnitude of the issue and the need to tackle it. Many of them have joined UNEP's Global

Partnership on Marine Litter (GPML) and the global plastic associations have signed a declaration to develop solutions to marine litter.

How Bad is Coastal Pollution?

With the inexorable movement of the world's population towards the coastal areas, the pollution of the ocean nearer the shores has reached alarming proportions. Thousands of tonnes of sewage and industrial effluents are directly discharged into the ocean in many parts of the world.

A few years ago, shrimp aquaculture was taken up on a large scale on the Indian coast. This industry requires fresh water as well as sea water and uses heavy doses of antibiotics. Within a short time, the effluents from the shrimp farms polluted large areas. The local soil and ground water were affected. Ultimately, diseases and court orders put a stop to coastal aquaculture, but the industry flourishes in inland areas.

> **Key Idea** Coastal and marine pollution has reached alarming proportions.

It is no wonder that the marine pollution finds its way into the fish that we catch. For example, three major shrimp species harvested off Mumbai's coastal waters have tested positive for lead and cadmium. The fish catch itself is declining in these waters, probably due to marine pollution.

What are the International Initiatives to Control Marine Pollution?

Since 1972, a number of international agreements and programmes have focused on controlling marine and coastal pollution:

- The 1972 London Dumping Convention: The purpose of this Convention is to control all sources of marine pollution and prevent pollution of the sea through regulation of dumping into the sea of waste materials. It prohibits all dumping, incineration of wastes at sea, and the export of wastes.
- The 1989 Basel Convention on the Control of Transboundary Movement of Hazardous Wastes and their Disposal: Until 1999, the Convention was principally devoted to setting up a framework for controlling the movement of hazardous wastes across international frontiers. It has now expanded its scope to include the active promotion and use of cleaner technologies and production methods and the prevention and monitoring of illegal traffic.
- Convention on the Prevention of Pollution from Ships (MARPOL): It is the main international convention covering prevention of pollution of the marine environment by ships from operational or accidental causes.
- Global Programme of Action for the Protection of the Marine Environment from Land-based Activities (GPA-LBA): This programme was adopted in 1995 by over 100 countries. The aim is to control contaminants like sewage, persistent organic pollutants, radioactive substances, heavy metals, oils, nutrients, sediments, and litter that enter the ocean from land.
- The UNEP Regional Seas Programme: This programme has fostered regional cooperation on behalf of the marine and coastal environment. It has stimulated the creation of Action Plans for sound environmental management in each region. India, Bangladesh, Maldives, Pakistan, and Sri Lanka are partners in the South Asian Seas Programme.

India is a party to all these agreements and programmes.

Ending on a Hopeful Note: Positive Stories

Rainwater harvesting is being successfully used in India to tackle the problem of fluoride contamination (Box 12.5).

BOX 12.5 HOPE: *Rainwater Harvesting Tackles Fluoride Problem*

We saw in the lead story of the chapter how widespread was the fluoride contamination of water. One successful solution is to use rain water in place of the contaminated water. Here are two examples:

1. The village of Balisanain Gujarat had been affected both by drought and fluoride contamination of water. With the help of the NGO Utthan, the villagers diverted rain water into an old tank. From the tank, the rain water was led to a recharge well. The water has recharged the local aquifer and the local wells now have potable water.
2. Many villages in Tumkur, Kolar, and Gadag districts of Karnataka have been suffering from fluoride contamination of ground water. In 60 of these villages, a joint project of the NGO BAIF and the state government now provides potable water to over 5500 families. The main approach is to harvest rain water from roofs and artificial catchment areas and use that water for domestic purposes. Other activities include excavating farm ponds as well as recharging borewells and aquifers directly with rain water. The project has been implemented with the active involvement of the local communities.

REVIEW: A SUMMARY OF THE KEY POINTS

- Most of the freshwater sources in the world like rivers, lakes, and ground water including those in remote regions are already polluted. The pollutants come from a variety of sources, mostly due to human activities.
- Excessive extraction of ground water in India and Bangladesh is leading to increasing contamination with fluoride and arsenic. This has extremely serious effects on the health of the people who consume the water.
- Every day, 2 million tonnes of human waste are disposed of in water bodies of the world. At least 1.8 billion people worldwide are estimated to drink water that is faecally-contaminated.
- Thanks to Swachh Bharat Abhiyan, the percentage of rural households with access to toilets in India increased from 77% in 2017–2018 to 94% in 2019–2020.
- There are several ways of treating and purifying water and sewage. Disposing of the toxic sludge that results is a major problem.
- Most of the Indian rivers are polluted and the National River Conservation Authority has launched Action Plans for several rivers.
- The adoption of ecological sanitation or composting toilets seems to be a way to solve the sanitation problem of the world.
- Human activities are responsible for heavy pollution of the ocean and the coastal zone; many international initiatives have been taken to control this pollution.
- The future looks grim with respect to water, soil, and marine pollution and this calls for urgent steps.

EXERCISES

Objective-type questions

For each question below, choose the best answer out of the given choices.

1. Which of the following is a nonpoint source of water pollution?

   (a) Oil spill
   (b) Sewage treatment
   (c) Open cast mine
   (d) Deep borewell plant

2. What does BOD stand for?
   (a) Biological Oxygen Demand
   (b) Basic Oxygen Dissolved
   (c) Biological Oxygen Decomposition
   (d) Biological Organic Demand
3. Which of the following statements is true with regard to wastewater treatment?
   (a) Waste water can be completely converted into fresh water.
   (b) Waste water can be treated, but some sludge will remain.
   (c) Primary wastewater treatment makes use of microorganisms.
   (d) Any sludge that remains after treatment can be easily processed.
4. Which of the following statements is **not** a method of purifying water?
   (a) Reverse osmosis
   (b) Ultraviolet radiation
   (c) Distillation
   (d) Evaporation from a pond
5. Which of the following statements is **not** true with regard to global sanitation?
   (a) About 45% of the global population lacks access to improved sanitation.
   (b) About 45% of the household wastewater generated globally is discharged without safe treatment.
   (c) contains About 500 million people still defecate in the open.
   (d) With regard to sanitation, Swachh Bharat Abhiyan was not successful..
6. Which of the following statements is true with regard to Ecological sanitation or EcoSan?
   (a) EcoSan toilet uses water to carry away the solid waste.
   (b) Ecosan considers human excreta as waste.
   (c) EcoSan increases the load on sewage plants.
   (d) EcoSan gives us pleasant-smelling compost.
7. Which of the following descriptions is true with regard to the Great Pacific Garbage Patch?
   (a) Millions of small and microscopic pieces of plastic floating over a large area.
   (b) Huge island of plastic trash visible from satellites.
   (c) A single patch of floating plastic.
   (d) A patch of dead birds and marine organisms.

Short-answer questions

1. How did the ground water in many places in India become contaminated with fluoride and arsenic?
2. How do fluoride and arsenic contamination of water affect the health?
3. Give any five major categories of water pollutants, their sources, and their effects.
4. Explain point and non-point sources of water pollution.
5. What is meant by eutrophication of lakes?
6. Describe three measures of water quality.
7. What is the status of sanitation in the world?
8. How can we provide sanitation facilities to the maximum number of people in the world?
9. How does soil become polluted and how can it be remedied?
10. What are the main sources of marine and coastal pollution?
11. Describe the programme Swachh Bharat Abhiyan regarding sanitation. Why was it successful to a great extent?

Long-answer questions

1. Write an essay on the various international conventions and agreements concerning water resources, both fresh water and marine waters. Use the information given in this chapter as well as in Chapters 4 and 5.
2. Describe the various ways of treating and purifying water and sewage.

Think critically: Deeper question for reflection and discussion

How can we make people aware of the fact that any pollution that we create ultimately comes back to us? How can we encourage people to avoid polluting water and soil—through regulation or education?

ENJOY AND EDUCATE YOURSELF

Watch these two films, both based on true stories:

1. A *Civil Action* (1998), starring John Travolta and Robert Duvall, a movie which dramatically relates the efforts of a dogged attorney to bring an industrial polluter to justice.
2. *Erin Brockovich* (2000), starring Julia Roberts, about a law office clerk, who uncovers evidence that a large electric utility has poisoned the water supply of a city with toxic chromium, causing disease and death among many locals.

ACCESS THE OUP ONLINE RESOURCE CENTRE FOR MORE

- The story of the red tides: Bloom that kills
- Additional text and other recommended references, websites, and films

13 Air Pollution, Noise, and Other Forms of Pollution

There's so much pollution in the air now that if it weren't for our lungs there'd be no place to put it all.

Robert Orben (1927–) American magician and professional comedy writer

MAIN QUESTIONS ADDRESSED

- What are the levels of outdoor and indoor air pollution in India and the world?
- What are the causes and effects of air pollution and how can they be controlled?
- What are the sources of noise pollution and what is being done about it in India?
- How did ozone depletion occur and how was it controlled through an international agreement?
- What are the causes and effects of acid rain and what can be done about it?

KEYWORDS AND PHRASES

acid rain, asthma, Bharat emission norms, chlorofluorocarbon (CFC), decibel, hybrid car, Montreal Protocol, Ozone Depleting Substance (ODS), Ozone Layer, Persistent Organic Pollutant (POP), photochemical smog, Polycyclic Aromatic Hydrocarbons (PAH), primary air pollutant, radioactive pollution, secondary air pollutant, smog, urban heat island effect, Volatile Organic Compound (VOC)

LEAD STORY

THE STORY OF JUVENILE ASTHMA: POLLUTED AIR, SUFFERING CHILDREN

Eight-year-old Moni caught pneumonia during winter rains three years ago and she is now an asthmatic, visiting the government hospital every week. Her father, who earns ₹60 per day, needs ₹80 per week for her treatment. The family of five cannot buy rations and the house rent is six months overdue.

Moni is not alone. Seven-year-old Umesh Kumar, one-year-old Mushtab, and many more children among the poor of Kanpur city are all asthmatics, condemned for a long period of medical treatment and unaffordable expenses. Anuj Rawal is perhaps among the few happy people of the city, since his medical shop sells ₹50,000 worth of asthma medicines every month!

Kanpur is one of the worst polluted cities in India. It is home to many textile mills and leather units. The most popular form of transport is the rickety three-wheeler tempo, which spews out volumes of smoke from old engines. Dust is thick in the air and the smog never goes away. And the hospitals are full of juvenile asthmatics. The story is the same in the shanties of Delhi, slums of Mumbai, or colonies of Chennai.

The World Health Organization (WHO) estimates that 10–15% of Indian children in the 5–11 age group suffer from asthma. It costs an average of ₹400 per month to buy a child's asthma medicines. Since there is little awareness of asthma among the poor and even health officials, often the disease is not even diagnosed. Even if it is diagnosed, the child is given steroids because they are cheap. Steroids usually have long-term adverse effects on their health.

Several studies have shown the link between pollution and asthma. Doctors see a direct connection between an increase in asthma cases and the worsening of air quality. More people are admitted to the emergency wards on days when the air pollution is high, particularly in winter.

Man saying: *"I am taking the kids out of town before the smog sets in."*

CLIMATE CHANGE AND WATER QUALITY

Climate change and air pollution are very different phenomena, but their causes are similar: the release of air pollutants from a variety of sources and activities. Burning fossil fuel is the major source common to both. Just as air pollution can have adverse effects on human health and ecosystems, it can also impact the earth's climate. Taking actions to reduce the pollution from fossil fuel burning will help improve air quality and address climate change.

What do we learn from the Juvenile Asthma case?

Indira Gandhi told the 1972 Stockholm Conference on the Human Environment that poverty was the worst form of pollution. The juvenile asthma case shows that when poverty and pollution come together the result is doubly tragic.

What is Air Pollution?

Air pollution is said to exist if the levels of gases, solids, or liquids present in the atmosphere are high enough to harm humans, other organisms, or materials. The pollution could have natural causes like a forest fire or the eruption of a volcano. Our primary concern, however, are human activities, which are today responsible for most of the air pollution. Further, much of the pollution caused by humans is concentrated in thickly populated urban centres (Box 13.1).

BOX 13.1 DISASTER: *The Story of Mexico City—Saving a Choked City*

Just living and breathing the air here is equivalent to smoking two packets of cigarettes a day. It is the second largest city in the world and it has also the second worst level of air pollution.

Mexico City is located in a bowl-shaped valley with mountains on three sides. It has a population of more than 20 million, which is constantly on the increase. There are more than 3 million vehicles that emit 3 million tonnes of pollutants annually. Many of the vehicles are old ones that emit more pollutants than normal.

Emissions from 36,000 industries and leakage of liquefied petroleum gas (LPG) from thousands of containers add to the air pollution. The air also contains particles of dried faecal matter from the millions of tonnes of sewage dumped on the land near the city.

The Mexican government has taken several steps to reduce the air pollution:

- The hillsides have been reforested to reduce the particulate matter produced by wind erosion; in all, 25 million trees have been planted.
- Some refineries have been closed, others upgraded.
- Cleaner fuel has been imported from the US and unleaded petrol has been introduced; old vehicles have been banned.
- Public transport is being improved and one day a week personal cars have been prohibited.

With these measures, there has been some improvement, but there is still a long way to go.

What are the types of air pollutants?

Primary air pollutants are harmful chemicals that are released directly from a source into the atmosphere. *Secondary air pollutants* are also harmful chemicals, but they are produced from chemical reactions involving the primary pollutants.

Primary air pollutants include the following:

- Particulate matter: This includes both solid particles and liquid suspensions. Soil particles, soot, lead, asbestos, and sulphuric acid droplets are examples.
- Oxides of carbon and nitrogen and sulphur dioxide
- Hydrocarbons like methane and benzene
- Volatile Organic compounds (VOCs): These are emitted as gases from certain solids or liquids. Many VOCs are human-made chemicals that are used and produced in the manufacture of paints, pharmaceuticals, and refrigerants.
- Polycyclic Aromatic Hydrocarbons (PAHs): These are a class of chemicals that occur naturally in coal, crude oil, and gasoline. They are released when we burn coal, oil, gas, wood, garbage, and tobacco. PAHs can bind to or form small particles in the air. Naphthalene is a manmade PAH used to make other chemicals and mothballs. Cigarette smoke contains many PAHs.

Secondary air pollutants include the following:

- Ozone: It is a form of oxygen and is a pollutant in the troposphere or the layer of the atmosphere closest to the earth's surface. (The Ozone Layer is discussed later in this chapter.)
- Sulphur trioxide: This is formed when sulphur dioxide reacts with oxygen. In turn, sulphur trioxide combines with water to form sulphuric acid.

Other important terms you should know regarding pollutants:

- Peroxyacetyl Nitrate (PAN): This is a component of photochemical smog, produced in the atmosphere, when oxidized volatile organic compounds combine with nitrogen dioxide. (Smog is discussed below.)
- Persistent Organic Pollutants (POPs): These are toxic chemicals that adversely affect human health and the environment around the world. Because they can be transported by wind and water, most POPs generated in one country can and do affect people and wildlife far from where they are used and released. They persist for long periods of time in the environment and can accumulate and pass from one species to the next through the food chain. (See also under Marine Pollution in Chapter 12.)

What are the Sources of Outdoor Air Pollution?

The sources of outdoor air pollution are:

- Burning of fossil fuels in

- automobiles, domestic cooking, and heating
- power stations and industries (primarily the chemical, metal, and paper industries)

- Mining activities leading to dust as well as fires (Box 13.2)
- Burning biofuels, tropical rainforests, wastes of all kinds, etc.
- Natural emissions from animals and decaying organic matter

BOX 13.2 DISASTER: *The Story of Jharia—City of Fire*

In 2000, the town's temple snapped in two and flames leapt out from underneath, spewing noxious gases. The underground fires that had been raging for several decades had reached the residents' doorsteps!

Jharia in the state of Jharkand is now a town surrounded by fires. Raging in the coal mines underground, the fires are now visible on the surface. At night, the smoky haze makes Jharia resemble a cremation ground. Every possible outlet from the mines spits fire. Danger lurks at every step.

Coal fires occur naturally like forest fires. Lightning, forest fires, or frictional heat inside the earth's crust can trigger the spontaneous combustion of coal. These fires burn away coal, raise the atmospheric temperature, and cause land subsidence. Smoke from these fires contains poisonous gases such as the oxides and dioxides of carbon, nitrogen, and sulphur. Jharia is today among the 10 most polluted towns of India.

Jharia has a 100-year history of coal fires. Neglected for long and stoked by relentless mining, the fires have consumed 40 million tonnes of India's best coking coal and rendered 1,800 million tonnes out of bounds. The fires now cover about 17 sq km. There have been many gas eruptions, accidents, and deaths of miners.

The estimate of the cost of extinguishing the fire ranges from ₹4 to 10 billion. It may be worthwhile because there is coal worth ₹30 billion still to be extracted in the area. Bharat Coking Coal Ltd, the public sector company that owns the mines, is said to have spent ₹1 billion so far to put out the fires, without much success.

The state government wants to evacuate the 300,000 people of Jharia, abandoning 100,000 houses. For the residents of Jharia, mere existence is now hell on earth. They live in constant fear of a major subsidence that could cause the entire town to collapse. Yet, they do not want to leave the town.

Will the entire town be evacuated so that mining can go on? Or will the fire be put out incurring high costs? Or more likely, will the precarious existence of the people continue without any action being taken?

Temporary, but severe, air pollution can occur due to disasters like earthquakes, volcano eruptions, dust storms, leak of gases (like the Bhopal gas tragedy case), and armed conflicts, etc. Even festivals (for example, Diwali with its crackers) can create air pollution. Dust storms are typically formed in desert areas and from there they can spread to places thousands of kilometres away (Box 13.3).

BOX 13.3 DISASTER: *The Story of Dust Storms—The Fifth Season*

Schools were closed, many flights had to be cancelled, and hospitals were crowded with patients suffering from breathing difficulties. This was the scene in Seoul, South Korea on April 12, 2002.

The cause was a huge dust storm that had originated in China. It marked the arrival of the 'fifth season', one of severe dust storms that the Koreans and the Chinese have come to fear. Such dust storms have now become a regular feature between winter and spring.

The amount of particulate matter in the Seoul air is normally 70 micrograms of dust per cu m. If this figure reaches 1000 micrograms, many would have breathing problems. On that day, the figure was 2070 micrograms per cu m.

Apart from affecting the health of many, such dust storms lead to worker absenteeism, lower retail sales, problems in dust-sensitive factories like the ones making computer chips, etc. Hence, they are a threat to the economy. On occasions, the storms from China have even reached the US.

The storms of course create havoc in China itself, including the capital Beijing. The real burden of the storms, however, falls on the Chinese farmers who live at their source. The dust and sand destroy crops, damage trees and orchards, kill animals, fill up water wells, and blow away fodder. Perhaps the worst effect is that they take away the topsoil.

Why do these storms occur? In its efforts to feed 1.3 billion people, China is overgrazing its rangelands, overploughing the cropland, overpumping the aquifers, and overcutting the forests. The land is becoming barren in northern and western China, and the strong winds of late winter and early spring generate these huge dust storms. They carry away the fine particles and deposit them in the lungs of bewildered Koreans or even Americans!

Efforts to halt the desertification through afforestation have had only a limited success. The key seems to be to relieve the pressure on the land created by the grazing of 290 million sheep and goats. How will the Chinese do it?

Industries and automobiles are by far the main contributors to outdoor air pollution across the world.

What is the Role of Automobiles in Creating Air Pollution and Other Environmental Problems?

The automobile is one of the most desired items of consumption today and the demand seems insatiable. From about 50 million in 1950, the numbers increased to more than 1.4 billion in 2023. The US alone has 20% of all the cars in the world. China is the second-largest car market in the world.

The automobile contributes to a range of environmental problems by increasing air and noise pollution, adding to solid waste, accelerating global warming, taking a heavy toll of life through accidents, using up natural non-renewable resources like oil and metals, etc.

Lead pollution caused by automobiles has been a serious problem. Lead was added to petrol for preventing the 'knocking' of the engine. Lead, however, is extremely poisonous and tends to accumulate in most biological systems. Large accumulation of lead in the body can result in paralysis, blindness, and even death. It can also affect the mental development of unborn children. Lead addition in petrol is now banned in most countries.

Automobiles need roads and highways, which have many adverse environmental effects. They use up land and consume resources like steel and cement, which require heavy energy inputs and pollute the environment. Congestion and traffic jams cause enormous loss of man-hours as well as fuel. In cities, automobile emissions are a major cause of smog.

What is Smog?

Smog is a form of outdoor pollution and the term was originally used to describe a combination of smoke, fog, and chemical pollutants that poisoned the air in industrialized cities like London. Now the term refers to the effects of air pollution not necessarily associated with smoke particles. It is used to describe air pollution that is localized in urban areas, where it reduces visibility.

What is common now in cities is photochemical smog formed by the chemical reactions between sunlight, unburnt hydrocarbons, ozone, and other pollutants. Photochemical smog can be seen as a hazy shroud on warm days in congested cities. It is an irritant to humans and very toxic to plants. In developing countries, leaded fuel, old engines, industrial emissions, and fuelwood burning combine to create severe smog.

What is Meant by the Urban Heat Island Effect?

Crowded urban areas (such as business districts) are warmer than the rural areas surrounding the city. We call such areas urban heat islands and they result from the following causes:

- The dark and tall buildings and the asphalt roads absorb a significant amount of light and radiation and emit it as heat, warming the city area.

Key Idea A range of human activities, including the use of automobiles, cause increasing air pollution in the world.

- Lack of trees and other vegetation prevents evaporative cooling that occurs in other green areas.
- Waste heat from vehicles, air conditioners, and generators release heat into the air.

Urban heat islands often have lower air quality because, along with the heat, there are also pollutants being pumped into the air. These pollutants are blocked from scattering and becoming less toxic by the buildings, roads, sidewalks, and parking lots. High-reflectivity coatings, green roofs, eco-friendly architecture, pedestrian-only areas, and other such measures can help reduce the heat island effect, but it is difficult to eliminate it completely.

What are the Levels of Outdoor Air Pollution in the World?

The 2022 World Air Quality Report released by IQAir (the technology partner of WHO) reviewed the status of air quality around the world for the year 2022. This report presented PM2.5 air quality data from 7323 cities across 131 countries, regions, and territories. The data used in this report was aggregated from over 30,000 regulatory air quality monitoring stations and low-cost air quality sensors. These monitoring stations and sensors are operated by governmental bodies, research institutions, non-profit non-governmental organizations, universities and educational facilities, private companies, and citizen scientists across the globe.

The key messages were:

- Air pollution continues to be the world's largest environmental health threat.
- Worldwide, poor air quality accounts for 93 billion days lived with illness and over six million deaths each year.
- The total economic cost equates to over $8 trillion dollars, surpassing 6.1 percent of the global annual GDP.
- Exposure to air pollution causes and aggravates several health conditions which include, but are not limited to, asthma, cancer, lung illnesses, heart disease, and premature mortality.
- Air pollution most severely impacts already vulnerable populations. More than 90% of pollution related deaths occur in low-income and middle-income countries. Children under 18 years old, pregnant women, and older adults all have increased risk of developing or worsening health conditions from air pollution exposure.
- 13 out of the 131 countries and regions included in this report have succeeded in achieving PM2.5 concentrations at or below the WHO guideline for annual PM2.5 concentrations of 5 μg/cu m.
- Much work has been done to combat air pollution; however, as evidenced by this report, there is still a long road ahead to ensure environmental equality. Citizens in only 10% of the global countries, regions and territories are breathing air that does not pose a risk to their health as indicated by the WHO.

What is the Level of air pollution in India?

India is now the second fastest growing auto market after China. The exponential growth of vehicles, outdated vehicle technology, bad fuel quality, poor maintenance of vehicles, poor traffic management and planning, all contribute to vehicular pollution. The problem is compounded by the unwillingness on the part of vehicle owners and the auto industry to accept emission norms and the lack of efficient public transport.

Trucks and buses run on diesel, which has high sulphur content. The old engines emit vast quantities of suspended particulate matter, leading to heavy air pollution over many cities.

The Central and State Pollution Control Boards have been measuring the Ambient Air Quality in Indian cities. They measure parameters such as suspended particulate matter (SPM), nitrogen oxide, and sulphur dioxide and compare the values with the National Standards. (SPM stands for extremely small particles and liquid droplets comprising of acids, organic chemicals, metals, and soil or dust particles.)

According to the 2022 World Air Quality Report published by IQAir, 14 Indian cities figure in the top 20 most polluted cities of the world (Table 13.1). In fact, in the top 50 list, 39 are Indian cities!

TABLE 13.1 Top 20 Most Polluted Cities (Ranking begins with the most polluted city)

Rank	City	Country/ Indian state	Rank	City	Country
1	Lahore	Pakistan	11	Ghaziabad	UP
2	Hotan	China	12	Dharuhera	Haryana
3	Bhiwadi	Rajasthan	13	Baghdad	Iraq
4	Delhi (NCT)	Delhi	14	Chapra	Bihar
5	Peshawar	Pakistan	15	Muzaffarnagar	UP
6	Darbhanga	Bihar	16	Faisalabad	Pakistan
7	Asopur	UP	17	Greater Noida	UP
8	N'Djamena	Chad	18	Bahadurgarh	Haryana
9	New Delhi	Delhi	19	Faridabad	Haryana
10	Patna	Bihar	20	Muzaffarpur	Bihar

What are the Effects of Outdoor Air Pollution?

Key Idea The air pollution in a large number of Indian cities is much more than the prescribed limits. 14 Indian cities figure in the top 20 most polluted cities of the world.

At low levels air pollutants irritate the eyes and cause inflammation of the respiratory tract. If the person already suffers from a respiratory illness, air pollution may lead to the condition becoming chronic at a later stage. It can also accentuate skin allergies.

Many pollutants also depress the immune system, making the body more prone to infections. Carbon monoxide from automobile emissions can cause headache at lower levels and mental impairment and even death at higher levels.

Particulate matter can reduce visibility, soil clothes, corrode metals, and erode buildings. On a larger scale, air pollution leads to acid rain, ozone layer depletion, and global warming.

How can Outdoor Air Pollution be Reduced or Controlled?

Outdoor air pollution can be reduced by adopting cleaner technologies, reducing pollution at the source, implementing laws and regulations to make people pollute less, introducing appropriate transportation policies, etc.

Automobile emissions can be reduced through various measures:

- Making cleaner and fuel-efficient cars (Read discussion below)
- Using lead-free petrol in existing cars
- Introducing policies that encourage the building and use of mass transit systems and discourage the use of personal transport (Examples are efficient and low-cost public transport, congestion charges

in city centres, separate lanes for car pools, heavy tax on personal cars, tax incentives on electric cars, etc.)

- Shifting from diesel to natural gas for trucks and buses (Read Box 13.4)

BOX 13.4 HOPE AND DESPAIR: ***The Story of Delhi's Air Pollution—Supreme Court Clears the Air***

Delhi had for long been an extremely polluted city. There was often a haze and many people had breathing problems. Responding to a public interest petition, the Supreme Court of India issued a series of orders beginning from 1985 to improve Delhi's environment. These orders included:

- mandatory use of the less-polluting Compressed Natural Gas (CNG) by all buses and commercial trucks
- shifting of all highly polluting industries out of Delhi
- phasing out of leaded petrol and of all commercial vehicles older than 15 years

After many delays and court interventions, the orders were implemented by December 2002. Gradually, the air became cleaner and it seemed to be a success story.

Delhi, however, seems to have lost all the gains made. The SPM in residential areas went up from 150 microgram per cu m in 2001 to 316 units in 2014. Some of the reasons for this worsening pollution are:

- Stubble burning in Haryana and Uttar Pradesh
- Adding 1000 new personal vehicles each day on its roads
- Growth in personal diesel vehicles, which pollute more than the petrol vehicles

The government has banned stubble burning, imposed fines and even suggested alternate uses for the straw and other crop residue. But farmers continue the practice.

The Delhi story shows how difficult it is to tackle air pollution in the major cities.

Particulate matter in the air can be reduced by:

- Fitting smokestacks with electrostatic precipitators, fabric filters, scrubbers, or similar devices
- Sprinkling water on dry soil that is being excavated during road construction

How can We Make Cleaner Cars?

There are options for making cars that would pollute less than current models: electric cars, hybrid cars, and hydrogen cars. All three types have been under development and prototypes have been made and tested.

The electric car is run by a motor powered by electricity. It produces virtually no emissions and the design is simple. The power usually comes from a battery inside the car. You can charge the battery using normal electric power. The battery needs recharging after running a certain distance (current models give about 400 km) and hence very long trips are not possible. One can move around within a city. Though there is no net reduction in pollution, the electric car certainly reduces the air and noise pollution in the city.

The electric car seems to be an ideal solution, but there is a catch. If the electricity that charges the batteries comes from a conventional thermal power plant, then we have only transferred the emission problem to the power plant. To produce the extra power needed for charging, the power plant puts out more emissions. Thus, the electric car can be considered to be clean, only if the electricity comes from a renewable source. The disposal of the discarded battery also poses an environmental problem.

A hybrid car is a petrol-and-electricity driven vehicle. It starts using the petrol engine, but switches automatically to the electric motor at low speeds or while idling. At normal speeds both engines contribute power. When the car slows down, the wheels run the generator to charge the batteries. Several carmakers have introduced hybrid models.

A car running on liquid hydrogen would be extremely clean, the only waste being water. In such a car, fuel cells (Chapter 8) combine hydrogen with oxygen in the air to produce electricity. The hydrogen car has no emissions and gives better performance since there is no waste during idling.

Where is the catch? As we saw in Chapter 8, hydrogen has to be first produced and that process consumes energy. If the hydrogen is made using non-renewable energy, then we are back to square one. The hydrogen car will make sense only if we use renewables like solar energy to obtain the hydrogen.

> **Key Idea** It is necessary to design and use automobiles that pollute much less than what current models do.

Experiments have been done to run cars with other less-polluting fuels like methane and biodiesel. It is, however, unlikely that the zero-emission wonder car running on low-cost, abundant, and renewable energy will soon arrive. Well before that happens, we will be forced to cut down on the number of cars on the road due to oil shortages, the reality of climate change, mounting solid waste, lack of space, and other problems.

How are Automobile Emissions Regulated in India?

The Indian government began regulating automobile emissions in 1991. In the year 2000, the government introduced Bharat emission norms modelled on the basic Euro norms of the European Union. Gradually, the norms were made stricter from Bharat-I to Bharat-IV.

Bharat-VI emission norms came into effect in on April 1, 2020. The Indian government decided to skip Bharat-V altogether and straight away shifted from Bharat-IV to Bharat-VI. The new norms introduced stricter limits on the emission of pollutants from vehicles and they had to be equipped with advanced emission control technologies such as particulate filters, selective catalytic reduction, and improved engine management systems. The Bharat-VI Phase 2 norms, which came into effect from April 1, 2023, focuses on real driving emissions and all the vehicles will now come with an OBD (On Board Diagnostic) system to monitor real-time emission levels.

> **Key Idea** India has been introducing progressively stringent norms for vehicle emissions.

What are the Causes and Effects of Indoor Air Pollution?

We give importance and attention to outdoor air pollution, but we do not realize that indoor pollution can be equally damaging.

Pesticides, mosquito repellents, cleaning agents, etc. used in urban households can cause toxic conditions. Building materials like asbestos, glass fibre, paints, glues, and varnishes are all health hazards. They can causc irritation of the eyes and skin, respiratory ailments, and cancer.

Air-conditioned rooms and offices cause a broad spectrum of health complaints because the sealed space accumulates various contaminants. Cigarette smoke affects both smokers and non-smokers (Box 13.5). The concentration of pollutants indoors may be five times more than outdoors.

BOX 13.5 WARNING: *The Story of Smoking—A Grave Matter*

It is a major cause of suffering and death among adults and it takes about 500 people every single hour to an early grave. What is shocking is that these deaths are completely preventable, if only people would stop smoking.

According to the WHO, cigarette smoking causes the premature death of 4 million people every year and this figure is expected to reach 10 million by 2030. Most of this increase will occur in the developing countries, China in particular. India is losing 800,000 to 900,000 lives every year due to tobacco. Worldwide cost of treating smoking-related illnesses is about US$200 billion per year.

Cigarette smoke is a mixture of hydrocarbons, carbon dioxide, carbon monoxide, cyanide, and particulate matter. In addition, it contains a small amount of radioactive material from the fertilizer used for the tobacco plant. All these substances are dangerous when the smoke is inhaled regularly. Nicotine in cigarettes is so addictive that only 10% of smokers who want to quit the habit actually succeed in doing so.

The connection between smoking and lung cancer has been well established. Smoking also leads to heart diseases and cancer of the bladder, mouth, throat, pancreas, kidney, stomach, voice box, and oesophagus.

Passive smoking, the chronic breathing of smoke from the cigarettes of others, also increases the risk of cancer, besides causing respiratory problems. Passive smoking is particularly harmful to infants, young children, pregnant women, seniors, and those with lung disease.

Smoking has declined in the US, Japan, and Europe. The tobacco companies are now aggressively exporting the habit to the developing countries. Smoking is on the increase in many of the poorer countries including India.

The Indian government has taken several steps to curb the advertisement and sale of tobacco products. From October 2, 2008, smoking has been banned in all public places (See also Box 13.8).

The most common pollutants in urban interiors are cigarette smoke, gases from stoves, formaldehyde (from carpets and furniture), pesticides, cleaning solvents, and ozone (from photocopiers). Organisms like viruses, bacteria, fungi, dust mites, and pollens also thrive in the many ducts found in office buildings.

Urban indoor pollution results in ailments like colds, influenza, and upset stomachs. Since these are common ailments, the connection with indoor pollution is often missed. Indoor pollution can also cause eye irritations, nausea, depression, etc., collectively called the 'Sick Building Syndrome'.

How bad is indoor air pollution in India?

According to WHO, the major sources of indoor air pollution in India are tobacco smoke and the smoke from the use of solid fuels with inefficient and leaky cook stoves. Annually, 400,000 to 2,000,000 premature deaths are attributable to indoor air pollution in India with a majority of deaths occurring in children under five due to acute respiratory infection.

In rural areas, indoor pollution is taking a toll on the health of women. Traditional stoves that use wood, coal, or animal dung spew out poisons that women inhale directly. This is equivalent to smoking 100 cigarettes a day! Many deaths take place in North India during winters when the doors and windows are closed shut and the poisonous smoke from the stove is not ventilated.

Key Idea Indoor air pollution is as damaging as outdoor pollution.

There have been campaigns to substitute these inefficient and polluting stoves with smokeless chulhas. The effort, however, has failed to make an adequate dent on this huge problem.

From air pollution let us move to noise pollution.

What is Noise Pollution and What are Its Sources?

Noise is defined as unwanted sound and it is an irritant and a source of stress. Most of the noise one hears originates from human activities. The main sources are:

- Transport sector: aircraft, trains, trucks, tractors, cars, three-wheelers, and motorcycles contribute the maximum noise.
- Industrial and construction machinery: factory equipment, generators, pile drivers, pneumatic drills, road rollers, and similar machinery.
- Special events: high-volume sound from loudspeakers during pop music performances, marriage receptions, religious festivals, public meetings, etc.

Noise pollution is increasing in industrial societies and in cities everywhere.

How is sound measured?

Sound is measured in decibel (db). It is not a linear, but a logarithmic scale. For example, a change from 40 db to 80 db represents a 10,000-fold increase in loudness. When the sound level reaches 140 db, you will start feeling pain in the ears. However, long exposure to noise even at 85 db can cause hearing loss.

Apart from loudness, the frequency or pitch of the noise also determines whether it is harmful or not. A modified scale called decibel-A (dbA) takes pitch into account. Hearing loss begins if a person is exposed more than 8 hours a day to a noise level of 80–90 dbA. A level of 140 dbA is painful and 180 dbA could kill.

Table 13.2 gives the typical intensity levels of common sources of sound.

TABLE 13.2 Typical Average Decibel Levels (dbA) of some Common Sounds (Where necessary, the distance of the source in metres is specified.)

Source	dbA	Source	dbA
Threshold of hearing	0	Motorcycle (10 m)	88
Rustling leaves	20	Food blender (1 m)	90
Quiet whisper (1 m)	30	Subway (inside)	94
Quiet home	40	Diesel truck (10 m)	100
Quiet street	50	Power mower (1 m)	107
Normal conversation	60	Pneumatic riveter (1 m)	115
Inside a car	70	Chainsaw (1 m)	117
Loud singing (1 m)	75	Amplified Rock and Roll (2 m)	120
Automobile (8 m)	80	Jet plane (30 m)	130

What are the Effects of Noise Pollution?

Noise can do physiological or psychological damage if the volume is high or if the exposure is prolonged. Loud, high-pitched noise damages the fine hair cells in the cochlea of the ear. The vibration of these hair cells in response to sound is transmitted to the brain by the auditory nerve. Since the body does not replace damaged hair cells, permanent hearing impairment is caused by prolonged exposure to loud noise.

Noise can also produce other effects like heart palpitation, pupil dilation, or muscle contraction. Migraine headaches, nausea, dizziness, gastric ulcers, and constriction of blood vessels are some of the other possible outcomes.

Noise can cause serious damage to wildlife, especially in remote regions, where the normal noise level is low. Ways in which animals are adversely affected by noise pollution include

- hearing loss, affecting their ability to avoid predators,
- masking, which is the inability to hear important environmental cues and animal signals,
- non-auditory physiological effects such as increased heart rate and respiration and general stress reaction, and
- behavioural effects, which could result in the abandonment of territory and lost reproduction.

What are the control measures against noise pollution?

Producing less noise is the best method of reducing this pollution. Almost all machinery can be redesigned to reduce noise. Another way is to provide shields and noise-absorbing material. Earplugs and earphones can shield the receiver from noise.

What is the Level of Noise Pollution in India?

In urban as well as rural areas, noise pollution is on the increase. Public meetings, festivals, marriage receptions, sound of televisions, automobile horns, general traffic movement, etc. have all become louder.

In the 1980s and 1990s, there were several court judgements in India restricting the generation of noise by industries, fire crackers, electric horns, etc. Finally, in 2000, the Indian government notified the Noise Regulation Rules (Box 13.6).

BOX 13.6 ENVIROFACT: ***Noise Regulation Rules in India***

In 2000, the Indian government notified the Noise Regulation Rules under the Environment (Protection) Act of 1986. Two types of noise standards are prescribed: ambient noise level standards and noise limits for designated types of machinery, appliances, and fire crackers.

The rules regulate noise levels in industrial (75 db), commercial (65 db), and residential zones (55 db), and also establish zones of silence (100 m) near schools, courts, hospitals, etc.

The rules specify that no permission could be granted by any authority for use of public address (PA) system in the open after 10.00 pm and before 6.00 am. After permission has been procured, the sound must fall within the sound limits prescribed in the Noise Rules.

An amendment to the Rules, made in January 2010, addresses the following issues:

1. Stress has been laid on making the night peaceful. The 'night time' has been defined (10.00 pm to 6.00 am) and restrictions have been imposed on the use of horns, sound-emitting construction equipment, and bursting of fire crackers during night time.
2. 'Public place' has been defined and the occupant of a public place has to restrict the volume of PA system, etc., so that the noise emitting from its activity would not exceed the noise limit more than 10 dbA.
3. Similarly, the occupant of a private place has to restrict the volume of music system, etc., so that the noise emitting from its activity would not exceed the noise limit by more than 5 dbA.
4. State governments must specify in advance the number and particulars of days, not exceeding 15 in a year, on which 2 hours exemption (10.00 pm to 12.00 midnight) would be operative for the use of PA system.

A National Ambient Noise Monitoring Network has been set up. It includes 10 monitoring stations in each of the seven cities: Mumbai, Delhi, Kolkata, Chennai, Bangalore, Lucknow, and Hyderabad.

Key Idea Noise pollution is on the increase in India and it has many adverse effects. We now have laws to control noise pollution

What is Radioactive Pollution?

Radiation is the emission of energy as electromagnetic waves or moving subatomic particles. Natural radiation comes from many naturally occurring radioactive materials found in soil, water, air, and in the body. Every day, people inhale and ingest forms of radiation from air, food, and water.

Radioactive pollution occurs when the natural radiation levels in the environment increase due to human activities. Such activities (that can release radiation) include mining, handling, and processing of radioactive materials, handling and storage of radioactive waste, generation of nuclear energy. Nuclear accidents and, of course, nuclear wars release enormous amounts of radiation covering large areas.

Currently, the most common artificial sources of human exposure to radiation are X-ray machines and radiopharmaceuticals used for diagnostic or radiotherapy and other medical devices. Mobile phones, phone towers, cordless phones, as well as TVs, computers, microwave ovens, broadcast antennas, military and aviation radars, satellites, and wireless internet are all sources of low-level radiation.

According to WHO, excessive exposure to radiation may damage living tissues and organs, depending on the amount of radiation received. The extent of the potential damage depends on several factors, including the following:

- Type of radiation
- Sensitivity of the affected tissues and organs
- Manner and length of time exposed
- Radioactive isotopes involved
- Characteristics of the exposed person (such as age, gender, and underlying condition).

The risk of developing adverse health effects depends on the radiation dose. The higher the dose, the higher the risk of adverse effects. If the radiation dose is low or it is delivered over a long period of time, the risk is substantially lower because the damage to cells and molecules will be repaired by the body.

What is the Problem of Ozone Layer Depletion?

Ozone is a poisonous gas made up of molecules consisting of three oxygen atoms. This gas is extremely rare in the atmosphere, representing just three out of every 10 million molecules. 90% of ozone exists in the upper atmosphere, or stratosphere, between 10 and 50 km above the earth.

The ozone layer in the atmosphere absorbs most of the harmful ultraviolet-B (UV-B) radiation from the sun. It also completely screens out the deadly UV-C radiation. The ozone shield is thus essential to protect life.

Depleting the ozone layer allows more UV-B to reach the earth. The result would be an increase in skin cancers, eye cataracts, weakened immune systems, reduced plant yields, damage to ocean ecosystems and reduced fishing yields, and adverse effects on animals.

In the 1970s, scientists discovered that CFCs, used as refrigerants and aerosol propellants, finally break apart in the atmosphere and release chlorine atoms. This causes ozone depletion. Bromine atoms released by halons (used in fire extinguishers) have the same effect. CFCs and halons are examples of Ozone Depleting Substances (ODS).

> **Key Idea** The ozone layer over the earth depletes due to the human use of certain chemicals. The depletion of the ozone layer has several harmful effects on human beings and ecosystems.

When measurements started in the early 1980s, scientists noticed that the ozone layer over the Antarctic was weakening. The land area under the ozone-depleted atmosphere increased steadily to more than 20 million sq km in the early 1990s and has varied between 20 and 29 million sq km since then. In 2000, the area of the ozone hole reached a record 29 million sq km.

While no hole has appeared elsewhere, the Arctic spring has seen the ozone layer over the North Pole thin by up to 30%. The depletion over Europe and other high latitudes varied between 5% and 30%.

What is the connection between climate change and ozone depletion?

Stratospheric ozone depletion has an influence on climate change since both ozone and the compounds responsible for its depletion are active greenhouse gases. In turn, climate change will affect ozone depletion through changes in atmospheric conditions that alter the chemical production and loss of stratospheric ozone.

What were the International Initiatives Against the Depletion of the Ozone Layer?

Inter-governmental negotiations for an international agreement to phase out ozone-depleting substances started in 1981 and concluded with the adoption of the Vienna Convention for the Protection of the Ozone Layer in March 1985.

The Vienna Convention encouraged intergovernmental cooperation on research, systematic observation of the ozone layer, monitoring of CFC production, and the exchange of information. The Convention committed the signatories to take general measures to protect human health and the environment against human activities that modify the ozone layer.

The Vienna Convention was a framework agreement and did not contain legally binding controls or targets. However, it set an important precedent. For the first time, nations agreed in principle to tackle a global environmental problem before its effects were felt, or even scientifically proven.

In May 1985, British scientists published their discovery of severe ozone depletion over the Antarctic. Their findings were confirmed by American satellite observations and offered the first proof of severe ozone depletion. The discovery of the ozone 'hole' shocked the world. It is regarded as one of the major environmental disasters of the twentieth century.

The governments now recognized the need for stronger measures to reduce the production and consumption of a number of CFCs and several halons. As a result, the Montreal Protocol on Substances that Deplete the Ozone Layer was adopted in September 1987.

Ninety-six chemicals are presently controlled by the Montreal Protocol and phase-out schedules. The Protocol was designed so that these schedules could be revised on the basis of periodic scientific and technological assessments.

In 2009, the Montreal Protocol became the first UN Treaty to achieve universal ratification (that is, by all the member countries), demonstrating the world's commitment to ozone protection, and more broadly, to global environmental conservation.

What has been the impact of the Montreal Protocol so far?

The Montreal Protocol has been an outstanding success. All the CFCs have been phased out since January 2010. Atmospheric abundance of most controlled ozone-depleting substances is decreasing. The 2022 Assessment Report from the UNEP Ozone Secretariat provides some good news (Box 13.7).

BOX 13.7 HOPE: ***The Success of Montreal Protocol***

The 2022 Assessment Report from the UNEP Ozone Secretariat provide the following key findings:

- Actions taken under the Montreal Protocol continued to decrease atmospheric abundances of controlled ozone-depleting substances (ODSs) and advance the recovery of the stratospheric ozone layer. The atmospheric abundances of both total tropospheric chlorine and total tropospheric bromine from long-lived ODSs have continued to decline since the 2018 Assessment.
- New studies support previous Assessments in that the decline in ODS emissions due to compliance with the Montreal Protocol avoids global warming of approximately 0.5–1°C by mid-century compared to an extreme scenario with an uncontrolled increase in ODSs of 3–3.5% per year.
- Actions taken under the Montreal Protocol continue to contribute to ozone recovery. Recovery of ozone in the upper stratosphere is progressing. Total column ozone (TCO) in the Antarctic continues to recover, notwithstanding substantial interannual variability in the size, strength, and longevity of the ozone hole. Outside of the Antarctic region, the limited evidence of TCO recovery since 1996 has low confidence.
- TCO is expected to return to 1980 values around 2066 in the Antarctic, around 2045 in the Arctic, and around 2040 for the near-global average (60°N–60°S). The assessment of the depletion of TCO

in regions around the globe from 1980–1996 remains essentially unchanged since the 2018 Assessment.

- Compliance with the 2016 Kigali Amendment to the Montreal Protocol, which requires phase down of production and consumption of some hydrofluorocarbons (HFCs), is estimated to avoid 0.3–0.5°C of warming by 2100. This estimate does not include contributions from HFC-23 emissions.

Up to 2 million cases of skin cancer will be prevented each year, thanks to the successful implementation of the Montreal Protocol. It is estimated that without the Protocol, by the year 2050, the amount of ODS in the atmosphere would have been five times greater. Ozone depletion would have risen to at least 50% in the northern hemisphere's mid-latitudes and 70% in the southern mid-latitudes, about 10 times worse than current levels.

Without the Protocol, the UV-B radiation reaching the earth would have doubled in the highly populated northern mid-latitudes and quadrupled in the southern latitudes. The implications of this would have been horrendous: it could have led to 20 million more cases of cancer and 130 million more cases of eye cataracts.

Key Idea The Montreal Protocol has been a great success and, as a result, the ozone layer could recover before the end of the century.

The Montreal Protocol has resulted in the phasing out of the ODSs. As most of these substances are also potent greenhouse gases, the Protocol has delivered substantial climate benefits too.

The success of ozone protection has been possible because science and industry were able to develop and commercialize alternatives to ozone-depleting chemicals. Developed countries ended the use of CFCs faster and with less cost than was originally anticipated.

What have been the lessons of the montreal protocol?

The efforts of the world community to protect the ozone layer are a fascinating example of how humanity can act as one to face a common danger. The Protocol offers many lessons that could be applied to solve other global environmental issues:

- Adhere to the 'Precautionary Principle' because waiting for complete scientific proof can delay action to the point where the damage will become irreversible.
- Send consistent and credible signals to industry (e.g., by adopting legally binding phaseout schedules) so that they have an incentive to develop new and cost-effective alternative technologies.
- Ensure that improved scientific understanding can be incorporated quickly into decisions about the provisions of a treaty.
- Promote universal participation by recognizing the 'common but differentiated responsibility' of developing and developed countries and ensuring the necessary financial and technological support to developing countries.
- Base control measures on an integrated assessment of science, economics, and technology.

What is Acid Rain?

When atmospheric water droplets combine with a range of man-made chemical air pollutants, acidic rain is formed. It could also be in the form of acidic mist or snow.

The main pollutants involved are oxides of nitrogen and sulphur. In nature, volcanoes, fires, and decomposing matter emit these substances in small amounts. However, since the advent of the Industrial Revolution, human activities have been releasing such pollutants in large quantities. Such emissions are very high in the major industrial centres and have been increasing rapidly since mid-twentieth century.

Automobiles and coal- and oil-fired power stations are major sources of acid-forming compounds. In fact, any burning of coal, oil, and (to a lesser extent) natural gas produces them.

The acid rain ultimately falls on the ground, sometimes hundreds of kilometres from the area in which it formed and generally one to four days later. The effects are quite damaging.

What is the effect of acid rain?

When soil is acidified, it leads to loss of productivity. The acidification damages plant roots and they are not able to draw in enough nutrients to survive and grow.

When trees, particularly conifers, are exposed to acid rain for several years, they lose their leaves and die. This is one of the several causes for the decline of forests in Europe, North America, and Japan. Plants like orchids, lichen, and moss are also very sensitive to acid.

Acid rain falling on lakes and rivers leaves them clear and lifeless. Thousands of lakes in Sweden, Norway, and Canada, for example, have been permanently affected by acid. Fish populations have died and so did species like otters, amphibians, and birds that depended on fish for their food.

Acid rain harms people directly when they breathe in the acidic air. Acid rain can also harm people indirectly when they eat fish caught in affected lakes or rivers.

Key Idea Acid rain is formed when atmospheric water droplets combine with a range of man-made chemical air pollutants. Acid rain had adverse effects on trees, fish populations, human beings, buildings, etc

Old buildings are also threatened by acid rain; the famous St Paul's Cathedral in London has decayed more in the last 50 years than in the previous two centuries. Some famous statues, such as the Lincoln Memorial and Michaelangelo's statue of Marcus Aurelius, have started deteriorating because of acid rain. The same is true of many historic buildings in Europe.

The Taj Mahal was also threatened by acid rain caused by factories in Agra. Thanks to the orders of the Supreme Court, some of these industries have been shifted or closed down.

A side effect of acid rain is the leaching of aluminium out of the soil into water bodies. Aluminium is very toxic to fish and the birds that prey on the fish. Sometimes, acidification leads to the leaching of cadmium and this can affect animals.

What can be done about acid rain?

Acid rain occurring in a place could be caused by emissions from far away. In most cases, acid rain formed in one country falls on some other country. It is also difficult to prove that a particular country or a factory was responsible, or to quantify the amount of contributing pollution from a source.

Pouring powdered limestone into water bodies is a rapid, but short-lived method of reducing acidity. A more permanent, but slow and expensive, method is the liming of surrounding soils.

Some technologies for reducing emissions are flue gas desulphurization in power stations and catalytic converters and engine modifications in automobiles. The best way, of course, is to reduce emissions.

Ending on a Positive Note: Hopeful Stories

1. Box 13.4 described how the air in Delhi improved in recent times (and became polluted again).
2. India is the first country to adopt the WHO Global Monitoring Framework on Noncommunicable Diseases (NCDs), including lung diseases caused by air pollution (Box 13.8).

BOX 13.8 HOPE: *Government Initiative—Going with the WHO Action Plan*

Every year, roughly 5.8 million Indians die from noncommunicable diseases (NCDs) such as heart and lung diseases, stroke, cancer, and diabetes. In fact, one in four Indians risks dying from an NCD before they reach the age of 70. The greatest risk factors contributing to NCD are unhealthy diets, physical inactivity, tobacco and alcohol use, and air pollution.

In line with WHO's Global Action Plan for the Prevention and Control of NCDs 2013–2020, India is the first country to develop specific national targets and indicators aimed at reducing the number of premature deaths from NCDs by 25% by 2025. A National Multisectoral Action Plan that outlines actions by various sectors in addition to the health sector, to reduce the burden of NCDs and their risk factors, is being developed.

The global action plan lists 9 targets for countries to set. But India has taken the unprecedented step of setting a tenth target to address household air pollution—a major health hazard in the Southeast Asian region due to burning of solid biomass fuel and second-hand smoke.

India's National Monitoring Framework for Prevention and Control of NCDs calls for a 50% relative reduction in household use of solid fuel and a 30% relative reduction in prevalence of current tobacco use by 2025.

Additionally, India has implemented WHO's Framework Convention on Tobacco Control aimed at reducing the demand for tobacco products. The country has prohibited sales of tobacco products around educational institutions, restricted tobacco imagery in films and TV programmes, banned some smokeless tobacco products and developed tobacco-free guidelines for educational institutions.

India also plans go a step further and require tobacco pictorial warnings to cover 85% of the package. If implemented, this effort will be an excellent example of a 'best buy' or cost effective, high impact intervention for combating NCDs.

REVIEW: A SUMMARY OF THE KEY POINTS

- While there are some natural sources of air pollution, most of the pollution today is caused by human activities.
- Burning fossil fuels in automobiles and industry is the major source of air pollution.
- Air pollution has many adverse effects on human health.
- Technologies are available to reduce automobile and industrial emissions.
- The zero-emission wonder car running on low-cost, abundant, and renewable energy is still a dream.
- The world will be forced to cut down on the number of cars on the road due to a variety of reasons.
- Indoor air pollution can be as damaging as outdoor pollution.
- As the number of automobiles increases rapidly in India, air pollution is becoming a serious problem. In particular, it is taking a heavy toll on the health of urban poor children.
- Spurred on by the courts, the Indian Government is introducing stringent rules to reduce automobile emissions.
- Noise pollution can have very damaging effects and the best way is to curb the generation of noise.
- The ozone layer in the atmosphere is getting depleted and an ozone hole has developed over the Antarctic.
- The depletion of the ozone layer has adverse effects on life.
- The Montreal Protocol on Substances that Deplete the Ozone Layer has been successful in reducing the production and consumption of such substances. The ozone hole is now closing.
- Acid rain is formed by the emission of pollutants from human activities. Acid rain has a number of adverse effects on the environment and living beings.

EXERCISES

Objective-type questions

In each question below, choose the best out of the given choices.

1. Which of the following statements is **not** true with regard to air pollution?
   (a) Air pollution is caused only by human activities.
   (b) Urban areas have high air pollution.
   (c) A burning forest produces air pollution.
   (d) Air pollution is caused by volcanoes.
2. Which of the following is **not** a primary air pollutant?
   (a) Methane
   (b) Sulphur dioxide
   (c) Ozone
   (d) Asbestos
3. Which of the following is an occasional cause of air pollution?
   (a) Mining
   (b) Driving automobiles
   (c) Cooking
   (d) Celebrating a festival
4. Which of the following statements is true?
   (a) Hybrid cars run on petrol and diesel.
   (b) The only emission from a hydrogen-powered vehicle will be oxygen.
   (c) An electric car has to be charged from the grid.
   (d) A diesel vehicle pollutes less than a petrol vehicle.
5. Which of the following statements is true with regard to noise and noise pollution?
   (a) Decibel is a linear scale of noise measurement.
   (b) A jet plane is one of the high-decibel sources of noise.
   (c) Noise will not affect the heart.
   (d) Noise cannot be shielded.
6. Which of the following statements is **not** true with regard to the ozone layer?
   (a) It has now recovered fully.
   (b) It absorbs most of the UV-B radiation.
   (c) It screens out the UV-C radiation.
   (d) Its depletion leads to more cancers.
7. Which of the following is the successful international agreement on ozone layer depletion?
   (a) Kyoto Protocol
   (b) Montreal Protocol
   (c) Vienna Convention
   (d) Copenhagen Accord
8. Acid rain is formed when
   (a) an acid mixes with rain.
   (b) man-made chemical air pollutants combine with atmospheric water droplets.
   (c) factories let out gases.
   (d) matter decomposes
9. Which of the following is **not** an effect of acid rain?
   (a) Death of trees
   (b) Plants lose productivity
   (c) Soil turns alkaline
   (d) Lakes turn lifeless
10. Which of the following toxic chemicals adversely affects human health and the environment around the world, because they can be transported by wind and water?
    (a) Volatile Organic compounds (VOCs)
    (b) Polycyclic Aromatic Hydrocarbons (PAHs)
    (c) Peroxyacetyl Nitrate (PAN)
    (d) Persistent Organic Pollutants (POPs)

Short-answer questions

1. What are primary and secondary air pollutants? Give examples.
2. What are the sources of outdoor air pollution?
3. What are the effects of outdoor air pollution?
4. How can outdoor air pollution be reduced or controlled?
5. What are the causes and effects of indoor air pollution?
6. What are the sources and effects of noise pollution?
7. Give an account of the rules framed by the government to control noise pollution.
8. What is ozone layer and why is it getting depleted?
9. Outline the provisions of the Vienna Convention and the Montreal Protocol.
10. What have been the results of implementation of the Montreal Protocol?
11. Explain the causes and effects of acid rain.

Long-answer questions

1. 'The automobile is one of the worst inventions made by humankind.' Write an essay supporting this statement. Focus on the environmental impact of

the automobile. Comment on the possible impact of the rapid increase of the number of cars in India and China. Review the approaches for making cleaner cars.

2. Describe the state of urban air pollution in India. What is its impact on health, especially on that of children? What are the measures the government is taking to reduce vehicle emissions? How did the quality of air improve in Delhi?

Think critically: Deeper question for reflection and discussion

What is the psychological basis for the great attraction of the personal car? How can that need be satisfied through public transport? How can cycling be promoted (even as the Chinese are giving up this healthy and ecofriendly habit)?

ENJOY AND EDUCATE YOURSELF

1. Relax with the children's book *The Lorax* by Dr Seuss, a great environmental story. You may like it for its message and its wacky verse.
2. Watch the animation movie version of *The Lorax* (2012), directed by Chris Renaud and Kyle Balda.

ACCESS THE OUP ONLINE RESOURCE CENTRE FOR MORE

- Additional text and other recommended references, websites, and films

UNIT 5

Climate Change

14 Climate Change: Causes and Impacts

We are not educated people, but I can sense something grave is happening around us. The land that I had tilled for years, that fed me and my family for generations, has vanished. We have moved to Sagar Island and are trying to rebuild our lives. Storms have become more intense than ever. Displacement and death are everywhere here. The land is shrinking and salty water gets into our fields. We feel very insecure now.

Tulsi Khara, A resident of the Sundarbans

MAIN QUESTIONS ADDRESSED

- What are the causes and effects of global warming and climate change?
- Why have the greenhouse gas emissions been going up steadily?
- What is the impact of climate change on India?

KEYWORDS AND PHRASES

Arctic, Carbon Footprint, climate change, climate justice, climate vulnerability, El Niño, global warming, greenhouse gas, man-made disaster, natural disaster, Tuvalu

LEAD STORY

THE STORY OF TUVALU: RISING SEA, SINKING ISLANDS

'I feel sad and angry at the same time, sad that eventually we will have to move, and angry because this is not our doing, but because of doings of others who don't care, who are looking after their own needs and not at the bigger picture.'

That was Paani Laupepa, the former Assistant Secretary for the Environment, Tuvalu. He was referring to the soon-to-come evacuation of Tuvalu before it disappears into the ocean as the world's first country-casualty of global warming.

Tuvalu is a chain of nine coral islands in the South Pacific with a total area of 25 sq km and a population of 11,000. It is one of the smallest and most remote countries, halfway between Hawaii and Australia. It has been described as a paradise with chalk-white beaches and coconut palms. Soon, however, it will be a paradise lost!

People calling out: *"Help us. Our island is almost gone!"*

Sea-level rise, caused by global warming and climate change, is already a fact in Tuvalu. The islands are made of porous fossil coral and water has started flowing up through holes in the ground. The tides are higher, and the storms are more frequent and severe.

Waves wash over the island's main roads. Coconut trees stand partly submerged. The small patches of cropland have been rendered unusable because of encroaching saltwater.

Thousands of journalists, researchers, and curious visitors now come to Tuvalu during high-tide months to see the big waves. These visitors bring valuable income to the country. They also spread awareness about climate change when they return to their countries.

The people of Tuvalu, who survive on agriculture and fishing, are not giving up yet. The residents and their government are constructing seawalls to protect their homes. They may, however, be forced to evacuate the islands within the next 40–50 years.

Tuvalu is not alone. Rising sea levels also threaten the other Pacific island nations such as Kiribati, Vanuatu, the Marshall Islands, the Cook Islands, Fiji, and the Solomon Islands. They have larger populations and where will they all go? (We also discussed in Chapter 1 the plight of people living on the vanishing islands of the Sundarbans.)

Tuvaluans feel that they are being punished for no fault of theirs. The reckless burning of fossil fuels by the rich countries has resulted in global warming and sea-level rise.

Tuvalu may well become the first nation in the world to disappear due to global warming. When the Tuvaluans leave their homes, who will compensate them for the loss of their culture, language, and way of life?

CLIMATE CHANGE: GRIM HUMOUR

Two planets meet.
Oh hello, says one, long time no see. How are you?
Not doing so well, says the other. I think I have Homo sapiens.
That's terrible, responds the first planet, I had that too. But don't worry, it doesn't last long.
– Author unknown
(*Homo sapiens* is the scientific name for the human species.)

What should the world learn from the story of Tuvalu?

The Tuvalu story shows how interconnected the world's ecosystems are. The effects of environmental degradation are worldwide. Anything we do—driving a car in the US, cutting down a rainforest in Amazonia, or conducting a nuclear test in India—has an impact on the rest of the world.

The story also shows that the people worst affected by global warming and climate change will be the poor of the world. They cause little environmental damage, but they will pay the price first.

In this chapter, we will look at the causes and consequences of major environmental effects like global warming and climate change. We begin with a short discussion on disasters because climate change is leading to more and more disasters.

What is a Disaster?

According to the UN Office for Disaster Risk Reduction (UNDRR), a disaster is a serious disruption of the functioning of a community or a society involving widespread human, material, economic, or environmental losses and impacts, which exceeds the ability of the affected community or society to cope using its own resources.

In other words, an event becomes a disaster, if:

- it is sudden, abrupt, or unpredictable;
- it causes human, material, economic, or environmental losses; and
- it exceeds the ability of the affected community to cope with them.

Disaster impacts may include loss of life, injury, disease, and other negative effects on human, physical, mental, and social well-being, together with damage to property, destruction of assets, loss of services, social and economic disruption, and environmental degradation.

India's Disaster Management Act of 2005 defines a disaster as follows:

'Disaster means a catastrophe, mishap, calamity or grave occurrence in any area, arising from natural or manmade causes, or by accident or negligence which results in substantial loss of life or human suffering or damage to, and destruction of, property, or damage to, or degradation of, environment, and is of such a nature or magnitude as to be beyond the coping capacity of the community of the affected area.'

What are the types of disasters?

Disasters can be broadly classified as natural disasters and technological disasters (primarily man-made).

Natural disasters include the following:

- Geophysical or geological: Earthquake, volcanic activity, tsunami
- Meteorological (Short-lived, micro- to meso-scale extreme weather and atmospheric conditions that last from minutes to days): Extreme temperature (heat wave, cold wave), fog, storm, tornado, dust storm
- Hydrological: Flood, landslide, wave action
- Climatological (Long-lived, meso- to macro-scale atmospheric processes ranging from intra-seasonal to multi-decadal climate variability): Drought, glacial lake outburst, wildfire
- Biological: Epidemic, pandemic, insect infestation

Technological (mostly man-made) disasters include the following:

- Industrial accidents: Chemical spill, explosion, fire, poisoning, gas leak (Example: Bhopal Gas Tragedy)
- Transport accidents: Accidents in air, on road, in water, in railways; oil spill
- Nuclear accidents: Chemical reactions during operation or testing (Example: Chernobyl in 1986); due to earthquake or tsunami (Japan in 2011)
- Disasters caused by conflicts and wars: Chemical warfare (Examples: Use of Agent Orange in Vietnam and depleted uranium in Iraq)

A natural disaster can trigger a technological disaster. For example, in 2011, a tsunami in Japan led to a nuclear accident.

Is the Global Climate Changing?

Weather is the condition of the atmosphere at a particular place and time, such as the temperature, humidity, rain, wind, etc. Climate is the long-term pattern of weather conditions for a given area.

The factors that influence global climate are the flow of solar energy, the condition of the atmosphere, the shape and rotation of the earth, and the currents and other processes of the ocean.

Until the middle of the twentieth century, the earth's climate was generally regarded as unchanging, but it is now known to be in a continuous and delicate state of flux. Further, there is now enough scientific evidence that global climate is changing—extreme events like cyclones, floods, and drought are becoming more common and severe. Even relatively small changes in climate can have major effect on our resources like food, energy, and water.

What is global warming and how does it occur?

Recall the way the carbon cycle works (Chapter 2). During photosynthesis, plants absorb carbon dioxide (CO_2) and release oxygen. Organisms breathe in this oxygen, and give out CO_2, which goes back to the plants. This is the carbon cycle in brief.

Normally, CO_2 and other such gases (called greenhouse gases) that surround the planet let the radiation from the sun reach the earth but prevent some of the heat from being reflected out again. Without these greenhouse gases, the earth would be far colder, largely covered in ice. When the amount of gases exceeds a limit, however, higher temperatures and global warming result.

Since the 1960s, each decade has been warmer than the previous one. In fact, the year 2014 was the warmest one (over both land and ocean surfaces) among all the years since record keeping began in 1880. The December 2014 combined global land and ocean average surface temperature was also the highest on record.

The average temperatures around the world have risen by about 0.5°C since the beginning of the twentieth century. If greenhouse gas emissions continue at the current rate, the temperature rise could be anything from 1.5 to 4.5°C in the twenty-first century.

> **Key Idea** Excessive burning of fossil fuels releases huge amounts of greenhouse gases, which leads to global warming and climate change.

> **Key Idea** We must limit the global temperature rise to 2°C and the CO_2 concentration to 350 ppm

The earth is a delicately balanced system and an increase of just 1.0 or 1.5°C in the mean global temperature could cause major changes in the climate with serious implications for our environment, health, and economy. The change is likely to be greater than anything experienced during the last 10,000 years.

Every degree (even half a degree) increase in average global temperature will result in more severe climate and greater loss and damage. Scientists believe that we must keep the temperature increase by the end of the century to 1.5°C. We can achieve that goal only if we take immediate measures to curb global warming. Otherwise, an increase of 2°C seems very likely.

Why and How has the CO_2 Concentration in the Atmosphere been Increasing?

By burning large amounts of fossil fuels, we release huge quantities of CO_2 into the atmosphere. Concurrently, deforestation also releases carbon trapped in the tissues of the trees. At the same time, loss of trees reduces the earth's capacity to absorb CO_2 through photosynthesis. Natural processes like volcano eruptions and earthquake-induced fires also contribute CO_2 emissions.

Due to these factors, the CO_2 concentration in the atmosphere has been rapidly increasing (Table 14.1).

TABLE 14.1 CO_2 Concentration in the Atmosphere (parts per million or ppm)

Year	Average CO_2 (ppm)
1750	280
1958	315
1992	355
2010	389
2014	398.5
2022	417

Some of the other greenhouse gases are far more effective than CO_2 in trapping heat. Chlorofluorocarbons (CFCs) are an example, but their role is greater in the depletion of the ozone layer (Chapter 13). Methane, released from swamps, garbage dumps, and human and animal waste is also a greenhouse gas, and its concentration is increasing. Similarly, human activities are causing a rapid increase in the amounts of thirty other greenhouse gases.

Why then are we focusing on CO_2 emissions?

There are two main reasons why CO_2 gets all the attention:

- CO_2 has caused most of the warming since 1750. The other greenhouse gases are far less abundant in the atmosphere and are also being added more slowly.
- CO_2 remains in the atmosphere for hundreds or even thousands of years—longer than the other major greenhouse gases emitted because of human activities. The emissions that we release today

from our cars and power plants will decide the climate for our children, grandchildren, and later generations.

Which are the Countries and Sectors with the Largest Greenhouse Gas Emissions?

The top three greenhouse gas emitters — China, the European Union, and the US — contribute 41.5% of total global emissions, while the bottom 100 countries only account for only 3.6%. Collectively, the top 10 emitters (which includes India) account for over two-thirds of global GHG emissions.

While the top emitters in total increased their emissions by 47% since 1990, the United States, European Union, Russia, and Japan have since peaked and Brazil seems to have stabilized their emissions. Although China, India, Indonesia, Iran, and South Korea are still increasing their emission, India and Indonesia have comparatively low greenhouse gas emissions per capita.

Emission growth slowed down globally since 2013, increasing by an average of 0.7% per year, compared to an average of 1.7% since 1990. This slowing of growth happened even as the global economy grew during the same period. However, greenhouse gas emissions are still on an upwards trend, illustrating the need for increased climate actions to see a decoupling of economic growth and carbon emissions.

> **Key Idea** China, the European Union and the US contribute 41.5% of total global emissions, while the bottom 100 countries only account for only 3.6%. The countries most seriously affected by climate change are often those that carry the least responsibility.

Many poor countries emit very small amounts. Often, the countries most seriously affected by climate change (like Tuvalu) are those that carry the least responsibility. These uneven contributions to the climate problem and unjustified negative impact on some countries are making it difficult for the world community to find effective and equitable solutions to climate change.

The energy sector—including electricity, transport, manufacturing, buildings, and fossil fuels—is the largest contributor to GHG emissions, representing 73% of global emissions.

In addition to Ecological Footprint (Chapter 1) and Water Footprint (Chapter 5), we also have the concept of Carbon Footprint (Box 14.1).

BOX 14.1 CONCEPT: *Carbon Footprint*

The Carbon Footprint measures the total greenhouse gas emissions caused directly and indirectly by a person, organization, event, product, or country.

Unlike Ecological Footprint, Carbon Footprint is not measured in area, but in tonnes of carbon dioxide equivalent (tCO_2e). The Footprint of a country does not just measure emissions that occur on its territory. Like Water Footprint, it includes emissions that occur in the production of all goods and services consumed in a country. It also includes international transport (ocean freight and aviation).

The table here gives the Carbon Footprint of selected countries.

Country	Carbon Footprint (tCO_2e)
US	28.6
Singapore	24.1
Canada	19.6
Germany	15.1
Japan	13.8
South Africa	6.0
China	3.1
India	1.8
Bangladesh	1.1
Global Average	**5.1**

You can calculate your personal Carbon Footprint and try to reduce it. (Visit www.carbonfootprint.com)

What is El Niño and How is it Related to Climate Change?

The phenomenon of El Niño is an oscillation of the ocean-atmosphere system in the tropical Pacific. Whenever it occurs, it has important consequences for weather around the globe.

Are all extreme weather events due to El Niño? Or should we blame global warming and climate change for all the freak events? Are they both responsible and is there a connection between the two? Many climate scientists believe that there is indeed a connection between climate change and the observed increase in strength and frequency of El Niño events since the late 1970s. Though they have not found a direct link so far, they say that, combined with a future El Niño event, climate change could strengthen or weaken the typical weather patterns associated with El Niño.

What is the Current Impact of Climate Change and What is Likely to Happen in the Future?

Climate change is already here and is set to become worse. The impact is and will be widespread and long-lasting:

Natural disasters

There were an unprecedented number of natural disasters during the 1990s and that trend continues in the twenty-first century. Direct and insured losses from weather- related disasters have increased substantially in recent decades, both globally and regionally. It is difficult to connect a specific meteorological or climatological disaster to climate change, though scientists are getting better and better at it.

Ocean and coasts

The ocean has become warmer and more acidic and sea levels are rising. The melting of polar ice caps is adding to the problem. Small islands like those of the Maldives, South Pacific, and Sundarbans are threatened. If sea levels continue to rise, coastal areas will be flooded in places like the Netherlands, Egypt, Bangladesh, and Indonesia, necessitating the evacuation of large populations.

Coral reefs are already dying all over the world due to human activities. A warmer and more acidic ocean will accelerate this process. Corals are home to 9 million different kinds of marine plants and animals. Their death will have a devastating effect on marine life and fisheries.

Melting of glaciers, ice caps, and permafrost

Glaciers continue to shrink worldwide. Permafrost is warming and thawing in high-latitude regions and in high-elevation regions. The most dramatic evidence of this change is the melting of the Arctic (Box 14.2).

BOX 14.2 ECOSYSTEM: ***The Story of the Arctic—Melting Ice, Hungry Bears***

The Arctic is the area around the North Pole. It is a vast ocean covered with ice and surrounded by treeless, frozen ground. The Arctic region is one of the last remaining areas of pristine nature.

The Arctic is full of organisms living in the ice: fish and marine mammals, birds, and land animals, besides human settlements. Its biological diversity is very valuable. The natural resources include oil, gas, minerals, forest, and fish.

The Arctic sea ice keeps the polar regions cool and helps moderate global climate. Sea ice has a bright surface, so 80% of the sunlight that strikes it is reflected into space. As sea ice melts in the summer, it exposes the dark ocean surface. Instead of reflecting 80% of the sunlight, the ocean absorbs 90% of the sunlight. The ocean heats up, and Arctic temperatures rise further.

A small temperature increase at the poles leads to still greater warming over time. This makes the polar regions to be most sensitive to climate change. According to scientific data, both the thickness and summer sea ice extent in the Arctic have shown a dramatic decline over the past 30 years. This is consistent with observations of a warming Arctic. The loss of sea ice also has the potential to accelerate global warming trends and to change climate patterns.

A melting Arctic has many adverse effects in the region:

- The indigenous people of the Arctic have never seen such weather before. They must travel far over the dangerously thin ice to hunt seals. They have even had to use boats! Accidents are increasing due to unusual conditions, resulting in injuries and death, loss of valuable equipment, and expensive rescues.
- Severe storms and coastal erosion are happening.
- Marine habitats are shrinking for ice-dependent seals, polar bears, and some seabirds. This may push some species to extinction.
- Polar bears need ice for protective cover and for a platform to hunt seals. During the summer, they eat very little while they wait for the ocean to freeze. Due to climate change, sea ice melts earlier in the spring, forcing the bears to move to land earlier in the season. This means they do not have enough fat reserves to survive the ice-free season. Changing ice conditions over the last 20 years have already reduced the number of polar bears, and the number of live births and the health of adult bears have declined.

Water, agriculture, and food

In many regions, changing precipitation or melting snow and ice are altering hydrological systems, affecting water resources in terms of quantity and quality. Negative impacts of climate change on crop yields have been more common than positive impacts.

Extreme floods and droughts are likely to have serious effects on water resources, agriculture, and food security:

- Loss of topsoil, erosion of soil, and desertification
- Overflow of sewage systems and resulting water pollution and epidemics
- Amount and location of fresh water affected by changing rainfall, melting ice, and more evaporation. (For example, if the Himalayan glaciers are gone, there will be no water for 500 million people.)
- Warmer water attracting more organisms and getting contaminated
- Sea-level rise bringing salt water into coastal marshes and aquifers

Animals, plant species, and human beings

Many terrestrial, freshwater, and marine species have shifted their geographic ranges, seasonal activities, migration patterns, abundances, and species interactions in response to climate change.

Key Idea Climate change is likely to result in massive increases in natural disasters, biodiversity loss, water scarcity, sea-level rise, and human migration

Thousands of animal and plant species will go extinct, unable to adjust quickly enough to the new conditions. Polar species may be the first to go, followed by those in the coastal zones everywhere.

Warming will increase photosynthesis activity leading to faster growth of plants and trees. Initially, the yields will be more, but too much heat will kill the crops.

Extreme weather will increase human migration. There will be many millions more of environmental refugees. People living on the coasts will suffer extensive damage due to sea-level rise and cyclones.

What is the Impact of Climate Change on India?

Geographic location, huge population, high dependence on agriculture, and huge income inequalities together make India very vulnerable to climate change. India is already being affected by climate change and its impact will be stronger in the coming years. Eight of the ten warmest years ever were recorded during the decade 2001–2010. Apart from sea-level rise, the meltdown of Himalayan glaciers is another effect of global warming.

Climate change has already affected our monsoon patterns. Since 1951, instances of very heavy rains have gone up every year. Spells of moderate rain are going down and extreme events have become 'normal'. This changing trend of the monsoon has made us more vulnerable to disasters such as floods and landslides and has also led to heavy crop losses.

In future, global warming could change the climate in ways we have never experienced. Frequencies and intensities of tropical cyclones in Bay of Bengal could increase, particularly in the post-monsoon period. Low-lying coastal areas could be flooded, displacing millions of people. Mumbai and other coastal cities could suffer severe losses.

> **Key Idea** India is especially vulnerable to climate change and its impact.

Some states are likely to get very heavy rains, while other states could experience severe droughts. The meltdown of glaciers would ultimately lead to water scarcity and severe fall in food production.

What is Meant by Vulnerability to Climate Change?

Vulnerability to climate change (also called climate vulnerability or climate risk vulnerability) is the propensity or predisposition to be adversely affected by climate change. The concept describes how strongly people or ecosystems are likely to affected by climate change.

Some ecosystems such as low-lying islands are vulnerable to the rise in sea level caused by global warming. Examples are the islands of the Sundarbans and the entire Maldives. The Arctic is very vulnerable due to the thinning of ice cover. Many Himalayan settlements are vulnerable because heavy rainfall would cause massive landslides. Cities that are on the coasts and those close to big rivers are also vulnerable. Poorer communities are vulnerable because they cannot overcome damage to their homes and lands or loss of livelihood.

What is the Global Climate Risk Index?

The Global Climate Risk Index is published every year by the NGO Germanwatch. The Global Climate Risk Index 2021 analysed and ranked to what extent countries and regions have been affected by impacts of climate related extreme weather events (storms, floods, heatwaves etc.). The most recent data available for 2019 and from 2000 to 2019 was considered.

The countries most affected in 2019 were Mozambique, Zimbabwe as well as the Bahamas. For the period from 2000 to 2019, Puerto Rico, Myanmar, and Haiti were worst affected, followed by Philippines, Mozambique, The Bahamas, Bangladesh, Pakistan, and Thailand.

The Climate Risk Index clearly shows that signs of escalating climate change can no longer be ignored – on any continent or in any region. Impacts from extreme-weather events hit the poorest countries hardest as these are particularly vulnerable to the damaging effects of a hazard, have a lower coping capacity and may need more time to rebuild and recover. The Global Climate Risk Index indicates a level of exposure and vulnerability to extreme weather events, which countries should understand as warnings to be prepared for more frequent and/or more severe events in the future.

The 2019 storms in Japan showed that even high-income countries were feeling climate impacts more clearly than ever before. Effective climate change mitigation and adaptation to prevent or minimize potential damage is therefore in the self-interest of all countries worldwide.

Where does India stand in the global climate risk index 2021?

Here are some references to India in the Report:

- India is among the top 10 countries worst affected by climate change in 2019.

- The floods caused by the heavy rains were responsible for 1800 deaths across 14 states and led to the displacement of 1.8 million people.
- Overall, 11.8 million people were affected by the intense monsoon season with the economic damage estimated to be US$10 billion.

What is Climate Justice?

We can discuss climate justice from diverse perspectives. The discussion below is based on the model developed at the University of California Center for Climate Justice, US.

Climate Justice recognizes the disproportionate impacts of climate change on low-income communities and communities of color around the world, the people, and places least responsible for the problem. It seeks solutions that address the root causes of climate change and in doing so, simultaneously address a broad range of social, racial, and environmental injustices.

These solutions can be organized into Six Pillars of Climate Justice:

1. **Just Transition**
   At its core, a just transition represents the transition of fossil fuel-based economies to equitable, regenerative, renewable energy-based systems. However, a just transition is not only centered around technological change. It emphasizes employment in renewable energy and other green sectors, sustainable land use practices, and broader political economic transformations. We should support policies that advocate and plan for a just transition and an equitable and sustainable future.

2. **Social, Racial, and Environmental Justice**
   Climate justice connects the climate crisis to the social, racial, and environmental issues in which it is deeply entangled. It recognizes the disproportionate impacts of climate change on low-income and BIPOC communities around the world, the people, and places least responsible for the problem.

   There are many other instances of interconnected marginalizations across the globe. The power of a climate justice approach is that by addressing the root causes of climate change, we simultaneously address a broad range of social, racial, and environmental injustices.

3. **Indigenous Climate Action**
   Indigenous communities around the world are facing some of the most severe climate impacts. Indigenous communities are not only reliant on their surrounding ecosystems for their lives and livelihoods; their identities are also deeply interwoven with the land and water. As a result, Indigenous Peoples are leading efforts in climate change mitigation and adaptation across the globe.

4. **Community Resilience and Adaptation**
   The most marginalized communities, who are least responsible for the climate crisis, are facing the most severe consequences of climate change. We must view community resilience and adaptation from a social justice and equity perspective. This would inspire models such as food sovereignty, common property forest management, and energy democracy. It would support local communities in developing their own solutions and allow them to benefit directly from local climate action.

5. **Natural Climate Solutions**
   Natural climate solutions recognize the importance of forests and agricultural lands as critical ecosystems for equitable climate action. From a climate justice perspective, natural climate solutions take a systems approach and include regenerative farming, agroforestry, permaculture, urban gardens, and forest restoration.

6. **Climate Education and Engagement**
Given the amount of denial and misunderstanding surrounding the climate crisis, widespread climate education and engagement is fundamental to addressing the root causes of climate change. We need education not only based on climate science but also on the ways in which climate change is deeply intertwined with a range of other social, racial, and environmental issues that define our daily lived experiences.

With a widespread perspective that centers on equity, we can build civic engagement to support candidates who recognize climate change as an urgent existential crisis, unite countries with science and a systems-thinking approach, and take bold steps toward deep decarbonization that do not further inequities. This approach, which unites people around equity, has the power to make real and lasting system-wide change.

Ending on a Positive Note: Hopeful Stories

1. **Growth in renewable energy production:** Renewable energy production hit record levels in 2022. The War in Ukraine and rising fossil fuel prices this year have undoubtedly pushed countries to look for alternative energy sources. Short on gas following the stoppage of Russian supply, the European Union has ramped up efforts to scale up renewable energy infrastructure, and the outcome is promising. In the second quarter of 2022, 43% of the bloc's energy mix came from renewables, with 19 of the bloc's member states achieving record wind and solar power generation. And while it's true that some countries returned to coal (even if only temporarily) amid the energy crisis, recent data shows that EU emissions in November have reached their lowest value in at least 30 years, showing that concerns about the bloc regressing on its climate commitments are unfounded.

But Europe was not alone. China, the US, and India – whose economic growth has largely been fueled by coal and gas – have also made great strides in their commitment to shifting to alternative energy in keeping with their net-zero targets.

According to the International Energy Agency's latest report, global growth has been so substantial that renewable energy is now on track to become the largest source of global electricity generation by 2025, and by 2027, the world will have twice as much renewable capacity as in the previous five years.

2. **The US passes the biggest climate bill in the country's history:** In August 2022, US President Joe Biden signed the Inflation Reduction Act (IRA) into law. The historic piece of legislation is the single largest investment in climate and energy in America's history, paving the way for a greener future in the US – the world's second-largest polluting nation after China – but ultimately also for the entire planet.

The IRA sets aside US$369 billion to fight the climate crisis. Experts predict a 40% reduction in US emissions by 2030 from 2005 levels, which would bring the country one step closer to its commitment to reach net zero by 2050.

The bill includes significant investments in renewables, particularly solar and offshore wind, as well as new credits for nuclear power production and clean hydrogen and incentives to develop more facilities that produce clean energy inputs, components, and finished products. It also provides tax breaks to make electric vehicles more affordable and help low-income households to turn away from gas-powered cars. Through these incentives for investment in clean energy, the government hopes to push consumers to make more sustainable choices. What's more, the IRA provides huge incentives for carbon capture, utilization, and sequestration projects and expands the eligibility for carbon capture and sequestration credits.

3. **UN Accord on compensation for climate change damages:** At the UNFCCC COP27 summit in Sharm El Sheikh, Egypt, countries reached a long-awaited deal to provide compensation for climate change damages to vulnerable developing nations. The final COP27 agreement included the long-awaited provision to establish a fund to help developing countries that are "particularly vulnerable" to global warming bear the immediate costs of climate change-fuelled events, such as storms and floods.

   Despite the historic win for poor nations, however, details as to who would pay, how much, and who would benefit won't be decided until next year, when a transitional committee is expected to make recommendations for countries to adopt at COP28 in November 2023.

REVIEW: A SUMMARY OF THE KEY POINTS

- Warming of the climate system is undeniable, climate change is already upon us, and is set to get worse.
- Human influence on the climate system is clear. Climate change is due to the excessive burning of fossil fuels.
- Continued emission of greenhouse gases will cause long-lasting climate change leading to severe, pervasive, and irreversible impacts for people and ecosystems.
- Climate change is likely to result in massive increases in natural disasters, biodiversity loss, water scarcity, sea-level rise, and human migration.
- India is already facing the impact of climate change and is among the top 10 vulnerable countries.

EXERCISES

Objective-type questions

For each question below, choose the best answer out of the given choices.

1. What is the main cause of global warming and climate change?
   (a) Photosynthesis
   (b) Climate change
   (c) Burning fossil fuels
   (d) Carbon Cycle
2. Your Carbon Footprint measures the
   (a) amount of carbon you consume.
   (b) land you need for sustaining yourself indefinitely.
   (c) greenhouse gas emissions caused by you.
   (d) the amount of travel you do.
3. Which of the following statements is **not** true about global warming and climate change?
   (a) The Arctic is melting fast.
   (b) Global warming will stop the moment we stop burning fossil fuels.
   (c) There are many extreme weather events now.
   (d) There is an overwhelming agreement among scientists that climate change is happening.
4. The safe limit for CO_2 concentration in the atmosphere is 350 ppm, but it has now reached this level:
   (a) More than 410
   (b) Between 350 and 360
   (c) Between 380 and 400
   (d) Exceeded 400, but now it is down to 380
5. Which is the truly safe limit for the increase in global average temperature?
   (a) 1°C
   (b) 1.5°C
   (c) 2°C
   (d) None of the above

Short-answer questions

1. What is global warming and how does it occur?
2. What are the possible effects of climate change?

3. What is vulnerability to climate change?
4. What is climate justice?

Long-answer question

Carry out a survey in your area and write an essay on the topic: How do educated people view climate change? Are there still some sceptics? How can we convince them of the urgency of climate change?

Think critically: Deeper question for reflection and discussion

Communities that contribute very little to global warming are often most vulnerable to climate change. How do we consider this fact when we make climate policies or arrive at international agreements on climate change?

ENJOY AND EDUCATE YOURSELF

1. Watch the movie *The Day After Tomorrow* (2004), directed by Roland Emmerich and starring Dennis Quaid. What happens if the most pessimistic climate change predictions come true? See for yourself in this movie!
2. Relax with *Flight Behavior* (2012) by Barbara Kingsolver, a riveting story about a young woman who experiences something she cannot explain, and how her discovery energizes various competing factions—religious leaders, climate scientists, environmentalists, politicians—trapping her in the centre of the conflict and ultimately opening up her world.

ACCESS THE OUP ONLINE RESOURCE CENTRE FOR MORE

- Additional text and other recommended references, websites, and films

15 Climate Change: Adaptation and Mitigation

A warming El Niño is expected to develop in the coming months, and this will combine with human-induced climate change to push global temperatures into uncharted territory. There is a 98% likelihood that at least one of the next five years, and the five-year period, will be the warmest on record. This will have far-reaching repercussions for health, food security, water management and the environment. We need to be prepared.

Petteri Taalas
Secretary-General of the World Meteorological Organization
May 17, 2023

MAIN QUESTIONS ADDRESSED

- How serious is the impact of climate change on India?
- What should be the global response global warming and climate change?
- What are the international and Indian efforts to tackle the issue of climate change?
- What are the key mitigation and adaptation measures about climate change?

KEYWORDS AND PHRASES

Adaptation, carbon budget, carbon capture, carbon credit, carbon intensity, carbon neutrality, carbon trading, Clean Development Mechanism, climate justice, Common But Differentiated Responsibility, energy intensity, Intended Nationally Determined Contribution (INDC), Intergovernmental Panel on Climate Change (IPCC), Kyoto Protocol, mitigation, National Climate Action Plan, net zero, resilience, UN Framework Convention on Climate Change (UNFCCC)

LEAD STORY

THE STORY OF EXTREME WEATHER EVENTS IN INDIA (2022)

In November 2022, the Centre for Science and Environment, New Delhi, released the Report "India 2022: An assessment of extreme weather events". The Report attempted to build an evidence base on the frequency and expanding geography of extreme weather events in India. The Report was based on data from the India Meteorological Department It has sourced its data on extreme events from two key government sources and the Disaster Management Division (DMD) of the Union Ministry of Home Affairs.

The key findings were:

- India saw a disaster nearly every day in the first nine months of 2022 - from heat and cold waves, cyclones, lightning to heavy rain, floods, and landslides. These disasters claimed 2755 lives, affected 1.8 million hectares (ha) of crop area, destroyed over

400,000 houses and killed close to 70,000 livestock. This estimation of loss and damage is probably an underestimate as data for each event is not collated, nor are the losses of public property or crop loss calculated.

- With an event every second day, Madhya Pradesh saw the highest number of days with extreme weather events; but Himachal Pradesh saw the highest number of human deaths (359). Madhya Pradesh and Assam saw 301 human deaths each.
- Assam reported the highest number of damaged houses and animal deaths. Karnataka, which experienced an extreme weather event on 82 days since the beginning of the year, accounted for more than 50% of the crop area affected in the country. Madhya Pradesh, as per the official records, did not report any crop area damage. This could be due to gaps in loss and damage reporting.
- The Central region reported the highest number of days with extreme weather events at 198, followed by the Northwest (195 days). In terms of human lives lost, the Central region saw the highest number of deaths at 887, followed by East and Northeast region (783 deaths).
- In 2022, India recorded its seventh wettest January since 1901. This March was also the warmest ever and the third driest in 121 years. It was also the country's third warmest April, 11th warmest August, and 8th warmest September since 1901.
- Eastern India and Northeast India saw its warmest and driest July in 121 years. The region also recorded its 2nd warmest August and 4th warmest September in 2022.

Record breaking!! Warmest, driest, highest number of cyclones, heavy rains

What should we learn from the CSE report?

The CSE Report tells us that we are in the middle of a serious climate crisis. The Report made the following observations:

- We should note the increased frequency of the events—an extreme event we saw once every 100 years has now begun to occur every five years or less. Worse, it is now all coming together—each month is breaking a new record. This in turn is breaking the backs of the poorest who are worst impacted and are fast losing their capacities to cope with these repeated and frequent events.
- All types of extreme weather were seen in the nine months—lightning and storms were spread over 30 states and claimed 773 lives. Then, every day of the three months of monsoon—from June to August - show heavy to very heavy and extremely heavy rainfall in some part of the country. This is why the flood devastation has not sparred any region— in Assam, for instance, vast parts of the state were submerged, and people lost life, homes, and sources of livelihoods.
- Heatwaves claimed 45 lives, but what is not captured in the data is the impact of the prolonged high temperatures on people's wellbeing in north India – from farmers to construction workers and how they would have coped (or not) because of the intense and searing heat.
- The impact of severe cold episodes and frost is worse for crop damage. Farmers must have adequate systems for compensation for weather-related losses. Without this, their livelihoods are threatened; every loss adds to their mounting debt burden and pulls them into the cycle of marginalisation and poverty.

- The good news is that fatalities because of cyclones were few—only two lives were lost according to available data from the cyclones that destroyed 95,000 ha in the country. This is because of the laudable work done by IMD for cyclone forecasting so that there is adequate warning to governments. It is also because state governments, particularly from the coastal regions of India, Odisha, Andhra Pradesh, and West Bengal, have vastly improved their systems of disaster management so that they can evacuate people quickly and provide them the assistance that is needed in the shelters.
- Each cyclone, however, takes away that development dividend that governments work so hard to build—from public schools to water and health facilities and road and communication infrastructure. It also destroys people's ability to cope as they lose livelihoods and resources.

The extreme weather report card is important to understand because it gives us information on the number and frequency of such events as well as the consequent cumulative and extensive damage. It also shows that we need systems to better account for the losses so that we see how climate change affects real people.

Given the Scale of the Climate Crisis, What should We Do Now?

Globally and in India, we must take the following steps:

- Scientific study: Continue to make a scientific assessment of global warming and climate change and to predict future events enabling better preparedness.
- Increase our climate resilience.
- Implement measures of mitigation and adaptation.

We will begin by explaining several new terms.

What is Meant by Climate Resilience, Mitigation, and Adaptation?

Climate resilience: This term refers to (successfully) coping with and managing the impacts of climate change while preventing those impacts from getting worse. A climate resilient society would be low-carbon and equipped to deal with the realities of a warmer world.

There's only one real way to achieve climate resilience: reduce emissions while adapting to unavoidable changes in the climate. We should do so in ways that make the world more equitable and just, not less.

Mitigation: The term mitigation means "the reduction of something harmful or the reduction of its harmful effects". Mitigation is reducing the emissions of greenhouse gases responsible for climate change, so that less change occurs. Given that we cannot now avoid an increase in global temperature, what would be the safe limit to aim for? In 1990, the Stockholm Environmental Institute suggested that, to avoid the worst impacts of climate change, the limit should be set at 2°C increase in global temperature. But the Report also warned that temperature increases beyond even 1°C may elicit rapid, unpredictable, and non-linear responses that could lead to extensive ecosystem damage. Thus, there is nothing necessarily 'safe' about a two-degree limit. However, limiting warming to no more than 2°C has now been widely accepted as the target for global climate policy.

Another target often suggested by scientists and environmentalists is to bring down the CO_2 concentration in the atmosphere to 350 ppm. They feel that unless we can reach the figure of 350 ppm this century, we risk triggering tipping points and irreversible impacts that could send climate change spinning truly beyond our control.

Reaching 350 ppm target or keeping the temperature increase to less than 2°C is not going to be easy. We need to reduce net greenhouse gas emissions to almost zero by 2050, if we wish to have a high probability of staying below two degrees.

There are many ways of climate mitigation. They include the shutting down coal and gas plants, shifting to renewable energy sources, using energy more efficiently, using less oil for transportation, expanding the use of public transportation and electric vehicles, and using land in ways that removes carbon from the atmosphere.

Adaptation: Since extreme weather events cannot be avoided, we must design and implement measures to adapt to actual or expected future climate. The goal is to reduce the risks from the harmful effects of climate change (like sea-level rise, more intense extreme weather events, or food insecurity).

Adaptation can consist of a wide variety of actions by an individual, community, or government to prepare for, or respond to, climate change impacts. Some examples are:

- Breed climate-resilient crop varieties, which are more tolerant of heat, drought, and water logging.
- Promote shore protection techniques and open space preserves that allow beaches and coastal wetlands to gradually move inland as sea level rises.
- Identify and improve evacuation routes and evacuation plans for low-lying areas, to prepare for increased storm surges and flooding.
- Protect and increase migration corridors to allow species to migrate as the climate changes.
- Increase energy efficiency to help offset increases in energy consumption.
- Implement early warning systems and emergency response plans to prepare for changes in the frequency, duration, and intensity of extreme weather events.
- Improve water use efficiency and build additional water storage capacity.
- Plant more trees to absorb carbon.

Mitigation and adaptation are complementary strategies for reducing and managing the risks of climate change.

What is Carbon Budget?

The carbon budget is the amount of carbon dioxide the world can emit while still having a likely chance of limiting average global temperature rise to 2°C above pre-industrial levels, an internationally agreed-upon target.

The total size of the global carbon budget is about 3000 gigatonnes of carbon dioxide ($GtCO_2$). The cumulative amount of CO_2 emitted so far since the Industrial Revolution is about 2000 $GtCO_2$ and the emissions to date have increased the concentration in the atmosphere from around 275 ppm to about 420 ppm today. Based on this, the best current estimate is that around two thirds of the total carbon budget has already been used. And, if emissions continue unabated, we will exceed it entirely in about 30 years. Blowing this budget would expose the world to more severe forest fires, extreme weather, sea level rise, and other climate impacts.

There is a close association between global surface temperature increases and the total carbon emitted into the atmosphere. It is also well established that the climate system response lags the point at which greenhouse gases are emitted to when the temperature has fully responded. This means that we are already committed to further climate change from what has been emitted so far.

In addition to CO_2, other greenhouse gases are also important. Emissions of methane and nitrous oxide have led to concentrations of these gases in the atmosphere exceeding the range of concentrations recorded in ice cores during the past 800,000 years. If warming is to be kept below 2°C above pre-industrial levels, the emissions of these gases will also need to be restricted.

There are also additional earth system feedbacks that could affect the future budget, such as the emissions of greenhouse gases from permafrost and methane hydrates. These are expected to place further limitations on the total global carbon budget.

What is Carbon Capture or Sequestration?

Carbon sequestration refers to the capture and the long-term storage of atmospheric CO_2 for mitigating global warming. Some examples of promoting carbon sequestration:

- Wetland restoration: Wetland soil is an important carbon sink; 14.5% of the world's soil carbon is found in wetlands, while only 6% of the world's land is composed of wetlands.
- Agriculture:
  - Zero tillage or no tillage farming: No-till farming has carbon sequestration potential through storage of soil organic matter in the soil of crop fields. Tilling results in soil organic matter being broken down much more rapidly, and carbon is lost from the soil into the atmosphere.
  - Enhancing carbon removal: Using the crop and its relation to the carbon cycle to permanently sequester carbon within the soil. This is done by selecting farming methods that return biomass to the soil and enhance the conditions in which the carbon within the plants will be reduced to its elemental nature and stored in a stable state. Methods for accomplishing this include using cover crops such as grasses and weeds as temporary cover between planting seasons and restoring degraded land, which slows carbon release while returning the land to agriculture or other use.
- Biochar burial: Biochar is charcoal created by pyrolysis of biomass waste. The resulting material is used as a soil improver. Biochar carbon relatively inert so that it remains sequestered in soil.
- Geological sequestration: Storage of CO_2 underground in depleted oil and gas reservoirs, saline formations, or deep, un-minable coal beds. CO_2 is captured from a gas or coal-fired power plant, compressed, and transported by pipeline to the place of storage. There are several large-scale carbon capture and sequestration projects that have demonstrated the viability and safety of this method of carbon storage.

What is meant by Energy Intensity, Carbon Intensity, Net Zero, Climate Neutral, and Carbon Neutral?

These terms are often used in connection with emissions.

Energy Intensity: This parameter is measured by dividing our total energy consumed by our GDP. Globally, the energy intensity has been going down in recent decades. Thus, we use less energy than before to achieve every unit of GDP.

Carbon Intensity: This parameter is the measure of CO_2 produced per unit of GDP. In other words, it is a measure of how much CO_2 we emit when we generate one rupee in our economy. A rapidly decreasing carbon intensity is good news for our environment and our economy. It means that energy consumption is growing increasingly efficient and that more of us are doing jobs that do not require us to burn fossil fuels.

Net Zero: A state in which the greenhouse gases going into the atmosphere are balanced by removal out of the atmosphere. This is the state at which global warming stops. The Paris Agreement (explained below) underlines the need for Net Zero, requiring states to 'achieve a balance between anthropogenic emissions by sources and removals by sinks of greenhouse gases in the second half of this century'.

For Net Zero to be effective, it must be permanent. Any greenhouse gas removals should not leak into the atmosphere over time, for example through the destruction of forests or the improper storage of removed carbon dioxide. Net Zero is the internationally agreed upon goal for mitigating global warming in this century.

Carbon Neutral: If an entity is carbon neutral, its net contribution to global CO_2 emissions is zero. Any CO_2 emissions attributable to an entity's activities are fully compensated by CO_2 reductions or removals exclusively claimed by the entity — irrespective of the time or the relative magnitude of emissions and removals involved. The entity could be an individual, an organization, a community, or a country.

Climate Neutral: An actor's activities result in no net effect on the climate system. Any GHG emissions or other activities with warming effects are fully compensated by GHG reductions or removals, or other activities with cooling effects — irrespective of the time or the relative magnitude of emissions and removals involved.

All the different terms (Net Zero, Carbon Neutral, Climate Neutral) point to the different ways in which emissions sources and sinks are accounted for.

What is the Scientific Assessment of Global Warming and Climate Change?

In 1988, the World Meteorological Organization (WMO) and the United Nations Environment Programme (UNEP) together created the UN Intergovernmental Panel on Climate Change (IPCC), a task force of over 2000 climate scientists from 154 countries. The scientists are divided into three working groups.

The IPCC does not conduct its own scientific inquiries, but reviews worldwide research, issues regular Assessment Reports, and compiles special reports and technical papers. Thus, the IPCC Reports come from the largest assessment of global climate research, and we must rely and act on their findings.

The IPCC issued its first Assessment Report in 1990. Since then, its Reports have become increasingly strong in stressing the seriousness of climate change and the need for action. However, the Reports have not been taken as seriously as they should have been.

What is the latest IPCC assessment of climate change?

During the Sixth Assessment (AR6), IPCC has published the following reports:

- The Working Group I contribution, *Climate Change 2021: The Physical Science Basis.*
- The Working Group II contribution, *Climate Change 2022: Impacts, Adaptation and Vulnerability.*
- The Working Group III contribution, *Climate Change 2022: Mitigation of Climate Change.*

On March 20, 2023, IPCC presented its final Synthesis Report of the Sixth Assessment. As the title implies, this Report synthesizes all the findings. The main messages of the Synthesis Report were:

A. Current Status and Trends

A.1 Observed Warming and its Causes:

Human activities, principally through emissions of greenhouse gases, have unequivocally caused global warming, with global surface temperature reaching 1.1°C above 1850–1900 in 2011–2020. Global greenhouse gas emissions have continued to increase, with unequal historical and ongoing contributions arising from unsustainable energy use, land use and land-use change, lifestyles and patterns of consumption and production across regions, between and within countries, and among individuals.

A.2 Observed Changes and Impacts:

Widespread and rapid changes in the atmosphere, ocean, cryosphere, and biosphere have occurred. Human-caused climate change is already affecting many weather and climate extremes in every region across the globe. This has led to widespread adverse impacts and related losses and damages to nature and people. Vulnerable communities who have historically contributed the least to current climate change are disproportionately affected.

A.3 Current Progress in Adaptation and Gaps and Challenges:
Adaptation planning and implementation has progressed across all sectors and regions, with documented benefits and varying effectiveness. Despite progress, adaptation gaps exist, and will continue to grow at current rates of implementation. Hard and soft limits to adaptation have been reached in some ecosystems and regions. Maladaptation is happening in some sectors and regions. Current global financial flows for adaptation are insufficient for, and constrain implementation of, adaptation options, especially in developing countries.

A.4 Current Mitigation Progress, Gaps, and Challenges:
Policies and laws addressing mitigation have consistently expanded since the Fifth Assessment Report (AR5). Global GHG emissions in 2030 implied by Nationally Determined Contributions (NDCs, explained below) announced by October 2021 make it likely that warming will exceed 1.5°C during the 21st century and make it harder to limit warming below 2°C. There are gaps between projected emissions from implemented policies and those from NDCs and finance flows fall short of the levels needed to meet climate goals across all sectors and regions.

B. Future Climate Change, Risks, and Long-Term Responses

B.1 Future Climate Change:
Continued greenhouse gas emissions will lead to increasing global warming, with the best estimate of reaching 1.5°C in the near term in considered scenarios and modelled pathways. Every increment of global warming will intensify multiple and concurrent hazards. Deep, rapid, and sustained reductions in greenhouse gas emissions would lead to a discernible slowdown in global warming within around two decades, and to discernible changes in atmospheric composition within a few years.

B.2 Climate Change Impacts and Climate-Related Risks:
For any given future warming level, many climate-related risks are higher than assessed in AR5, and projected long-term impacts are up to multiple times higher than currently observed. Risks and projected adverse impacts and related losses and damages from climate change escalate with every increment of global warming. Climatic and non-climatic risks will increasingly interact, creating compound and cascading risks that are more complex and difficult to manage.

B.3 Likelihood and Risks of Unavoidable, Irreversible or Abrupt Changes:
Some future changes are unavoidable and/or irreversible but can be limited by deep, rapid, and sustained global greenhouse gas emissions reduction. The likelihood of abrupt and/or irreversible changes increases with higher global warming levels. Similarly, the probability of low-likelihood outcomes associated with potentially very large adverse impacts increases with higher global warming levels.

B.4 Adaptation Options and their Limits in a Warmer World:
Adaptation options that are feasible and effective today will become constrained and less effective with increasing global warming. Losses and damages will increase, and human and natural systems will reach adaptation limits. Maladaptation can be avoided by flexible, multi-sectoral, inclusive, long-term planning and implementation of adaptation actions, with co-benefits to many sectors and systems.

B.5 Carbon Budgets and Net Zero Emissions:
Limiting human-caused global warming requires Net Zero CO_2 emissions. Cumulative carbon emissions until the time of reaching Net Zero and the level of greenhouse gas emission reductions this decade

largely determine whether warming can be limited to 1.5°C or 2°C. Projected CO_2 emissions from existing fossil fuel infrastructure without additional abatement would exceed the remaining carbon budget for 1.5°C.

B.6 Mitigation Pathways:
All global modelled pathways that limit warming to 1.5°C with no or limited overshoot, and those that limit warming to 2°C, involve rapid and deep and, in most cases, immediate greenhouse gas emissions reductions in all sectors this decade. Global Net Zero CO_2 emissions are reached for these pathway categories, in the early 2050s and around the early 2070s, respectively.

B.7 Overshoot: Exceeding a Warming Level and Returning:
If warming exceeds a specified level such as 1.5°C, it could gradually be reduced again by achieving and sustaining net negative global CO_2 emissions. This would require additional deployment of carbon dioxide removal, compared to pathways without overshoot, leading to greater feasibility and sustainability concerns. Overshoot entails adverse impacts, some irreversible, and additional risks for human and natural systems, all growing with the magnitude and duration of overshoot.

C. Responses in the Near Term

C.1 Urgency of Near-Term Integrated Climate Action:
Climate change is a threat to human well-being and planetary health. There is a rapidly closing window of opportunity to secure a liveable and sustainable future for all. Climate resilient development integrates adaptation and mitigation to advance sustainable development for all and is enabled by increased international cooperation including improved access to adequate financial resources, particularly for vulnerable regions, sectors and groups, and inclusive governance and coordinated policies. The choices and actions implemented in this decade will have impacts now and for thousands of years.

C.2 The Benefits of Near-Term Action:
Deep, rapid, and sustained mitigation and accelerated implementation of adaptation actions in this decade would reduce projected losses and damages for humans and ecosystems, and deliver many co-benefits, especially for air quality and health. Delayed mitigation and adaptation action would lock-in high-emissions infrastructure, raise risks of stranded assets and cost-escalation, reduce feasibility, and increase losses and damages. Near-term actions involve high up-front investments and potentially disruptive changes that can be lessened by a range of enabling policies.

C.3 Mitigation and Adaptation Options across Systems:
Rapid and far-reaching transitions across all sectors and systems are necessary to achieve deep and sustained emissions reductions and secure a liveable and sustainable future for all. These system transitions involve a significant upscaling of a wide portfolio of mitigation and adaptation options. Feasible, effective, and low-cost options for mitigation and adaptation are already available, with differences across systems and regions.

C.4 Synergies and Trade-Offs with Sustainable Development:
Accelerated and equitable action in mitigating and adapting to climate change impacts is critical to sustainable development. Mitigation and adaptation actions have more synergies than trade-offs with Sustainable Development Goals. Synergies and trade-offs depend on context and scale of implementation.

C.5 Equity and Inclusion:
Prioritising equity, climate justice, social justice, inclusion and just transition processes can enable adaptation and ambitious mitigation actions and climate resilient development. Adaptation outcomes

are enhanced by increased support to regions and people with the highest vulnerability to climatic hazards. Integrating climate adaptation into social protection programs improves resilience. Many options are available for reducing emission-intensive consumption, including through behavioural and lifestyle changes, with co-benefits for societal well-being.

C.6 Governance and Policies:

Effective climate action is enabled by political commitment, well-aligned multilevel governance, institutional frameworks, laws, policies and strategies and enhanced access to finance and technology. Clear goals, coordination across multiple policy domains, and inclusive governance processes facilitate effective climate action. Regulatory and economic instruments can support deep emissions reductions and climate resilience if scaled up and applied widely. Climate resilient development benefits from drawing on diverse knowledge.

C.7 Finance, Technology, and International Cooperation:

Finance, technology, and international cooperation are critical enablers for accelerated climate action. If climate goals are to be achieved, both adaptation and mitigation financing would need to increase many-fold. There is sufficient global capital to close the global investment gaps but there are barriers to redirect capital to climate action. Enhancing technology innovation systems is key to accelerate the widespread adoption of technologies and practices. Enhancing international cooperation is possible through multiple channels.

What are the International Initiatives for Tackling Climate Change?

Climate change is obviously the most urgent issue that calls for an international agreement. All the countries are affected by it and most countries contribute to the worsening situation. Yet, the world community has been unable to agree on emission reductions.

The early IPCC Reports spurred governments to create the UN Framework Convention on Climate Change (UNFCCC), which came into force in 1994. The Convention sets an overall framework for intergovernmental efforts to tackle the challenges posed by climate change. It recognizes that the climate system is a shared resource whose stability can be affected by industrial and other emissions of CO_2 and other greenhouse gases.

IPCC Reports are used as the basis for decisions made under the UNFCCC, and they played a major role in the negotiations leading to the Kyoto Protocol.

What was the Kyoto Protocol?

The Kyoto Protocol was an international agreement to reduce the greenhouse gas emissions. It was negotiated under the UNFCCC during a meeting held Kyoto, Japan, in 1997 and came into force in 2005. The first commitment period was 2008-2012. The Doha Amendment launched a second commitment period, which ended in 2020.

The key features of the Kyoto Protocol were:

- The Protocol 'operationalized' the UNFCCC. It committed the industrialized countries to stabilize greenhouse gas emissions based on the principles of the Convention.
- The Protocol set binding emission reduction targets for 37 industrialized countries and the European community (Annex I Parties) in its first commitment period of 2008–2012. Overall, these targets added up to an average of 5% emissions reduction compared to 1990 levels over the five-year period.
- The Protocol only bound the developed countries because it recognized that they were largely responsible for the current high levels of GHG emissions in the atmosphere, which were the result of more

than 150 years of industrial activity. It placed a heavier burden on developed nations under its central principle of 'common but differentiated responsibility'.

- Commitments under the Protocol varied from nation to nation. For example, the target for the European Union was 8%, while for the US it was 7%.
- Developing countries were not legally bound to emissions reduction targets initially, because these countries had historically been responsible for only a small portion of the global greenhouse gas emissions.
- Countries were to meet their targets primarily through national measures. However, the Protocol also offered them an additional means to meet their targets by way of market-based mechanisms (outlined below).

International Emissions Trading and Carbon Credit: This mechanism allowed countries that had emission units to spare—emissions permitted to them but not 'used'—to sell this excess capacity to countries that were over their targets. Thus, a new commodity was created in the form of emission reductions. Since carbon dioxide is the principal greenhouse gas, we talk of carbon market, where carbon is tracked and traded like any other commodity.

Clean Development Mechanism (CDM): The CDM allowed an Annex I country with an emission-reduction or emission-limitation commitment under the Protocol to implement an emission-reduction project in developing countries. A CDM project activity might involve, for example, a rural electrification project using solar panels or the installation of more energy-efficient boilers. Such projects could earn saleable certified emission reduction (CER) credits, each equivalent to one tonne of CO_2, which could be counted towards meeting Kyoto targets.

CDM was the first global, environmental investment and credit scheme of its kind, providing a standardized emissions offset instrument, the CER. The mechanism stimulated sustainable development and emission reductions, while giving industrialized countries some flexibility in how they met their emission reduction or limitation targets.

The CDM was designed to meet two objectives:

- Help Annex I Parties to cost-effectively meet part of their emission reduction targets under the Kyoto Protocol
- Assist non-Annex I Parties in achieving sustainable development.

While CDM projects created CERs that project participants could sell to Annex I Parties to help them meet their Kyoto Protocol targets, they could also provide complementary benefits to non-Annex I Parties such as new investment, the transfer of climate-friendly technologies and knowledge, the improvement of livelihoods and skills, job creation, and increased economic activity.

Joint Implementation: This mechanism allowed a country with an emission reduction or limitation commitment under the Protocol to earn emission reduction units (ERUs) from an emission-reduction or emission removal project in another such Party, each equivalent to one tonne of CO_2, which could be counted towards meeting its Kyoto target. Joint implementation offered Parties a flexible and cost-efficient means of fulfilling a part of their Kyoto commitments, while the host Party benefitted from foreign investment and technology transfer.

What was the fate of the Kyoto Protocol? Most countries did not meet the targets for emission reductions assigned for the first commitment period of 2008–2012. Hence, the Protocol's impact on the rising trend in global emissions was very small. Even if the Protocol had been fully implemented, the 5% reduction in emissions would have done little to contain climate change.

Has CDM benefited the world? A 2012 analysis by UNFCCC showed that the mechanism had provided carbon reductions equivalent to the emissions from about a fifth of the world's cars over one year and saved at least US$ 3.6 billion in emissions reduction costs. It had mobilized US$ 215 billion of investment in developing countries. In September 2012, the CDM passed the milestone of reducing 1 billion tCO_2e of greenhouse gases - roughly equal to the whole of Japan's emissions in 2009 or the yearly emissions of all the cars in six major EU economies. UNFCCC claimed, 'The CDM is the undisputed heavyweight carbon offset champion of the world.'

There is, however, another side to CDM and carbon trading. With the US not ratifying the Protocol, the other big emitters like China and India not obliged to cut emission under the Protocol, and Europe facing a recession, there were few buyers of carbon credits. By 2012, the carbon market virtually collapsed. Indian companies, which invested in carbon market, also faced a loss.

With the signing of the Paris Agreement (discussed below) and the consequent expectation of more action to cut emissions, there is hope that the carbon market will revive. China and some other countries are also setting up national emissions trading systems.

What is REDD+?

REDD+ stands for Reducing Emissions from Deforestation and Forest Degradation in Developing Countries. The UN Collaborative Programme on REDD+ was launched in 2008 and builds on the convening role and technical expertise of UN FAO, UNDP, and UNEP. The overall development goal of the Programme is to reduce forest emissions and enhance carbon stocks in forests while contributing to national sustainable development.

The UN-REDD+ Programme supports nationally led REDD+ processes and promotes the informed and meaningful involvement of all stakeholders, including indigenous peoples and other forest-dependent communities, in national and international REDD+ implementation.

Over 60 countries (including India) spanning Africa, Asia-Pacific and Latin America are now partners in the Programme, which supports partner countries through:

- Direct support to the design and implementation of National REDD+ Programmes.
- Complementary tailored support to national REDD+ actions.
- Technical capacity building, support through sharing of expertise, common approaches, analyses, methodologies, tools, data, best practices, and South-South knowledge sharing.

What is the Forest Carbon Partnership Facility?

The Forest Carbon Partnership Facility (FCPF) is a global partnership of governments, businesses, civil society, and Indigenous Peoples focused on reducing emissions from deforestation and forest degradation, forest carbon stock conservation, the sustainable management of forests, and the enhancement of forest carbon stocks in developing countries.

> **Key Idea** The Kyoto Protocol was a welcome agreement to cut greenhouse gas emissions, but the targets set were woefully inadequate and even those targets were not met

The four strategic objectives of the FCPF are:

- Assist countries in their REDD+ efforts by providing them with financial and technical assistance in building their capacity to benefit from possible future systems of positive incentives for REDD+.
- Pilot a performance-based payment system for REDD+ activities, with a view to ensuring equitable benefit sharing and promoting future large-scale positive incentives for REDD+.
- Test ways to sustain or enhance livelihoods of local communities and to conserve biodiversity.

- Disseminate broadly the knowledge gained in the development of the Facility and the implementation of Readiness Preparation Proposals (RPPs) and Emission Reductions Programs (ERPs).

What Happened with Climate Negotiations After 2012?

After the expiry of the Kyoto Protocol in 2012, the annual UNFCCC Conferences tried (without much success) to come up with a better agreement. At the core of the disagreement was the North–South Conflict—the differences between the rich countries of the North and the poor ones of the South.

The industrialized countries wanted everyone to chip in and reduce emissions, while the developing countries wanted the rich ones to own responsibility for causing climate change and pay for global emission reduction. The issue was further complicated by countries like China, India, Brazil, and South Africa, which have been developing rapidly and consequently releasing huge emissions. The basic and unresolved question is: whose responsibility is it to reduce emissions, by how much, when, and who would pay for it?

Given the urgency expressed in the IPCC Fifth Assessment, the UNFCCC Meeting (COP21) in Paris in December 2015 had to come up with a binding international agreement.

What is meant by Intended Nationally Determined Contribution (INDC)?

As an important step towards reaching a new universal agreement on climate change in Paris at the end of 2015, UNFCCC had invited the countries to submit their intended contributions on climate action. In the course of 2015, many governments submitted their Intended Nationally Determined Contributions (INDCs) to the UNFCCC.

An effective agreement called for ambitious actions by all countries, as well as a plan to measure their combined effects in advance of the Paris meeting. UNFCCC recognized that every nation was unique in how it contributed to climate action and was affected by climate change, yet there was an urgent call for collective global action to confront the effects of rising greenhouse gases. A country's INDC was to provide information on its strategic efforts to combat climate change through actions tailored to its own national circumstances.

What would be the aggregate effect of the submitted INDCs? 147 Parties responded to the invitation and submitted INDCs before the Paris Meeting. The collective impact of the INDCs was assessed as follows:

- Fully implemented, these plans together would begin to make a significant dent in the growth of greenhouse gas emissions.
- The INDCs will bring global average emissions per capita down by as much as 8% in 2025 and 9% in by 2030.
- The INDCs could deliver sizable emissions reductions and slow emissions growth over the next 10 years.
- Their implementation will not result in aggregate annual emissions consistent with the 2°C scenarios levels.
- UNEP estimated that the INDCs would put the world on track to a temperature rise of around 3°C by 2100.

What was COP21 and the Paris Agreement on Climate Change?

COP21 was the 21st Conference of the Parties to UNFCCC held in Paris in December 2015. It was attended by all the Parties and many world leaders including President Obama of the US and PM Narendra Modi.

After two weeks of negotiations, the conference adopted an Agreement. The key provisions of the Agreement are given in Box 15.1.

BOX 15.1 Key Provisions of the Paris Agreement on Climate Change

The Agreement ends the strict differentiation between developed and developing countries that characterized earlier efforts, replacing it with a common framework that commits all countries to put forward their best efforts and to strengthen them in the years ahead.

The Agreement

- Reaffirms the goal of limiting global temperature increase well below 2 degrees Celsius, while urging efforts to limit the increase to 1.5 degrees;
- Establishes binding commitments by all parties to make 'nationally determined contributions' (NDCs), and to pursue domestic measures aimed at achieving them;
- Commits all countries to report regularly on their emissions and progress made in implementing and achieving their NDCs, and to undergo international review;
- Commits all countries to submit new NDCs every five years, with the clear expectation that they will represent a progression beyond previous ones;
- Reaffirms the obligations of developed countries under the UNFCCC to support the efforts of developing countries, while for the first time encouraging voluntary contributions by developing countries too;
- Extends the current goal of mobilizing $100 billion a year in support by 2020 through 2025, with a new, higher goal to be set for the period after 2025;
- Extends a mechanism to address 'loss and damage' resulting from climate change, which explicitly will not 'involve or provide a basis for any liability or compensation'; and
- Calls for a new mechanism, like the Clean Development Mechanism under the Kyoto Protocol, enabling emission reductions in one country to be counted toward another country's NDC.

What would be a balanced assessment of the Paris Agreement?

Many world leaders, business leaders, and environmental groups hailed the Agreement as a success. On the positive side, it was a historic and landmark agreement, since 194 countries accepted the need to act on climate change and adopted a common deal.

There were, however, many voices of dissent. According to the critics, the proposed steps, even if fully implemented, will not prevent severe climate change from occurring, due to these reasons:

- The agreement does not bind any country (developed or developing) to specific targets for emission reduction. All such targets are voluntary.
- There is no mention of the global carbon budget and each country's fair share.
- There are no clear provisions on financing the mitigation measures.

What is the status of the Paris Agreement?

- The Agreement was open for signature and ratification by each country from 22nd April 2016 onwards. India, China, and the US were among the 177 Parties who signed the Agreement on the opening day.
- The Agreement entered into force on November 4, 2016, the 30th day after the date on which at least 55 Parties to the Convention accounting in total for at least an estimated 55% of the total global greenhouse gas emissions had deposited their instruments of ratification, acceptance, approval, or accession with the Depositary.
- Currently, 189 countries and 195 signatories have joined the Paris Agreement.

What is meant by 'Common But Differentiated Responsibility' and What is the Status of this Concept?

The principle of 'Common But Differentiated Responsibility' (CBDR) evolved from the notion of the 'Common Heritage of Mankind' (Chapter 4) and is a manifestation of general principles of equity in international law. The principle recognizes historical differences in the contributions of developed and developing States to global environmental problems, and differences in their respective economic and technical capacity to tackle these problems. Despite their common responsibilities, important differences exist between the stated responsibilities of developed and developing countries.

CBDR was first expressed in the Rio Declaration, issued at the end of the Earth Summit in 1992. It states: 'In view of the different contributions to global environmental degradation, States have common but differentiated responsibilities. The developed countries acknowledge the responsibility that they bear in the international pursuit of sustainable development in view of the pressures their societies place on the global environment and of the technologies and financial resources they command.'

Similar language exists in the UNFCCC: Parties should act to protect the climate system 'based on equality and in accordance with their common but differentiated responsibilities and respective capabilities.'

The principle of 'Common But Differentiated Responsibility' includes two fundamental elements:

- The first concerns the common responsibility of States for the protection of the environment, or parts of it, at the national, regional, and global levels.
- The second concerns the need to consider the different circumstances, particularly each State's contribution to the evolution of a particular problem and its ability to prevent, reduce, and control the threat.

Over the years of climate change negotiations, the concept of CBDR weakened and it was not emphasized at all in the Paris Agreement.

What has India Done about Tackling Climate Change?

Former Prime Minister Dr Manmohan Singh established the PM's Council on Climate Change in 2007 to evaluate and alleviate the effects of climate change. But the Council had very few meetings and was not effective.

In 2008, the same PM unveiled the National Action Plan on Climate Change, which included eight national missions. When the new government came to power in 2014, the PM's Council was reconstituted, and four more national missions were added (Box 15.2). The implementation of the 12 missions is awaited.

BOX 15.2 ENVIROFACT: *National Action Plan on Climate Change*

On June 30, 2008, former Prime Minister Manmohan Singh released India's first National Action Plan on Climate Change (NAPCC) outlining existing and future policies and programmes addressing climate mitigation and adaptation. The Plan identified eight core 'national missions' and directed the ministries to submit detailed implementation plans to the PM's Council on Climate Change.

While emphasizing the overriding priority of maintaining high economic growth rates to raise living standards, the Plan also pledged that India's per capita greenhouse gas emissions 'will at no point exceed that of developed countries even as we pursue our development objectives.'

National Missions

1. National Solar Mission: The Plan aims to promote the development of solar energy with the ultimate objective of making solar competitive with fossil-based energy options.

2. National Mission for Enhanced Energy Efficiency: Building on the Energy Conservation Act of 2001, new initiatives were to be implemented.
3. National Mission on Sustainable Habitat: The Plan promotes energy efficiency as a core component of urban planning.
4. National Water Mission: With water scarcity projected to worsen because of climate change, the Plan proposes improvement in water use efficiency through pricing and other measures.
5. National Mission for Sustaining the Himalayan Ecosystem: The Plan aims to conserve biodiversity, forest cover, and other ecological values in the Himalayan region, where glaciers that are a major source of India's water supply are projected to recede because of global warming.
6. National Mission for a 'Green India': Goals include the afforestation of degraded forest lands and expanding forest cover.
7. National Mission for Sustainable Agriculture: The plan aims to support climate adaptation in agriculture through the development of climate-resilient crops, expansion of weather insurance mechanisms, and agricultural practices.
8. National Mission on Strategic Knowledge for Climate Change: To gain a better understanding of climate science, impacts, and challenges, the Plan envisions a new Climate Science Research Fund, improved climate modelling, and increased international collaboration.

In early 2015, the new government added four more missions:

1. Wind Energy Mission: To produce 50,000–60,000 MW of power by 2022.
2. Human Health Mission: To assess impact of climate change on human health and build up capacities to respond to it.
3. Coastal Resources Mission: To prepare integrated coastal resource management plan and map vulnerabilities along the entire shoreline.
4. Waste-to-energy Mission: To incentivize efforts towards harnessing energy from waste, lower dependence on coal, oil, gas, and make power production a more earth-friendly process.

What is the National Clean Development Mechanism Authority (NCDMA)?

The establishment of a designated national authority is one of the requirements for participation by a Party in the CDM. This authority is the organization granted responsibility by a Party to authorise and approve participation in CDM projects. The main task of the authority is to assess potential CDM projects to determine whether they will assist the host country in achieving its sustainable development goals, and to provide a letter of approval to project participants in CDM projects. This letter is submitted to CDM Executive Board to support the registration of the project.

The Indian Government has constituted the National Clean Development Mechanism Authority (NCDMA). This Authority receives projects for evaluation and approval as per the guidelines and general criteria laid down in the relevant rules and modalities pertaining to CDM in addition to the guidelines issued by the CDM Executive Board and Conference of Parties to the UNFCCC.

The evaluation process of CDM projects includes an assessment of the probability of eventual successful implementation of CDM projects and evaluation of extent to which projects meet the sustainable development objectives, as it would seek to prioritize projects in accordance with national priorities.

What is the state of CDM in india?

- India hosts the second largest number of CDM projects (after China). From 2003 to 2011, a total of 2295 projects (one-quarter of the global total) had been registered with NCDMA.
- India has adopted a 'laissez faire' approach to governing CDM, neither actively promoting nor discouraging CDM project implementation in different states. In contrast, China's national policy steers CDM investment toward the country´s priorities, such as renewable energy and economically backward provinces.

- CDM projects are concentrated in states that are more industrialized, such as Gujarat and Maharashtra. In contrast, poorer and less industrialized states generally implement fewer CDM projects.

What was India's Intended Nationally Determined Contribution (INDC)?

The main features of India's INDC submitted to UNFCCC in 2015 were:

- India pledged to improve the emissions intensity of its GDP by 33–35% by 2030 below 2005 levels.
- It also pledged to increase the share of non-fossil fuels-based electricity to 40% by 2030.
- It agreed to enhance its forest cover to the extent that it will absorb an additional 2.5 to 3 billion tonnes of carbon dioxide by 2030.
- India agreed to enhance investments to adapt in vulnerable sectors like agriculture, water resources, coastal regions, health, and disaster management.
- India has also reiterated its need for international finance and technology support to meet its climate goals. The country would require at least USD2.5 trillion (at 2014–15 prices) to meet its climate change actions between now and 2030.

What were the Gains and Losses for India and the Developing Countries as far as the Paris Agreement was Concerned?

Gains:

- Considering the failure of all the previous meetings, just getting an agreement adopted by all the countries was a gain.
- Terms such as CBDR, equity, and climate justice still find a place in the Agreement, but in a weakened context.
- Marginal differentiation between the developed and developing countries is expressed in this way: Developed country Parties should continue taking the lead by undertaking economy-wide absolute emission reduction targets. Developing country Parties should continue enhancing their mitigation efforts and are encouraged to move over time towards economy-wide emission reduction or limitation targets in the light of different national circumstances.

Losses:

- There is no target set for developed countries to take more aggressive cuts to reduce their (already large) contributions to the growing stock of emissions in the atmosphere.
- The phrase 'historical responsibility' has been erased from the agreement. This weakens the obligations of developed countries to take actions to mitigate the impact of their past emissions. They have no legally binding targets for emissions cuts or for providing finance for the developing countries.
- The Agreement makes it clear that the loss and damage due to climate change 'does not involve or provide a basis for any liability or compensation'. Thus, developing countries, particularly the Small Island Developing States, which are the innocent victims of climate change, cannot claim any compensation from the developed countries, whose emissions are now causing loss and damage.

What was India's Third Biennial Update Report to UNFCCC?

Under the Paris Agreement, each country is required to submit biennial update reports (BURs) to UNFCCC. India's Third BUR was submitted to UNFCCC in February 2021 (Box 15.3).

BOX 15.3 India's Third Biennial Update Report to UNFCCC (2021)

The Key Messages of the Report were:

- In 2016, India's total GHG emissions were 2,838.89 m tonne CO_2e. India's contribution to global emissions, both cumulative and on annual basis are well below its equitable share of the global carbon budget by any criterion of equity.
- India's emission intensity of gross domestic product (GDP) has reduced by 24% between 2005 and 2016.
- India is implementing one of the largest renewable energy expansion programmes with a target of achieving 175 GW of renewable energy capacity by 2022 and later up to 450 GW.
- India's commitment to the expansion of renewable energy has not been affected by the economic contraction due to the COVID-19 pandemic.
- Coal will continue to be an integral part of India's energy requirements, both for electricity generation and non-electricity uses and remains essential for India's developmental needs and energy security. This is in keeping with India's claim to a fair share of the global carbon budget and India's significant underutilization of this share thus far.
- Forest and tree cover sequestered 331 $MtCO_2$ in 2016 which is around 15% of total carbon dioxide emissions occurring in the country.
- The Department of Heavy Industry is administrating Faster Adoption and Manufacturing of (Hybrid) and Electric Vehicles (FAME) India Scheme for promotion of electric/hybrid vehicles in India since 1 April 2015.
- India's climate action is widely acknowledged by independent, international assessments to be among the few that are compatible with the well below 2oC warming target of the Paris Agreement.
- India's commitment to multilateral efforts and global cooperation in climate action is amply demonstrated by its initiation of, and the provision of resources to, the International Solar Alliance (ISA) in partnership with France.
- India has initiated the Coalition for Disaster Resilient Infrastructure (CDRI), announced at the UN Climate Action Summit in 2019. India also co-leads with Sweden the leadership group for Industry Transition in hard-to-abate sectors initiated in the preparation for the UN Climate Action Summit in 2019.
- Taken together, India's mitigation actions speak of the enormous effort that the country is undertaking, through its own resources, without any significant support from developed countries in terms of climate finance, technology transfer or capacity building.

What were the commitments made by India at the 2021 UNFCCC COP26 Conference?

In his speech to the 2021 UNFCCC COP26 Conference in Glasgow, PM Narendra Modi made the following commitments:

1. India will reach its non-fossil energy capacity of 500 GW by 2030.
2. India will meet 50% of its energy requirements from renewable energy by 2030.
3. India will reduce the total projected carbon emissions by one billion tonnes from now onwards till 2030.
4. By 2030, India will reduce the carbon intensity of its economy by less than 45%.
5. By 2070, India will achieve the target of Net Zero.

What is India's REDD+ strategy?

In August 2018, MoEFCC released an updated National REDD+ Strategy. According to the document, the 'Strategy indicates Government of India's commitment to implement REDD+ by optimally exploring the mitigation potential of forestry sector in the country. It also recognizes the active participation of local communities and Indigenous people. The Strategy will also contribute towards green skill development and job creation in forestry sector.'

The activities proposed in the Strategy include:

- Reducing deforestation and forest degradation
- Enhancement and conservation of forest carbon stocks

- Sustainable management of forests
- Forest productivity enhancement through research
- Capacity building and training; building a cadre of community foresters
- Use of funds from CAMPA, green India Mission, National Afforestation Programme, and UN Green Climate Fund

The new initiatives for the enhancement of forest stocks include:

- Forestry intervention in the Ganga) through the Namami Gange Programme) and in other major river catchments
- Green Highways (Plantation, Transplantation, Beautification, and Maintenance) Policy, 2015
- Green Skill Development Programme

Environmentalists have criticised the Strategy on the following grounds:

- While the Strategy rightly supports the role of communities in protecting forest resources, it fails way short in giving them decision making power.
- Though the Strategy mentions that all the existing legal and customary rights of the indigenous communities will be respected as per the existing laws of the land, when it comes to implementation of the forest conservation programmes, it's too forest bureaucracy-centric.
- While it mentions the Joint Forest Management (JFM) committees, formed under a programme of the government, it grossly undervalues the existence of thousands of Community Forest Management (CFM) initiatives in the country that have been sustainably managing natural forests for hundreds of years.

How can We Use Indigenous Knowledge for Climate Change Assessment and Adaptation?

In recent years, there is a move to make use of indigenous knowledge in responding to climate change. Indigenous knowledge is that which a community (for example, a tribal group, a forest community, or a mountain community) has accumulated through years of interacting with the land, the waters, the air, etc. It could include answers to questions such as:

- What are the best seeds to plant during which times of the year and on which part of the land?
- Who among the community has the special ability to choose and plant the best seeds?
- How do the phases of the sun and the moon affect the crops?
- Which animals can sense a storm before it arrives?
- What will the next harvest be like, given the current climate?
- What types of birds or plants will be abundant next season?
- What is the rainfall expected based on the movement of the clouds, plants, and temperature changes?

Indigenous people with their knowledge gained over generations may know answers that science cannot provide. Indigenous knowledge has sustained communities for hundreds of years of fluctuating weather and climate. Such knowledge can be used to increase our resilience and to implement adaptation measures.

Is There Any Hope on the Climate Change Front?

While governments have been delaying action, there is some good news too:

- The Paris Agreement and later agreements have raised hopes of emission reductions by countries.

- The cost of solar energy is dropping, rooftop solar units are becoming popular, and consumers are getting credit for feeding solar power into the grid.
- Efficient electric cars are being made in large numbers.
- Many businesses are turning green.
- Cities across the world are taking independent steps to tackle climate change.
- Huge rallies of indigenous and other groups affected by development and climate change have been taking place, demanding action by the governments.

What are the Connections between Climate Change and the COVID-19 Pandemic?

There are three important connections between climate change and COVID-19 pandemic:

1. The COVID-19 pandemic has spotlighted inadequacies of both governments and international institutions to cope with transboundary risks. The same is true of climate change since it affects the whole world - the rich and the poor countries.
2. Governments have not seized the opportunity for a green recovery from COVID-19. They are mobilizing more than USD12 trillion for COVID-19 pandemic recovery. As a comparison, annual investments needed for a Paris-compatible emissions pathway are estimated to be US$1.4 trillion.
3. A COVID-19 recovery strategy and economic stimulus based on growth first and sustainability second is not likely to lead to the emissions reductions needed to meet Paris goals.

Ending on a Positive Note: Hopeful Stories

1. **New European Union regulations to fight climate change:** New bloc-wide laws and regulations put the European Union (EU) at the forefront of international efforts to fight climate change. Throughout 2022, the EU – the world's third-largest emitter behind China and the US – has undoubtedly positioned itself as an indisputable leader in the fight against global warming. As part of the European Green Deal, a plan that sets out a clear path towards the bloc's ambitious targets of a 55% reduction in carbon emissions compared to 1990 levels by 2030 and carbon neutrality by mid-century, the EU passed sweeping legislation and adopted new rules that will put its 27 member states on track to achieve their climate goals.

   In October 2022, the European Parliament and Council reached an agreement that effectively bans all sales of fossil fuel cars and vans by 2035, a crucial step forward considering that the transportation sector accounts for about 30% of the bloc's total greenhouse gas emissions and almost two-thirds of oil used. The EU is effectively the world's first (and for now only) region to go all-electric. Similar legislations were recently adopted by California and the State of New York, as both US states announced that they will ban the sales of gas-powered cars by 2035.

   More recently, the EU announced new bloc-wide regulations on packaging waste – which currently accounts for 36% of all municipal solid waste – and proposed a new plan to certify carbon removal projects, though key details will be worked out at a later point. EU lawmakers also agreed to add the shipping industry to the bloc's Emission Trading System (ETS), a decision that effectively forces vessels to pay for their carbon dioxide, methane, and nitrogen dioxide emissions for voyages within the bloc and that adds pressure to scale up green infrastructure and technologies.

   Lastly, EU countries agreed on a world-first carbon-border tariff targeting imported goods including steel, aluminium, cement, fertilizers, and electricity, which requires overseas and domestic companies to buy permits to cover the CO_2 emissions associated with them.

2. **UN Accord to provide critical financing to save the world's biodiversity:** In December 2022, representatives from 195 countries gathered in Montreal, Canada, for COP15 of the Convention on Biological Diversity. COP15 was tasked with securing a global action plan to halt and reverse biodiversity loss by the end of the decade.

   Besides the 30 × 30 goal – an ambitious plan to protect at least 30% of the world's land, inland waters, coastal areas, and oceans by 2030, the countries agreed on allocating US$200 per year for biodiversity initiatives both from the private and public sector. Developed countries also pledged to provide $25 billion annually starting in 2025 and $30 billion by the end of the decade to poorer nations through a new biodiversity fund that will be created under the Global Environment Facility.

3. **Lula's election brings hope for the Amazon:** After years of persistent deforestation and a sharp increase in wildfires under climate denier Jair Bolsonaro, Lula's astonishing comeback marked a turning point in Brazil's fight against climate change and spurred hope for the future of the Amazon, the world's largest rainforest and one of the most biologically diverse ecosystems, home to three million species of plants and animals.

   During Bolsonaro's presidency, deforestation of the Amazon soared to a 15-year high, with scientists warning that the forest was nearing a tipping point beyond which there would be irreversible consequences that would be felt across the globe. September 2022 marked yet another record-breaking month, as nearly 1,455 sq km of coverage were lost. This marked a staggering 48% increase from just a year ago and more than the current record, which was hit in September 2019.

   During his election campaign, Lula da Silva vowed to fight Amazon deforestation and crack down on illegal gold miners, loggers, and ranchers responsible for widespread environmental destruction and the displacement of indigenous communities.

   The newly elected president made a meaningful appearance during the second week of UNFCCC's COP27, saying that climate change would have the highest profile in his government: "There is no climate security for the world without a protected Amazon. We will do whatever it takes to have zero deforestation and the degradation of our biomes."

(Source: earth.org)

REVIEW: A SUMMARY OF THE KEY POINTS

- India is now facing a regular occurrence of extreme weather events.
- Mitigation and adaptation measures are essential to meet the challenge of climate change.
- IPCC's Sixth Assessment paints a grim picture of climate change.
- The Kyoto Protocol set modest targets for the reduction of greenhouse gases, but the targets were not met.
- The 2015 Paris Agreement reaffirms the goal of limiting global temperature increase well below 2 degrees Celsius, while urging efforts to limit the increase to 1.5 degrees.
- India has adopted a National Action Plan on Climate Change.
- India has made bold commitments to reduce emissions.
- Limiting climate change would require substantial and sustained reductions in greenhouse gas emissions.
- We must limit the global temperature rise to 2°C and the CO_2 concentration to 350 ppm.

EXERCISES

Objective-type questions

For each question below, choose the best answer out of the given choices:

1. Which of the following statements is **not** true about the Kyoto Protocol?
   (a) It commits countries to specified reductions in emissions.
   (b) It has not been implemented seriously.
   (c) It concerns specified greenhouse gases.
   (d) It has a uniform emission reduction target for all.
2. Which of the following statements is **not** true about the Intergovernmental Panel on Climate Change (IPCC)?
   (a) It conducts research.
   (b) It comes out with periodical assessment reports.
   (c) It consists of scientists from many countries.
   (d) It provides a basis for UNFCCC meetings
3. Mitigation of climate change includes:
   (a) Reduce emissions
   (b) Capture more carbon
   (c) Reduce coal use
   (d) All the above
4. The Paris Agreement on climate change:
   (a) Reaffirms the goal of limiting global temperature increase well below 2 degrees Celsius, while urging efforts to limit the increase to 1.5 degrees;
   (b) Establishes binding commitments by all parties to make 'nationally determined contributions' (NDCs), and to pursue domestic measures aimed at achieving them;
   (c) Commits all countries to report regularly on their emissions and progress made in implementing and achieving their NDCs, and to undergo international review;
   (d) All the above
5. INDC stands for:
   (a) International Neutrally Determined Contribution
   (b) Intended Notionally Determined Climate
   (c) Intended Nationally Determined Contribution
   (d) Intended Nationality Dependent Contribution

Short-answer questions

1. Outline the main messages of the IPCC Sixth Assessment Report.
2. What were India's commitments in response to climate change?
3. What is meant by 'Common But Differentiated Responsibility' and what is the status of this concept?

Long-answer questions

1. How can we persuade the UN members to take urgent action on climate change instead of blaming each other?
2. How do we raise funds for mitigation and adaptation?

Think critically: Deeper question for reflection and discussion

An African diplomat once told the delegates of the rich countries, 'If you do not share your wealth with us, we will share our poverty with you.' Currently, the rich countries are responsible for most of the greenhouse gas emissions. How should they support the poorer countries to develop and use cleaner technologies?

ENJOY AND EDUCATE YOURSELF

Here are some recent novels on the theme of climate change. Read the blurbs and choose what you like:

1. *The High House* by Jessie Greengrass
2. *Line* by Niall Bourke
3. *Something New Under the Sun* by Alexandra Kleeman

ACCESS THE OUP ONLINE RESOURCE CENTRE FOR MORE

- Full text of the IPCC Synthesis Report (Sixth Assessment)
- Additional text and other recommended references, websites, and films

16 Environmental Law and Environmental Management

The more laws and order are made prominent, the more thieves and robbers there will be.

Lao Tzu
Chinese philosopher (6th Century BCE)

MAIN QUESTIONS ADDRESSED

- How did environmental legislation evolve in India and what are the important environmental laws and regulations?
- What is meant by environmental ethics and environmental justice?
- What is the role of cultural and religious ethics in environmental conservation?

KEYWORDS AND PHRASES

eco-label, Ecomark, environmental ethics, Environmental Impact Assessment, environmental justice, environmental management, ISO 14000, judicial activism, National Green Tribunal, Pollution Control Board, public interest litigation, sacred grove, Taj Trapezium

LEAD STORY

THE STORY OF THE TAJ TRAPEZIUM: PUBLIC INTEREST LITIGATION

The Taj Mahal, one of the most beautiful monuments on the earth and a UNESCO World Heritage Site, has been showing black spots and a yellowish tinge, due to the pollution caused by Mathura Refinery, iron foundries, glass, and other chemical industries in the area. The sulphur dioxide released by the industries reacts with rainwater to become acid rain, which falls on the monument. In fact, because of very high toxic emissions from these industries, the Taj Mahal, Agra Fort, and Fatehpur Sikri, and 255 other historic monuments within the Taj Trapezium area have been facing serious threat because of acid rain (Chapter 13). The Taj Trapezium Zone (TTZ) is a 10,400 sq km trapezium-shaped area covering the five districts of the Agra region.

Reporter saying: *Here is the new Taj Mahal: Yellow in colour!*

In 1984, environmental lawyer M.C Mehta filed a Writ Petition in the Supreme Court, seeking appropriate directions to be given to the concerned authorities to take immediate steps to stop air pollution in the area and save the Taj Mahal. In a historic judgement delivered in December 1996, the Apex Court gave various directions including banning the use of coal and coke and directing the industries to switch over to Compressed Natural Gas (CNG). The Court based its verdict on the reports of the Varadharajan Committee (1978), Central Pollution Control Board (1981), and National Environment Engineering Research Institute (1990).

In January 1993, the Court directed the Uttar Pradesh Pollution Control Board to make a detailed list of all the industries and foundries active in the region and to make sure that pollution control measures were employed by the industries and foundries. Notices were issued to all the 511 industries regarding pollution control. The Court ordered the shutting down of the industries until necessary pollution control devices were installed.

The Court also asked the UP State Industrial Development Corporation to look for sites outside the Taj Trapezium Zone where the industries could be shifted. The creation of a green belt in the area was also to be undertaken. The Court said that its orders were based on the 'Precautionary Principle' and 'Polluter Pays Principle'. The onus of proof was on the developer/industrialist to show that his action was environmentally benign.

The closure of 212 coal based industrial units and shifting out of a thermal power plant as per the initial orders of the Court reduced the pollution levels by 1994. But there has been a steady increase in the levels of SPM after 1994, due to the emissions from the Mathura Oil Refinery, increase in the number of vehicles, and the use of diesel generators during power cuts.

In 2015, the Court pulled up the UP government for tree felling and inadequate tree planting in the TTZ. Though the Court issued many orders, the different stake holders have not been able to implement the same in its entirety. The Taj Protection Mission, set up as a joint venture between the UP government and the Centre in 1996 (based on a Supreme Court order), remains a non-starter.

What can we learn from the Taj Mahal pollution case?

- Not just our lives, but our very heritage is under threat due to pollution.
- Faced with the inaction (and even detrimental actions) of the government and civic agencies, the only recourse citizens often have in environmental matters is to approach the courts.
- Even the orders of the Supreme Court can be flouted by the authorities.

We will review in this chapter the major environmental laws that we have. We will also discuss judicial activism, environmental management, and environmental ethics.

What are the Indian Constitutional Provisions Regarding the Environment?

The Constitution (Forty-Second Amendment) Act of 1976 explicitly incorporates environmental protection and improvement. Article 48A, which was added to the directive principles of state policy, declares: 'The state shall endeavour to protect and improve the environment and to safeguard the forests and wildlife of the country'.

Article 51A(g), in a new chapter entitled 'Fundamental Duties', imposes a similar responsibility on every citizen 'to protect and improve the natural environment including forests, lakes, rivers, and wildlife, and to have compassion for living creatures'.

> **Key Idea** The Indian Constitution contains two important provisions concerning environmental protection.

In addition, Article 21 of the Constitution states: 'No person shall be deprived of his life or personal liberty except according to procedure established by law.' This Article protects the right to life as a fundamental right.

The courts have interpreted this Article to mean that the enjoyment of life, including the right to live with human dignity, encompasses within its ambit the protection and preservation of environment.

Do we have an Environmental Policy?

In 1980, the Union Government established the Department of Environment. It became the Ministry of Environment and Forests in 1985. It was renamed again in May 2014, when the new government came to power, as the Ministry of Environment, Forests, and Climate Change (MoEFCC).

MoEFCC initiates and oversees the implementation of environmental policies, plans, laws, and regulations. Over the years, the Government of India has announced several policies and plans directly or indirectly concerned with the environment, such as the following:

- National Forest Policy, 1988
- National Conservation Strategy and Policy Statement on Environment and Development, 1992
- Policy Statement on Abatement of Pollution, 1992
- National Environmental Action Programme, 1994
- National Agriculture Policy, 2000
- National Population Policy, 2000
- National Water Policy, 2002
- Wildlife Conservation Strategy, 2002

Building on and extending such documents, the Ministry came out with a National Environment Policy in 2006.

What was the Beginning of Environmental Legislation in India?

The UN Conference on the Human Environment held in Stockholm in June 1972 was the first international meeting to address environmental issues. The participating countries agreed to take appropriate steps for the preservation of the natural resources of the earth. In consonance with this decision, India began enacting environmental laws.

Initially, the laws were not very different from the general body of law. For example, the Water Act of 1974 was very much like other laws and created another agency-administered licensing system to control effluent discharges into water.

The Bhopal Gas Tragedy changed the situation. In the 1990s, many laws were passed covering new areas like vehicular emissions, noise, hazardous waste, transportation of toxic chemicals, and Environmental Impact Assessment.

Further, the old licensing regime was supplemented by regulatory techniques. The new laws included provisions like public hearings, citizens' right to information, deadlines for technology changes (in motor vehicles, for example), workers' participation, and penalties on higher management of companies.

Key Idea After the Bhopal Gas Tragedy, India enacted several environmental laws.

The powers of the enforcing agencies like the Pollution Control Boards were also increased to levels much higher than before. For example, previously a board had to approach a magistrate to get a factory to close. Now, it was given the power to order closure, leaving the polluter to challenge the order in court.

Let us now briefly review the main environmental laws of the country.

What Powers does the Environment (Protection) Act of 1986 Give to the Central Government?

This Act is an *enabling* law, that is, it provides powers to the executive to frame various rules and regulations. The Act authorizes the central government to protect and improve environmental quality, control, and reduce pollution from all sources, and prohibit or restrict the setting and/or operation of any industrial facility on environmental grounds.

The Act defines terms such as environment, environmental pollutant, and hazardous substance. According to the Act, the Central Government has the power to

- take measures to protect and improve environment;
- give directions (such as to close, prohibit, or regulate any industry, operation, or process); and
- make rules to regulate environmental pollution (air, water quality standards, prohibition or restriction in handling hazardous materials, siting of industry, etc.).

The chapter on the prevention, control, and abatement of environmental pollution includes controlling discharge of environmental pollutants, enforcing compliance with procedural safeguards, power of entry and inspection, and power to take samples, setting up of environmental laboratories, appointing environmental analysts, and prescription of penalties for contravening the Act.

What are the Environment (Protection) Rules, 1986?

These rules set the standards for emission or discharge of environmental pollutants. In addition, more stringent standards may be laid down for specific industries or locations.

There are rules regarding the prohibition and restriction on the location of industries and the carrying on of processes and operations in different areas. Factors to be taken into consideration include topographic and climatic features of an area, environmentally compatible land use, the net adverse impact likely to be caused by an industry, proximity to areas protected under various other laws, proximity to human settlements, etc.

What are the Provisions of the Air (Prevention and Control of Pollution) Act of 1981?

The objective of this Act is to provide for the prevention, control, and abatement of air pollution. The Act defines air pollution as the presence in the atmosphere of any solid, liquid, or gaseous substance (including noise) in such concentration as may be injurious to human beings, other organisms, property, or the environment.

The provisions of the Act are to be implemented by the Central Pollution Control Board along with the state boards. The Act lists several functions for the Board including the setting of air quality standards, collecting data on air pollution, organizing training and awareness programmes, establishing laboratories, etc. The Board can specify air pollution control areas and set standards for vehicle emissions.

The Act lays down penalties for violation of its provisions. This applies to companies and their owners and managers as well as to government departments. Citizens can file complaints with the Board.

What are the Water-related Environmental Laws in India?

The early Acts concerned with water issues were the following:

- The Easement Act of 1882 allowed private rights to use ground water by viewing it as an attachment to the land. It also states that all surface water belongs to the state and is a state property.
- The Indian Fisheries Act of 1897 established two sets of penal offences whereby the government can sue any person who uses dynamite or other explosive substance in any way (whether coastal or inland) with intent to catch or destroy any fish or poisons fish to kill.
- The Merchant Shipping Act of 1970 deals with waste arising from ships along the coastal areas within a specified radius.

What are the objectives of the Water (Prevention and Control of Pollution) Act of 1974?

The objectives of the Water Act are to prevent and control water pollution and the maintenance or restoration of the wholesomeness of water. The Act defines water pollution as the contamination of water, alteration of its physical, chemical, or biological properties, or the discharge of any sewage or trade effluent or any other liquid, gaseous, or solid substance into water which may render such water harmful to public health or to domestic, commercial, industrial, agricultural, or other legitimate uses, or to the life and health of organisms.

The Act establishes an institutional structure for preventing and abating water pollution. It establishes standards for water quality and effluent. Polluting industries must seek permission to discharge waste into effluent bodies.

The implementation is like the Air (Prevention and Control of Pollution) Act with the Central Pollution Control Board being the main agency. In fact, the Central Pollution Control Board (CPCB) was constituted under this Act.

What does the Forest Conservation Act of 1980 Specify?

This Act, along with the Forest (Conservation) Rules of 1981, provides for the protection and conservation of forests. The Act specifies the requirements that should be met before declaring an area as a Protected Forest, Wildlife Sanctuary, or a National Park.

Under the Act, a state government may regulate or prohibit in any forest the clearing of land for cultivation, pasturing of cattle, or clearing the vegetation for any of the following purposes:

- protection against storms, winds, floods, and avalanches, for the preservation of the soil on the slopes, the prevention of landslips or of the formation of ravines and torrents, or the protection of land against erosion
- maintenance of a water supply in springs, rivers, and tanks
- protection of roads, bridges, railways, and other lines of communication
- preservation of public health

The Act makes it mandatory for the owner of a forest to seek permission before converting it to any non-forest purposes such as the cultivation of tea, coffee, spices, rubber, palms, oil-bearing plants, horticultural crops, or medicinal plants.

In 2022, new rules were promulgated by the government under the Act. These rules seem to make it easier for companies to take over forest land and use it for other purposes. Environmentalists have protested the introduction of these rules.

The Forest (Conservation) Amendment Bill, 2023 was introduced in Lok Sabha on March 29, 2023. The Bill amends the Forest Conservation Act, 1980 which provides for the conservation of forest land. The Bill adds and exempts certain types of land from the purview of the Act. Further, it expands the list of activities permitted to be carried out on forest land. The legislation also focuses on ending the practice of considering seismic surveys as non-forest activities.

The proposed amendment will give a boost to the oil and gas exploration activity in the country as it would offer explorers prompt access to thousands of sq km of forest areas for seismic surveys by obviating the need for time-consuming permits. This change will have enormous impact on the forest cover.

What are the Objectives of the Wildlife Protection Act of 1972?

The Wildlife Protection Act of 1972 (amended in 2006) defines wildlife to include any animal, bees, butterflies, crustaceans, fish, and moths; and aquatic or land vegetation, which form part of any habitat.

The Act, along with the Wildlife Protection Rules, provides for the protection of birds and animals and for all matters that are connected to it whether it be their habitat or the waterhole or the forest that sustain them.

The Act provides a powerful legal framework for:

- Prohibition of hunting
- Protection and management of wildlife habitats
- Establishment of protected areas and reserves such as national parks, wildlife sanctuaries, tiger reserves, conservation reserves, and community reserves
- Regulation and control of trade in parts and products derived from wildlife.
- Management of zoos.

The Act provides for stringent punishment for any violation of the rules.

How do Our Laws Support the Conservation of Forests and Nature Reserves by Local and Tribal Communities?

Local communities in India had been traditionally conserving forests, mountains, rivers, wetlands, trees, birds, and animals in various inventive ways. But planned and unplanned development, eroding traditional values, decline of traditional knowledge systems, and the establishment of protected areas have marginalized local efforts at conservation.

Some of the laws and policies, however, protect the rights of local communities and provide for their involvement in conservation. Here are some examples:

- Scheduled Tribes and Other Traditional Forest-Dwellers (Recognition of Forest Rights) Act, 2006: Communities can create local institutions and rules and regulations for protection of forests that they have been traditionally conserving.
- Biological Diversity Act, 2002: Provision to form Biodiversity Management Committees (BMCs) at the village level for the management, protection, and documentation of local biodiversity.
- Forest Conservation Act, 1980: Provision for formation of village forests.
- Wildlife (Protection) Act, 1972: Provisions for establishment of community-oriented protected areas, either on government land (Conservation Reserve) or on land owned by individuals or communities (Community Reserve).
- National Forest Policy, 1988: Recognition of people's need to access forests and resources for their livelihoods and mandatory involvement of local people in the management of forests.

What are the Other Acts and Rules Concerning the Environment?

The following are the other important environment-related Acts and Rules:

- Hazardous Waste (Management and Handling) Rules of 1989 control the generation, collection, treatment, import, storage, and handling of hazardous waste.
- Manufacture, Storage, and Import of Hazardous Chemical Rules of 1989 set up an Authority to inspect, once a year, the industrial activity connected with hazardous chemicals and isolated storage facilities.
- Manufacture, Use, Import, Export, and Storage of Hazardous Micro-organisms, Genetically Engineered Organisms or Cells Rules of 1989 were introduced with a view to protect the environment, nature, and health, in connection with the application of genetic engineering.

- Public Liability Insurance Act and Rules of 1991 and Amendment, 1992 were drawn up to provide for public liability insurance for the purpose of providing immediate relief to the persons affected by accident while handling any hazardous substance.
- National Environmental Tribunal Act of 1995 was created to award compensation for damages to persons, property, and the environment arising from any activity involving hazardous substances.
- Biomedical Waste (Management and Handling) Rules of 1998 constitute a legal binding on the health care institutions to streamline the process of proper handling of hospital waste such as segregation, disposal, collection, and treatment.
- Coastal Regulation Zone Notification of 1991 regulates various activities, including construction, in the coastal zone. It gives some protection to the backwaters and estuaries.
- The Draft Solid Waste Management Rules were published in 2015 for public comments. These Rules will supersede the Municipal Solid Waste Management and Handling Rules of 2000. The new rules shall apply to every urban local body in the country.

What are the Functions and Powers of the Central and State Pollution Control Boards?

The Central Pollution Control Board (CPCB), set up in 1974, provides technical services to the Ministry about the provisions of the Environment (Protection) Act, 1986. The main functions and powers of CPCB are to:

- Advise the Central Government on any matter concerning prevention and control of water and air pollution and improvement of the quality of air.
- Plan and execute nation-wide programmes for the prevention, control, or abatement of water and air pollution.
- Coordinate the activities of the State Pollution Control Boards.
- Provide technical assistance and guidance to the State Boards, carry out and sponsor investigation and research relating to problems of water and air pollution, and for their prevention, control, or abatement.
- Organize, through mass media, a comprehensive mass awareness programme on the prevention, control, or abatement of water and air pollution.
- Collect, compile, and publish technical and statistical data relating to water and air pollution and the measures devised for their effective prevention, control, or abatement.
- Prepare manuals, codes, and guidelines relating to treatment and disposal of sewage and trade effluents as well as for stack gas cleaning devices, stacks, and ducts.

The State Pollution Control Boards have similar functions and powers at the state level.

What is Eco-labeling of Products and Ecomark of India?

An eco-label is used to mark a consumer product to indicate that it is environment-friendly about its manufacture and use. The label means that the product satisfies certain eco-friendly criteria laid down by the government, association, or a certification agency. The BEE energy rating mentioned in Chapter 8 is an example of eco-labelling. An eco-label enables the consumer to choose the right product.

Eco-labeling is a voluntary method of environmental performance certification and labelling that is practiced around the world. A manufacturer attaches an approved eco-label on his product to promote the fact that his product is genuinely environment friendly. Eco-labels can guide our purchasing choices and thus reduce waste.

In 1991, the Government of India launched its first eco-label called Eco-mark for easy identification of environment-friendly products. The Ministry administers the programme with technical advice from the Central Pollution Control Board (CPCB). The Ecomark scheme is linked to the product quality and safety standards of Bureau of Indian Standards (BIS). This scheme distinguishes itself from other international ecolabeling schemes, which are independent. Ecomark has some product specific requirements that include clauses on energy conservation in the production process. The criteria follow a cradle-to-grave approach, that is, from raw material extraction, to manufacturing, and to disposal. The Ecomark label is awarded to consumer goods that meet the specified environmental criteria and the quality requirements of Indian Standards.

FIGURE 16.1 Ecomark Logo

An earthen pot was chosen as the logo for the Ecomark scheme in India (Fig. 16.1). The familiar earthen pot uses a renewable resource like earth, does not produce hazardous waste, and consumes little energy in making. Its solid and graceful form represents both strength and fragility, which also characterises the eco-system.

Due to many reasons the Eco-mark scheme has not been successful. The BEE energy rating, however, has been adopted by many manufacturers of consumer products (like refrigerators) and is now used by many consumers to make buying choices.

How are the Environmental Laws being Enforced?

We saw that there is no dearth of laws for protecting and conserving the environment. However, the implementation of these laws continues to be poor. The government agencies have vast powers to regulate industries and others who are potential polluters. They are, however, reluctant to use these powers to discipline the polluters.

The Parliament and the state assemblies are ready to pass environmental laws, but do not provide funds for their implementation. Nor do they demand that the governments enforce the laws strictly.

The poor performance of the government agencies in enforcing the laws has compelled the courts to play a proactive role in the matter of environment. They have directly responded to the complaints of citizens or public interest litigation and assumed the roles of policy makers, educators, administrators, and, in general, friends of the environment. The environmental lawyer M.C. Mehta has played a remarkable role in this process (Box 16.1).

BOX 16.1 INSPIRATION: *The Story of M.C. Mehta—The Green Avenger*

Mahesh Chandra Mehta visited the Taj Mahal for the first time in early 1984 and was shocked to see that the monument's marble had turned yellow and was pitted because of pollutants from nearby industries. Being a lawyer, he filed an environmental case in the Supreme Court of India on the issue. (See Lead Story of this chapter)

Mehta did not stop with the Taj case. In 1985, he filed a petition on the Ganga. As we saw, many positive actions to prevent the pollution of the river resulted from this case.

Mehta has continued his crusade and at the last count, his cases numbered more than 50 in the Supreme Court alone. He has successfully fought cases against industries that generate hazardous waste and succeeded in obtaining a court order to make lead-free gasoline available. He has also been working to ban intensive shrimp farming and other damaging activities along India's coast.

Through his work, Mehta has set the national agenda in the fields of water and air pollution, vehicular emission control, conservation of the coastal zone, and the translocation of heavy industry away from urban areas. Almost single-handedly, he has obtained more than 40 landmark judgements and numerous orders from the Supreme Court against polluters. In addition, responding to his petition, the Court has ordered the inclusion of environmental studies as a compulsory subject in all the schools, colleges, and universities of the country.

No other environmental lawyer in the world has perhaps done this much. He has inspired many lawyers in the lower courts to take up environmental cases. Mehta won the Goldman Environmental Prize in 1996 and the Ramon Magsaysay Award for Public Service in 1997.

Mehta has set up the M.C. Mehta Environmental Foundation for the protection of the environment, the rights of the people to clean and fresh water and air, the promotion of sustainable development, and the protection of the cultural heritage of India.

Many petitions filed in courts by individual citizens, groups, and voluntary organizations have led to major decisions given by the courts forcing the state governments to act against pollution and degradation of the environment. The Supreme Court, for example, has in numerous cases issued directions to close or shift factories, change to less-polluting technologies, implement environmental norms, etc. Examples are the Taj Trapezium Case (See lead story) and the Shrimp Aquaculture Case (Box 16.2).

BOX 16.2 CONTROVERSY: *The Story of Shrimp Aquaculture—Mediating in Prawn Wars*

Shrimp aquaculture production in India increased from 30,000 tonnes in 1990 to 102,000 tonnes in 1999, made possible by a rapid increase in the area under semi-intensive farms. The expansion was driven by the high profitability of shrimp farming, and it attracted a wide range of investors ranging from individual farmers converting paddy fields to multinational companies investing in large-scale, semi-intensive and intensive shrimp farming.

Coastal areas are ideal for shrimp aquaculture since it needs both fresh water and sea water. The rapid expansion of shrimp aquaculture on the coast, particularly in Tamil Nadu and Andhra Pradesh, created many social and environmental problems:

- Polluted salty water from the prawn tanks was discharged into fields killing the soil and the crops. Wells became contaminated and the water undrinkable. Villagers were forced to walk many miles to fetch fresh water.
- The salty water resulted in salinization leading to the collapse of mud houses of the poor.
- The wastes from prawn farms containing pesticides, fertilizers, and antibiotics were often pumped back into the sea, polluting the breeding zones for the fishes.
- The inlet and outlet pipes extending into the sea caused problems for fishing nets and boats.
- In many places, the farms prevented access for the fisherfolk to go to the sea.
- Mangrove areas were converted into aquaculture farms. During the 1990s, shrimp aquaculture accounted for about 80% of the conversion of mangrove land.

In 1994, S. Jagannathan, a Gandhian social worker from Tamil Nadu, filed a writ petition in the Supreme Court in public interest. The petition sought the enforcement of Coastal Zone Regulation Notification of 1991 and stoppage of intensive and semi-intensive type of prawn farming in the ecologically fragile coastal areas, prohibition from using the wastelands/wetlands for prawn farming, and the constitution of a National Coastal Management Authority to safeguard marine life and coastal areas.

The Supreme Court bench, headed by Justice Kuldip Singh, issued many injunctions and directions. The shrimp aquaculture industry was prohibited in the coastal zone and existing farms were directed to be demolished. The workers, rendered unemployed, were to be compensated by the owners. Agricultural lands, salt-pan lands, mangroves, wetland, forestlands, and land for village common purposes were not to be converted into shrimp ponds. The Court also directed the government to set up an Aquaculture Authority to regulate the industry.

Following the judgment, the government set up an Aquaculture Authority in 1997 to regulate new aquaculture farms and implement the Supreme Court directions with respect to closure of aquaculture farms that were violating coastal regulations. However, a few months after its constitution and after the deadline for closure of aquaculture farms had expired, the government changed its charter. The Authority no longer had the responsibility for the closure of existing aquaculture farms that were violating coastal regulations.

The last word has not been said on this issue.

Key Idea The implementation of environmental laws in India has been poor, forcing the people to turn to public interest litigation.

As a result of such 'judicial activism', hundreds of factories have installed effluent treatment plants and there is a much greater environmental awareness among the bureaucracy, police, and municipal officials, all of whom are involved in implementing the Court's orders. Judicial activism has certainly helped the cause of environment, but there is also the view that the courts should not be taking over the role of the executive.

Many of the laws and the rules have been amended over the years—in some cases they have been made more stringent, while in other cases they have been relaxed.

Laws, regulations, and public interest litigations cannot save the environment if there is lack of environmental ethics among the citizens, government officials, companies, and industries.

What is the National Green Tribunal?

The Indian government established a National Green Tribunal in October 2010, headed by a former judge of the Supreme Court. It is a tribunal exclusively dedicated to environmental issues. This Body, established by an Act of Parliament (National Green Tribunal Act of 2010), will have circuit benches across the country to try all matters related to and arising out of environmental issues.

The Tribunal shall also consist of members who are experts in the field of environmental and related sciences. It has been empowered to issue directions for the compensation and restitution of damage caused from actions of environmental negligence. In doing so, this is the first body of its kind that is required by its parent statute, to apply the 'polluter pays' principle and the principle of sustainable development.

What is Environmental Impact Assessment?

Environmental Impact Assessment (EIA) is the assessment of the environmental consequences (positive and negative) of a plan, policy, program, or project prior to the decision to move forward with the proposed action. EIA began in India during 1978–79 with the impact assessment of river valley projects. Subsequently, the scope was enhanced to cover other developmental sectors such as industries, thermal power projects, mining schemes etc.

The comprehensive Environmental Impact Assessment Notification (EIA Notification) was issued in 2006 under the Environmental (Protection) Act, 1986. Subsequently, several amendments were made to the EIA Notification.

EIA is now mandatory for 29 categories of developmental activities involving investments of ₹50 crores and above. The crucial aspect is that the project proponents must obtain prior environmental clearance before undertaking any construction. Projects have been classified into Category A that will be assessed by MoEFCC and Category B, which are handled by the State-level Expert Appraisal Committee (SEAC).

What is the EIA Procedure? After the submission of an application by a project authority along with all the requisite documents, there are four stages in the process:

Screening: The state SEAC will determine whether the project or activity requires further environmental studies for preparation of an EIA.

Scoping: SEAC will determine detailed and comprehensive Terms of Reference (TOR) addressing all relevant environmental concerns.

Public Consultation: The concerns of local affected persons and others who have plausible stake in the environmental impacts of the project are ascertained.

Appraisal: This stage begins after the project proponent has submitted the revised EIA report and an Environment Management Plan after the public consultation stage. The SEAC examines all the documents and may approve or reject the proposal. If the project is approved, environmental clearance is given subject to implementation of the stipulated environmental safeguards.

In recent years, the EIA Rules have been repeatedly amended, relaxing many conditions, and making it easier to get environmental clearance. NGOs have protested such changes.

The drawbacks of the current EIA process are:

- The EIA reports are prepared by consultants engaged by the project proponents and hence cannot be unbiased.
- Many proponents choose the option of 'Rapid EIA', which is often inadequate.
- Lack of cumulative assessment of the impact of multiple projects in the area.
- Poor quality of EIA reports
- Cases of plagiarism and inadequate assessment
- Lack of accountability of the EIA consultants
- Ineffective and improper public consultation
- Weak appraisal mechanism (unqualified Committee members)
- Poor monitoring of compliance.

Overall, EIA is used presently as a project justification tool rather than as a project planning tool to contribute to achieving sustainable development. Even further relaxation of the rules is in the offing.

What are the major changes proposed in the Draft EIA Rules of 2020?

The important changes proposed are:

- Public consultation has been made optional for several toxic industries.
- Such industries are allowed to come up in proximity to densely populated and protected areas.
- Several conditions that allow ex post facto clearances have been inserted which are perhaps illegal. Such clearance goes against the Supreme Court order in the case of Alembic industries versus Rohit Prajapati.
- Relaxation of EIA for mining based on its area.
- Over 25 red and orange category toxic industries are brought under Category B2, which needs neither public consultation nor a report by an Expert Assessment Committee.
- Exemption for over 40 industries from prior environmental clearance.
- Dilution of general conditions such that several red and orange toxic industries can now operate as close as 0–5 Km from a Protected Area.
- Expansion of an industry up to 50% allowed without public consultation.
- Validity period for mining increased from 30 to 50 Years.

What is an Environmental Management System?

An Environmental Management System (EMS) is a framework that helps an organization achieve its environmental goals through consistent review, evaluation, and improvement of its environmental performance. The assumption is that this consistent review and evaluation will identify opportunities for improving and implementing the environmental performance of the organization. The EMS itself does not dictate a level of environmental performance that must be achieved; each organization's EMS is tailored to its own individual objectives and targets.

Following ISO 14000 standards is typically a part of an organization's EMS.

What is ISO 14000?

ISO 14000 is a global green standard, a voluntary environmental management system. The ISO 14000 family of standards provides practical tools for companies and organizations looking to manage their environmental responsibilities. Any organization can choose to seek certification under this standard.

The ISO 14000 standards have been developed by the International Organization for Standardization (ISO). The standards do not themselves specify environmental performance goals. These must be set by the organization itself, considering the effects it has on the environment, and the views of its stakeholders.

The standards define the key elements of a management system that will help an organization address the environmental issues it faces. The management system includes the setting of goals and priorities, assignment of responsibility for accomplishing them, measuring, and reporting on results, and external verification of claims. By getting certified under ISO 14000, the organization tells its customers and other stakeholders that it is committed to the protection of the environment. There are more than 300,000 certifications to ISO 14001 in 171 countries around the world.

What is Meant by Environmental Ethics?

Ethics are concerned with what is wrong and what is right, irrespective of the culture and society. For example, it is ethical to have reverence for all forms of life and any killing is unethical.

Morals reflect the predominant feelings of a culture about ethical issues. For example, in most cultures, it is morally right to kill enemies in a war, though it is unethical.

Environmental ethics try to define the moral basis of environmental responsibility. There are three possible viewpoints:

- Anthropocentric view: Our environmental responsibility is to ensure that the earth remains hospitable and pleasant for human beings. This is the development ethic, the basis of the Idea of Progress (Chapter 1). In this view, nature has value only when humans utilize it.
- Biocentric view: All forms of life—humans, animals, and plants—have an inherent right to exist and live without hindrance. This is the preservation ethic, which recognizes that nature has an intrinsic value apart from its use as a resource for humans.
- Ecocentric view: Environment deserves care and consideration by itself and not out of the interests of humans, animals, and plants. This is the conservation ethic, which extends the preservation ethic to the entire earth and for all time.

It should be our aim to move from the current (widely held) anthropocentric view to an ecocentric view. That will change our relationship to nature and conserve the environment.

What is the role of cultural and religious ethics in environmental conservation?

Our view of nature and our relationship to it are strongly influenced by our cultures, faiths, and beliefs. Hence, cultural beliefs and religious teachings could play a role in environmental conservation.

The Alliance of Religions and Conservation (ARC) is a secular body that helps the major religions of the world to develop their own environmental programmes, based on their core teachings, beliefs, and practices. ARC helps the religions link with key environmental organisations—creating powerful alliances between faith communities and conservation groups. Twelve faiths (covering about 85% of the world's population) have joined the Alliance.

As part of the Alliance, each of the faiths has compiled its own statement summarizing its relationship with and beliefs about the environment. Here are excerpts from some of the statements:

- Buddhism: This is a religion of love, understanding, and compassion and is committed toward the ideal of non-violence. As such, it also attaches great importance to wildlife and the protection of the environment on which every being in this world depends for survival.
- Christianity: Every human act of irresponsibility towards creatures is an abomination. According to its gravity, it is an offence against that divine wisdom which sustains and gives purpose to the interdependent harmony of the universe.
- Hinduism: The Hindu scriptures are permeated with a reverence for life and an awareness that the great forces of nature—earth, sky, air, water, and fire as well as various orders of life including forests and animals are all bound together within the great rhythms of nature.
- Islam: Mankind's role is that of a trustee of God. We are not masters of this earth; it does not belong to us to do what we wish.
- Judaism: The sun, moon, stars, plants, animals, and ultimately man were created with a rightful and necessary place in the universe. They were not to encroach on each other.

Given that the theme of this book is climate change, we must also add that, in June 2015, Pope Francis issued a detailed and unprecedented statement (called encyclical) on environment. It is a powerful, prophetic, and personal plea for governments, religions, businesses, and individuals to work together to address climate change.

Cultural traditions in India have also supported environmental conservation. Three examples are:

- The case of the Bishnois as protectors of nature (Chapter 3, Box 3.2).
- The residents of Kokkerebellur in Karnataka, who are famous for adopting the spot-billed pelican (Kokkare in Kannada) as their heritage and taking care of the nesting and breeding of these birds. (ORC)
- The tradition of sacred groves (Box 16.3).

BOX 16.3 INSPIRATION: *The Story of Sacred Groves—Conservation by Faith!*

It could be just a few trees or a whole forest. No tree or plant is cut here, no animal or bird is killed, and no form of life is harmed. No one would dare because it is protected by the local deity. Some even have a temple within.

The sacred groves of India are a unique traditional institution devoted to the conservation of forests and biodiversity. They are referred to in the ancient texts and thousands of them must have existed. They were protected by local communities through social traditions and taboos that incorporate spiritual and ecological values.

Preserved over the course of many generations, sacred groves represent native vegetation in a natural or near-natural state. They are thus rich in biodiversity and are banks of species and genetic diversity. They often contain species that have disappeared in other places. Rare medicinal plants are also found in the groves.

Many groves have water sources that help the local communities. The groves absorb water during the monsoon and release it slowly during the dry period.

Over time, hundreds of these groves have disappeared under the pressure of population and development. However, according to one survey, over 13,000 groves still survive as patches across the country. Other estimates give the number as being between 100,000 and 150,000. Only groves in remote parts remain undisturbed, while others need protection.

In recent years, there has been an increasing interest in documenting and conserving the sacred groves.

What is Environmental Justice?

Environmental justice has been defined as equal justice and equal protection for all under the environmental laws and regulations without discrimination based on race, caste, ethnicity, or socio-economic status.

There are three categories of environmental equity issues.

- Procedural Injustice: This refers to the uniform application of governing rules, regulations, and evaluation criteria. Examples of procedural injustice are:
  - 'stacking' boards and committees with pro-business interests
  - holding hearings in remote locations to minimize public participation
  - using English-only material to communicate to non-English speaking communities
- Geographical Injustice: Some neighbourhoods, communities, and regions receive direct benefits, such as jobs and tax revenues, from industrial production while the costs, such as the burdens of waste disposal, are sent elsewhere. Communities hosting waste-disposal facilities receive fewer economic benefits than communities generating the waste.
- Social Injustice: Environmental decisions often mirror the power arrangements of larger society For example, toxic or waste dumps could be in poor neighbourhoods because the local people are unable to protect and resist the move.

> **Key Idea**
> Environment is basically an ethical issue, and we need to move from an anthropocentric view to an eco-centric view. We also need to promote environmental justice.

Environmental justice is about social transformation directed towards meeting basic human needs and enhancing our quality of life—economic quality, health care, housing, human rights, environmental protection, and democracy. In linking environmental and social justice issues, the environmental justice movement seeks to challenge the abuse of power which results in poor people having to suffer the effects of environmental damage caused by the greed of others.

What Lies Ahead?

Judicial intervention alone cannot bring about systemic changes in such a large and complex country like India. It is one of many tools for promoting the environmental agenda. Public education, lobbying, and political action by organizing citizens may be far more effective in some cases.

In the long run, we need political commitment for conserving the environment shown in the form of substantial budgetary allocations for enforcing environmental laws. Courts can only supplement, and not replace, the administrative enforcement mechanism.

Ending on a Hopeful Note: Positive Stories

1. In many cases of public interest litigation and citizen action on environmental issues, there is victory, but often a partial one. This was true of the Taj Trapezium Case, Shrimp Aquaculture Case, and the Kodaikanal Mercury Case (Box 16.4).
2. Faced with rapid fall of the water table, the Punjab Government enacted in 2009 the Punjab Preservation of Subsoil Water Act. This Act prohibits the farmers from sowing paddy in nurseries before May 1 and transplanting paddy before June 10. Essentially, the Law delays the transplanting almost until the arrival of the monsoon and thus prevents the depletion of ground water. The law has arrested the further decline of water table.

BOX 16.4 DISASTER: *The Story of Kodaikanal Mercury Case—Send It Back!*

Normally, the waste would have slowly contaminated the soil and caused problems for years. In this case, however, the mercury was sent back to the US for recycling—thanks to a citizens' campaign and environmental litigation.

Hindustan Lever Ltd, a subsidiary of the Anglo-Dutch multinational Unilever, shut down a mercury thermometer factory in Watertown, New York and moved it to the hill station Kodaikanal, in Tamil Nadu in 1983. It imported mercury from the US and exported the finished thermometers back to the US. By 1997, the plant was making 125,000 thermometers every year.

In 2001, the local people discovered tonnes of mercury waste from broken thermometers that had been dumped on a dirt lot near the factory. The community immediately purchased the mercury as evidence and informed the Tamil Nadu Pollution Control Board (TNPCB). The company initially denied it was their waste, but later admitted that it had been 'inadvertently sold'. The company had in fact sold the mercury to a scrap dealer over four years.

When liquid mercury is spilled, it forms droplets that can accumulate in the tiniest of spaces and then emit vapours into the air. Health problems caused by mercury depend on how much of it has entered the body. Hence, regardless of quantity, all mercury spills should be treated seriously.

In March 2003, the TNPCB ordered the company to ship the mercury-laden waste back to the US for proper disposal. Under close supervision, some 300 tonnes of mercury-contaminated waste were packed into containers and taken to a mercury recycling plant in the US.

The story was not over yet. At a public hearing held in September 2002, the former workers of the factory said they had never been told about the poisonous nature of mercury and demanded that their health problems be addressed. 23 workers had died young, and their symptoms had been those of mercury poisoning. Over 550 workers still living in Kodaikanal exhibit similar symptoms.

In 2006, the Ex-Mercury Employees Welfare Association filed a petition in the Chennai High Court seeking rehabilitation and healthcare treatment for all the ex-employees. The company has dismissed the workers' symptoms as having nothing to do with mercury exposure. The case is still on.

In September 2004, the Hazardous Waste Monitoring Committee appointed by the Supreme Court visited Kodaikanal. It ordered a clean-up of the site as well as medical aid for the affected people. The company admitted that over 360 kg of mercury remain spread over the factory site but has not cleaned up the site yet.

Meanwhile, studies have shown that mercury levels in the Kodaikanal lakes are abnormally high. Will the factory's mercury convert into an even more dangerous form, methylmercury? Will it get into the food chain? The citizens are worried.

REVIEW: A SUMMARY OF THE KEY POINTS

- India has many laws to protect the environment, but the implementation has been poor.
- Responding to public interest litigation by citizens and groups, the courts have been taking a proactive role to enforce environmental laws in India.
- We have constitutional provisions to safeguard the environment.
- The Bhopal Tragedy gave the impetus for passing several environmental laws incorporating regulatory mechanisms.
- The Environment (Protection) Act of 1986 is an enabling law, providing powers to the executive to frame various rules and regulations.
- An Environmental Impact Assessment (EIA) is mandatory for certain types of projects.
- We have specific laws concerning air, water, forests, wildlife, hazardous waste, etc., but the enforcement of all these laws is poor. These laws are also being reviewed to make clearances easier.
- Environmental ethics try to define the moral basis of environmental responsibility.

EXERCISES

Objective-type questions

For each question below, choose the best answer out of the given choices.

1. Which of the following statements is true about the Constitution of India?
   (a) It contains one provision regarding environmental protection.
   (b) It contains no provision regarding environmental protection.
   (c) It contains two provisions regarding environmental protection.
   (d) According to it, right to life is not a fundamental right.
2. Which event gave an impetus for enacting many environmental laws in India?
   (a) Stockholm conference
   (b) Bhopal Tragedy
   (c) Arrival of the British
   (d) Independence
3. Which of the following statements is **not** true about the Environment (Protection) Act?
   (a) It is an enabling law.
   (b) It sets the standards for emission or discharge of environmental pollutants.
   (c) It provides powers to the executive to frame various rules and regulations.
   (d) It authorizes the central government to protect and improve environmental quality.
4. An Environmental Impact Assessment is required for:
   (a) All projects
   (b) All tourism projects
   (c) All mining projects
   (d) Specified categories of projects
5. Which of the following views about the environment is currently dominant?
   (a) Anthropocentric view
   (b) Eco-centric view
   (c) Biocentric view
   (d) Ethical view

Short-answer questions

1. Outline the Indian constitutional provisions regarding the environment.
2. Describe the beginnings of environmental legislation in India.
3. Explain the requirement of an Environmental Impact Assessment for certain types of projects.
4. What are the main provisions of the following Acts?
   (a) Environment (Protection) Act
   (b) Air (Prevention and Control of Pollution) Act
   (c) Wildlife Protection Act
   (d) Water (Prevention and Control of Pollution) Act
   (e) Forest Conservation Act
5. Give two examples of public interest litigation and judicial activism in enforcing environmental laws in India.
6. Explain environmental ethics and the three different ways of viewing environmental responsibility.
7. What is Environmental Impact Assessment and how is it conducted?
8. What is Environmental Management System?
9. Why was the earthen pot chosen as the Ecomark Logo of India?

Long-answer question

Write an essay on judicial activism in India. Give examples of cases in which the courts have assumed the roles of policymakers, educators, or administrators, and given directives that the government or the enforcement agency should have issued in the first instance.

Think critically: Deeper questions for reflection and discussion

Is judicial activism to be welcomed, given that the governments are not implementing the laws properly? How long can the courts continue to play the role of administrators? Will the fear of courts force the governments to enforce the laws strictly or will they let the court take on that task?

ENJOY AND EDUCATE YOURSELF

1. Watch the movie *Dersu Uzala* (1975), made by the famous Japanese film director Akira Kurosawa. It is the portrait of a man living in harmony with nature, struggling against the forces of modernity and 'progress'.
2. Relax with the novel *Immediate Harm* by James Thornton, a legal thriller about the threat posed by genetically modified corn.

ACCESS THE OUP ONLINE RESOURCE CENTRE FOR MORE

- The story of Kokkerebellur in Karnataka where citizens protect the migrating pelicans.
- Additional text and other recommended references, websites, and films

UNIT 7 **Sustainable Development**

17 Sustainable Development and Global Initiatives

You tell us to take land in Gujarat. You tell us to take compensation. For losing our lands, our fields, for the trees along our fields. But how are you going to compensate us for our forest? How will you compensate us for our river—for her fish, her water, for the vegetables that grow along her banks, for the joy of living beside her? What is the price for this? Our gods, and the support of our kin—what price do you put on that? Our adivasi life—what price do you put on that?

Excerpt from a letter written in 1994 by Bava Mahalia of Jalsindhi, one of the Narmada Dam-affected villages, to the Chief Minister of Madhya Pradesh

MAIN QUESTIONS ADDRESSED

- How serious is the issue of displacement of people caused by development projects including dams?
- Why do programmes for the resettlement and rehabilitation of displaced people fail in most cases?
- What are the alternative models of development that aim toward sustainability?
- What are the steps being taken toward a Green Economy?

KEYWORDS AND PHRASES

Ceres Principles, Circular Economy, Global Reporting Initiative, Green Business, Green Economy, Manibeli, Millennium Development Goals, Narmada Project, UN Sustainable Development Goals

LEAD STORY

THE STORY OF MANIBELI: DISPLACEMENT AND RESISTANCE

'My children will never till the hill slopes. It is unthinkable. My father tilled here. I walked by his side as a child, knowing that I would be doing the same when I grow older. I cannot give my children these assurances. I cannot give them anything because whatever I have is suddenly not mine', said Jatrabhai, a 70-year-old resident of Manibeli village in North Maharashtra.

Manibeli, with 140 residents, was the first village to be affected by the Sardar Sarovar Dam project on the River Narmada. For the tribal people of Manibeli, it had been a long struggle. The authorities had tried to resettle these villagers right from 1983. About 100-odd families were moved to Parveta. The land offered to them as compensation was in a very bad condition and the monetary compensation was less than half of what was promised.

Meanwhile, the Narmada Bachao Andolan (NBA) had been formed and the fight for proper resettlement and rehabilitation had begun. Manibeli became famous during the *satyagraha* undertaken by the people in June 1991. With the waters steadily rising, the first batch of the NBA's Samarpit Dal ('drowning squad') sat in *dharna* in a hut at the lowest level. This hut became the NBA headquarters in July 1991. On August 3, district police raided Manibeli and arrested 63 people.

By March 1992, hundreds of policemen virtually laid siege to the village. There were forcible evictions and a number of other atrocities. During July–September 1992, the second Manibeli *satyagraha* was organized. Rains lashed the area and the water level began to rise in the hut where the *satyagrahis* sat. But they did not move. In December, the authorities served fresh eviction notices, which were challenged in the courts.

The final siege of Manibeli by the police occurred in May–June 1993, when only 14 families were left in the village. Their demand for adequate compensation had not been met and they would not compromise.

On July 16, 1993, the river rose rapidly and submerged the huts of the 14 villagers. Manibeli, which had become synonymous with the NBA's struggle against the Sardar Sarovar Project (SSP), disappeared along with the 1000-year-old Shurpaneshwar temple.

The remaining villagers shifted to a higher level. As the height of the dam increased, the waters rose higher up the hill slope. When the water level reached too close for comfort, the villagers would dismantle their homes and move further up the hill. In this way, the residents relocated their homes and fields thrice.

Once they reached the very top of the hill, they had literally nowhere to go. In August 2006, the river fully encircled and covered the Manibeli hill. It was the end of a saga.

Manibeli, however, lives on as the symbol of resistance and struggle. On October 3, 1994, over 2000 NGOs from 44 countries issued the Manibeli Declaration calling for a moratorium on World Bank funding of large dam projects.

The story of displacement and distress is common to many of the affected villages of Narmada Valley. Nobody knows exactly how many families are affected by the project. Estimates are 35,000 in Madhya Pradesh and about 5000 each in Gujarat and Maharashtra, but the real numbers are likely to be much more. Further, the numbers keep going up as the dam height is increased. The numbers also do not tell the story of repeated relocation of some families. In general, the resettlement and rehabilitation process has been incomplete and unsatisfactory.

True development means moving higher up the hill!

Since 1994, the Narmada Control Authority has been raising the height of the main Sardar Sarovar Dam in steps to the full height of 138.64 m. More and more people are being displaced and larger areas are being submerged.

NBA's long struggle to save the people and the river seems to be ending in heartbreak. However, NBA drew national and international attention to the question: *What is true development?* That, perhaps, has been its great contribution.

CLIMATE CHANGE AND SUSTAINABLE DEVELOPMENT

Climate change and sustainable development are reciprocally connected. On one hand, climate change influences key natural and human living conditions and thereby also the basis for social and economic development. On the other hand, society's priorities on sustainable development influence the greenhouse gas emissions that are causing climate change.

What are the lessons of the Narmada case?

The story highlights the problems faced by poor people who are displaced by development projects. Such stories are common to many large projects in different parts of the world. There are many other aspects of dams like the high costs, loss of biodiversity, radical changes in the ecosystem, siltation, impact on fishing, etc. There are also the possible benefits like generation of power, supply of water for drinking and irrigation, and promotion of tourism.

In this chapter, we will consider the issues of displacement, resettlement, and rehabilitation. We will then raise the question whether this kind of development could ever be sustainable. That will lead us to alternative concepts such as Green Business and Green Economy.

What are the Reasons for Displacement of Populations?

Millions of people have had to leave their homes and move to other places, cities, or foreign countries for a variety of reasons:

- Conflicts like wars between countries, civil wars, ethnic conflicts, and religious persecution
- Natural disasters like cyclones, hurricanes, tsunamis, floods, earthquakes, volcano eruptions, and droughts
- Environmental disasters like industrial mishaps, nuclear accidents, pollution of water bodies, toxic contamination of sites, and oil spills
- Development projects in various sectors:
  - Water supply (dams, reservoirs, irrigation)
  - Urban infrastructure (roads, flyovers, beach resorts, etc.)
  - Transportation (roads, highways, canals)
  - Energy (mining, power plants, oil exploration and extraction, pipelines)
  - Agricultural expansion
  - Forests (conversion into national parks and reserves)
- Economic needs (in search of a livelihood or for improving the quality of life)
- Forcible relocation by the government under population redistribution schemes as it happened in South Africa under apartheid, China during the Cultural Revolution, and the Soviet Union in the Stalinist era.

The reasons for displacement are often interconnected. For example, a family displaced by the construction of a dam loses its livelihood and hence moves to another place for economic reasons.

When people leave an area, they may leave behind environmental problems like abandoned agricultural land. Their migration also poses environmental problems in the area into which they move. There are large refugee camps in the world that have become permanent settlements lacking in basic amenities. In other cases, the refugee group upsets the balance of the area by making unsustainable demands on the natural resources.

The UN High Commissioner for Refugees (UNHCR) predicts that economic and environmental refugees will continue to make up a significant percentage of the total refugee populations around the world, and that the number will only increase as more damage is done to the environment and as more countries become globalized and offer better opportunities than their host countries.

What are the Displacement Problems Created by Development Projects?

People who are forced to flee from a disaster or conflict usually receive sympathetic attention and international aid. The same cannot be said about the millions of people worldwide who have been displaced by development, even though the consequences they face may be every bit as grave as those faced by people displaced by other forces.

In the past, the dominant view was that large-scale development projects accelerated the pace toward a brighter and better future. If people were displaced along the way, that was deemed a necessary evil.

In recent times, however, a new development paradigm has been articulated, one that promotes poverty reduction, environmental protection, social justice, and human rights. In this paradigm, development is seen as both bringing benefits and imposing costs. Among its greatest costs has been the displacement of millions of vulnerable people.

The World Bank estimates that every year since 1990, roughly 10 million people worldwide have been displaced by development projects for a variety of reasons. During the last 50 years, development projects have displaced 25 million people in India and 40 million in China (of whom, 13.6 million were displaced in the 1990s alone). Read about China's Three Gorges Dam in Box 17.1.

BOX 17.1 HOPE OR DESPAIR? *The Story of the Three Gorges Dam*

Until recently, Huang Zongjin was a poor farmer cultivating rice and vegetables on the banks of the Yangtze river near Wushan town in China. One day, his world changed, suddenly and totally. He has now become Huang the boatman, ferrying tourists up the Yangtze.

The Government had decided to build a dam on the Yangtze (known in China as 'the dragon'), just downstream from the place known as Three Gorges. Huang and more than 700,000 others were asked to move, leaving their homes and fields, which were to be submerged in water.

If completed, the Three Gorges Dam on the Yangtze will be the largest hydroelectric dam in the world. It will stretch nearly 1.5 km across and tower 200 m above the world's third longest river. Construction began in 1994 and is scheduled to take 20 years and cost over US$24 billion. The river is no longer seen as an unstoppable force, but as a dragon, which can be tamed by technology.

The expected benefits of the dam include the prevention of the devastating Yangtze basin floods, which have killed millions of people, and the generation of 18,200 MW of electricity, supplying a tenth of China's needs. The power generated would be equivalent to operating more than a dozen nuclear power plants or burning 50 million tonnes of coal. It is a remarkable feat of engineering.

Outside China, the project has been strongly criticized for the corruption, secrecy, financial incompetence, human rights violations, and possible environmental consequences. The reservoir will partially or completely inundate 2 cities, 11 countries, 140 towns, 326 townships, and 1351 villages.

Between one and two million people will have to be resettled, accounting for about one-third of the project's cost. Many critics believe resettlement would fail and create reservoir refugees. The forced migration would raise social unrest. Many of the residents to be resettled are peasants. They would be forced to move from fertile farmland to much less desirable areas.

By October 2003, the second stage was over, the water had risen, 700,000 people had been relocated, and the dam was finally producing electricity. The Dam reached its maximum reservoir water level of 175 m in October 2010. It should now be able to generate full power.

Most of the people seem to be either positive or fatalistic about the dam. Huang Zongjin used his compensation money to buy the dilapidated boat. The government has built the family a new, far bigger, hillside home, but as yet it has no running water or electricity. The land is too steep to be cultivated.

Huang, however, is sanguine. 'I may float over my old home every day, but I never think about it. What's the point?' he says. 'We can't change anything. And besides, life is better now. We have a new home, more space and more money. The dam has been good for us.'

Is it good for everybody? Is it good for the environment? Will the dam surprise everybody one day with its secrets?

> **Key Idea** Millions of people in the world have been displaced from their homes and lands due to development projects and environmental changes.

The displaced people may not have crossed a border and may not be considered to be in 'refugee-like' circumstances within their own country. Nevertheless, they have been evicted from their homes or places of habitual residence, had their lives and livelihood disrupted, and face the uncertainties of resettling in unfamiliar and often inhospitable locations.

What are the Special Problems with Regard to Displacement by Dams?

After a multi-year study, the World Commission on Dams (WCD) listed the following social impacts of dams in its report published in 2000:

- Dams have physically displaced some 40–80 million people worldwide.
- Millions of people living downstream from dams—particularly those reliant on natural floodplain function and fisheries—have also suffered serious harm to their livelihood and the future productivity of their resources has been put at risk.
- Many of the displaced were not recognized (or enumerated) as such, and therefore were not resettled or compensated.
- Where compensation was provided, it was often inadequate, and where the physically displaced were enumerated, many were not included in resettlement programmes.
- Those who were resettled rarely had their livelihood restored, as resettlement programmes have focused on physical relocation rather than the economic and social development of the displaced.
- The larger the magnitude of displacement, the less likely it is that even the livelihood of affected communities can be restored.
- Even in the 1990s, impacts on downstream livelihood were, in many cases, not adequately assessed or addressed in the planning and design of large dams.

The WCD report noted that poor people, other vulnerable groups, and future generations were likely to bear a disproportionate share of the social and environmental costs of large dam projects without gaining a commensurate share of the economic benefits:

- Indigenous and tribal people and vulnerable ethnic minorities have suffered disproportionate levels of displacement and negative impacts on livelihood, culture, and spiritual existence. The outcomes have included loss of assets, unemployment, debt-bondage, hunger, and cultural disintegration.
- Affected populations living near reservoirs as well as displaced people and downstream communities have often faced adverse health and livelihood outcomes from environmental change and social disruption.
- Among affected communities, gender gaps have widened and women have frequently borne a disproportionate share of the social costs and were often discriminated against in the sharing of benefits.

The Report concluded, 'impoverishment and disempowerment have been the rule rather than the exception with respect to resettled people around the world.' The Report gave specific recommendations to national government, NGOs, affected people's organizations, private sector, aid agencies, and development banks on all aspects including displacement and resettlement.

What are the Issues Concerning the Resettlement and Rehabilitation of Displaced Groups?

The majority of displacement and resettlement programmes involving large populations has occurred in the developing countries. The reasons are the massive development projects financed by foreign aid and international agencies and high densities of population.

Some of the problems faced by the displaced people are the following:

- The compensation for the lost land is often not paid or delayed, and even if paid, the amounts are pitifully small. The oustees are rarely able to start new lives with the compensation. To add to the problem, agents and corrupt officials deprive the poor of the full compensation.
- Generally, the new land that is offered is of poor quality and the refugees are unable to make a living.

- Basic infrastructure and amenities are not provided in the new area. Very often, temporary camps become permanent settlements.
- When tribal groups are displaced, they do not get any compensation, since they have no legal title to the land.
- Ethnic and caste differences make it difficult for the refugees to live peacefully with the communities already living in the area.

Key Idea Resettlement and rehabilitation of displaced people have generally been unsatisfactory.

In India, we are in the process of rapid economic development. Poor people are being increasingly displaced from their homes and lands to make way for a variety of projects: mines, large industries, Special Economic Zones, highways, airports, power plants, educational institutions, dams, canals, national parks, reserve forests, and so on. We have to ask ourselves: Is this unceasing development, displacement of people, and exploitation of natural resources sustainable? What are their real costs?

Is Sustainable Development Still a Meaningful Concept?

In Chapter 1, we introduced the concept of sustainable development. Recall the definition of sustainable development given by WCED in 1987:

Sustainable development is development that meets the needs of the present without compromising the ability of future generations to meet their own needs.

This definition contains within it two key concepts:

- The concept of needs, in particular the essential needs of the world's poor, to which overriding priority should be given.
- The idea of limitations imposed by the state of technology and social organization on the environment's ability to meet present and future needs.

The definition implies that unceasing economic development and environmental conservation could go together. But such a concept seems to be a contradiction in terms. If we continue with the current model of economic growth and development, we cannot sustain it indefinitely. If we use the natural resources in a sustainable way, we cannot show continuous economic growth.

Key Idea The popular Brundtland definition of sustainable development reads well but is perhaps impossible to implement.

While the term 'sustainable development' continues to be used, newer concepts such as New Economics, Green Economy, Green Business, Sustainable Business, and Eco-economy are gaining currency. They are often projected as answers to the challenge posed by global warming and climate change (Chapters 14 and 15).

The alternative approaches raise and try to answer questions such as the following:

- In the face of the environmental devastation being caused by current economic systems, how can we move to more sustainable economic models?
- What do the concepts of ecological sustainability and sustainable development really mean and how can they be achieved?
- Can the value of an environment be measured?
- Is GDP the appropriate measure of 'growth'? What is the real 'growth' of a society we should aim at?
- What tools for change exist within the current system?
- How can we make the transition from a global to a local economy, from efficiency to sufficiency?

The objectives that seem to be common to many of these alternative models are to:

- achieve full employment by providing an ongoing means of livelihood for all job seekers.
- protect and restore the environment for present and future generations.
- ensure healthy communities based on the sustainable use of local resources for local consumption and regional trade, the availability of meaningful work, and the opportunity for creative, diverse cultural expression.
- measure the success of the economy by the improvement in the well-being of all people and the development of healthy, vibrant, diverse communities, rather than by the total monetary value of economic activity.

We can 'green' the economy by modifying our businesses and infrastructure such that we get proper returns on our natural, human, and economic investments, while at the same time, reducing greenhouse gas emissions, extracting and using less natural resources, creating less waste, and reducing social disparities.

A green economy would focus on areas such as:

- Promoting renewable energies including wind, solar, geothermal, and biomass
- Working towards sustainable transport options including hybrid vehicles, high-speed rail, and bus rapid transit systems
- Restoring and conserving the planet's ecological infrastructure, including fresh waters, forests, soils, and coral reefs
- Supporting sustainable agriculture, including organic farming
- Improving the energy efficiency of old and new buildings

Is Green Economy being Promoted in Any Way?

There are Green Economy initiatives being taken by international agencies, countries, corporate associations, and companies. Here are some examples:

UNEP Green Economy Initiative (GEI): The GEI is designed to assist governments in 'greening' their economies by reshaping and refocusing policies, investments, and spending towards a range of sectors, such as clean technologies, renewable energies, water services, green transportation, waste management, green buildings, and sustainable agriculture and forests. GEI activities include providing advisory services to countries and regions producing research reports, and engaging in partnerships to effectively promote and implement green economy strategies.

UNESCAP Green Growth Initiative: With the support of the UN Economic and Social Commission for Asia and the Pacific (UN ESCAP), the Governments in the Asian and Pacific region have unanimously agreed to respond to the challenges of simultaneously improving people's lives and conserving natural resources through the promising path of environmentally sustainable economic growth, or 'Green Growth'. This is a strategy to foster creative sustainability responses for the region. The Green Growth Initiative proposes to harness the power of economic growth while guiding it in a way that will enhance the immense possibilities provided by innovative technologies and industries, so that progress can be registered in more than gross domestic product increases alone.

UN Sustainable Development Goals: The Millennium Development Goals (MDGs) were eight international development goals that were established following the UN Millennium Summit in the year 2000. The eight MDGs were:

1. Eradicate extreme poverty and hunger
2. Achieve universal primary education
3. Promote gender equality and empower women
4. Reduce child mortality
5. Improve maternal health
6. Combat HIV, malaria, and other diseases
7. Ensure environmental sustainability
8. Develop a global partnership for development

Countries were expected to meet the MDGs by 2015, but the implementation was not very effective. Further, the MDGs failed to consider the root causes of poverty, gender inequality, or the holistic nature of development. The goals made no mention of human rights, nor specifically addressed economic development.

As 2015 neared, the UN conducted a large consultation to come up with Sustainable Development Goals, which would follow and build on the MDGs (Chapter 1, Box 1.3).

Country initiatives

Here are some examples:

- Denmark is moving away from fossil fuels (Visit the ORC for this story).
- Iceland is working towards a hydrogen economy (Visit the ORC for this story).
- South Africa, after holding a Green Economy Summit held in May 2010, is developing a Green Economy Plan. The country is investing on 'green' jobs, railways, energy efficient buildings, and water and waste management.
- Kenya is implementing a US$99 million restoration of the entire Mau Forest Complex, the largest closed-canopy forest ecosystem in Kenya covering over 400,000 ha. The country has committed to go totally green by 2017 and to restore the forest cover to 10% by 2020. Currently, the government has launched a green energy campaign and mobilized $1 billion to construct a 280MW geothermal power plant.
- Rwanda, Uganda, and other African countries are investing in green economic sectors such as renewable energies and energy efficiency improvements, sustainable agriculture, and better management of water and waste.
- India announced in 2008, a National Action Plan on Climate Change (Chapter 14, Box 14.4). This Plan has many features of a Green Economy.

Many developing countries report success stories, which are described in the UNEP Green Economy Report. UNEP believes that such green investments and policies, if scaled up and integrated into a comprehensive strategy, could offer an alternative development pathway, one that is pro-nature, pro-jobs, and pro-poor.

Ceres (pronounced 'series')

This is a national network of investors, environmental organizations, and other public interest groups working with companies and investors to address sustainability challenges such as global climate change. The mission of Ceres is to integrate sustainability into capital markets for the health of the planet and its people.

The Ceres Coalition of over 130 investor groups, environmental organizations, and investment funds engages directly with companies on environmental and social issues. Ceres companies seek to attain long-term business value and to improve management quality through stakeholder engagement, public disclosure, and performance improvements.

In 1989, Ceres announced the creation of the Ceres Principles, a 10-point code of corporate environmental conduct to be publicly endorsed by companies as an environmental mission statement or ethic (Box 17.2). Over 70 companies have endorsed the Ceres Principles.

BOX 17.2 HOPE: ***The Ceres Principles—Greening the Corporation***

Ceres offers 10 principles as a comprehensive statement of environmental values for businesses within any industry sector. They are intended to help companies formalize their dedication to environmental awareness and accountability, and actively commit to an ongoing process of continuous improvement in environmental performance, dialogue, and comprehensive, systematic reporting.

The 10 CERES Principles cover the following themes:

- Protection of the Biosphere
- Sustainable Use of Natural Resources
- Reduction and Disposal of Wastes
- Energy Conservation
- Risk Reduction
- Safe Products and Services
- Environmental Restoration
- Informing the Public
- Management Commitment
- Auditing and Reporting

(For details, visit www.ceres.org)

By endorsing the Ceres Principles or adopting their own comparable code, companies not only formalize their dedication to environmental awareness and accountability, but also actively commit to an ongoing process of continuous improvement, dialogue, and comprehensive, systematic public reporting.

In 1997, Ceres, in partnership with UNEP, established the Global Reporting Initiative (GRI) with the mission of developing globally applicable guidelines for reporting on the economic, environmental, and social performance of corporations, governments, and non-governmental organizations (NGOs). GRI incorporates the active participation of corporations, NGOs, accountancy organizations, business associations, and other stakeholders from around the world.

GRI has become the *de facto* international standard in sustainability reporting and currently, more than 1500 companies and organizations worldwide issue GRI-based sustainability reports.

Interface

Ray Anderson was the Chairman and founder of Interface, the world's largest manufacturer of commercial carpets, located in the US. The way he began turning Interface into a totally sustainable corporation is a remarkable story (Box 17.3). More companies are following the path of sustainability.

BOX 17.3 INSPIRATION: ***The Story of Ray Anderson—Building a Sustainable Corporation***

Ray Anderson was the Chairman and founder of Interface, the world's largest commercial carpet manufacturer. The company has 26 factories in six countries. In 1994, Anderson realized that, as the head of a company, he was 'plundering' the natural resources of the world. He decided to convert Interface into a totally sustainable green corporation. What he did has now become a legend.

Anderson came up with Ecosense, a vision for 2020. He wanted Interface to become totally sustainable by 2020 and also to help others to become sustainable. He planned the following steps:

- Reduce, reuse, reclaim, redesign
- Adopt best practices, share them
- Develop sustainable technologies
- Challenge suppliers to follow

Since his change of heart, Anderson implemented hundreds of projects in the company with these objectives in mind:

- Zero-waste generation
- Minimum energy use
- Eventual zero use of fossil fuels

Interface now leases out carpets instead of selling them. For a monthly charge, the company installs, cleans, and maintains the carpets. It repairs worn-out tiles and recycles old carpets into new ones.

The company has developed a new carpet material called solenium, which can be completely recycled. It requires 40% less raw material and energy, generates very little waste, and lasts much longer.

By 2009, Interface had reached a sound position:

- It was halfway towards the goal of total sustainability.
- It has sharply reduced energy use and waste generation and saved millions of dollars, and costs are down.
- The products were the best they have ever been.
- Its people were galvanized around a shared higher purpose.
- The company's goodwill in the marketplace was far better than what any amount of advertisement could have brought.

Interface was ranked first in the Sustainability Survey, a survey of global sustainability thought leaders conducted by GlobeScan.

Anderson himself gave up his luxury car for a hybrid car and built a home without a grid connection. He was named one of TIME International's 'Heroes of the Environment' in 2007. He was co-chairman of the President's Council on Sustainable Development and was an architect of the Presidential Climate Action Plan, a 100-day action plan on climate that was presented to the Obama Administration.

The company is a model to follow, because, even as it moved towards sustainability, it tripled its profits. Green business can also be good business!

Ray Anderson died of cancer in 2011 before realizing his full vision for Interface. His family has launched the Ray Anderson Foundation with a mission to create a brighter, sustainable world through the funding of innovative projects that promote and advance the concepts of sustainable production and consumption.

What can India Do to Promote a Green Economy and Green Jobs?

Lack of employment is the main source of poverty in India. A study by the Centre for Science and Environment, New Delhi, suggests that the key to generating employment lies in promoting productive and sustainable livelihood based on natural resources. We should renew and revive the key livelihood areas of agriculture, forestry, livestock, fishing, and horticulture, by promoting sustainable occupations in these sectors. The existing impediments to such development should be removed.

Some examples of such green livelihood that would generate employment and income and at the same time, conserve the environment are:

- Bamboo: It is an exceptionally versatile plant with about 1500 uses, including as a building material and for making paper, handicrafts, and agricultural appliances. It generates 10 million jobs presently and can provide 8.6 million jobs more. The main hurdle is that it remains a monopoly of the forest department. It should be declared as an agricultural item, permitting people to cultivate, harvest, process, and sell it in various forms.
- Fuelwood: Wood plantations on degraded land can be promoted and managed by the women head-loaders (Chapter 6) or the community and fuelwood trade can be legitimized. Apart from generating huge employment, we will also be promoting renewable energy in a big way. The plantations will also give timber for homes and village industries and help regenerate the soil.
- Tree plantations for pulp and paper sector: An area of about 1 million ha can produce the 5 million tonnes of raw material the industry needs every year. This could generate employment for 550,000 families.

Key Idea There are attempts in different parts of the world by different groups to move towards a more sustainable 'green' economy.

For such green livelihood to succeed, changes in laws and policies are needed. There should be a shift from conservation to sustainable utilization of natural resources. Laws that prohibit the growing, transporting, and marketing of trees like the bamboo should be repealed or modified.

What is a Circular Economy?

We saw in Chapter 1 that we are now using resources faster than they can regenerate and creating waste faster than it can be absorbed. We can call it a linear economy, in which we take resources, make things, consume them, and throw them away. This way of living uses up finite raw materials and produces vast quantities of waste.

According to the World Economic Forum, a Circular Economy is an alternative to this linear economy. In a Circular Economy, products are used again and again, which reduces our use of precious raw materials and cuts CO_2 emissions. In such an economy, things are made and consumed in a way that minimizes our use of the world's resources, cuts waste, and reduces carbon emissions. Products are kept in use for as long as possible, through repairing, recycling, and redesign – so they can be used again and again. At the end of a product's life, the materials used to make it are kept in the economy and reused wherever possible.

Moving to a Circular Economy will not be easy. It will require a deep system change. Consumers, businesses, and politicians all need to make changes to how goods are designed, produced, sold, manufactured, and reused.

Ending on a Hopeful Note: Positive Stories

While the general displacement and rehabilitation scene is depressing, there are some success stories too, like that of Tawa Matsya Sangh in Madhya Pradesh. Even here, the initial success has been followed by disappointment later (Box 17.4).

BOX 17.4 HOPE AND DESPAIR: *The Story of Tawa Matsya Sangh—From Forests to Fisheries*

Most people displaced by development projects end up losing everything—their lands, livelihood, and shelter. In most cases, they do not get any compensation for their lands and even if they do, the amount is grossly inadequate. This story, from Madhya Pradesh, however, is one of hope.

A dam on the River Tawa, a tributary of Narmada, submerged 20,000 ha and displaced over 4000 *adivasi* families in 44 villages. More than half the villages were on forestland and hence the people got no compensation at all.

Normally, these oustees would have migrated to other villages or towns in search of livelihood. This group, however, campaigned for and secured fishing rights in the reservoir created by the dam. The *adivasis* learnt how to spread nets, use boats, and do the fishing operations.

They formed the Tawa Matsya Sangh (TMS), a federation of primary fishermen's cooperative societies with 1200 members. In 1996, TMS was given a five-year lease by the government. TMS was in charge of overall management and was responsible for stocking the reservoir with fish. It also took care of transport and sale of fish, regulatory measures for conservation, and members' welfare.

The former hunter-gatherers became good fishermen and the harvest was good. TMS made profits and shared it with the members. It even paid wages to them during the lean season, between June and August when there was an agreed ban fishing. TMS was also able to pay the agreed royalty to the government.

It was a rare case of dam oustees doing well in a new occupation, but troubles were ahead. When the lease was renewed, the government steeply increased the royalty amount. In return, however, the government agency did little to improve the infrastructure. Even the promised ice factory was not built. Under the new terms, TMS was also subject to greater government control. In fact, the government appointed a review committee to evaluate the performance of TMS, but did not share the report with them. In December 2006, TMS lost its licence. Later, the area came under the Satpura Tiger Reserve, fishing was banned, and that was the end of TMS.

Though short-lived, TMS is a great example of how displaced people could come together and rehabilitate themselves.

REVIEW: A SUMMARY OF THE KEY POINTS

- There is increasing displacement of populations due to a variety of reasons.
- The resettlement and rehabilitation of displaced people have been poor in most projects.
- New concepts such as Green Economy and Green Business have emerged in our search for sustainability.
- UN Sustainable Development Goals would follow and build on the Millennium Development Goals.
- Green Economy initiatives are being taken by international agencies, countries, corporate associations, and companies.
- India can follow its own path in developing a Green Economy.

EXERCISES

Objective-type questions

For each question below, choose the best answer out of the given choices.

1. What is the importance of the village Manibeli?
   (a) It is in Maharashtra part of the Narmada Dam project.
   (b) The villagers had to leave Manibeli in 2003.
   (c) It was submerged in the waters in 2006.
   (d) It has become a symbol of resistance and struggle against displacement and lack of proper resettlement.
2. Which of the following **may not** be a case of displacement due to development projects?
   (a) Dam oustees moving to another area.
   (b) Forest tribals resettled outside the forest.
   (c) Poor people migrating to cities looking for work.
   (d) People leaving an area due to the coming of a new airport.
3. Which of the following statements is **not** true with regard to people displaced due the construction of dams?
   (a) They are always resettled and rehabilitated well.
   (b) The compensation is often poor or not paid.
   (c) The new land that is offered is often of poor quality.
   (d) Very often, temporary camps become permanent settlements.
4. Which of the following **cannot** be a valid and meaningful approach for the world?
   (a) Being sustainable.
   (b) Exploit nature without limit.
   (c) Consume less.
   (d) Respect nature.
5. Which of the following activities would **not** be acceptable in a green economy?
   (a) Generating solar energy
   (b) Organic agriculture
   (c) Burning LPG
   (d) Promoting public transport
6. Which of the following is very clearly a Sustainable Development Goal?
   (a) Reduce child and maternal deaths
   (b) Achieve universal education
   (c) Promote gender equality
   (d) Take action to combat climate change

Short-answer questions

1. Explain the reasons for the displacement of populations and its impact.
2. Describe the special problems of displacement caused by dams.
3. Discuss the issues concerning the resettlement and rehabilitation of displaced groups.

4. What are the questions raised by those who propose alternate models of economy?
5. Describe any two Green Economy initiatives.
6. Give two examples of green livelihood that would generate employment and income and at the same time conserve the environment in India.
7. Compare linear economy and circular economy.

Long-answer question

Write an essay on the impact of dams on people. What are the usual expected benefits? What are the negative impacts on people? What does the World Commission on Dams say on the topic? What do the cases of Narmada and the Three Gorges dams illustrate?

Think critically: Deeper question for reflection and discussion

If constant economic growth is neither possible nor desirable, what kind of 'growth' should a society aim for? Are Gandhiji's ideas relevant to this question?

ENJOY AND EDUCATE YOURSELF

1. Watch the movie *Wild River* (1960), starring: Montgomery Clift and Lee Remick. The story is about the building of a dam across the Tennessee River, displacement of people, and the resistance by one octogenarian lady.
2. Relax with the novel *The Shaping of Water* by Ruth Hartley. The plot is about a decision by the government of Rhodesia (now Zimbabwe) to build a dam across the mighty Zambezi. The dam creates a vast man-made lake, displaces the river people (the Tongas), and forever changes the ecology of the region.

ACCESS THE OUP ONLINE RESOURCE CENTRE FOR MORE

- 1994 Manibeli Declaration Calling for a Moratorium on World Bank Funding of Large Dams
- Transcript of 1994 Letter Dictated by Bava Mahalia of Jalsindhi Village, addressed to the Chief Minister of Madhya Pradesh
- List of UN Decades with reference to the environment.
- Additional text and other recommended references, websites, and films

UNIT 8

Project and Field Work

18 Project Work and Case Studies

MAIN QUESTIONS ADDRESSED

- How should you carry out field work and document your observations and conclusions?
- Where are the case studies and what could be the discussion questions?

Why should You Carry out Field Work?

In this book, we have covered a wide variety of environmental problems facing India and the world. You may not have imagined that the state of the environment was so serious. You may not even believe that all that has been said in this book is true.

How does one verify and validate the various descriptions and ideas presented in the book? One way of doing this would be to embark on field work and carry out a project. It can be either undertaken individually or as a group activity.

Field work gives you an opportunity to find out for yourself how things are in the real world. In doing the project, you will be involving yourself in a micro-level situation. You will then begin to appreciate the real nature and complexity of the environmental problems facing us today. You will also have the satisfaction of moving from being a part of the problem to becoming a part of the solution.

A group project also gives you the chance to work together with others who may not always agree with you. The lessons you will learn in working in a team will be of great value to you in your career and of course, in your life itself.

How should You Choose the Project for your Field Work?

Choose a project that you can complete in the time that you have. It is far better to do a thorough job with a small project, instead of taking on a big one and leave it unfinished at the end.

Here are some criteria you can use while choosing a project. They are given in the form of a checklist of questions you can ask yourself:

- Attraction of topic: Do I have a basic interest in the topic? Am I going along just because others have chosen the topic?
- Usefulness: Will I be able to make a modest and yet useful contribution to a given real-life situation?
- Specialist knowledge needed: Does the project need any specialist information and if so, can I equip myself with it before I begin the work? Are there accessible experts whom I can consult?
- Work already done by other groups: Are there reports prepared by others who have been to the site earlier? Does the project sound interesting, judging from these reports?

- Measurability: Will I be able to measure the impact of my work?
- Accessibility and facilities: Is the project location easily accessible? If I am carrying out the project on a full-time basis, is there any accommodation available at or near the project site?
- Weekend projects: If it is going to be a weekend project, will I be able to do some work each week, adding up to a meaningful whole?
- Future work: Given the short time frame, it may not be possible for me to achieve all my objectives; is there scope to do things later as follow-up measures?

If the answer is 'yes' to many of these questions, the project is worth doing.

At the end of each chapter in this book, suggestions for project work were given. More ideas are listed below:

- Documenting environmental resources like river, forest, grassland, hill, mountain in a specific area
- Study of a polluted site in an urban, rural, industrial, agricultural area
- Study of simple ecosystems: ponds, rivers, hill slopes

Project ideas classified by discipline of student:

- English: Study of fiction on the theme of environment
- Botany/Zoology: Study of plants, insects, birds, etc. in a specific area; tracing the origins of different plants, trees, vegetables, and fruits available in an area; study of any seed bank preserving indigenous species.
- Chemistry: Testing water quality in an area
- Engineering: Design or study of a composting unit, wastewater treatment facility, etc.
- Geography: Resource mapping of a village
- Philosophy: Studies on environmental ethics
- Economics: Study of alternative economic models
- Architecture: Study of buildings designed using ideas of ecological architecture
- Design, fine arts, crafts, etc.: Designing products with waste material, improving the design of solar energy products like lanterns and cookers.
- Performing arts: Effective ways of communicating to people and mobilizing them for preserving our environment (staging street performances or designing a brochure on a specific topic).

Should you seek a project within an organization?

It is best to work as a volunteer/project trainee with an organization that has been working in the area or site. It could be a voluntary organization (NGO), a government department, or even a company that is funding and managing an environmental or social project.

How should You Prepare Yourself for the Project Work?

- Get access to a tablet or laptop with internet access.
- Define objectives: Start with a list and revise it as you go along.
- Formulate the questions: List the questions you expect to answer through the project.
- Conduct a literature survey: Do a thorough study of the literature available on the topic (books, reports, news items, etc.).
- Maintain a bibliography: Remember to enter in a computer file the full bibliographic details right when you access any item of information—in a book, periodical, or website. Otherwise, you will be desperately searching for the details while writing the report.

- Don't believe everything you find on the Internet: There is a mix of reliable and unreliable information on websites. Hence, cross-check the facts. Rely mostly on reports by international organizations including UN agencies.
- Keep notes: During the literature survey and throughout the project period, keep entering your findings on files.
- If you do not have easy access to a laptop: Use cards of about 10 cm × 15 cm size to write your notes. Each card should contain one main idea and should carry the name of the topic/subtopic at the top right corner. This way it will be easy to shuffle and arrange the cards according to the topic. It will enormously simplify the writing process at the end.
- Meet concerned persons: If you are going to interview a person, go prepared with a set of questions. Take a digital recorder along but take the person's permission before recording the interview.
- Obtain any permission needed for entering the project site.
- Letter from college/university: Always carry a letter of introduction from your institution and your identity card.
- Collect any equipment needed for the project.

How should You Conduct the Field Study?

- Plan each visit or trip meticulously.
- Keep a diary and make detailed notes at the end of each day.
- Take photos or short videos on a regular basis, especially to show the situation before and after an intervention.
- Always be punctual and keep any deadlines you have agreed to.
- Keep your guides/supervisors (on site and at your institution) informed of the progress and seek their advice.
- At the end of the project, make sure that you return all borrowed material and leave the organization on a pleasant note.
- Take a certificate about your work from the organization. Your institution may ask for it and it will also be useful to you later.
- Later, remember to give the organization a copy of your report.

How should You Write the Report?

- Time frame: Allow yourself enough time to write a good report. Ultimately, what you have done comes out only through the report.
- The general format of the report could be the following, but follow any guidelines set by your institution or guide:
  - Executive summary
  - Contents
  - Acknowledgements
  - Preface
  - Introduction: The problem or ecosystem in brief; objectives of study
  - Background: literature survey
  - Observations and results
  - Conclusions and recommendations

- References (books, articles, websites, etc.)
- Photographs and videos

- Language and style: Read the slim volume *Elements of Style* by Strunk and White. It is a classic with very useful tips. Keep the language as simple as possible. If your language abilities are weak, get the draft corrected by a professional.
- Word processing: Do not depend too much on the software to correct the grammar and usage.
- Approval of the draft report: Get the draft approved by the organization, and your guides.
- Revision and final version: Check for typographical errors.
- Printing and submission: Follow any guidelines given on the size, number of copies, etc.

How should You Prepare for a Viva-voce Examination, if There is One?

- Prepare presentation slides for a computer presentation.
- Each slide should have not more than 10 lines of text. Do not read out what everyone can see. The points on a slide are only to trigger your memory.
- Prepare ahead for possible questions.

In Which Other Ways can You Use the Project Work and the Report?

- A good project report can be used in job interviews and in applications for admission to courses.
- If you are looking for a career in environment, send an electronic copy of the report to organizations that have openings.
- Write an article on your work for the appropriate journal, magazine, newspaper, or website.

Ideas for Project Work

General

1. Study your neighbourhood, your town, or your ancestral village. What are the key environmental issues faced by the place? What are the conflicting interests in each case?
2. Participate in tree plantation drives and nature camps organized by environmental NGOs.

Ecosystems

1. Choose a small ecosystem like a pond or a garden that is relatively undisturbed. Observe the ecosystem over three months or more and keep a log of your observations. Try to identify the producers, consumers, and decomposers.
2. Choose a small animal or bird that you can watch in your back garden or a nearby park. Observe the behaviour of the organism regularly and keep a journal of your observations. Watch what the organism eats, what it rejects, where does it live, over which area does it move, how does it reproduce, which organisms are its predators, etc.

Forest Resources

1. If possible, spend your vacation in a forest area, observing the biotic species and abiotic conditions, the lives of the local people, and efforts of environmental groups. Write a report on the environmental and social problems in the area and suggest solutions.
2. Many states have programmes to promote joint forest management (JFM). With the permission of the concerned forest department, study any one programme. Spend a few days or weeks living with

the forest communities. Interview local people as well as foresters. Write a report evaluating the JFM. Focus on the situation before and after the implementation of JFM.

3. Study any movement against a specific development or conservation project in a forest area like the construction of a dam or the establishment of a protected area. Write a report giving your assessment of the situation. Suggest alternatives that may be acceptable to the government and the people.

Wetlands

Locate a wetland and study it over a period of (at least) three months as an ecosystem. Trace the inflow and outflow of water. What are the plant and animal species found in the ecosystem? What kind of services does the wetland provide? What are the threats faced by the system and how best to face them? Write a report on your study.

Water Resources

1. Choose a village, town, or city as a unit for study. Examine the water situation in the place by finding answers to the following questions and write a report.
   - Where does the water the people use come from? What is its ecological footprint?
   - How much does it cost the users?
   - How much does it cost to supply the water?
   - What is the pattern of water use by the people?
   - Where does the waste water go?
2. Examine the water usage of a small community (a village, a locality in a city, an apartment block) and write a report on actions that could be taken for conserving water:
   - How can the demand for water be reduced?
   - How can the ecological footprint of the water they get be reduced?
   - What other environment-friendly ways of getting water can one implement?
   - How can the quality of the water be protected?
   - How can people reuse and recycle water?
   - How can you educate the users about the proper use of water?
3. Examine the water usage in your college (as in S.No 2).

Agriculture

Spend some time at an organic farm and a 'normal' farm that follows the Green Revolution approach. Study the methods used in the farms and compare them. Write a report detailing the environmental and economic aspects. Describe also how the 'normal' farm can convert itself into an organic one.

Energy

Do an energy audit of your college. Examine the consumption of all forms of energy over three months and find out how much energy each activity consumes. Find out also the cost aspects. Come up with proposals for (a) reducing the demand, (b) increasing the energy efficiency, and (c) ways of using renewable energy.

Biodiversity

1. Select a small park or garden in your area. Prepare a biodiversity register: List all the species found in the place, find their scientific names with the help of a botanist and a zoologist. Interview long-term users of the place and find out if any loss of biodiversity has been observed or whether they

have noticed new species. Write a report describing your observations and your recommendations for conserving the biodiversity of the place.

2. Choose a small village and prepare a detailed biodiversity register listing the species found within the boundaries of the village. Take the help of a biologist to identify the plants. Before starting the project, discuss the issues of biodiversity and biopiracy with the villagers and explain the advantages of preparing a register. Involve the villagers, especially the youth, in the project.
3. Document the biodiversity of your college campus. Collect specimens of species, find out their scientific names and other details and exhibit them in the science lab.

Pollution

1. Trace the path of the waste that you dump in your street bin. Interview conservancy workers, municipal officials, rag-pickers, waste dealers, etc. Write a report answering questions such as:
   - Where does the truck take the waste?
   - Is it treated in any way or is it just dumped on land?
   - What do the rag-pickers collect, how much, and where do they sell it? How can we assess the role of this unorganized sector in waste management?
   - Does the waste contaminate soil, water, and air?
   - How much of the waste is recycled and what are the processes used? Is there a waste from recycling?
   - What is the economics of the recycling trade?
2. Approach the National River Conservation Authority and volunteer your services. Join a team that is implementing an Action Plan for a river in your state or in a neighbouring one. Spend at least three weeks working with the team or any ecologist in the team. Write a report describing the state of the river, the sources of pollution, the Action Plan, methods used for field-level implementation, problems encountered, results achieved, etc.
3. Volunteer your services to the Central Pollution Control Board for its programme of monitoring the air quality in the cities. Work with the monitoring unit for two or three weeks and write a report on your experience. Include in your report a description of the measuring equipment, the parameters that are measured, how the parameters changed over the period you were involved, etc.
4. Study the solid waste disposal, sanitation, and sewage treatment in your college campus and propose improvements.

Environmental Law

Get in touch with any individual or group of environmental lawyers in your area. Volunteer your services for a few weeks and help them with a case. Write a report on the case. What were the issues? Who are the parties to the case? Which of the laws are involved?

Sustainable Development

Visit the site of any project that has displaced people. Study the project documents and examine the plans and reports regarding resettlement and rehabilitation. Interview some of the oustees and record their experiences. Write a report outlining what was promised and what was delivered as far as resettlement and rehabilitation were concerned. What are your recommendations?

Case Studies for Discussion

The national and international case studies described in this book are listed in Tables 18.1 and 18.2 respectively. Note that, in these tables, ORC refers to the Online Resource Centre.

TABLE 18.1 National Case Studies

S No	Title	Chap	Location
1	The Story of Ghoramara: Climate Change And Vanishing Islands	1	Lead Story
2	CONNECTIONS: Vultures, Cows, Wild Dogs, And Rabies	1	Box 1.4
3	The Story of Kalahandi: From Forests To Famine	1	ORC
4	The Story of The Himalayas: Climate Change And Melting Glaciers	2	Lead Story
5	The Story of Sunderlal Bahuguna	2	ORC
6	UN World Restoration Flagship Programmes	2	ORC
7	The Story of The Western Ghats	3	Lead Story
8	INSPIRATION: The Story of The Bishnois	3	Box 3.2
9	HOPE: The Story of Silent Valley	3	Box 3.3
10	The Story of The Gulf of Mannar	4	Lead Story
11	ECOSYSTEM: The Story of Bengaluru's Lakes	4	Box 4.5
12	ECOSYSTEM: The Story of Chilika Lake	4	Box 4.6
13	Namami Gange Programme	4	Box 4.7
14	The Story of Lake Victoria: Reap What You Sow	4	ORC
15	The Story of Cherrapunji	5	Lead Story
16	INSPIRATION: The Story of Plachimada	5	Box 5.4
17	Controversy: Interlinking Indian Rivers	5	Box 5.5
18	The Ken-Betwa Project	5	Box 5.6
19	INSPIRATION: Water Conservation In India	5	Box 5.9
20	The Story of Water Conservation In Rajasthan By Rajendra Singh And Tarun Bharat Sangh	5	ORC
21	The Story of the Andaman and Nicobar Islands	6	Lead Story
22	INSPIRATION: The Story of Chipko	6	Box 6.4
23	INSPIRATION: The Story of Thimmakka	6	Box 6.5
24	The Story of Punjab: Poverty of Plenty?	7	Lead Story
25	CONTROVERSY: The Story of Bt Brinjal	7	Box 7.4
26	ECOSYSTEM: The Story of The Aravalli Hills	7	Box 7.5
27	INSPIRATION: The Story of Cuba	7	Box 7.6
28	INSPIRATION: Nammalvar	7	Box 7.7
29	The story of Ramesh Dagar	7	ORC
30	The Story of Women Headloaders	8	Lead Story
31	INSPIRATION: The Story of A Solar Campaign	8	Box 8.3
32	The Story of The Indian Small Farmer	9	Lead Story
33	The Story of Olive Ridley Turtles	10	Lead Story
34	HOPE: The Story of The Kanis	10	Box 10.1
35	INSPIRATION: The Story of Romulus Whitaker	10	Box 10.5
36	The Story of Alang	11	Lead Story

(Contd.)

TABLE 18.1 (*Contd.*)

S No	Title	Chap	Location
37	INSPIRATION: The Story of Vellore Srinivasan	11	Box 11.3
38	Hope: Swachh Bharat Abhiyan	11	Box 11.4
39	The Story of Fluoride Contamination	12	Lead Story
40	DISASTER: The Story of Arsenic Poisoning	12	Box 12.1
41	Success of Swachh Bharat Abhiyan	12	Box 12.2
42	HOPE: The Story of Ecosan	12	Box 12.3
43	HOPE: Rainwater Harvesting Tackles Fluoride Problem	12	Box 12.5
44	The Story of Juvenile Asthma	13	Lead Story
45	DISASTER: The Story of Jharia—City of Fire	13	Box 13.2
46	HOPE AND DESPAIR: The Story of Delhi's Air Pollution	13	Box 13.4
47	The Story of Extreme Weather Events In India (2022)	15	Lead Story
48	The Story of The Taj Trapezium	16	Lead Story
49	INSPIRATION: The Story of M.C. Mehta	16	Box 16.1
50	CONTROVERSY: The Story of Shrimp Aquaculture	16	Box 16.2
51	INSPIRATION: The Story of Sacred Groves	16	Box 16.3
52	DISASTER: The Story of Kodaikanal Mercury Case	16	Box 16.4
53	The Story of Kokkerebellur In Karnataka	16	ORC
54	The Story of Manibeli	17	Lead Story
55	HOPE and DESPAIR: The Story of Tawa Matsya Sangh	17	Box 17.4

TABLE 18.2 International Case Studies

S No	Title	Chap	Location
1	STATE OF THE PLANET: Doomsday Clock - 90 Seconds to Midnight	1	Box 1.1
2	Connections: Get rid of malaria, but invite the plague	1	ORC
3	Connections: Drink coffee in US and make the songbird vanish in South America!	1	ORC
4	ECOSYSTEM: The Story of the Arctic National Wildlife Refuge	3	Box 3.1
5	DISASTER: The Story of the Aral Sea	4	Box 4.4
6	The Story of Wangari Mathaai of Kenya	6	ORC
7	The Story of Julia Butterfly Hill	6	ORC
8	INSPIRATION: Litre of Light	8	Box 8.4
9	Stories of focus on renewable energy in Denmark and Iceland	8	ORC
10	ECOSYSTEM: The Story of Disappearing Frogs	9	Box 9.2
11	DISASTER: The Story of the Blue Whale	9	Box 9.3
12	ECOSYSTEM: The Story of Disappearing Birds	9	Box 9.4
13	The Case of New York City	9	ORC

(*Contd.*)

TABLE 18.2 *(Contd.)*

S No	Title	Chap	Location
14	The Story of the Passenger Pigeon	9	ORC
15	HOPE: The Story of CITES	10	Box 10.2
16	The Story of Biodiversity Conservation in Bhutan	10	ORC
17	The Story of Kalundborg	11	ORC
18	The Story of Khian Sea	11	ORC
19	DISASTER: The Great Pacific Garbage Patch	12	Box 12.4
20	DISASTER: The Story of Mexico City	13	Box 13.1
21	DISASTER: The Story of Dust Storms	13	Box 13.3
22	HOPE: The Success of Montreal Protocol	13	Box 13.7
23	The Story of Tuvalu	14	Lead Story
24	ECOSYSTEM: The Story of the Arctic	14	Box 14.2
25	HOPE OR DESPAIR? The Story of the Three Gorges Dam	17	Box 17.1
26	INSPIRATION: The Story of Ray Anderson	17	Box 17.3

Discussion Questions: (Use what is applicable to the particular case)

- What is or was the core environmental issue?
- What is the scale of the issue? (Micro-, meso, synoptic, or planetary)
- What were the indicators that measured the impact of the issue? (For example, hectares of forest, concentration of a toxic substance, or number of people affected by the issue)
- Does it involve human beings or nonhuman species?
- How were the humans and/or non-humans affected in the case?
- What are the national laws or international agreements applicable to the case?
- What were the solutions proposed or implemented?
- Were the local communities consulted on the proposed solution?
- What were the actions taken by governments or international organizations?
- What was the effectiveness of the solution(s)?

19 Field Work: Activities

The way to get started is to quit talking and begin doing.

Walt Disney (1901–1966) American film producer and animator

Suggested Group Activities

General

1. Make a good beginning for the semester by setting up an eco-club in your college. Write down its aims and possible activities. Elect a secretary and a small committee. Plan activities. You can get ideas from the UN special programme for youth, called TUNZA.
2. Observe Earth Day on April 22 to create awareness in your neighbourhood or institution about environmental issues. Earth Day has been an annual event for people around the world to celebrate the earth and our responsibility toward it. More than half a billion people participate in the campaigns every year. Your club can do a variety of things to observe Earth Day. Here are some examples:
   a. Volunteer for environmental action such as tree planting.
   b. Begin making your institution a green campus.
   c. Help launch a community garden.
   d. Urge your corporation councillors, MLAs, and MPs to take environmental issues seriously.

Forest Resources

1. Join any forests-related group action (such as the Save Western Ghats Campaign) that may be going on in your area.
2. Observe July 1-7 as Vanamahotsava Week: The idea of observing a Vanamahotsava Week was started in India several decades ago. As the name implies, it was to be a forest festival with the participation of the people. Over the years, however, the practice lost its original appeal and has now become a mere ritual. Take the lead in putting some fresh life into this festival and promote planting and protecting trees in your college or in your neighbourhood.
3. Observe March 21 as World Forestry Day. This day is celebrated in forests around the world for people to consider the benefits of forests to the community such as catchment protection, providing habitat for animals and plants, areas for recreation, education and scientific study, and as a source of many products including timber and honey. World Forestry Day also aims to provide opportunities for people to learn how forests can be managed and used sustainably for these purposes

Mountain Biomes

Observe December 11 as International Mountain Day: The UN General Assembly designated December 11 as the International Mountain Day from 2003. Each year the observance focuses on a theme. For more information, access the website: www.fao.org/forestry/internationalmountainday/en/.

Aquatic Ecosystems

1. If you are in a coastal town, join voluntary groups engaged in activities like beach clean-up.
2. If there are ponds, lakes, or wetlands in or near your area, there could be groups trying to save them. If there is no group and if a water body is in peril, organize a group to make representations to the government and to create awareness in the community.
3. Observe February 2 as World Wetlands Day, which marks the date of the signing of the Convention on Wetlands in 1971, in the Iranian city of Ramsar. On this day, government agencies, non-governmental organizations, and citizens undertake actions aimed at raising public awareness of wetland values and benefits in general and the Ramsar Convention in particular. For more information, access the Ramsar website www.ramsar.org.
4. Observe June 8 as World Oceans Day as adopted by the UN General Assembly. The Ocean Project and the World Ocean Network have helped to promote and coordinate World Oceans Day events worldwide with aquariums, zoos, museums, conservation organizations, universities, schools, and businesses. For more information, access the website www. theoceanproject.org.

Water Resources

1. On a regular basis, check all the public taps and pipelines in your area and arrange to plug the leaks.
2. Observe World Water Day on March 22, as designated by the UN. The objectives of World Water Day is to focus attention on the need to:
   - address the problems relating to drinking water supply;
   - increase public awareness on the importance of conservation, preservation, and protection of water resources and drinking water supply. For more information, access the website www. worldwaterday.org.
3. Join The World Youth Parliament for Water. This is a network of young people acting for water. It is active in 71 countries, with a mission to advocate for youth participation in the water sector, and to implement concrete actions for water. The members act at all levels from local communities, where they implement concrete actions and lay the foundations for universal access to water and sanitation, to the UN General Assembly, where they advocate for youth participation in the water sector. For more information, access the website http://www.pmje-wypw.org/

Energy Resources

1. Observe December 14 as National Energy Conservation Day.
2. Organize activities under the UN Decade of Sustainable Energy for All (2014–2024).
3. Choose a slum in your area and launch a Liter of Light project. You can seek help from an NGO involved in such a project in India.

Food and Agriculture

1. Observe October 16 as World Food Day (WFD), which is a worldwide event designed to increase awareness, understanding, and informed, year-around, and long-term action on the complex issues of food security for all.
2. You can observe WFD by increasing awareness, understanding, information, services, support, advocacy, and networking with regard to food issues. You can get more information and help from the FAO website: www.fao.org/wfd/.

3. Observe November 21 as World Fisheries Day. It was initiated by the World Forum of Fish Harvesters and Fish Workers (WFF). The World Fisheries Day is observed with the idea of highlighting preservation of marine ecology, creating and sustaining public awareness, and initiating and strengthening action at various levels. This day is not only for the fish-harvesters and fish-workers but also for all who care for and wish to nurture this planet.
4. Observe June 17 as the World Day to Combat Desertification and Drought (For information, access the website www.unccd.int).
5. Find out more about citizens' movements aimed at conserving biodiversity and join one of them as a volunteer. For example:
   a. If you are in south India, join the movements to save the Silent Valley and the Western Ghats.
   b. If you are in Odisha, join the groups trying to save the Olive Ridley turtles.
   c. If you are in Chennai, find out if you can help the Madras Snake Park or the Crocodile Bank; you can also join the Turtle Watch on the Chennai beach.
6. Volunteer for the 'Kids for Tigers' Programme, promoted by Sanctuary Asia magazine. The programme aims to bring out the vital connection between the survival of the tiger and the ecological security of the Indian subcontinent. (www. kidsfortigers.org)

Biodiversity

Observe the International Day of Biological Diversity on May 22. This observance is supported by the Secretariat for the Convention on Biological Diversity. It is an opportunity to strengthen people's commitment and actions for the conservation of the world's biological diversity. Each year, the Secretariat chooses a theme and provides posters and promotional materials.

You could celebrate the day by organizing:

- meetings and lectures on the theme of biodiversity,
- an excursion to a biodiversity-rich area with experts as guides,
- activities for children,
- environmental clean-up activities.

You could also plan the day as a people's event with colourful activities such as street rallies, bicycle parades, green concerts, essays, and poster competitions in schools, media events, tree planting, and public events in parks, nature conservancies, and botanical gardens.

Suggested Campus Activities

Energy Management

- Do an energy audit of your campus.
- Suggest steps for improving energy efficiency and reducing the electricity charges.

Water Management

- Do a water audit of your campus measuring the water usage for various purposes. Suggest ways of reducing water consumption.
- Suggest rainwater harvesting.

Solid and Liquid Waste Management

- Examine the campus sewage system
- Suggest waste water treatment and reuse of water for gardens

Note: These activities have also been listed as potential projects in Chapter 18.

Suggested Individual Activities

What is the LiFE Movement?

The Union Government launched the 'Lifestyle for the Environment (LiFE) Movement' for Adoption of Environment-Conscious Lifestyle on June 5, 2022.

The idea of LiFE was first introduced by the Prime Minister during the 26th UN Climate Change Conference of the Parties (COP26) in Glasgow in 2021. The idea promotes an environmentally conscious lifestyle that focuses on 'mindful and deliberate utilisation' instead of 'mindless and wasteful consumption'. It hopes to be an India-led global mass movement to nudge individual and community action to protect and preserve the environment.

The LiFE Movement aims to utilise the power of collective action and nudge individuals across the world to undertake simple climate-friendly actions in their daily lives. The LiFE movement also seeks to leverage the strength of social networks to influence social norms surrounding climate. The Mission plans to create and nurture a global network of individuals, namely 'Pro-Planet People' (P3), who will have a shared commitment to adopt and promote environmentally friendly lifestyles. Through the P3 community, the Mission seeks to create an ecosystem that will reinforce and enable environmentally friendly behaviours to be self-sustainable. In five years there would be one billion Pro-Planet People in India.

The Mission envisions replacing the prevalent 'use-and-dispose' economy—governed by mindless and destructive consumption—with a circular economy, which would be defined by mindful and deliberate utilization.

The Mission will be incubated, curated and piloted by NITI Aayog and subsequently implemented by MoEFCC, in a non-linear and non-sequential manner. While a proceeding phase will organically feed into the next phase of Mission LiFE, all phases are equally simultaneous in nature.

A comprehensive and non-exhaustive list of 75 individual LiFE actions across seven categories is given in Table 19.1.

TABLE 19.1 LiFE Actions

Energy Saved	
1	Use LED bulbs/tube-lights
2	Use public transport wherever possible
3	Take the stairs instead of an elevator wherever possible
4	Switch off vehicle engines at red lights and railway crossings
5	Use bicycles for local or short commute
6	Switch off irrigation pumps after use
7	Prefer CNG/EV vehicle over petrol/diesel vehicles
8	Use carpooling with friends & colleagues
9	Drive in the correct gear. Keep your foot off the clutch when not changing gears
10	Install a solar water or solar cooker heater on rooftops
11	Switch off appliances from plug points when not in use
12	Use biogas for cooking and electricity needs
13	Keep temperature of Air Conditioners to 24 degrees

(Contd.)

TABLE 19.1 (*Contd.*)

14	Prefer pressure cookers over other cookware
15	Keep your electronic devices in energy-saving mode
16	Use smart switches for appliances which are used frequently
17	Install community earthen pots for cooling water
18	Defrost fridge or freezer regularly
19	Run outdoors instead of on a treadmill
Water Saved	
20	Adopt cultivation of less water intensive crops like millets
21	Participate in recharge of rural water bodies through Amrit Sarovar Scheme
22	Practice crop diversification. Move from rice & wheat cultivation to pulse & oil seed cropping system.
23	Use efficient water saving technologies (like micro-irrigation, bunding, farm ponds, zero tillage, direct seeded rice, alternate wetting, and drying and others)
24	Create rainwater harvesting infrastructure in home/schools/offices
25	Use drip irrigation systems created with waste materials, wherever possible
26	Reuse water from washed vegetables to water plants and other purpose
27	Pre-soak heavy pots and pans before washing them
28	Do not discard unused stored water every time there is fresh water coming in taps
29	Use buckets instead of hose pipes to water plants/floors/vehicles
30	Fix leaks in flushes, taps, and waterpipes
31	Use water-efficient fixtures for taps, and showerheads, and toilet flush units
32	Invest in a water meter for your house to measure water consumption regularly
33	Reuse water drained out from AC/RO for cleaning utensils, watering plants and others
34	Prefer a water purification system that wastes less water
Single Use Plastic Reduced	
35	Use cloth bag for shopping instead of plastic bags
36	Carry your own water bottle wherever possible
37	Reuse glass containers/packaging plastic items as storage boxes
38	Participate in and mobilize participation for clean-up drives of cities and water bodies
39	Prefer using non-plastic eco-friendly cutlery during gatherings and events
40	Turn off running taps when not in active use
41	Use menstrual cups instead of sanitary napkins
42	Use recycled plastic over virgin plastic, wherever possible
43	Use steel/recyclable plastic lunch boxes and water bottles
44	Cut the packaging bags used for milk, buttermilk, etc. only partially to avoid plastic bits from mixing into biodegradable waste
45	Opt for bamboo toothbrushes and neem combs

(*Contd.*)

TABLE 19.1 (*Contd.*)

	Sustainable Food Systems Adopted
46	Include millets in diets through Anganwadi, Mid-Day meals, and PD scheme
47	Compost food waste at home
48	Create kitchen gardens/terrace gardens at homes/schools/offices
49	Prepare organic manure from cow dungs and apply to farms
50	Prefer locally available and seasonal foods
51	Use smaller plates for daily meals to save food wastage
	Waste Reduced (Swachhata Actions)
52	Contribute cattle waste, food waste, and agricultural waste to biogas plant (provided under GOBARDHAN)
53	Practice segregation of dry and wet waste at homes
54	Use agricultural residue, animal waste for composting, manuring, and mulching
55	Recycle and reuse old newspapers, magazines
56	Feed unused and uncooked vegetables leftovers to cattle
57	Set printer default to double-side printing
58	Repair, reuse, and recycle old furniture
59	Buy paper products made from recycled paper
60	Donate old clothes and books
61	Do not discard waste in water bodies and in public spaces
62	Do not let pets defecate in the public places
	Healthy Lifestyles Adopted
63	Encourage use of millets in food and indigenous herbs and medicinal plants for nutrition and well being
64	Prefer consuming natural or organic products
65	Start biodiversity conservation at community level
66	Plant medicinal plants such as neem, tulsi, giloy, mint, curry leaves, ashwagandha, curry leaves etc. within household premises
67	Practice natural or organic farming
68	Plant trees to reduce the impact of pollution
69	Avoid purchasing products/souvenirs made from skin, tuskers, and fur of wild animals
70	Create and volunteer at community food and cloth banks, and at animal shelters
71	Initiate and/or join green clubs in your residential area/school/office
	E-Waste reduced
72	Repair and use electronic devices over discarding the devices
73	Discard gadgets in nearest e-recycling units
74	Use rechargeable lithium cells
75	Prefer cloud storage over a pen drive/hard drive

UNIT 9

Conclusion

20 Conclusion: Another World is Possible

Very few people on earth ever get to say: 'I am doing, right now, the most important thing I could possibly be doing'. If you'll join this fight that's what you'll get to say.

Bill McKibben (1960–)
American environmentalist and author

How can You Move from Despair to Hope?

This (last) chapter is addressed directly to you, the reader. The book has been a catalogue of environmental destruction, sprinkled with signs of positive change. The state of the world can easily drive you to despair. But how can you move from a sense of despair to one of hope, from crisis to cure?

The first step is to realize that you have the power to change things. Mahatma Gandhi said, 'The difference between what we do and what we are capable of doing would suffice to solve most of the world's problems.'

There are three levels at which you can exercise the power you have:

- Power of One: You can take right actions as an individual.
- Power of a Group: You can join (or create) a group or community of like-minded people working for positive changes.
- Power of a Movement: You can join any one of the social and environmental movements that are determined to change the world.

Why is There a General Lack of Public Awareness about Environmental Issues?

There are many factors that limit our awareness of environmental issues. To the millions of poor people, the problems of daily existence are more important than environmental degradation. On the other hand, the more prosperous are afraid that, in the name of environment, their comforts may be taken away. In any case, most of us do not pay the real costs of exploiting nature.

There is also false anti-environment propaganda by people with vested interests like the large corporations, for whom constant growth is vital. At the political level, parties are more interested in short-term gains and votes in elections and would not take unpopular measures for conserving the environment. Further, in this age of extreme specialization very few can look at the larger picture of what is happening to the world. There is also paucity of reliable and clear information on the environment. To make matters worse, economic indicators like Gross Domestic Product give us a misleading picture of what is desirable.

Who is the Real Enemy?

Before you can act, you have to ask yourself: Who is really responsible for the environmental crisis? Who is the real enemy?

- Rich societies like that of the US that consume and pollute a lot?
- Governments and political parties that are only concerned about the next elections and hence do not take the necessary tough decisions?
- Companies that use natural resources and just throw away the waste?
- Corrupt officials who let the companies pollute?
- Municipalities that do not clear the garbage?
- Your neighbour, who throws the garbage on the street?

It is easy enough to blame others for the crisis and, of course, some or many of them may well deserve a share of the blame. However, a little reflection shows that, at the very basic level, you are the cause and each one of us is the cause. As the cartoon character Pogo puts it, 'We have seen the enemy and it is us!'

The root causes of the crisis include:

- Your consumption and desire for more.
- The waste that you create and throw away mindlessly.
- Your NIMBY (Not In My BackYard) syndrome: The practice of objecting to something that would affect you or take place in your locality, even though it would benefit many others.
- The corruption that you support, directly or indirectly.

Your actions such as these lead to increasing production of goods and services, overexploitation of natural resources, more waste and pollution, and so on.

If you agree that you are part of the problem, one could ask you, 'Can you become a part of the solution?' Your response could well be, 'What can I do? I am just a powerless individual. How can I fight against the bureaucrats, politicians, or industrialists?'

What is the Power of One?

Many individuals all over the world have indeed tried to become part of the solution. They have acted to save the environment and brought about real changes. There are many such inspiring stories, some of which were given in the previous chapters.

Many more such environmental heroes can be found across the world. True stories of this kind have many uses:

- They can inspire us to act in our lives and in our context.
- By presenting environmental issues in the context of real places and events, they are more effective in spurring action than mere fear-inducing information.
- Through the stories, we understand the differences and commonalities of environmental problems and solutions around the world.
- The stories can be a great tool in education and creation of awareness among children and the youth.

Reading these extraordinary stories, we may be tempted to ask, 'What makes ordinary individuals take up seemingly impossible tasks in the face of heavy odds?' Clearly, given the depressing data, the driving force could not be just optimism, which arises from the head.

It can only be hope that springs from the heart, as described by Vaclav Havel, writer and first President of the Czech Republic:

Hope is an orientation of the spirit, an orientation of the heart; it transcends the world that is immediately experienced, and is anchored somewhere beyond its horizons.

Havel (who led resistance groups against the Soviet Union), Gandhiji (who led our freedom struggle), Nelson Mandela (who led the struggle against apartheid in South Africa), Martin Luther King, Jr, (who led the Civil Rights Movement in the US) and others like them went on with their work, even against great odds, not by a sense of optimism, but undying hope. That hope did triumph at the end. In the same way, the environment may also be saved from a disaster by the actions of all of us.

What steps can you take?

You could become an inspiring hero, but until then you can still do your bit in healing this planet. You could take three steps:

- Be informed: Read books and magazines and scour websites to find out for yourself where the world stands.
- Examine yourself and your lifestyle from an environmental point of view.
- Take action at home and workplace, in the neighbourhood, in your city, and so on. Chapter 19 gives many suggestions for action.

What is the Power of a Group?

Every city has many NGOs that take up local environmental issues and conduct campaigns during weekends. There is strength in numbers and you may see better results when you work with such groups. The famous anthropologist Margaret Mead said, 'Never doubt that a small group of thoughtful committed citizens can change the world. Indeed, it is the only thing that ever has.'

You can also go beyond just working with local environmental groups and move into a community or create one. Often, such a community grows from the vision of an individual or a small and dedicated group. Some have ecology as a focus, while others are oriented towards religion and spirituality. Other communities concentrate on social work. In India, there are also Gandhian communities, inspired by the ideals of the Mahatma. Box 20.1 gives examples of communities that focus (among other things) on the environment. There are many more, large and small as well as old and new.

BOX 20.1 INSPIRATION: ***Examples of Ecological Communities***

Gaviotas It was established in 1971 by Paulo Lu-gari on 25,000 acres of land on the impoverished eastern plains of Colombia. The Gaviotans are about 200 researchers, students, and workers and they produce 70% of food and energy needed. The place is run by consensus and unwritten rules. The residents get good wages, free meals, medical care, schools, and housing. Over the years, Gaviotans have come up with an extraordinary number of inventions including efficient wind turbines, solar devices, self-cooling rooftops, cooling wind corridors, corkscrew manual well digger, and so on. Since Gaviotas does not patent its inventions, its ideas have spread in the region, from Central America to Chile.

Auroville Also called the City of Dawn, this is an international township in Tamil Nadu, near Puducherry, dedicated to human unity. It was founded in 1968 by the French visionary known as 'The Mother', a spiritual collaborator of the sage Sri Aurobindo. It is a remarkable story of ecological transformation achieved by a group of people (now about 2000 in number) from 35 different countries including India. They have planted three million trees to convert barren land into lush greenery. They have also experimented with a range of environment friendly technologies covering water, energy, waste, building, and farming. Local biodiversity and medicinal knowledge are being recorded and revived.

Timbaktu Collective This community was established in 1990 on 32 acres of dry, degraded land in the drought-prone Anantapur district of Andhra Pradesh. Slowly over the years not only Timbaktu but also the surrounding hills have greened themselves while insects, birds, and animals have reappeared. A small community of volunteers, committed to developmental and ecological regeneration, has settled here. Timbaktu's vision is to stop the degradation of the land in the area and to find ways to reverse it. The aim is also to develop alternative lifestyles that are sustainable and provide more liberty and happiness, than those based upon exploitation.

What is the Power of a Movement?

If the planet is to be saved from destruction, we need many Chipko-type people's movements. Paul Hawken, who has been studying such movements, believes that there are up to 2 million organizations in the world working toward ecological sustainability, social justice, and indigenous rights. 'It is a global humanitarian movement arising from the bottom up. It is in fact a coherent, organic, self-organized, worldwide movement involving tens of millions of people dedicated to positive change.'

Hawken puts it this way, 'If you look at the science that describes what is happening on earth today and aren't pessimistic, you don't have the correct data. If you meet the people in this unnamed movement and aren't optimistic, you haven't got a heart.'

Joanna Macy, American Buddhist scholar and peace activist, is sure that a 'Great Turning' is occurring in the world. 'This turning is a shift from the industrial growth society to a life-sustaining civilization. Future generations will look back at the epochal transition we are making to a life-sustaining society. It is happening now. To see this as the larger context of our lives clears our vision and summons our courage.'

David Korten, Macy's colleague and author of the book *The Great Turning,* believes that everything is going to change. He suggests that we should embrace the crisis as an opportunity and 'move from Empire to Earth Community, from Dominator story to Partnership story, and from Competition to Cooperation' (Box 20.2).

BOX 20.2 HOPE: ***Change the Story, Change the Future***

Every society essentially plays out a story. One story has the theme, 'Man is an integral part of nature and is not separate from it.' This was the story of many indigenous peoples of the world. Today the dominant story tells us again and again in every way:

- Produce more and more products and services, be a strong economy and a powerful nation.
- Make more money, be happier.
- Consume more, enjoy more, that is your right.
- Compete or you will perish.
- We can change the story to a new one that tells us:
- We are the stewards of the earth.
- Degrading the earth with the waste products of our luxurious living is a sin.
- The right path is to live as frugally and simply as possible.
- Reducing consumption is not a sacrifice; it is an elevating experience.
- Partnership and cooperation are the keys to survival.

What is Stopping You from Acting to Save the Planet?

Taking actions suggested in this book is necessary, but not sufficient. A profound change is possible only if all of us change our mindsets. Albert Einstein said, 'You cannot solve a problem with the same mindset which created it in the first place.'

We mistakenly see a difference between other beings and ourselves, between nature and ourselves. When we truly begin to see ourselves as an indivisible part of the universe, there will be a fundamental shift in our mindsets.

Perhaps the first step in saving the planet is to fall in love with its beauty. The second step is to hear within us the sounds of the earth crying. The third step is to put this new understanding into action. Begin doing what you wish others would do to save the environment.

Begin changing yourself and you will then find that *another world is possible!*

Farewell

Power, politics, and even people may not be able to save this planet. But poetry just might, because it touches our hearts and could change our mindsets.

As an end-piece, here is the poem *Bashundhara* (1893) by Rabindranath Tagore, in which he evokes the image of the earth as the mother who sustains us at every stage:

Bashundhara

Take me back to your lap O Earth
Bless me within your shadow
I exist within your beauty and radiate
Myself all around life the joy of spring.
Quivering, gurgling, radiating myself
With the rays of light I flow in joy
To the far corners of the earth
In joyous play I extend
Language to every wave and direction
I spread myself on the pinnacles
Of the snowy cliffs in silence
O Earth my heart has sung aloud
In joy, aspired to clasp you close to me
To kiss every single bud, to embrace
Every blade of grass
The joy of the whole world
I wish to feel with all of mankind
Clasp me close to your heart
Where joy evolves in every beat
In every nook and corner
Do not keep me away.

(Source: Accessed from www.museindia.com and reproduced with the permission of the translator Dr. Amrit Sen.)

APPENDIX A

Glossary

Abiotic components or conditions The non-living components or conditions of an ecosystem such as the natural resources and the atmospheric conditions.

abiotic conditions

Abyssal zone The cold and dark zone at the bottom of the ocean.

Acid rain Rain, mist, or snow formed when atmospheric water droplets combine with a range of man-made chemical air pollutants.

Adaptation Adjustment in natural or human systems in response to actual or expected climatic stimuli or their effects, which moderates harm or exploits beneficial opportunities.

Aflatoxin Poisonous and carcinogenic chemical produced by certain moulds.

Agent Orange A compound herbicide used by the US Army in the Vietnam War to kill all vegetation.

Agroforestry A system of land use that combines growing crops along with trees.

Albedo The reflection of light from a surface, measured as the fraction of the incident light that a surface reflects back.

Algal bloom A population explosion of some pigmented marine algae seen as an explosion of colour on the ocean – orange, red, or brown.

Allopatric speciation The process of one species becomes two due to the formation of geographical barriers such as land separation, mountain formation, emigration, or human interference.

Anthropocene The new geological epoch in which humanity has overwhelmed the forces of nature.

Aquaculture The artificial production of fish in ponds or underwater cages.

Aquatic life zone The non-terrestrial part of the biosphere including wetlands, lakes, rivers, estuaries, inter-tidal zone, coastal ocean, and open ocean.

Aquifer An underground layer of rock or sand that contains water.

Asbestos A fibrous silicate mineral used as construction material and insulation. It is very dangerous to health when the fibres are inhaled.

Autotroph Green plant or producer that makes its own food.

Background extinction The process of natural and low-level extinction that goes on continuously due to changes in the environmental conditions.

Barrel The unit used in the US for petroleum.

Bathyal zone The dimly lit middle level zone in the ocean, roughly between 200 m and 1500 m in depth.

Benthos Bottom-dwelling organisms adapted to living on the floor of a water body.

Bio-intensive farming Intensive garden cultivation using deep-dug beds.

Biodegradable waste Any waste item that breaks down into the raw materials of nature and becomes part of the environment in reasonable time.

Biodiversity (Biological diversity) The numbers, variety, and variability of living organisms and ecosystems, covering diversity within species, between species, as well as the variation among ecosystems.

Biodiversity Hotspot An area, especially rich in biodiversity with a large number of endemic species, that is threatened with the loss of that biodiversity.

Biodynamic farming A type of organic farming that exploits bio- and solar rhythms, based on the ideas of Rudolf Steiner.

Bioenergy Energy extracted from biomass.

Biofertilizers The use of soil microorganisms to increase the availability and uptake of mineral nutrients for plants.

Biofortification The process by which the nutritional quality of food crops is improved through agronomic practices, conventional plant breeding, or modern biotechnology.

Biofuel Fuel obtained by converting biomass into liquid fuel.

Biogas Gas produced by the process of anaerobic digestion of organic material such as cow dung and vegetable waste.

Biogeochemical cycle A cycle (with biological, geological and chemical interactions) through which matter moves through ecosystems, powered directly or indirectly by solar energy.

Bioinformatics The application of information technology to the management of biological information.

Biointensive farming A type of organic farming involving intensive garden cultivation using deep-dug beds.

Biological capacity or biocapacity Ecosystems' capacity to produce biological materials used by people and to absorb waste material generated by humans, under current management schemes and extraction technologies.

Biological diversity See Biodiversity

Biological extinction The complete disappearance of a species, an irreversible loss with not a single member of the extinct species being found on Earth.

Biological Oxygen Demand (BOD) Measure of the oxygen used by microorganisms to decompose organic waste.

Biological pest control The intentional introduction of predators, diseases, or parasites to control pests.

Biomagnification The increasing concentration of pollutants in organisms as we move up the food chain.

Biomass gasification Incomplete combustion of biomass resulting in production of combustible gases.

Biome A terrestrial and regional ecosystem with a distinct climate and a distinct biological community of plants, animals and other organisms.

Biomedical waste Waste that originates mainly from hospitals and clinics and includes blood, diseased organs, poisonous medicines, etc.

Biopesticide Pesticides derived from animals, plants, bacteria, and certain minerals.

Biopiracy The appropriation of traditional knowledge of biodiversity by outsiders, including the fraudulent patenting of such biological resources for profit.

Bioremediation The use of biotechnology to clean up wastes and toxic pollutants.

Biosphere That part of the earth where life exists.

Biosphere reserve Area of land or water that is protected by law in order to support the conservation of the ecosystem.

Biota The living component of an ecosystem, also called the biotic community. The biotic community includes the plants, animals and microorganisms.

Biotechnology Technology that manipulates living organisms or cells to create a product or an effect.

Biotic components The living components of an ecosystem.

Bottom trawling The practice of fishing by scraping the sea floor with a net.

Brent Crude The sweet and light crude oil that serves as a major benchmark price for purchases of oil worldwide.

Brominated flame retardant Chemical added to consumer products such as mattresses and electronic items in order to reduce fire-related injury and property damage.

Bunker fuel Fuel consumed for international marine and air transport.

Bycatch The species caught in the fishing nets along with the targeted ones.

Canopy The more or less continuous cover of branches and foliage formed collectively by the crowns of adjacent trees.

Carbon budget The cumulative amount of carbon dioxide emissions permitted over a period of time to keep within a certain temperature threshold.

Carbon capture The process of trapping carbon dioxide at its emission source, transporting it to a usually underground storage location, and isolating it there.

Carbon credit A certified carbon dioxide emission displacement credit supposed to be equal to one tonne of CO_2 removed from the environment.

Carbon cycle Cyclic movement of carbon in various forms from the environment to organisms and back to the environment.

Carbon Footprint Total greenhouse gas emissions caused directly and indirectly by a person, organisation, event, product, or country.

Carbon intensity The amount of carbon by weight emitted per unit of energy consumed.

Carbon neutrality Having a balance between emitting carbon and absorbing carbon from the atmosphere.

Carbon sequestration The process of removing carbon from the atmosphere and depositing it in a reservoir.

Captive breeding Reproduction of threatened animals in captivity.

Carbon trading A market-based system aimed at reducing greenhouse gases, particularly carbon dioxide, emitted by burning fossil fuels.

Carnivore Organism that feeds on other consumers.

Carrying Capacity The maximum number of individuals of a given species that an area's resources can sustain indefinitely without significantly depleting or degrading those resources.

Cell respiration The process in which the molecules of glucose combine with water and oxygen to release energy and create carbon dioxide and water.

Checkdam or *johad* A small structure of earth and stones that blocks the path of any flow of water and helps recharge the groundwater.

Chlorofluorocarbon (CFC) A type of chemical that is used as a refrigerant or aerosol propellants. When it breaks apart in the atmosphere and releases chlorine atoms, it causes ozone depletion.

Circular economy An economy that keeps materials, products, and services in circulation for as long possible.

Clean Development Mechanism The UN mechanism that allows a country with an emission-reduction or emission-limitation commitment under the Kyoto Protocol to implement an emission-reduction project in developing countries.

Climate change A significant and persistent change in the mean state of the climate or its variability.

Climate justice A term and a movement that acknowledges climate change can have differing social, economic, public health, and other adverse impacts on underprivileged populations.

Climate resilience Strengthening the ability of human and non-human systems to withstand and respond to changes in the earth's climate.

Climate vulnerability The propensity or predisposition to be adversely affected by climate change.

Climax ecosystem Ecosystem that has reached a steady state.

Coastal zone The area extending from the high tide mark on land to the edge of the continental shelf, where there is a sharp increase in the depth of water.

Commensalism A symbiotic relationship between two species in which one species benefits from the relationship and the other is neither benefitted nor harmed.

Common But Differentiated Responsibility A principle within the UN Framework Convention on Climate Change that acknowledges the different capabilities and differing responsibilities of individual countries in addressing climate change.

Common Effluent Treatment Plant (CETP) A common plant where the waste of several units from an industrial estate is collected and made safe by treatment.

Common Heritage of Mankind A principle of international law which holds that defined territorial areas and elements of humanity's common heritage (cultural and natural) should be held in trust for future generations and be protected from exploitation by individual nation states or corporations.

Community Populations of different species (plants, animals, and microorganisms) living and interacting in a given area at a given time.

Competition The interaction between two or more species that seek the same resource for survival.

Composting The process of converting organic waste into fertilizer.

Conifer Tree on which the seeds are borne in a cone.

Coniferous forest A type of forest with an abundance of coniferous trees like spruce, fir, pine, and hemlock.

Consumer An organism that feeds on producers or other organisms, also called heterotroph.

Continental shelf The submerged part of the continent at the edge of the coastal zone, where there is a sharp increase in the depth of water.

Coral bleaching The process when corals lose their colour due to various stressors, such as changes in temperature, light, or nutrients.

Coral reef Colourful protective crust of limestone formed by colonies of tiny organisms called polyps.

Critically Endangered species A threatened species facing an extremely high risk of extinction in the wild.

Crude birth rate The number of live births per 1000 people in a population in a given year.

Crude death rate The number of deaths per 1000 people in a population in a given year.

Cyclone Violent tropical storm in which strong winds move in a circle.

DDT (Dichloro-diphenol-trichloroethane) A toxic insecticide that protects crops and human beings from insects.

Decibel (db) A logarithmic scale for measuring the intensity of sound.

Deciduous tree Tree that sheds all its leaves in winter.

Decomposer An organism that digests and breaks down dead organisms and wastes of living organisms.

Demographic Dividend Boost in economic growth that can result from changes in a country's population age structure.

Desertification Land degradation in arid and semi-arid areas caused by human activities and climatic changes.

Detrivore A consumer that feeds on detritus, which refers mainly to fallen leaves, parts of dead trees, and faecal wastes of animals.

Dioxin A highly toxic chemical compound that occurs as contaminants in a number of industrial processes and products; also formed in the burning of waste, plastics, coal or cigarettes.

Disaster management Effective way of managing disasters including mitigation, preparedness, response, and recovery.

Disaster mitigation Reducing the effects of potential disasters through suitable measures.

Displacement The movement of people from their homes to new locations.

DNA The molecule of an organism that contains information about its characteristics and behaviour.

E-waste See Ewaste

Eco-label A label used to mark a consumer product to indicate that it is environment-friendly with regard to its manufacture and use.

Eco-sensitive zone A peripheral area around a Protected Area that is considered ecologically fragile enough to justify some regulation of human activities.

Ecological architecture Architecture that seeks to minimize the ecological footprint of the house, building, or complex.

Ecological balance The fine balance between the biota and abiotic conditions of an ecosystem, enabling it to remain stable and for all its organisms to survive and prosper.

Ecological extinction The state of a species when so few members are left that the species can no longer play its normal ecological role in the community.

Ecological Footprint A measure of the ecological impact of an entity, expressed as the extent of land needed to completely sustain the entity.

Ecological niche All the physical, chemical, and biological factors that a species needs in order to live and reproduce.

Ecological pyramid A graphical representation of the change that occurs as we move from one trophic level to the next in a food chain.

Ecological sanitation (EcoSan) A sustainable closed-loop sanitation system that uses dry composting toilets.

Ecological succession The orderly process of transition from one biotic community to another in a given area.

Ecologist A scientist who works in the field of ecology.

Ecology The study of the relationships and interactions between organisms and their environment.

Ecomark Eco-label established by the Indian government for easy identification of environment-friendly products.

Ecosystem A defined area in which a community (with its populations of species) exists with interactions taking place among the organisms and between the community and its non-living physical environment.

Ecosystem diversity The variety of habitats found in an area, that is, the variety of forests, deserts, grasslands, aquatic ecosystems, etc., that occurs in the area.

Ecosystem service The ecological service provided by an ecosystem such as the maintenance of the biogeochemical cycles, modification of climate, waste removal and detoxification, and control of pests and diseases.

Ecotone The transitional zone between adjoining ecosystems.

Edge effect The presence of rich and unique biological diversity found in an ecotone.

El Niño An abnormal warming of the surface ocean waters in the eastern tropical Pacific in some years.

Electromagnetic radiation A form of energy radiated as waves and caused by changing electric and magnetic fields.

Endangered species A threatened species facing a very high risk of extinction in the wild.

Endemic species A species is found only in a specific geographical location and not found anywhere else.

Endosulfan A highly toxic pesticide used to protect many crops from pest attacks.

Energy flow Flow of energy in a food chain from one organism to the next in a sequence.

Energy intensity A measure of the energy inefficiency of an economy, calculated as units of energy per unit of GDP.

Environment The natural world in which people, animals, and plants live.

Environmental conservation All the ways in which we protect nature and reverse the damage caused to the natural environment.

Environmental degradation This term refers to the damage caused to the natural environment by human action and otherwise.

Environmental education A subject concerned with all environmental issues, including the social aspects.

Environmental ethics Moral principles that try to define our responsibility towards the environment.

Environmental health Those aspects of human health that are determined by physical, chemical, biological, social, and psychosocial factors in the environment.

Environmental Impact Assessment (EIA) The study of the likely short-term and long-term impact of a new project on the natural and social environment.

Environmental justice The fair treatment and meaningful involvement of all people regardless of race, colour, national origin, or income, with respect to the development, implementation, and enforcement of environmental laws, regulations, and policies.

Environmental management The practice of organizing human activities in order to limit their impact on the natural environment.

Environmental refugee A person who has been displaced due to environmental degradation or a development project,

Environmental Science The systematic and scientific study of our environment and our role in it.

Environmental stability The maintenance of natural processes in a state of balance. Forests contribute to environmental stability.

Environmental Studies The branch of study concerned with environmental issues and includes the social aspects of the environment.

Environmentalist A person who helps in the conservation of the environment.

Epiphyte A plant that derives its moisture and nutrients from the air and rain and grows usually on another plant.

Estuary The wide part of a river where it flows into the sea.

Euphotic zone The upper part of the open ocean where there is enough light for the phytoplankton to carry out photosynthesis.

Eutrophication The excessive addition of chemical nutrients like nitrogen or phosphorus into the soil or a standing water body, which promotes the excessive growth of some species leading to the death of others.

Evergreen tree Tree that retains its leaves all year and for several years.

Ewaste Waste from discarded electrical and electronic equipment.

Ex-situ (off-site) conservation Conservation, which attempts to preserve and protect the species in a place away from their natural habitat.

Exotic species A tree species introduced from a different place.

Exponential growth The growth of a quantity with time in such a way that the curve is relatively flat in the beginning, but becomes steeper and steeper with time.

Extinct species A known species, no member of which is found anywhere on earth.

Extractive reserve Protected forest, in which local communities are allowed to harvest non-timber products in ways that do not harm the forest.

Fauna All the animals that live in a particular area time period or environment.

Flora All the plants that live in a particular area time period or environment.

Fluorosis An ailment caused by the excess intake of fluoride.

Food chain A sequence of species, in which each is the food for the next in the chain.

Food web An interconnected set of food chains.

Forest certification A system for certifying forests that adopt sustainable management practices.

Fossil fuel Remains of organisms that lived 200–500 million years ago that were converted by heat and pressure into coal, oil, and natural gas.

Fuel cell An electrochemical unit that generates electricity from hydrogen and oxygen.

Genetic diversity The variety in the genetic makeup among individuals within a species.

Genetic engineering The manipulation of the genes in an organism to change its characteristics, for example, moving a favourable gene from one organism to another.

Genetic Modification (GM) Direct modification of the genetic makeup of an organism by introducing foreign genes into the gene pool of the organism.

Genetically Modified food (GM Food) Food derived from genetically modified organisms, which have had specific changes introduced into their DNA by genetic engineering.

Genome The complete set of DNA within a single cell of an organism.

Genomics A discipline in genetics that applies biotechnology to sequence, assemble, and analyse the function and structure of genomes.

Geothermal energy Energy from the hot liquid rock under the Earth's crust tapped from the hot water that comes to the surface.

Global warming Warming of the earth's atmosphere due to an abnormal increase in the concentration of greenhouse gases.

Global warming potential (GWP) An index representing the combined effect of the differing time periods for which greenhouse gases remain in the atmosphere and their relative effectiveness in absorbing outgoing infrared radiation.

Grassland Region where the average annual precipitation is high enough for grass and a few trees to grow.

Green business Enterprise that has no negative impact on the global or local environment, community, society, or economy.

Green Economy Economic activity related to reducing the use of fossil fuels, decreasing pollution and greenhouse gas emissions, increasing the efficiency of energy usage, recycling materials, and developing and adopting renewable sources of energy.

Green livelihood Productive and sustainable livelihoods based on natural resources.

Green Revolution A way of agriculture that greatly increases crop yields, using new seed varieties, large quantities of chemical fertilizers, pesticides, and water.

Greenhouse gas A gas like carbon dioxide that surrounds the Earth and prevents some of the Sun's heat from being reflected back out again.

Gross World Product The total value of all the products made and services offered in the world.

Groundwater Water contained underneath the Earth's surface.

Habitat The area where a species is biologically adapted to live.

Habitat fragmentation The process by which continuous areas of species habitat are reduced in extent or divided into patchwork of isolated fragments due to human impact.

Herbivore An organism that feeds directly on producers.

Heterotroph Any consumer.

Home range Area in which an organism lives and finds what it needs for its survival.

Homeostasis The tendency or ability of an ecosystem to maintain internal stability in the face of disturbances.

Hubbert Curve A curve proposed by the geophysicist M.King Hubbert that describes the pattern of oil availability in a field over time.

Hurricane Violent storm with very strong winds experienced mainly in the western Atlantic Ocean.

Idea of Progress The belief that humankind would move on an unceasing path of better material conditions and a better life through economic and industrial development, exploiting natural resources.

In-situ (on-site) conservation Conservation, which tries to protect species where they are, that is, in their natural habitat.

Indicator species A species whose presence, absence, or abundance reflects a specific environmental condition.

Indigenous knowledge The traditional and local knowledge held by the members of a given community.

Intended Nationally Determined Contribution (INDC) A non-binding national plan highlighting climate change mitigation, including climate-related targets for greenhouse gas emission reductions.

Intertidal zone The area of shoreline between the low and high tides. It is the transition between the land and the ocean.

Invasive species Any plant, fungus, or animal species that has entered (or invaded) an area to which the species is not native.

Joint Forest Management Sustainable management of forests involving local communities in the planning and execution of the conservation programme.

Judicial activism The pro-active role of the judiciary in responding to the complaints of citizens or public interest litigation.

Keystone species A species that has a disproportionately large effect on the communities in which it occurs and determines the ability of a large number of other species in the community to survive.

Land Degradation Neutrality (LDN) A state whereby the amount and quality of land resources, necessary to support ecosystem functions and services and enhance food security, remains stable or increases within specified temporal and spatial scales and ecosystems.

Landfill An area, usually located just outside the city, on which municipal waste is dumped.

Landslide The sliding down of soil and rocks on a mountain slope.

Local extinction The state of a species when it is no longer found in the area it once inhabited. It is, however, present elsewhere in the world.

Mangrove A unique salt-tolerant tree with interlacing roots that grows in shallow marine sediments.

Marine Protected Area (MPA) Area set up by a country to protect a marine ecosystem, its natural processes, habitats, and species.

Marine upwelling The process of water replacement in ocean, when strong winds push the water away drawing to the surface the cold water from below, which is rich in nutrients.

Marsh Wetland with few trees.

Mass extinction A global and catastrophic event, with more than 65% of all species becoming extinct over some millions of years.

Mesosphere This layer occupies the space above the stratosphere up to about 80 km above the Earth's surface.

Methyl Isocyanate (MIC) Highly poisonous chemical used in pesticide manufacture.

Mitigation In the context of climate change, a human intervention to reduce the sources or enhance the sinks of greenhouse gases.

Monocropping Planting only a single species over a piece of land.

Montane Growing in or inhabiting mountain areas.

Municipal Solid Waste (MSW) Waste collected by a municipality or disposed of at the municipal waste disposal site.

Mutualism A symbiotic relationship between two species in which both species benefit and they rely on each other for survival.

Natural farming No-tillage and organic farming, pioneered by Masanobu Fukuoka of Japan.

Natural gas A fossil fuel often found above the oil deposit in wells.

Nautical mile The unit of distance used in the ocean. One nautical mile equals 1.85 km.

Nekton The strong swimmers of the ocean including all the larger organisms like fishes, turtles and whales.

Net energy yield The usable amount of high-quality energy that can be extracted from an energy source.

Net Zero A state in which the greenhouse gases going into the atmosphere are balanced by removal out of the atmosphere.

NIMBY (Not In My BackYard) syndrome Practice of objecting to something that would affect one or take place in one's locality, even though it would benefit many others.

Non-renewable energy source An energy source that is limited in supply and gets depleted by use.

Nonpoint-source of water pollution A large area over which water flows and picks up pollutants.

Nuclear radiation Energy particles or rays that are given off from a radioactive element, such as uranium, as it decays.

Nutrient Any food, element, or compound that is essential for an organism to live and grow.

Ocean Thermal Energy Conversion (OTEC) Energy generation using the difference in temperature between the ocean surface water and the colder deep ocean water.

Old-growth forest Forests that have not been seriously disturbed by human activities or natural disasters for several hundred years or more.

Omnivore An organism that eats producers as well as other consumers.

Open ocean The area of the ocean beyond the coastal zone.

Organic farming A method of farming that does not use chemical fertilizers and chemical pesticides.

Organism Any living thing - an animal, a plant, or a microbe.

Overshoot The result of an ecosystem being exploited more rapidly than it can renew itself.

Ozone Depleting Potential (ODP) The amount of ozone depletion caused by a substance.

Ozone layer A layer of ozone that exists in the upper atmosphere, or stratosphere, between 10 and 50 km above the Earth.

Parasitism A symbiotic relationship between two species in which one species (parasite) benefits at the expense of another species (host).

PCBs (Polychlorinated biphenyls) Group of toxic chemical compounds that are very stable, have good insulation qualities, are fire resistant, and have low electrical conductivity.

Peak oil The maximum rate of the production of oil in any area under consideration, recognising that it is a finite natural resource, subject to depletion.

Permaculture Consciously designed landscapes which mimic the patterns and relationships found in nature, while yielding an abundance of food, fibre, and energy for provision of local needs.

Persistent Organic Pollutants (POPs) A group of persistent, toxic chemicals that can accumulate in organisms and can contaminate sites far removed from their source.

Photochemical smog A form of outdoor air pollution formed by the chemical reactions between sunlight, unburnt hydrocarbons, ozone, and other pollutants.

Photosynthesis The process in which green plants take in carbon dioxide from the atmosphere, water from the soil and energy from the Sun to make food.

Photovoltaic (PV) cell A device that converts solar energy directly into electricity.

Phytoplankton Photosynthetic producers forming the basis of the ocean's food web.

Pioneer species Hardy species which are the first to colonize a previously disrupted or damaged ecosystem.

Planetary boundaries The boundaries for certain processes that regulate the stability and resilience of the earth system.

Plankton Free-floating microorganisms that cannot swim easily and are buffeted about by the waves and currents.

Plant Genetic Resources Genetic material of plant origin with actual or potential value for food and agriculture.

Point-source of water pollution Specific places like factories that discharge pollutants into water bodies.

Polluter Pays Principle A principle by which a polluter is made to pay for or repair the damage caused to the environment.

Polychlorinated biphenyls (PCBs) Toxic chemicals widely used in electrical equipment, which remain in the environment for long.

Polyp Tiny organism that forms the coral.

Population The members of a species living and interacting within a specific geographical region.

Precautionary Principle A principle used to avoid any proposed action that has the potential to harm the environment, even if there is yet no conclusive proof of harm occurring.

Precipitation All the forms in which water comes down on Earth, including rain, snow, and hailstorm.

Primary air pollutant Harmful chemical that is released directly from a source into the atmosphere.

Primary forests (or old-growth forest) Forests of native tree species where human activities have not made an impact and the ecological balance remains undisturbed.

Producer An organism such as a green plant that can produce food from simple inorganic substances through photosynthesis. Also called autotroph.

Propagule (of a tree) A portion of the tree such as a cutting or a seed that propagates the tree.

Protected area Area in which the biodiversity and wildlife are protected from human exploitation.

Public Interest Litigation (PIL) Petitions filed in courts by individual citizens, groups, and voluntary organizations seeking justice in matters involving public interest.

Pyramid of Biomass A graphical representation of the reduction in biomass of organisms as we move from one trophic level to the next.

Pyramid of Energy A graphical representation of the reduction in usable energy of organisms as we move from one trophic level to the next.

Pyramid of Numbers Pyramid that shows that the number of organisms drops drastically from one trophic level to the next.

Rainforest A type of forest found in the hot and humid regions near the Equator.

Rainwater harvesting Harvesting rainwater where it falls, either by collecting and storing it, or by letting it recharge the groundwater.

Rangeland Land that is not suitable for crop production and is used for grazing by animals.

Recombinant DNA Technology that combines two or more different strands of DNA to create a new strand.

Recycle To convert waste back into a useful form.

Rehabilitation The provision of opportunities and facilities to displaced people to help them find livelihoods and shelter in the new area.

Renewable energy Type of energy (like solar energy) that is replaced by natural processes and can be used forever.

Renewable energy source An energy source that is replenished by natural processes and hence can be used indefinitely.

Reuse To extend the life of an item or to find a new use for it.

Reverse Osmosis or RO Method Purifying water by forcing it through a semi-permeable membrane.

Richter scale A measure of the severity of an earthquake. It is a measure of the amount of energy released, which is indicated by the vibrations in a seismograph.

Sacred grove A forest that is protected by the local community through social traditions and taboos that incorporate spiritual and ecological values.

Salinization of soil The building up of salt in the soil flowing the evaporation of excess water.

Sanitary landfill A site where waste is isolated from the environment until it is safe.

Savannah Tropical grasslands with widely scattered clumps of low trees. They are marked by low rainfall and prolonged dry periods.

Second-growth forest A forest that results from secondary ecological succession that takes place when forests are cleared and then left undisturbed for long periods of time.

Secondary air pollutant Harmful chemical that is produced from chemical reactions involving primary pollutants.

Secondary forests (or second-growth forest) Forests that emerge when primary forests are removed by human action or natural causes and are then regenerated.

Seed bank A kind of gene bank that stores seeds of food crops or any rare species of plants.

Seismograph An instrument that measures the amount of energy released in an earthquake by sensing the vibrations.

Sentinel species Species that are very sensitive indicators of environmental problems.

Shale gas Natural gas that is trapped within shale formations, which are fine-grained sedimentary rocks

Shale oil Crude oil stored in a rock formation called shale.

Sink Any process, activity or mechanism which removes a greenhouse gas, an aerosol or a precursor of a greenhouse gas from the atmosphere.

Sludge The toxic material left behind after the treatment of sewage.

Smog A form of outdoor pollution that is localized in urban areas, where it reduces visibility.

Social forestry The planting of trees, often with the involvement of local communities, in wasteland or common land.

Speciation The formation of new species due to the genetic changes in an existing species.

Species A group of similar organisms.

Species diversity The variety of plant and animal species present in a community or ecosystem.

Species extinction The situation in which no members of the species are found to exist anywhere on Earth.

Stratosphere This layer is above the troposphere and extends to about 50 km above the Earth's surface.

Sulphur cycle The cyclical movement of sulphur in the environment.

Sustainable development Development that meets the needs of the present without compromising the ability of future generations to meet their own needs.

Sustainable Forest Management The use of the world's forests in such a way that that they continue to provide resources now without depriving future generations of their needs.

Swamp Wetland dominated by trees and shrubs.

Symbiosis Any intimate relationship between two or more species in a community.

Sympatric speciation The formation of new species where the genetic modification is based on a single ancestor.

Tar sands Sands containing oil-rich bitumen.

Temperate forest A type of forest with seasonal variations in climate, freezing in winter and warm and humid in summer.

Temperate Having temperatures that are not too hot or too cold.

Terminator seed technology Genetic modification of plants to make them produce sterile seeds.

Thermal pollution of water Sudden increase or decrease in temperature of any natural body of water caused by human activity.

Thermosphere This is the space above the mesosphere up to about 600 km above the Earth's surface.

Threatened species A species that is facing a high risk of global extinction.

Tidal energy Energy produced by the surge of ocean waters during the rise and fall of tides

Tight oil Same as shale oil

Tonne of oil equivalent The amount of energy released by burning one tonne of crude oil.

Topsoil Topmost layer of the soil, where most plant roots, microorganisms, and other animal life are located.

Toxic waste Waste that contains poisons, which could kill certain organisms.

Trophic level The specific feeding stage of an organism in the ecosystem.

Troposphere The part of the atmosphere up to a distance of 17 km from the Earth's surface.

Tsunami An undersea high-energy wave set off by an (undersea) earthquake; when the wave hits the coast, giant waves result.

Tundra The forests in the Arctic. They occur in the extreme northern latitudes, where the snow melts seasonally.

Typhoon Violent storm with very strong winds experienced mainly in western Atlantic Ocean.

Understory An underlying layer of vegetation that grows beneath a forest's canopy.

Urban heat island A city area that is significantly warmer than its surrounding rural areas due to human activities.

Urban sprawl The unplanned and uncontrolled spreading of urban development into areas adjoining the edge of a city.

Urbanization The process by which more and more people live and work in cities rather than in the rural areas.

UV method Use of ultraviolet radiation to kill harmful organisms in water.

Vermicomposting or Vermiculture Composting organic waste efficiently using earthworms.

Virtual water Water that goes into the production of the food and non-food items that we use or consume.

Vulnerable species A threatened species facing a high risk of extinction in the wild.

Wasteland reclamation The process by which any wasteland is brought again under vegetative cover and made productive.

Water cycle A process that continually recycles and transports water among the atmosphere, land, and ocean.

Water Footprint Total volume of freshwater that is used to produce the goods and services consumed by an individual or community or produced by a business.

Water harvesting The process of catching the rain when and where it falls.

Watershed A region from which water flows (or drains) into a stream, lake, reservoir, wetland, or other body of water.

Wave energy Energy generated from the up-and-down motion of waves.

Wetland Land surface covered or saturated with water for a part or whole of the year.

Zooplankton Primary consumers that feed on phytoplankton.

Zooxanthellae The tiny single-celled algae that live inside the tissues of the polyps that form the corals.

APPENDIX B

Answers to Objective-Type Questions

1. Global Environmental Change, Current Crisis and Responses

1. (b) 2. (c) 3. (d) 4. (a) 5. (d)
6. (b)

2. Ecosystems and Natural Resources

1. (a) 2. (c) 3. (a) 4. (d) 5. (a)
6. (b) 7. (c) 8. (c)

3. Biomes: Forests, Grasslands, and Deserts

1. (c) 2. (a) 3. (d) 4. (a)

4. Aquatic Ecosystems: Ocean, Rivers, Lakes, and Wetlands

1. (d) 2. (a) 3. (c) 4. (a) 5. (d)
6. (c)

5. Water Resources

1. (a) 2. (d) 3. (c) 4. (c) 5. (b)
6. (c) 7. (d) 8. (a) 9. (d) 10. (a)

6. Forest Resources

1. (b) 2. (d) 3. (d) 4. (a) 5. (c)
6. (c) 7. (a)

7. Land, Soil, and Mineral Resources

1. (a) 2. (d) 3. (d) 4. (b) 5. (c)
6. (b) 7. (b) 8. (d) 9. (b) 10. (a)

8. Energy Resources

1. (a) 2. (b) 3. (c) 4. (d) 5. (c)
6. (c) 7. (a) 8. (d)

9. Introduction to Biodiversity

1. (c) 2. (a) 3. (c) 4. (a) 5. (c)
6. (b)

10. Biodiversity Conservation

1. (d) 2. (c) 3. (a) 4. (d)

11. Solid Waste and Soil Pollution

1. (a) 2. (b) 3. (d) 4. (c) 5. (a)
6. (d) 7. (b) 8. (a) 9. (a) 10. (d)

12. Water and Marine Pollution

1. (c) 2. (a) 3. (b) 4. (d) 5. (d)
6. (d) 7. (a)

13. Air Pollution, Noise, and Other Forms of Pollution

1. (a) 2. (d) 3. (d) 4. (c) 5. (b)
6. (a) 7. (b) 8. (b) 9. (c) 10. (d)

14. Climate Change: Causes and Impacts

1. (c) 2. (c) 3. (b) 4. (a) 5. (d)

15. Climate Change: Adaptation and Mitigation

1. (d) 2. (a) 3. (d) 4. (d) 5. (c)

16. Environmental Law and Environmental Management

1. (c) 2. (b) 3. (b) 4. (d) 5. (a)

17. Sustainable Development and Global Initiatives

1. (d) 2. (c) 3. (a) 4. (b) 5. (c)
6. (d)

APPENDIX C

Question Bank 1

For University Examinations

Part A: Objective-type Questions

1. Which of the following statements refers to the global population?
   (a) It has been increasing gradually over centuries.
   (b) It has been doubling every 100 years.
   (c) It has not been growing in recent decades.
   (d) It has been increasing exponentially since the 17th century.

2. What is the image of India's Ecomark?
   (a) Earthen pot
   (b) Rice plant
   (c) Plough
   (d) Lotus

3. Which of the following is **not** a biome?
   (a) Desert
   (b) Ecosystem
   (c) Grassland
   (d) Tundra

4. ISO 14000 Environmental Management Standards are:
   (a) Compulsory for companies in India.
   (b) Standards that specify limits for the environmental performance of companies.
   (c) Voluntary standards that can help an organization to fulfil its environmental responsibilities.
   (d) Applicable only to industries.

5. What is **not** true of the ocean now?
   (a) Increased temperatures in the ocean are affecting marine life and corals.
   (b) Since 1978, summer sea ice in the Arctic has considerably decreased.
   (c) Carbon dioxide absorption has turned the ocean very acidic.
   (d) 75% of the global fish stocks have recovered from the earlier over-exploitation.

6. What would be a **wrong** way of viewing water?
   (a) Water is the basis of life.
   (b) Water belongs to all living beings on earth.
   (c) Water is private property.
   (d) Water is a common resource for the sustenance of all.

7. What is **not** true of global biodiversity?
   (a) Biodiversity is affected by climate change.
   (b) Biodiversity supports and provides many ecosystem services.

(c) Biodiversity contributes to both climate-change mitigation and adaptation.
(d) Biodiversity is fully documented.

8. What is **not** true of global generation of solid waste?
   (a) Solid waste is the by-product of a resource-intensive, consumer-based economic lifestyle.
   (b) As a country's affluence increases, paper and plastic waste generally decreases, while organic waste increases.
   (c) The amount of municipal solid waste is growing even faster than the rate of urbanization.
   (d) China is the world's largest waste generator.

9. Noise regulation rules in India
   (a) Limit noise levels in only industrial zones.
   (b) Allow the use of public address systems at any time provided permission has been taken.
   (c) Establish zones of silence in specified areas.
   (d) Allow noise from firecrackers without any limit during festivals.

10. What is **not** true of India's sacred groves?
    (a) The local community can take any plant from a sacred grove.
    (b) Sacred groves represent native vegetation in a natural state.
    (c) Sacred groves are banks of species and genetic diversity.
    (d) Rare medicinal plants are found in the sacred groves.

Part B: Short-answer Questions

1. List any five Sustainable Development Goals proposed by the UN for transforming the world by 2030.
2. What is the difference between the meaning of the terms 'species' and 'populations'?
3. What are the on-going environmental changes in the Himalayas and why are they happening?
4. List four biogeochemical cycles and describe any one of them.
5. Explain the term 'Idea of Progress'.
6. What happened to the Indian vulture in the decade of the 1990s?
7. Explain the environmental and social consequences of building the Three Gorges Dam in China.
8. What is meant by Carrying Capacity?
9. What is wasteland reclamation?
10. What is thermal pollution of water?
11. What are landslides and how do they occur?
12. How does exposure to nuclear radiation impact health?
13. What is meant by adaptation to climate change?
14. What is climate resilience?
15. Explain the main provisions of ISO 14000 standards.
16. What is 'carbon credit'?
17. What is Clean Development Mechanism?
18. What are the functions and powers of the Central and State Pollution Control Boards?
19. Describe the Great Pacific Garbage Patch.
20. What is eco-labelling of products?

Part C: Essay Questions

1. What were the major findings of the IPCC Sixth Assessment of Climate Change?
2. Explain the concept of Green Economy giving examples.
3. Describe the ecological and social issues concerning the Western Ghats including the Silent Valley.
4. What is the state of the ocean? What are the human activities that cause adverse effects on the ocean?
5. What is the importance of Antarctica and the Arctic for the global environment and what is happening there?

Answers to Part A

1. (d) 2. (a) 3. (b) 4. (c) 5. (d) 6. (c) 7. (d) 8. (b) 9. (c) 10. (a)

APPENDIX D

Question Bank 2

UPSC Civil Services Preliminary Examination General Studies Paper I

(The syllabus for UPSC General Studies Paper I includes the topic 'General Issues on Environmental Ecology, Biodiversity and Climate Change'. Given below are model objective questions on this topic following the pattern of the examination. Answers to the questions will be found in this textbook.)

Each question is followed by four possible responses. Choose the one you consider to be the best.

1. Which of the following statements are true regarding the global environment?
   1. Two billion people do not have access to safely managed drinking water services.
   2. The current extinction rate of species is estimated to be more than 10,000 times the rate at which species naturally disappear.
   3. At least 1 billion people in the world breathe unhealthy air and 3 million die annually due to air pollution.
   4. Overfishing and ocean acidification is placing all marine life at risk.

   Select the correct answer using the code given below:
   (a) 1, 2, 3, and 4
   (b) 1, 3, and 4 only
   (c) 3 and 4 only
   (d) 1, 2, and 3 only

2. Which of the following are among the primary causes of global environmental degradation?
   1. The Idea of Progress
   2. Unrestrained growth of human population
   3. Unsustainable exploitation of natural resources
   4. Increase in the number of automobiles

   Select the correct answer using the code given below:
   (a) 2, 3, and 4 only
   (b) 3 and 4 only
   (c) 1, 2, 3, and 4
   (d) 1, 2, and 3 only

3. How can we best describe the concept of Carrying Capacity?
   1. Carrying Capacity is concerned about the present and the future.
   2. Carrying Capacity refers to the maximum population of a species that a given land or marine area can support.
   3. Carrying Capacity is very similar to Ecological Footprint of a population.
   4. It is difficult to calculate the Carrying Capacity of humanity because our resource consumption keeps changing over time and space.

Select the correct answer using the code given below:
(a) 1, 2, and 3 only
(b) 2 and 3 only
(c) 1, 2, 3, and 4
(d) 1, 2, and 4 only

4. Which of the following statements correctly describe the roles and functions of the Intergovernmental Panel on Climate Change (IPCC)?
   1. IPCC synthesizes worldwide research carried out on climate change.
   2. IPCC is a panel of climate scientists responsible for conducting original research on climate change.
   3. IPCC prepares an Annual Assessment Report on climate change.
   4. UN member countries are bound to adopt IPCC's recommendations.

   Select the correct answer using the code given below:
   (a) 1 only
   (b) 2 and 3 only
   (c) 1, 2, 3, and 4
   (d) 3 and 4 only

5. What was true of the Kyoto Protocol?
   1. It was an international agreement to reduce the greenhouse gas emissions.
   2. It was negotiated in Kyoto, Japan, in 2015.
   3. It was not a legally binding agreement for the countries that signed it.
   4. Under the Protocol, developing countries were also required to cut emissions.

6. Sea levels are rising due to global warming. Which of the following places are experiencing heavy erosion and submergence due to sea-level rise?
   1. Tuvalu
   2. The Sundarbans
   3. Kiribati
   4. Marshall Islands

   Select the correct answer using the code given below:
   (a) 1 only
   (b) 2 and 3 only
   (c) 1, 2, and 4 only
   (d) All of them

7. What are the primary causes of climate change?
   1. Excessive burning of fossil fuels
   2. Exploding number of automobiles driven by oil
   3. Increasing solar flares
   4. Heavy deforestation

   Select the correct answer using the code given below:
   (a) 3 only
   (b) 1, 2, and 4 only
   (c) 1, 2, 3, and 4
   (d) 1 and 4 only

8. Which countries are among the top five in carbon dioxide emissions?
   1. China
   2. US
   3. Germany
   4. India

   Select the correct answer using the code given below:
   (a) All of them
   (b) 1, 2, and 4 only
   (c) 1, 2, and 3 only
   (d) 1 and 2 only

9. The key messages of the IPCC's Sixth Assessment Report were:
   1. Human activities, principally through emissions of greenhouse gases, have unequivocally caused global warming.
   2. Human-caused climate change is already affecting many weather and climate extremes in every region across the globe.
   3. Adaptation planning and implementation has progressed across all sectors and regions.
   4. Limiting human-caused global warming requires Net Zero CO_2 emissions.

   Select the correct answer using the code given below:
   (a) 1, 2, and 4 only
   (b) 1, 2, and 3 only
   (c) All of them
   (d) 1 and 2 only

10. What are the incontrovertible impacts of climate change on India?
    1. The year 2022 was the fifth warmest year on record since 1901 and the past decade (2013–2022) was the warmest decade.
    2. Himalayan glaciers are melting.
    3. A tsunami occurred in 2004.
    4. Unseasonal heavy rains and hailstorms are occurring across the country.

    Select the correct answer using the code given below:
    (a) 1, 2, and 4 only
    (b) 1, 2, and 3 only
    (c) All of them
    (d) 1 and 2 only

11. What has been the impact of Green Revolution in India?
    (a) The number of cultivated crop varieties has gone up steeply.
    (b) The number of cultivated crop varieties has gone down.
    (c) There are now more rice varieties and less wheat varieties.
    (d) There are now more wheat varieties and less rice varieties.

12. What are the major factors that determine the degree of diversity in an ecosystem?
    1. Habitat stress
    2. Geographical isolation
    3. Dominance by one species
    4. Availability of ecological niches
    5. Edge Effect
    6. Geological history

Select the correct answer using the code given below:
(a) 1, 2, 3, 4, and 6 only
(b) 1, 2, and 3 only
(c) All of them
(d) 1, 2, 3, and 4 only

13. Which of the following are examples of ecosystem services provided to us by nature?
1. Provisioning services such as water
2. Regulating services such as flood control
3. Supporting services such as soil formation
4. Cultural services such as recreation

Select the correct answer using the code given below:
(a) 1, 2, 3, and 4
(b) 1, 2, and 3 only
(c) 2, 3, and 4 only
(d) 1 and 4 only

14. Which of the following are among the mega-biodiversity countries of the world?
1. Brazil
2. US
3. China
4. Egypt
5. Costa Rica
6. India

Select the correct answer using the code given below:
(a) 1, 2, 3, and 4
(b) 1, 3, 5, and 6 only
(c) 2, 3, and 4 only
(d) 1, 3, and 4 only

15. What is the meaning of ecological extinction of a species?
(a) The species is no longer found in the area it once inhabited.
(b) It is the same as biological extinction.
(c) It is endemic to an area.
(d) So few members are left that the species can no longer play its normal ecological role in the community.

16. Which statements are true regarding keystone species?
1. They play roles affecting many other organisms in an ecosystem.
2. They determine the ability of many other species to survive.
3. When a keystone species becomes extinct, it could result in a cascade of extinctions of other species.
4. They are indicator species.

Select the correct answer using the code given below:
(a) 1, 2, 3, and 4
(b) 1 and 3 only
(c) 1, 2, and 3 only
(d) 1, 3, and 4 only

17. Which of the following statements are correct regarding ISO 14000?
    1. ISO 14000 is a voluntary environmental management system.
    2. ISO 14000 standards specify environmental performance goals.
    3. If a manufacturing company has ISO 14000 certification, its products will be environmentfriendly.
    4. ISO 14000 standards provide practical tools for organizations looking to manage their environmental responsibilities.

    Select the correct answer using the code given below:
    (a) 1, 2, 3, and 4
    (b) 2 and 3 only
    (c) 2, 3, and 4 only
    (d) 1 and 4 only

18. Which of the following statements are true regarding the concept of peak oil?
    1. Peak oil refers to the maximum rate of the production of conventional oil in an area.
    2. Peak oil is related to the Hubbert Curve.
    3. Peak oil applies to the production of both conventional and non-conventional oil in an area.
    4. Peak oil refers to the running out of oil in an area.

    Select the correct answer using the code given below:
    (a) 1, 2, 3, and 4
    (b) 2 and 3 only
    (c) 1 and 2 only
    (d) 1 and 4 only

19. The Decade of Sustainable Energy for All is the initiative of
    (a) United Nations
    (b) India
    (c) Germany
    (d) World Bank

20. What is true of OPEC?
    1. It stands for the Petroleum Exporting Countries of the Middle East.
    2. It consists only of Iran, Iraq, Kuwait, Libya, Qatar, Saudi Arabia, and the United Arab Emirates.
    3. It stands for the Organization of the Petroleum Exporting Countries.
    4. It includes Algeria, Angola, Ecuador, and Venezuela.

    Select the correct answer using the code given below:
    (a) 1, 2, 3, and 4
    (b) 2 and 3 only
    (c) 1 and 2 only
    (d) 3 and 4 only

Answers

1. (b)	2. (c)	3. (d)	4. (a)	5. (a)	6. (d)	7. (b)	8. (b)	9. (c)	10. (a)
11. (b)	12. (c)	13. (a)	14. (b)	15. (d)	16. (c)	17. (d)	18. (c)	19. (a)	20. (d)

Index

About the Author

Prof. R. Rajagopalan holds a B.E. (Honours) degree in Mechanical Engineering from the University of Madras and M.Tech. and Ph.D. degrees in Industrial Management from the Indian Institute of Technology (IIT) at Kanpur, India. He taught for over 30 years at IIT Kanpur and IIT Madras, handling a variety of courses on industrial engineering, management, environment, and development.

About 25 years ago, he shifted his focus to environmental issues. At IIT Madras, he was also the Director of International Ocean Institute (IOI India) and coordinated several international ocean and environment-related courses and workshops. He was a member of the Governing Board of the International Ocean Institute, Malta, during 2003–2009.

Prof. Rajagopalan continues to be active, giving presentations and conducting workshops on environment for different groups. He is a regular facilitator at Initiatives of Change, Panchgani, where he has made presentations on environment to over 300 IAS and other Civil Services officers since 2008. More than 200 participants have attended the workshop on 'Exploring a Sustainable Future' that he co-directs at Auroville, near Puducherry.

Prof. Rajagopalan has published more than 20 books on environment for schools, colleges, and the public. This university-level book, *Environmental Studies: From Crisis to Cure*, has often been a bestseller on Amazon.in.